# The Ethnic History of Chicago

MELVIN G. HOLLI, *Editor*

## Advisory Board

*Josef Barton*

*Kathleen Niels Conzen*

*Lawrence J. McCaffrey*

*William McCready*

# The Jews of Chicago

# Irving Cutler

לא תרצה

לא תנאף

לא תגנב

לא תענה

Other Works by Irving Cutler

*The Chicago-Milwaukee Corridor*

*The Chicago Metropolitan Area: Selected Geographic Readings* (editor)

*Chicago: Transformations of an Urban System* (coauthor)

*Illinois: Land and Life in the Prairie State* (contributor)

*Urban Geography*

*Urban Communities* (coauthor)

*The Sentinel's History of Chicago Jewry, 1911–1986* (contributor)

*Ethnic Chicago* (contributor)

*Synagogues of Chicago* (coeditor)

*Chicago: Metropolis of the Mid-Continent*

# The Jews of Chicago

## From Shtetl to Suburb

UNIVERSITY OF ILLINOIS PRESS *Urbana & Chicago*

Excerpts from

*World of Our Fathers,*

copyright © 1976

by Irving Howe,

reprinted by permission

of Harcourt Brace and

Company. Excerpts

from *Life Is with People,*

by Mark Zborowski

and Elizabeth Herzog

(New York: Schocken

Books, 1952), quoted

by permission of

International Universities

Press, Inc.

© 1996 by the Board of Trustees of the University of Illinois

Manufactured in the United States of America

C  5  4  3  2

*This book is printed on acid-free paper.*

Library of Congress Cataloging-in-Publication Data

Cutler, Irving.

  The Jews of Chicago : from shtetl to suburb / Irving Cutler.

    p.    cm. — (The Ethnic history of Chicago)

  Includes bibliographical references and index.

  ISBN 0-252-02185-1

  1. Jews—Illinois—Chicago—History. 2. Chicago (Ill.)—Ethnic relations.

I. Title. II. Series.

F548.9.J5C87    1996

977.3'11004924—dc20        94-47591

                    CIP

TO OUR CHILDREN & GRANDCHILDREN

*So that they may know*

# Contents

# Preface

Chicago for many years had the third largest Jewish population among the cities of the world. Yet in the course of giving numerous talks and tours on Jewish Chicago over a long period of time, I found that, though interest in this major Jewish community was great, knowledge about it was typically very limited. This was especially the case among the younger generations. This book will, I hope, enable the young to learn and their elders to reminisce and expand their knowledge of the people, neighborhoods, institutions, and events that shaped today's Chicago Jewish community – and their own lives. It is quite a remarkable story.

Jewish immigrants who came to Chicago had in the main fled from Old World areas where conditions for them were often harsh, sometimes brutal. In Chicago they struggled, worked hard, and persevered so that their offspring could become educated and have a better life. Their children, grandchildren, and great grandchildren now generally live quite comfortably, mainly and increasingly in Chicago's suburbs, far from their roots and often barely aware of the contributions of their forebears.

Who were these Jews who first came to Chicago around the time of the city's incorporation and where did they come from? How did they live? What problems did they face and how did they adjust their lives to the New World? What were their neighborhoods like? What were their beliefs? What did they contribute and who were the major contributors? How did they lay the foundation for the present Jewish community and what is it like today? What progress has been made, and what problems does the community face? These are among the topics upon which this book will focus.

The book's strong emphasis upon Jewish neighborhoods reflects their importance to the Jewish immigrants and their offspring. Before the present era of mobility, Jewish life centered mainly around the neighborhood, which was a vibrant, closely knit community. It had almost everything one needed, from synagogues and schools to social life and stores, and it sometimes even had much of the flavor, spirit, openness, and infrastructure of a Jewish shtetl or town transplanted from the Old World. When I served as curator for the Jewish Life in America exhibit at the Museum of Science and Industry in Chicago in 1985, I noticed that the largest and most enthusiastic crowds seemed to congregate around the photos and maps of old Chicago Jewish neighborhoods. I understood the attraction, for I consider myself fortunate to have lived in a number of the major Chicago Jewish communities – Maxwell Street, Lawndale, and neighborhoods to the south and north.

A book such as this cannot hope to cover the whole story. Many important places and events and many noteworthy individuals, living and dead, unfortunately could not be included here. Perhaps they will be covered by future writers. The attempt here is to give a general picture of the growth and development of the Chicago Jewish community from its Old World roots to the present, including its blemishes and weaknesses as well as its successes and strengths. It is said that knowing where you come from will often help you understand where you are going and why you think, feel, and act the way you do. If this book helps to achieve even a part of such an understanding it will have served its purpose.

I wish to express my appreciation to those individuals and institutions that assisted in its preparation. A number of Chicago-area libraries provided valuable sources, especially the Asher Library and the Chicago Jewish Archives, both in the Spertus Institute of Jewish Studies. I also visited and received assistance from the personnel at the library of the American Jewish Historical Society at Waltham, Massachusetts; the American Jewish Archives on the campus of the Hebrew Union College in Cincinnati; and the facilities of YIVO and the Leo Baeck Institute in New York City. Publications of the Jewish Federation of Metropolitan Chicago and of *The Sentinel* were a frequent source of information. The Chicago Historical Society also provided useful information and interesting photographs.

I learned much from the publications of the Chicago Jewish Historical Society and from the society's many knowledgeable members. Dr. Irwin Suloway, longtime editor of the society's quarterly publication, read my manuscript, offered helpful, detailed criticism, and was always available as a reliable source of answers to questions. Walter Roth, the president of the society, also read the manuscript and offered useful suggestions, as did Norman Schwartz, a past president, who in addition carefully checked the manuscript for factual accuracy. Professor Melvin G. Holli, chair of the history department at the University of Illinois at Chicago and the editor of the Ethnic History of Chicago series that includes this book, guided the project from its inception and was very supportive with his wise counsel and critique of the manuscript. I would also like to thank Sheldon Robinson for answering many questions about religious institutions, and Joseph Kubal, a former student of mine, who very painstakingly and accurately converted my sketched maps into finished products.

To my family I owe a special debt for their patience during the period of writing and for their help in so many ways. My son, Dan, helped with the photographs; my daughter, Susie, offered many valuable suggestions and perceptive comments as she read and reread the manuscript. Special appreciation goes to my wife, Marian, for her constant encouragement, her untiring efforts in reading, typing, and proofreading the manuscript, and her continued good advice.

# The Jews of Chicago

# 1

# The First Wave

## The German-Speaking Jews

INTRODUCTION

First in a trickle and then in a torrent, the Jews poured into Chicago. By 1930 there were almost 300,000 Jews, comprising 9 percent of the city's population; Chicago then had the third largest Jewish population of any city in the world – exceeded only by New York and Warsaw. The Jews had come from virtually every country in Europe and the Middle East, but especially from Germany and the countries of Eastern Europe. In Chicago they formed a very diverse group even within the city's large immigrant diversity.

Like other immigrant groups, the Jews left Europe because of economic, political, and religious difficulties. For Jewish immigrants, however, such difficulties were often compounded by a virulent anti-Semitism that sometimes culminated in massacres. Because of this harsh treatment and because they usually were considered aliens in their homeland even though they may have lived there for centuries, Jews particularly welcomed the opportunity to emigrate to America. While the more affluent and educated members of other immigrant groups often remained in their homelands and occupied secure and respected positions, Jews of all economic and educational levels migrated to America. Unlike other immigrants, Jews left the Old Country with no thoughts of ever returning to their place of birth, despite sentimental attachments. Even with the initial difficulties many Jews experienced in their new environment, America offered freedom and opportunities they had never known before.

### EARLY CHICAGO

While most European Jewish immigrants settled along the East Coast, especially in New York City, a sizable number made their way westward to the relatively accessible and thriving community of Chicago. The first Jews arrived in Chicago shortly after its incorporation in 1833 as a town of some 350 people. In that year Chicago was described by a Scottish traveler, Patrick Shirreff, as follows:

> Chicago consists of about 150 wood houses, placed irregularly on both sides of the river, over which there is a bridge. This is already a place of considerable trade, supplying salt, tea, coffee, sugar, and clothing to a large tract of country to the north and west; and when connected with the navigable point of the river Illinois, by a canal or railway, cannot fail of rising to importance. Almost every person I met regarded Chicago as the germ of an immense city, and speculators have already bought up, at high prices, all the building ground in the neighborhood.[1]

But in 1833 black bears were still being killed in what is today's Loop area and wolves were seen prowling about.

The early Chicago to which the first Jews arrived was a flat, marshy area developing around the mouth of the Chicago River where it flowed into Lake Michigan and where Fort Dearborn had first been erected in 1803. Growth was slow until the Black Hawk War of 1832 evicted the Indians from the area. Thereafter, the city started to grow rapidly, reaching a population of 30,000 by 1850 and 112,000 by 1860 — with half the population foreign born.

Its growth was abetted by its excellent location near the geographic center of a vast fertile plain at the southwestern tip of Lake Michigan, where the Chicago and the Calumet rivers flowed into the lake. Its location made it a hub of water transportation and later of rail transportation, rendering the area very accessible for both people and products. The construction of the Illinois and Michigan Canal, completed in 1848 and connecting the Great Lakes with the Illinois–Mississippi River waterway system at Chicago, further enhanced Chicago's symbiotic relationship with its rich farm hinterland and also its position as a transportation center, in addition to creating thousands of canal construction jobs.

The author John Lewis Peyton described the burgeoning Chicago of 1848 as follows:

. . . The city is situated on both sides of the Chicago River, a sluggish slimy stream, too lazy to clean itself, and on both sides of its north and south branches, upon a level piece of ground, half dry and half wet, resembling a salt marsh, and contained a population of 20,000. There was no pavement, no macadamized streets, no drainage, and the three thousand houses in which the people lived were almost entirely small timber buildings painted white, and this white much defaced by mud. . . .

. . . Chicago was already becoming a place of considerable importance for manufacturers. Steam mills were busy in every part of the city preparing lumber for buildings which were contracted to be erected by the thousand the next season. Large establishments were engaged in manufacturing agricultural implements of every description for the farmers who flocked to the country every spring. A single establishment, that of McCormick, employed several hundred hands, and during each season completed from fifteen hundred to two thousand grain-reapers and grass mowers. Blacksmith, wagon and coachmaker's shops were busy preparing for a spring demand, which with all their energy, they could not supply. Brickmakers had discovered on the lake shore near the city and a short distance in the interior, excellent beds of clay, and were manufacturing, even at this time, millions of bricks . . . and the Illinois Central Railway employed large bodies of men in driving piles and constructing a track and depot on the beach. Real estate agents were mapping out the surrounding territory for ten and fifteen miles in the interior, giving fancy names to the future avenues, streets, squares, and parks.[2]

It was this young, bustling, growing commercial and industrial center of great potential that attracted the first Jews to Chicago. They came mainly from what is now Germany, with a smaller number originating in adjacent central European areas such as Bohemia and Austria.

## THE JEWS OF GERMANY

Germany has long had great significance in Jewish history. It is from the Hebrew word for Germany – *Ashkenaz* – that the term Ashkenazim was applied to almost all of the Jews of Europe except for the Sephardic Jews, who lived largely in the Mediterranean countries. It was in medieval Germany that Yiddish developed – the language that was to become the mother tongue of the great majority of European Jews. It was in Germany that the Jewish secular enlightenment and cultural renaissance movement, led primarily by Moses Mendelssohn, drew much of its early impetus, and where Jewish religious reform began. Many Jews became "Germans of the Mosaic faith," and achievement and assimilation reached a very high level, only to be followed by virtual annihilation.

Jews have lived in what is now Germany for more than a millennium. Their status there varied from periods of peaceful acceptance, to grudging tolerance when they were useful for certain purposes, to periods of outright persecution and massacres, such as during the Crusades and later, during the Black Death,

*The synagogue at Worms, Germany, was built in the eleventh century. It was destroyed by the Nazis in 1938 and reconstructed in 1961.*

(Courtesy of the Kulturinstitut, Worms.)

when they were accused of having poisoned the wells from which the general populace obtained water. During the times of persecution, synagogues were destroyed and homes looted; Jews were abused and killed, or baptism was forced upon them. Jews were sometimes confined to ghettos or were banished from most of the larger German cities and from whole provinces. But because of the political fragmentation of Germany, when the Jews were driven from one German area they were usually able to find refuge in another. For centuries the majority of the German Jews lived in small towns and villages while most of the large cities were *Judenrein,* free of Jews.

Ludwig Boerne, a prominent writer born in 1786 and raised in the crowded Frankfurt ghetto, *Judengasse,* later wrote sarcastically of his Jewish boyhood memories of the "benevolent" German government:

> They [the Jews] dwelt in their own little street, without doubt the most thickly populated dot on the face of the earth. There they rejoiced in the tender watchful care of the government. On Sundays they were prohibited from leaving the ghetto land, to spare them from being beaten up by drunkards. Before the age of twenty-five they were forbidden to marry, in order that their offspring prove sound and sturdy. On public holidays they had to reenter the ghetto gate by sharp six in the evening, lest over-exposure to the sun ruin their complexions. They were forbidden to stroll in the fields beyond the city wall, so as to run no risk of being attracted to the life of a farmer. When a Jew walked the city streets and a Christian cried Mach Mores, Jud! ("Your manners, Jew!"), he needs must remove his hat; in this way the proper politeness was maintained between the two faiths. Then, too, a great many of the streets – because their bumpy pavement was bad for the feet – were altogether closed to him.[3]

Despite periods of precarious existence, the Jews managed to maintain a flourishing intellectual life centering often on their talmudic studies. Barred from owning land and from the professions, except sometimes from medicine, and excluded from the guilds, many of the Jews became peddlers, hawkers of haberdashery, cattle dealers, pawnbrokers, and money lenders (an occupation closed to Christians). Some Jews, therefore, became useful to the German rul-

*The Judengasse in Frankfurt am Main in the 1840s. This area's Jewish ghetto was abolished in 1811 and the Judengasse torn down in 1854.*

(Courtesy of the Leo Baeck Institute, New York.)

ers and were given a certain protected and privileged status, a few as court Jews. But while a small number of Jews were prosperous, the masses were poor. A survey at the dawn of the nineteenth century showed that two-thirds of the Jewish population were petty tradesmen and peddlers; 10 percent were domestics; 8 percent were handicraft workers; and at least 84 percent of the Jewish population were of the poor classes.[4] For most Jews life was insecure, subject to occupational and civil restrictions, heavy taxation, and sometimes even limits on the number that could marry.

In 1789, on the eve of the French Revolution, three-quarters of the 400,000 Jews of Western Europe were living in Germany. The French Revolution, with its cry of "Liberty, Equality, Fraternity," and the subsequent Napoleonic era, had a profound effect on the Jews throughout the German states, especially in western Germany, which had been conquered by the French. The Jews were emancipated, many restrictions on commerce and residence were removed, and the Jews' social position was improved to the point where many of them were readily assimilated into the German culture and language. Some embraced Reform Judaism, which broke with many of the tenets of the prevailing Orthodox Judaism.

The fall of Napoleon, however, shattered the Jews' hope of full emancipation. Some of the reforms remained and a few individual Jews experienced success, but Jews were generally associated with the humiliation of the German army and also with increased competition in the commercial realm –

factors leading to a retrogression in the civil rights they had recently attained. Growing German nationalism brought with it a renewal of anti-Jewish sentiment resulting in attacks on Jews, such as during the Hep! Hep! riots of 1819. Conditions were particularly bad in the large kingdom of Bavaria where there were frequent calls for the Jews to get out and go to America. And in 1816 the Prussian minister of finance said: "It would be desirable not to have any Jews at all among us. Since we have them, however, we have to put up with them; but we must strive incessantly to render them as powerless as possible. The conversion of Jews to the Christian faith must be facilitated; all civil rights flow from that. But as long as the Jew remains a Jew, he cannot obtain a position in the state."[5]

These attitudes plus continued official government discrimination and economic restrictions, including special "Jew-taxes," were major factors in the decision of many German-speaking Jews to migrate to America. The image of America – often reinforced by enthusiastic letters from those who had already settled there – was that of an idyllic land of great economic opportunity, freedom, and adventure. Immigration increased markedly after the defeat of the revolutionary movements in Europe in 1848.

At first mainly from Bavaria, then from the Rhenish Palatinate, Prussia, Austria, Bohemia, and the Posen region of Poland, German-speaking Jews started migrating to America. They were primarily from the smaller towns of Germany. They came along with the German Christians but proportionately in much greater numbers. Their migration often adversely affected the communities they left, for many towns became depleted of their young Jews and found it difficult to maintain their Jewish institutions. But the departure of the Jews made many Germans jubilant, as noted in the following article from a German-Jewish newspaper of that period:

> Cases of emigration to America are ever and ever increasing in number. As often, and that is almost daily, as good letters come in from emigrants, more people make up their minds anew to take up their wanderer's staff. From tiny Hagenbach, a townlet in central Franconia, twelve young men are leaving after Passover. In Warbach nearby there are almost no young folks to be found any longer, save those who are without means. . . . Besides, not only artisans and merchants are emigrating but also men of the learned class, since the prospects for rabbinical or medical positions are not particularly bright owing to the vast number of candidates.

> Indeed we hear that many papers are jubilant over the departure of such large groups of Jews and express the joyous and pious wish that those remaining behind may follow those who have gone ahead; but we reply to them that to get rid of a companionship like theirs involves for us at least the exercise of self-control and self-denial, which cost the emigrants few tears, and which will some day perhaps give them some happy hours.[6]

Leaving the homeland of many generations, despite all of the problems there, was usually a sad occasion for the Jews. A local reporter wrote in the Stuttgart *Israelitische Annale* of 1839:

On last Sunday, June 16 about fifty men and women of the Mosaic persuasion in Ebenhauser – eight hours from Stuttgart – started their journey to the United States of North America. Throngs of onlookers poured from far and near to witness their departure. Not an eye remained dry; deep anguish filled every breast. For not merely young people were setting out, as they did some weeks before, but heads of families with their wives and children. It was truly heartrending to see a grey-beard of eighty bid a last farewell to all but one of his twelve children and to his fourteen grandchildren – the youngest barely two months old. Ebenhausen has a population of about 500 Israelites; so far 92 have emigrated. The present group carried with them their Torah scroll.[7]

## THE FIRST JEWISH ARRIVALS IN CHICAGO

The Jews who started arriving in Chicago during the 1830s, when Chicago was first incorporated, included a Jewish peddler, J. Gottlieb, who arrived at the swampy community in 1838. He is believed to have moved west to California after a short stay. The names of Morris Baumgarten, Peter Cohen, Aaron Friend, and Isaac Hays also appeared in documents of that decade, such as the *Chicago Directory,* voters' lists, newspaper subscription lists, and advertisements. The men were identified as peddlers and merchants; however, besides their Jewish-sounding names there is little direct evidence to show that they were Jewish. A few of these settlers evidently stayed in Chicago only briefly; for the others there is no record of their participation in the Jewish institutions that were beginning to be organized in the 1840s.[8]

The first authenticated permanent Jewish settlers in Chicago arrived in 1841. They were Benedict Shubart, Philip Newburgh, Isaac Ziegler, and Henry Horner. All came from Bavaria except for Horner, who came from Bohemia. All settled in the vicinity of Lake and Clark streets and through the years became active in the growing Chicago Jewish community. Many of the early Jewish immigrants started out as peddlers with packs on their backs and later they opened dry-goods, clothing, or grocery stores, often along the main commercial streets of early Chicago – Lake and Clark streets. They usually lived above or behind their stores.

Benedict Shubart and Philip Newburgh, brothers-in-law, were in their late twenties when they arrived in Chicago. Shubart started a merchant tailoring store at 187 Lake Street that soon became the city's most fashionable shop. He became prosperous and was able to build a brick residence, a rarity for the period. His sideburns and general resemblance to a Scotsman caused him to be called "Scott Benedict" by the gentiles and he consequently advertised his business under that name. Philip Newburgh also opened a tailoring establishment, at 153 Lake Street, near La Salle Street, but he was not very successful and subsequently became a tobacco merchant. His daughter Pauline and son Henry, both born in the 1840s, are believed to be the first Jewish children born in Chicago.

Isaac Ziegler, after first peddling in the Chicago area, opened a grocery store

Henry Horner was one of
the earliest Jewish settlers in
Chicago.
(From Hyman L. Meites, ed.,
*History of the Jews of Chicago;* all
photos from this publication are
reproduced with permission of
the Meites family.)

at Madison and Clark streets. It is said that he was very well liked for his willingness to help extricate horse teams that got stuck in the mud in front of his store and for being instrumental in having such signs as "Bottomless" and "Road to China" placed on the road.[9]

After clerking in a clothing store for two years, Henry Horner opened a retail and wholesale grocery store at the corner of Randolph and Canal at the western fringe of settlement, a business that was to become one of the largest wholesale grocery establishments in the area. Horner was also one of the founders of the Chicago Board of Trade. In addition to his business skills he had a great love for books and, in the turbulent days of early Chicago, had one of the city's finest collections. His attempt to save his library during the Great Fire of 1871 almost cost him his life. His grandson and namesake served as governor of Illinois from 1933 to 1940.

A few other German-speaking Jews who came to Chicago in the early 1840s, usually after first spending some time in eastern cities, were Levi Rosenfeld, Jacob Rosenberg, and the three Kohn brothers, Julius, Abraham, and Meier. Rosenfeld and Rosenberg soon formed a partnership and opened a retail and wholesale dry-goods store under their names at 155 Lake Street, next door to Philip Newburgh's store. Their business prospered and their relationship was further enhanced when each married a sister of Michael Reese. Jacob Rosenberg's marriage to Hannah Reese in 1849 was the first Jewish wedding in Chicago. The Kohns opened a successful clothing store, first at 85 Lake Street and later at 111 Lake Street.

Early Chicago was a city of many immigrants and lacked an ingrained social structure. The Jews, unlike those in Europe, were accepted in the social

milieu as well as in civic affairs. Jacob Rosenberg later served as an alderman and Abraham Kohn was city clerk under Mayor John Wentworth.

A few Jews, influenced by the aims of an organization in New York, the Colonization Society, whose goal was to lift the Jews out of some of their traditional economic pursuits such as peddling, arrived for the purpose of becoming farmers on a tract of land in nearby Schaumburg, which had been purchased by the society. But the Schaumburg project did not get very far and a number of Jewish farmers left and bought small farm holdings of their own. A few, such as Henry Meyer and Mayer Klein, came to Chicago. Henry Meyer, the first Jew to buy land in Cook County and farm it, became the first Jewish real-estate dealer in Chicago, and Mayer Klein was the first cantor in Illinois.

In 1847 there were twelve Jewish businesses located between 83 Lake Street and 202 Lake Street, divided equally between clothing-tailoring stores and dry-goods stores. Other Jews lived on nearby streets at or near their businesses or at the various hotels.

## THE EMERGENCE OF A COMMUNITY AND ITS INSTITUTIONS

By 1845 there were enough Jews in Chicago to be able to bring together the required ten adult males to constitute the city's first *minyan* for religious services on Yom Kippur – the Day of Atonement. The services were held in a room above a store at Wells and Lake streets. This bare minyan of ten men included two Jews who had come in from nearby Illinois areas outside of Chicago; whenever anyone left the room, services were suspended. The holy Sefer Torah was provided by the Kohn brothers, who had received it from their devout mother when they left their native Bavaria. The next minyan was not gathered until the following Yom Kippur, in 1846, when, as an indication of the growing Jewish population, there was not only a minyan but also a few to spare. The men met again, this time above the store of Rosenfeld and Rosenberg at 155 Lake Street, a site that was to be the center of much Jewish activity in early Chicago.

*Mrs. Dilah Kohn emigrated to Chicago from Bavaria in 1846. Her strict adherence to the Jewish dietary laws was an important factor in the formation of the city's first Jewish congregation that would be able to maintain a rabbi and a* shochet *(ritual meat slaughterer).*
(From Meites, ed., *History of the Jews of Chicago.*)

The first Jewish organization in Chicago, the Jewish Burial Ground Society, was formed in 1845, and in 1846 it purchased – for forty-six dollars – an acre of land adjacent to the lake, north of North Avenue. The land was in what is now the southern part of Lincoln Park but was then outside the city limits. The site, however, proved unsatisfactory because sand blown from the nearby lake shore frequently covered the graves. In 1851 the Hebrew Benevolent Society was organized to aid the sick and provide for burials. It purchased three acres in the town of Lake View, just south of the present Graceland Cemetery, and laid out a burial plot that is still extant, the oldest local Jewish cemetery.[10]

The Jewish community of early Chicago was small and closely knit. Most Jews came from neighboring localities in Europe and now lived in small frame dwellings in even closer proximity to each other. They were frequent visitors to each other's homes, especially on Friday evening and Saturday when their businesses were closed. They exchanged news about their European homeland and about relatives in the East and discussed means of helping newcomers to Chicago.

The Jewish population in Chicago continued to grow steadily, often increased by relatives coming from the old country. The three Kohn brothers soon brought over three more brothers, a sister, and their pious mother, Dilah. Dilah Kohn's strict observance of the dietary laws did not allow her to eat any meat because there was no *shochet* (ritual meat slaughterer). Alarmed by her frail physical condition, her son Abraham Kohn and other family members began to push for the formation of a congregation that would be able to maintain a rabbi and *shochet*.

On November 3, 1847, some twenty men met at Rosenfeld and Rosenberg's store to organize a congregation. At that time the Jewish population of Chicago

was less than a hundred in a total population of about seventeen thousand. They called the congregation Kehilath Anshe Maariv (Congregation of the Men of the West), designating the geographical location of their new community, unlike many of the later congregations, which were often named after areas in their native lands or on the basis of religious and charitable qualities. Nevertheless, all of the original members were Jews from the same general area in Germany.

The following day a constitution was approved for Kehilath Anshe Maariv and signed by the following fourteen members:[11] Abraham Kohn, Jacob Rosenberg, Samuel Cole, Morris L. Leopold, Philip Newburgh, Benedict Schubart, Leon Greenebaum, Levi Rosenfeld, Jacob Fuller, M. Becker, Isaac Wormser, B. Stern, M. Braunschild, and Julius Kohn. The Jewish Burial Ground Society merged with the new congregation and ceded its property to it. Abraham Kohn made a trip to New York to secure the services of a spiritual leader. The man selected was Reverend Ignatz Kunreuther. Kunreuther was born in Germany in 1811 and was the son of an ultra-Orthodox rabbi. Reverend Kunreuther served as a reader and rabbi for Kehilath Anshe Maariv and as a *shochet* for the entire Jewish community. He had good Talmudic training and was strictly observant of Jewish laws.

For the next few years the congregation met above the store on the southwest corner of Lake and Wells streets, in a room that was fitted out as a synagogue. The Orthodox ritual of the old country was followed – the *Minhag Ashkenaz* prayer book was used and women sat separately, with most members observing the traditional Sabbath and holidays by closing their places of business and posting signs in their windows reading "Closed on Account of Holiday."[12]

*(Left) Abraham Kohn (1819–71), an immigrant from Bavaria, helped to organize Chicago's first Jewish congregation.* (From Meites, ed., *History of the Jews of Chicago*.)

*(Right) The German-born Reverend Ignatz Kunreuther (1811–84) in 1847 became the first rabbi, reader, and shochet of KAM Congregation.* (From Meites, ed., *History of the Jews of Chicago*.)

The year 1848 was a notable one in Chicago history. It marked the completion of the Illinois and Michigan Canal, the arrival of the city's first railroad and telegraph, and the opening of the Chicago Board of Trade.[13] Of the Jews who arrived in Chicago from Germany that year, two young brothers, Elias and Henry Greenebaum, were destined to play important roles in both the Jewish community and the larger community for over sixty years. After starting out as store clerks and salesmen, they later founded what was to become a major bank. Both were active in a number of Jewish synagogues and organizations and contributed generously to a variety of philanthropic causes. Henry also was to hold a number of government positions, including alderman and park commissioner.

In 1848 and into the next year Chicago experienced one of its periodic disastrous cholera epidemics, probably caused by contaminated water. The outbreak claimed many lives, including that of Dilah Kohn, who had been so instrumental in the formation of Kehilath Anshe Maariv. In 1850 Chicago obtained its first Jewish teacher, Leopold Mayer. "Lehrer Mayer" was a graduate of a teachers' seminary in Germany, and in Chicago he taught Hebrew and German. Almost fifty years after his arrival in Chicago, Mayer, in a paper read before the Council of Jewish Women on "Jews and Judaism in Early Chicago Days," recounted the following:

When I came to Chicago, the Jews numbered possibly two hundred. The congregation had 28 contributing members and on the very first day I was introduced to most of them including the president and minister. The congregation provided for a reader, a chazan and a shochet. The German arrangement of prayers was in vogue, but it was so diversified that it often depended on the reader what prayer was read, although the addition or omission of a certain prayer created a row in the synagogue.

Instruction in both the tenets and the morals of Judaism was lacking. Every Jew was his own teacher and rabbi. A religious school for children was not necessary, as there were but few children of school-age here.

The two previous years, 1848–49, had been trying for the Jewish colony on account of the cholera which not only bore away a number of its members but left the survivors in constant dread of its return. A burial ground had been purchased from the city as early as 1846. It is remarkable how anxious the Jews are to provide a resting place for their dead when as yet they have scarcely a foothold for the living. This is noticeable through all their history. To the praise of the Jews then here, I must say, that they clung together in sorrow and in joy. The good fortune of one was the happiness of the other, while the gloom of one cast a shadow over all. Thus, on my first Friday night in Chicago, I watched, with one of my brothers, at the bedside of the sick child of a friend.

The place of worship was then located on the southwest corner of Lake Street and what is now Fifth Avenue [Wells Street], on the third floor. The narrow, uninviting entrance was unpleasantly obstructed by the goods of an auctioneer who occupied the store floor below. Already at this period the Sabbath was more or less violated. It is true that most of the women and many of the men were regular attendants, but the latter as a usual thing, left hurriedly for their places of business. Many stores were already open, and the younger men, engaged as clerks, were invisible in the synagogue. The younger women, likewise, were few, and of children under fifteen, there were scarcely any.

Mr. Mayer did manage to give private lessons, and in 1850, he recalled:

> I tried to organize a religious school from the few scholars I already had and the few more I might gather around me. To show the necessity for this, one incident will suffice. To make known my purpose, I went to the president of the congregation to ask leave to post on the door of the synagogue a notice to the effect that I would open a school to teach religion. In all seriousness he, the president, asked me what I intended to teach, and I found that my first lesson must be given to the head of the congregation.[14]

The rented quarters of the Kehilath Anshe Maariv Congregation soon became too small to handle its slowly but steadily increasing membership, and so a lot was leased on the northeast corner of Clark and Quincy streets (now the site of the Kluczynski Federal Building) and construction started on a small frame synagogue. However, because it was difficult to raise adequate funds from the small membership during an economic recession period, the congregation decided to send out appeals for financial assistance to other Jewish communities, especially those in the East.

The appeal read as follows:

To the Israelites and friends of the House of Jacob, throughout the United States – Greetings: –

> The undersigned in behalf of the Congregation Anshi Mayriv [sic] of the City of Chicago, most respectfully appeal to your generosity and solicit from you in the name of the God of our fathers, to extend to us your helping hand by liberal subscription toward defraying the cost of erecting a house of worship so that this, and generations to come, may pray to the Lord of Israel in the same, and that he may pour out his blessings on you and all the descendants of Jacob forever.

A. Kohn
L. Grunebaume
L. Rosenfeld[15]

The synagogue, the first in Illinois, was completed at an estimated cost of $12,000 and had a seating capacity of 450 people. The one-and-one-half-story building had a balcony where the women sat that extended on three sides of the interior. In the center of the synagogue was a raised pulpit (the *bimah*). The worshipers entered from Clark Street and prayed facing east toward Jerusalem, as was the tradition.

The new synagogue was dedicated on June 13, 1851, an historic event well publicized in the two local newspapers and attended by many non-Jews – a number of clergy and civic and political leaders of the city. The traditional rites for the dedication of a new synagogue were followed, including the prayers, the marching in with the scrolls of the Torah, and the circling around the *bimah* seven times before the scrolls were placed in the Holy Ark. The dedicatory sermon was given by the Reverend Isaacs, an English Jew who had settled in New York and who was brought in for the occasion. He fulfilled the task of impressing the importance of the occasion on both Jew and gentile.

The following day the *Daily Democrat* reported the dedication of the synagogue as follows:

> The ceremonies at the dedication of the first Jewish synagogue in Illinois, yesterday, were very interesting indeed. An immense number had to go away, from inability to gain admittance. There were persons of all denominations present. We noticed several clergymen of different religious denominations.
>
> The Jewish ladies cannot be beaten in decorating a church. The flowers, leaves and bushes were woven into the most beautiful drapery that Chicago ever saw before. The choir, consisting of a large number of ladies and gentlemen, did honor to the occasion and to the denomination. . . .

As for possible prejudice or anti-Semitism in Chicago, the newspaper went on with considerable enthusiasm:

> No person that has made up his mind to be prejudiced against the Jews ought to hear such a sermon preached. It was very captivating and contained as much real religion as any sermon we ever heard preached. We never could have believed that one of those old Jews we heard denounced so much could have taught so much liberality towards other denominations and earnestly recommended a thorough study of the Old Testament (each one for himself) and entire freedom of opinion and discussion.

The similarity between Judaism of this variety and some Protestant sects was not missed by the Chicago journalist who commented:

> We would sooner have taken him for one of the independent order of free thinkers than a Jew. Mr. Isaacs is an Englishman and is settled in New York City. There are Jewish synagogues as far west as Buffalo and Cleveland.
>
> The Jews in our city are not numerous, but are wealthy, very respectable and public spirited.
>
> The Jewish Sabbath is on Saturday, and very interesting service takes place today. The whole Mosaic law written on parchment (they never have it printed for church services) will be unrolled from a large scroll and read from. Rev. Mr. Isaacs will again preach. The service will commence at 8 A.M. and last until 11 A.M. The earlier part of the service will be the most interesting.
>
> Gentlemen are requested to keep their hats on, and to take seats below. The ladies will take seats upstairs, according to the Jewish custom of separating the sexes.[16]

In 1853 the congregation organized a day school. Two of its best-loved teachers, Gleason and Brewster, were Irish. The two men instructed Chicago's first-born Jewish generation in not only the grammar school curriculum but also some rudimentary Hebrew, which they taught with zeal but with questionable pronunciation. The school continued until 1873 when a Sabbath school, for religious instruction only, replaced it.

The congregation continued to grow in its new building, which was moved to Adams and Wells in 1853 when its land lease expired. An influx of newcomers, some of whom had fled Germany after the Revolution of 1848 had failed there, helped the congregation's growth. Soon, however, some members began agitating to bring about reform in the traditional rituals. In addition, the Bavarian Jews of Kehilath Anshe Maariv dominated the synagogue numerically and administratively to the extent that the congregation also became known as the "Bayerische Shul" (Bavarian synagogue). The Bavarians held themselves aloof from the increasing number of German-speaking Jews who had started arriving from the Posen area of Polish Prussia.

The impending changes distressed Reverend Kunreuther. Though not an intolerant man, he was one who clung tenaciously to the Orthodox traditions. In 1853 he severed his connection with the congregation and entered the real estate and loan business and became successful. He continued, however, to observe the Orthodox traditions and customs throughout his life.

### THE FORMATIVE YEARS

By 1852 there were just slightly over two hundred Jews in Chicago, but enough "Polish" Jews were discontented with their status at KAM to form their own congregation of twenty members, which they called Kehilath B'nai Sholom (Congregation of the Children of Peace). The congregation initially met in rooms above the clothing store of Solomon Harris, its first president, at 189 Lake Street – just a few short blocks north of KAM. Henry Greenebaum, though from the German Rhineland area, was active in many organizations and also joined the new congregation, serving as its first secretary. However, after being threatened with a loss of membership in KAM because of his dual membership, he resigned from Kehilath B'nai Sholom.

Kehilath B'nai Sholom was more Orthodox than KAM and used the Polish *Siddur* (prayer book). In 1856 some of its members formed another burial society, Chevra Gemilath Chassodim Ubikkur Cholim, and bought an acre of land from the Hebrew Benevolent Society. Kehilath B'nai Sholom grew steadily but was less affluent than KAM. It was not able to have its own synagogue until 1864, when it moved into a new $20,000 building at Harrison and Fourth Avenue (Federal Street). Like KAM, it had solicited funds from other Jewish communities. An article appeared in the Cincinnati *Israelite* on May 4, 1857, extending the appeal for contributions.[17] On the new building's completion, the dedication address was given by Dr. Isaac Mayer Wise, who came in from Cincinnati where he later helped organize the Union of American Hebrew Congregations and the Hebrew Union College.

Soon there was another breakaway by a group of KAM members – this time because it was felt that KAM was too Orthodox. Within KAM was a group of

CHICAGO.—A CIRCULAR—Our friends of the congregation *Bene Shalom* have issued the following circular, calling on all pious men for aid in building up a Synagogue—which we gladly lay before the community, hoping that the praying congregation will be supported by our brethren. Every Synagogue is a monument to Judaism, and every Israelite should contribute his mite toward the erection of another monument to Judaism.

## אל הקורא

הכבוד אחינו בני ישראל, היהודים החרים היושבים בערי
לפראות נרח ושלמו ל"ח אלוהינכם כל פניכם יגילו ש
לבורא קץ מאיבכם הרוזה ל"ח ותעו יי פקרים ושכנתי
ברכם מלוה ח' חנן רל תבמלו ישרם לח חבו ל"ה נבוד
כבו, קוו מנחה ובאו לחצרהזיו הקרובים והרחקים
באחרים.

" Vow and pay unto the Lord your God; let all that
" be round about Him bring presents unto Him, that
" ought to be feared. Bring an offering to the Lord,
" and let them make me a sanctuary, that I may dwell
" among them. He that hath pity upon the poor lend-
" eth unto the Lord, and that which he hath given,
" will He pay him again. Give unto the Lord, the glo-
" ry that is due unto His name; bring an offering, and
" come into His courts, the nearest and farthest from
" your brethren."

A small number of the children of Israel congregated on the western shores of Lake Michigan, in the great emporium of the Northwest, under the humble name *Kehilath Bene Shalom,* (sons of peace) struggled along for several years without having a house of worship, using a room for the purpose, which we can not keep any longer. We intend to lease a piece of ground in some part of the city, and if we are fortunate enough to raise the necessary funds for building a house, we will dedicate it to the service of God and to the education of our children. Our private means are limited, our numbers are few; we, therefore, appeal to your generous hearts, brethren of our faith, in particular, to solicit your assistance. We, the Board of Officers of the congregation, hope and trust that our American co-religionists, so prone to appreciate and support noble and generous institutions, will not fail to lend us a helping hand in this grand undertaking, not only to assist us on the present occasion, in the cause of the Almighty, but will respond to our appeal in a manner of the great nation of the American. Donations will be thankfully received by the undersigned President, and by the Editor of the Israelite.

For the congregation,

D. WETKOWKEY, Pres't. of K. B. S.
REV. A. ALEXANDER, Prof., Sec K. B. S.

This article was an appeal to other communities for contributions to help build a sanctuary for Kehilath B'nai Sholom.

traditionalists who felt very strongly that Judaism should be perpetuated essentially as it had been practiced and passed down through the generations. There was also a growing group who felt that Judaism had to be reformed and modernized in order to adapt better to the present society; they espoused the progressive nature of Jewish law.

The Reform movement had been started in the early decades of the nineteenth century in Germany by Jews who were generally of higher economic and social status. It had been advocated in the United States by Rabbi David Einhorn in Baltimore and by Dr. Bernhard Felsenthal in Chicago in his pamphlet *Kol Kore Bamidbar* (A Voice Calling in the Wilderness).

Each group in KAM believed fervently in its philosophy and religious position, to the detriment of harmony within KAM. Compromise became impossible and, in 1859, Dr. Felsenthal and others founded the *Judischer Reformverein* (Jewish Reform Society), which in 1861 formed the Sinai Reform Congregation with Dr. Felsenthal as its first spiritual leader. Felsenthal was not an ordained rabbi but was a graduate of a teachers' seminary in his native Germany. He had emigrated to the United States in 1854, and after teaching in Madison, Wisconsin, he arrived in Chicago in 1858 with the expectation of becoming a bank clerk while continuing his Talmudic studies.

Sinai Temple was founded by a group of twenty-six men who had seceded from KAM, including such prominent members as Henry and Elias Greenebaum and Leopold Mayer. The secessionists advocated a more westernized prayer book; the maintenance of decorum and uniformity in prayer in-

**1861.**

| | | | | |
|---|---|---|---|---|
| Sept. | 29 | To cash bal. handed in by the preceding Board, | $55 81 | |
| | | " Donation of the new Board, | 5 00 | |
| | | " Contribution of K. B. S., | 19 00 | |
| Oct. | 13 | " " Ramah Lodge, | 60 00 | |
| | | " " H. B. Society, | 100 00 | |
| | 20 | " " Young Ladies' Association, | 25 00 | |
| | | " " Relief Society No. 2, | 8 37 | |
| Nov. | 2 | " Collection at Funerals, | 18 00 | |
| | 28 | " " of L. Silverman, | 22 50 | |
| | | " " of Ladies' Benevolent Association, | 25 00 | |
| | | " " at Moor's Dinner Party, | 1 75 | |
| Dec. | 15 | " Collecting Committee at Large, | 763 22 | |
| | 12 | " " Eisendrath, | 2 75 | |
| **1862.** | | | | |
| April | 6 | " Collected at Funerals, | 4 00 | |
| | | " " Private Party, | 10 00 | |
| | | " " of Young Ladies' Association, | 25 00 | |
| May | 6 | " " at Funerals, | 8 00 | |
| | | " " | 2 00 | |
| July | | " " from Administration of Silverberg, | 11 00 | |
| | | " " at Funerals, | 2 50 | |
| Aug. | | " " B. B. Party, | 12 00 | |
| | | " " at Funerals, | 1 50 | |
| | | " " | 2 00 | |
| | | " " | 1 50 | |
| | | Interest of $500.00, | 20 00 | $1205 50 |
| | | *Balance in Treasury,* | | 21 83 |

| | | | | |
|---|---|---|---|---|
| **1861** | | *Reserve Fund.* | | |
| Sept. | 29 | To Cash bal. paid in by the preceding Board | 19 69 | |
| **1862** | | " Interest of $700.00 for one year, | 70 00 | |
| Aug. | | | | |
| | | To two Notes Invested, | 700 00 | $789 39 |
| | | *Balance in Treasury,* | | 89 69 |
| | | *Standing of Finances to-day:* | | |
| | | To Cash in hand of the Treasurer, in Relief Fund, | $21 83 | |
| | | " " " " in Reserve Fund, | 89 69 | $111 52 |

| 1st 6 months | 2d 6 months | Whole year 1861-62. | | 1st 6 months | 2d 6 months | Whole amt. |
|---|---|---|---|---|---|---|
| 28 | 20 | 48 | By Expenditures in Cash | $157 89 | $100 74 | $259 63 |
| 42 | 15 | 57 | " Groceries and Flour, | 132 35 | 56 69 | 189 04 |
| 12 | 6 | 18 | " Medicine, | 2 59 | 9 98 | 12 87 |
| 6 | 9 | 15 | " Rail Road Tickets, | 42 00 | 37 75 | 79 75 |
| 8 | 9 | 17 | " Rent for Dwelling, | 24 50 | 31 00 | 55 50 |
| 1 | 1 | 1 | " Funeral Expenses, | 5 00 | | 5 00 |
| 22 | 3 | 25 | " Wood and Coal, Excepting Orders, | 56 00 | 14 00 | 50 00 |
| 5 | 8 | 13 | " Strangers, | 51 93 | 25 75 | 57 68 |
| 8 | | 8 | " Board at the Hospital, | 22 50 | 8 50 | 22 00 |
| 8 | | 8 | " Wearing Apparel and Bedding, except the Goods Donated, | 14 42 | | 14 42 |
| 18 | | 18 | " Flour, except the Orders Donated, | 20 56 | | 20 56 |
| | | | " Stoves and Furniture, | 7 62 | | 7 62 |
| 5 | | 5 | " Matzos, | 32 97 | | 32 97 |
| 16 | | 16 | " Sanitary Committee, Camp Douglas and Pittsb'g Landing, | 20 00 | 15 00 | 35 00 |
| 1 | 1 | 2 | " Ticket to Europe, | | 20 00 | 20 00 |
| | 1 | 1 | " Drs. Valenta and Spungel, | | 18 50 | 18 50 |
| 2 | 2 | | " Assisting a sick woman, | | 6 38 | 6 38 |
| 1 | 1 | | " Drayage for wood, coal, &c., | | | 10 85 |
| | | | " 12 months' Salary to Bergman, | | | 36 00 |
| | | | " for Printing last year's Report, | | | 42 45 |
| 4 | 4 | | Discount on money collected, | | | 65 |
| | | | By 30 Cords Wood for next Winter, | | | 150 00 |
| | | | Cash in Treasury this day, | | | 21 83 |
| | | | By expending for goods to peddle, | | | 45 00 |
| | | | *Cash on hand,* | $21 83 | | $1205 50 |
| | | | *Reserve Fund.* | | | |
| | | | By Investment in Real Estate Security, | | | $700 00 |
| | | | By Interest on above for one year, | | | 70 00 |
| | | | By bal. of preceding Board, | | | 19 69 |
| | | | Total, | | | $789 69 |
| | | | *Cash on hand,* | $89 69 | | |
| | | | Besides the amount of Receipts and Expenditures of our Relief Fund, as above stated, we have received and expended Groceries, Flour, Shoes, Hardware and Clothing, Orders, valued at, | $400 00 | | |
| | | | Quilts and Sundries of the Ladies' Sewing Society | 200 00 | | |
| | | | Medicines of Dr. Mahla, | 20 00 | | |
| | | | 18 Cords Wood of the preceding Board, | 72 00 | | |
| | | | Total, | | $692 00 | |
| | | | Which, when added to the above, will make the whole amount of Receipts and Expenditures about, | | | $1,900 00 |

stead of each man being more or less on his own; greater use of the mother tongue intelligible to the members or the language of the country; acquisition of an organ and choir; and the removal of head coverings during services. They wanted to eliminate from Judaism some of its old customs and rituals and to place less stress on religious dogma and more emphasis upon the social and political issues of their country.

Sinai Temple was first located in a former church on Monroe Street just west of Clark Street. Partly because some of the members objected that they had to sit facing the north wall instead of east, in 1863 Sinai Congregation built a new temple at Van Buren Street and Plymouth Court for $7,000. The following year Dr. Felsenthal, now nationally known in Jewish Reform circles, resigned when the congregation refused to renew his contract for more than one year. That same year he became rabbi of the newly formed Zion Congregation, with Henry Greenebaum as its first president. The new congregation soon erected a building on Chicago's west side – on Des Plaines Street between Madison and Washington streets. Dr. Felsenthal served as the spiritual leader of Zion Congregation for twenty-three years. Very active on the Jewish scene, he was one of the founders of the Jewish Publication Society of America and of the American Jewish Historical Society and was one of the first Reform rabbis to participate in the Zionist movement.

By 1860 there were about 1,500 Jews in Chicago, out of a total population of 112,000. The Jewish community was no longer centered around Lake and Wells streets. A small number of Jews now lived north of the river; the older

*Third Annual Financial Report of the Executive Board of the United Hebrew Relief Association, issued October 19, 1862.*
(Courtesy of Michael Reese Hospital archives.)

Chicago's downtown looking west between Randolph and Washington streets from La Salle Street, 1858. Many Jews lived in this area and some had their stores there. (Photo by Alexander Hesler, courtesy of the Chicago Historical Society.)

settlers, who were generally well established, lived on the southern edge of the downtown; and a smaller number lived on its western fringe. Newer Jewish immigrants moved into the area being abandoned by earlier arrivals.

The German Jews who settled in early Chicago showed a propensity for forming organizations and by the 1860s there were numerous Jewish-sponsored organizations in the city. The first of many B'nai B'rith lodges, Ramah 33, was organized in 1857. Henry Greenebaum, the first Jewish political officeholder (alderman), was one of the organizers of the lodge and later wrote, "Here some of the best minds of German and Polish Jews joined hands to remove the miserable provincial barriers existing in Chicago, and the motto of the order, 'Benevolence, Brotherly Love and Harmony' became the living motto of all their actions in the outside world."[18]

In 1859 the leaders of the Ramah Lodge successfully promoted the founding of the first central Jewish relief organization in Chicago, the United Hebrew Relief Association (UHRA). It was established by a convention with delegates from most of the Jewish organizations in Chicago. The fifteen organizations that soon affiliated with the UHRA – and a good indication of the scope of Jewish organizations at the time – were the Ladies Sewing Circle, Frauen Wohlthaetigkeits Verein, Young Ladies' Hebrew Benevolent Association, Sisters of Peace, Ramah Lodge, Hillel Lodge, Hebrew Benevolent Society, Relief Society No. 1, Relief Society No. 2, Washington Irving Literary Association, Chevra Kadisha Ubikkur Cholom, and Congregations KAM, B'nai Sholom, Sinai, and Zion.[19]

Although by the 1860s there were Jewish cemeteries, there was as yet no Jewish hospital. One of the first major acts of the United Hebrew Relief Association was to purchase land in 1865 on La Salle Street between Goethe and Schiller streets for the erection of a hospital. Numerous fund-raising meetings were held and the $135,000 needed for the hospital construction was collected. The cornerstone was laid during a ceremony in 1867 after a parade that included many Jewish organizations and Mayor Rice of Chicago. The Jewish Hospital was opened in 1868 and pledged to admit all cases "irrespective of creed or race." Unfortunately the hospital perished almost at birth, being completely destroyed in the Great Fire of 1871.

Also in the 1860s, the Jews of Chicago became strongly active concerning a foreign issue. It was one of the first times they became involved in such a cause. A treaty with Switzerland, approved by the U.S. Senate and by President Pierce in 1855, allowed the Swiss government to refuse to accord to Jewish citizens of the United States the same privileges given other U.S. citizens. The treaty aroused the ire of many Jews throughout the country. In Chicago, Abraham Kohn, M. M. Gerstley, Samuel Cole, and others vehemently protested against the treaty, wrote letters and editorials for newspapers, met with Senator Stephen A. Douglas, and attended national meetings called to fight the treaty restrictions against Jews – a provision that was changed a number of years later.

Some Jews were also active in the antislavery movement. Michael Greenebaum, who opposed the Fugitive Slave Law, aided a runaway slave to escape in defiance of the law.

### THE CIVIL WAR PERIOD

In the crucial presidential election of 1860, Jews divided their support between Lincoln and Douglas. Just before Lincoln's inauguration, Abraham Kohn, the recently appointed city clerk of Chicago, presented the president-elect with a satin American flag on which he had inscribed verses 4–9 of the first chapter of Joshua, which includes the passage "as I was with Moses, so I will be with thee; I will not fail thee, nor forsake thee. Be strong and of good courage."

When the Civil War broke out, Chicago Jews rallied to the support of the Union. Some of them belonged to army units that were made up predominantly of German gentiles. The German Jews were on friendly terms with the non-Jewish Germans and identified with them in a number of ways. They spoke the

# Contributors to Fund for Equipping Jewish Company in Civil War

| Name | $ | Name | $ | Name | $ |
|---|---|---|---|---|---|
| David Adams | 25 | Mrs. A. Hart | 10 | Henry Newburger | 10 |
| E. Adler | 25 | Mrs. H. Hart | 10 | Oppenheimer & Metzger | 100 |
| Levi Alshuler | 10 | Heilbronner | 10 | Joe Peiser | 20 |
| American & Smith | 50 | J. H. Henoch | 50 | M. Peisser | 50 |
| H. Bachmann | 25 | Mrs. Henoch | 10 | Wolff Perez | 15 |
| Balzheimer | 10 | Daniel Herman | 25 | S. Price | 25 |
| A. Barnard | 20 | A. Herzog & Co. | 100 | Louis Rau | 25 |
| A. Basch | 15 | E. Hoffman | 20 | G. Rubel | 25 |
| S. Bateman | 50 | Ignatz Herzog | 100 | Regensberger & Co. | 25 |
| Beierdorf | 25 | Higher | 25 | Moses Reineman | 25 |
| Berlinsky | 15 | L. Hirchburger | 50 | Simon Reinman | 25 |
| Bockwitz | 50 | D. Isaacs | 25 | S. W. Rice | 25 |
| B. Brunneman | 15 | Jacob Jacobs | 10 | Moses Rosenberg | 15 |
| Mrs. J. M. Brunswick | 10 | E. A. Jessel | 100 | Rosenfeld & Rosenberg | 200 |
| Z. Boskowitch | 100 | G. A. Jessel | 50 | Hyman Rosenthal | 10 |
| E. Brunswick | 35 | Simon Klein | 25 | Julius Rosenthal | 25 |
| Charles Cahn | 10 | Julius A. Kohn | 100 | Rosenthal & Co. | 10 |
| A. Cohn & Co. | 100 | A. and H. Kohn | 50 | J. Rothschild | 25 |
| S. Cole and H. Leopold | 150 | H. A. Kohn & Bro. | 100 | Rubenstein | 15 |
| Mrs. H. Cole | 10 | M. Kohn (volunteer) | 10 | R. Rubel | 100 |
| Clayburgh | 25 | A. Kuh | 20 | Rubel Brothers | 100 |
| Coadowitch & Schnadig | 25 | Captain Jacob La Salle | 100 | L. Ruben | 50 |
| Michael Cowen | 20 | Mrs. La Salle | 10 | Major Salomon | 25 |
| A. Danzig | 10 | Leopold, Meyer & Guthman | 100 | S. Sanci | 10 |
| L. Daube | 25 | J. Lehman | 25 | M. Schwarzenberg | 10 |
| David Dyer | 10 | Mrs. Levi | 10 | A. Schmalz | 25 |
| N. Eisendrath | 100 | James Levy | 25 | B. & S. Schlossman | 100 |
| S. Florsheim | 25 | L. Levy | 15 | B. Schoeneman | 50 |
| L. Frieberger | 25 | M. Levy | 10 | Schoenfeld Bros. | 50 |
| Isaac Freeman | 20 | Newman Levy | 20 | Smith & Schwab | 100 |
| Jacob Frost | 50 | A. Lewis | 50 | Sigmund, Hyman & Hirsch | 100 |
| Freedman and Gutkind | 100 | Isaac Liebenstein | 100 | Lazarus Silverman | 10 |
| R. Foreman | 50 | M. Libenstein | 10 | Lyon Silverman | 50 |
| Frank & Son | 50 | H. Liebenstein | 100 | L. Silverman & J. D. Goodman | 150 |
| Mrs. B. Felsenthal | 10 | J. Liebenstein | 10 | G. Simons | 10 |
| S. M. Fleishman | 25 | M. Lindauer | 25 | J. S. Sheltheimer & M. Selz | 500 |
| Folks Bros. | 20 | M. Loeb | 50 | Shottenfels & Co. | 100 |
| Foreman Bros. | 100 | M. Loeb | 25 | Shoyer & Co. | 200 |
| L. Friesleben | 10 | Mrs. M. Loeb | 10 | Snydacker & Co. | 100 |
| Joseph L. Gatzert | 10 | L. F. Leopold | 25 | M. Solkey | 25 |
| M. M. Gerstley | 75 | Miller and Liebenstein | 100 | J. M. Stein | 50 |
| N. D. Goldberg | 25 | Simon and Leon Mandel | 25 | D. Strauss | 10 |
| Louis Goodman | 50 | Julian Mar | 25 | Dr. W. E. Strauss | 20 |
| Mrs. Goodman | 10 | A. Marcus | 25 | C. Summerfield | 50 |
| Mrs. L. Goodman | 10 | Theo. Marcuse | 10 | L. Theisl | 10 |
| David Greenebaum | 10 | L. Marcuse & Son | 25 | Van Bicur | 10 |
| Isaac Greenebaum | 50 | Isaac Marks | 50 | Vanhern | 10 |
| E. Greenebaum & Foreman | 100 | Alexander Mayer | 25 | J. M. Verosier | 10 |
| Michael Greenebaum | 25 | Chas. Mendel | 25 | S. Wampold | 25 |
| Henry Greenebaum | 100 | Simon Mendelsohn | 10 | Moses Weil | 100 |
| Greensfelder & Rosenthal | 50 | M. Mengass | 15 | Weinstein & Bernhard | 50 |
| Philip Goldstein | 20 | Isaac Miraslowsky | 10 | Wineman, Frank & Co. | 200 |
| Goldsmith, Morais & Co. | 50 | Nelson Morris | 25 | D. Witkowsky | 25 |
| Isaac Guthman | 10 | Jonas Moore | 25 | S. Witkowsky | 25 |
| Haas & Powell | 200 | Julian Moos | 25 | S. Witkowsky, Jr. | 25 |
| S. Harris | 50 | D. Morgentheim | 25 | M. Willstein & Lederer | 50 |
| Hart Bros. | 100 | L. Moss | 25 | Wolfner | 15 |

The Chicago Jewish community in 1862 quickly raised $11,000 to equip the Jewish company of soldiers, the Concordia Guards.
(From Meites, ed., *History of the Jews of Chicago*.)

same language and in many instances they had been forced by common political views to leave Germany in the aftermath of the unsuccessful Revolution of 1848. They read German newspapers, attended the German theater, and belonged to the same associations. But despite the good relations, the Jews had their own organizations and soon decided to raise their own company of soldiers.

A mass meeting on August 13, 1862, held at the Concordia Club, a newly organized Jewish social and civic club founded by Henry Greenebaum and

A Chicago Tribune *article in 1862 reported the formation of a volunteer company of Jewish soldiers to fight for the Union in the Civil War.*

located at Dearborn and Monroe streets, resulted in the establishment of a volunteer company of Jewish soldiers, the Concordia Guards, to fight for the Union in the Civil War. Ninety-six men out of the city's fifteen hundred Jewish residents joined the unit. Very few were native born. The Jewish community helped finance the unit's expenses and pay bounties to the company. It raised $11,000 for the outfit in two days. On August 16, 1862, the *Chicago Tribune* published a tribute to the Jews of Chicago.[20]

The unit became Company C of the Eighty-second Illinois Volunteer Infantry Regiment and participated in the battles of Fredericksburg, Chancellorsville, Gettysburg, and Chattanooga and joined Sherman's march to the sea. Serving with distinction with the unit was Colonel Edward S. Salomon, an immigrant from Germany, who at the time of his enlistment was alderman of the Sixth Ward and who was possibly the first Chicago Jew to become a lawyer. In the war he had two horses shot from under him during the Battle of Gettysburg. After the war he was elected Cook County Clerk and in 1869 he was appointed governor of the Washington Territory by President Grant.

Another Jewish officer of the Eighty-second Illinois was Captain Joseph B. Greenhut, who, although wounded in the war, continued to serve and rose to the rank of adjutant general. In 1891 he was honored by being chosen to deliver the dedicatory address at the unveiling of a monument honoring Illinois soldiers at Gettysburg.

Also serving in the war was Dankmar Adler, who had enlisted at the age of eighteen. He was the son of Rabbi Liebman Adler, the rabbi of KAM. Dankmar Adler was wounded at Chickamauga but his experience with the army engineers in the war served him well in his architectural career, which brought him world renown for works such as the Auditorium Building in Chicago, designed with his partner, Louis Sullivan.

(Left) Dankmar Adler
(1844–1900), the renowned
architectural engineer, was
born in Germany and came
to the United States in
1854, settling in Chicago
in 1859.
(Irving Cutler Collection.)

(Right) Marcus Spiegel
(1829–64) was born in
Germany and in 1849 came
to America, where he en-
gaged in the dry-goods
business. After his death in
the Civil War, his brother
Joseph opened the store that
he and Marcus had planned
together, which eventually
evolved into the Spiegel
Catalog Company.
(Courtesy of Jean Powers
Soman.)

Marcus Spiegel, one of the founders of the Hebrew Benevolent Society in
Chicago, enlisted in the Union army and rose to the rank of colonel. He was
severely wounded at Vicksburg but insisted on returning to active service. He was
killed in battle in 1864, just as papers promoting him to brigadier general had
been prepared. After Marcus's death, his brother Joseph opened the store that the
two men had originally planned together and which eventually evolved into the
Spiegel Catalog Company. Caroline Spiegel, Marcus's wife, was formerly a Quaker
from Ohio, where she had met Marcus, who was then an immigrant peddler from
Chicago. In 1853 she had been among the first in Chicago to be converted to
Judaism by a rabbinical-controlled board. Mrs. Spiegel continued to be very active in the Chicago Jewish community long after her husband had been killed.

Despite ardent Jewish support of the Union in the Civil War, there were a
number of instances of wartime discrimination against Jews. Jews were not
allowed to serve as army chaplains until Lincoln changed the policy. In 1862
General Grant issued an order barring Jews from Union-occupied areas in the
South that he commanded. Because of the alleged misdealings of a few Jewish
merchants near army camps, the "Jews, as a class" – as Grant described them –
were expelled from the area without a trial or even a hearing. When President
Lincoln was made aware of this order, he had the War Department in 1863 send
a letter on his behalf to Dr. Bernhard Felsenthal of Sinai Congregation disclosing
the rescinding of Grant's order.

When the war ended, General Salomon and what was left of the Eighty-second

*Letter from the War Department in 1863, on behalf of President Lincoln, to Dr. Bernhard Felsenthal, regarding the rescinding of General Grant's infamous order that expelled Jews from Union-occupied territories in the South in 1862.*
*(Courtesy of Chicago Sinai Congregation.)*

Regiment returned to Chicago in June 1865 to a huge welcoming reception where Mayor "Long John" Wentworth spoke. His speech included the following:

> A few years since, there was a cry raised that "foreigners" could not be trusted, and an attempt was made to disenfranchise you, but when at last the time came that tried men's souls – when native-born Americans proved false to their allegiance to their flag, and tried their utmost to tear down and trample under foot the noble structure their fathers fought and died to rear up, then you "foreigners" came forward and showed yourselves true men. You have done honor to your native and to your adopted countries. I say it: you have proved that this country owes its existence to foreign immigrants.[21]

In the decade of the Civil War, Chicago's population tripled, reaching about 300,000 by 1870. The Jewish population also grew, bolstered by more Jews not only from Germany but also from Holland; some started coming from Eastern Europe, especially from Latvia and Lithuania (the Litvaks). The Jewish population also began to spread out geographically, and in 1867 the first synagogue north of the river was built on Superior Street near Wells Street. This synagogue, composed largely of the older German-speaking Jews of the area, was called North Chicago Hebrew Congregation (now Temple Sholom).

The Yiddish-speaking Eastern European Jews – mostly peddlers initially, like the German-speaking Jews who preceded them – could not find a synagogue that was as Orthodox as they were. Thus in 1865 they organized a synagogue called B'nai Jacob on the southern fringes of what is today's Loop, and the following year established another, Beth Hamedrash Hagodol. In 1867 the two synagogues merged and became Beth Hamedrash Hagodol Ub'nai Jacob. It met for a few years on the first floor of the home of David Zemansky at 183 Fourth Avenue, near Polk Street. Zemansky had recently arrived from New York and was in the business of outfitting "Litvak" peddlers with packs. The synagogue soon established a *cheder* (Hebrew school) for the religious instruction of its youth. The Yiddish-speaking Jews, unlike their German-speaking brethren, did not readily enter into the secular life around them.

Factionalism and differences existed among the Yiddish-speaking Jews just as they did among Jews who spoke German. Often the division was based on the rivalry of those from different towns in Europe, people who believed that their ritual or their rabbi was superior to that of the others. An example is an event that evidently occurred in 1870 at Beth Hamedrash Hagodol. A congregant came to services and, instead of wearing the customary black felt hat, he wore a light straw hat, at the time considered inappropriate by the synagogue officials, who ordered him out. He left, very upset, and was followed out of the synagogue by his fellow countrymen from the town of Mariampol (in southern Lithuania). The Mariampol group proceeded to secede from Beth Hamedrash Hagodol and to form its own synagogue, Ohave Sholom Mariampol. Through the years there were many synagogues that split for various reasons, including differences of religious philosophies, personal conflicts often of national origin, or dislike of the rabbi. Usually the breakaway group would meet first in a home, then in a storefront, school, or hotel, eventually building a synagogue.

Another Orthodox synagogue formed before the Great Fire of 1871 was Ohave Emuno Congregation (Love of Faith). However, because members were seen pulling up in their horse-drawn wagons to attend Sabbath services and then pulling away to continue their business, the synagogue became known as Die Halbe Emuno (the half-faith congregation). Sermons and meeting minutes were in Yiddish at the Eastern European synagogues, in contrast to the German used in the early German-speaking synagogues.

While the little Eastern European Orthodox synagogues were being established to the south and southwest of the downtown, the older synagogues founded by German Jews were growing and changing. The oldest congregation, KAM, moved farther south in 1868 into a former church building at Wabash and Peck (Eighth Street). In 1874 it joined the Union of American Hebrew Congregations, the national organization of Reform Judaism. KAM's president from 1861 to 1891 was the indefatigable M. M. Gerstley, and its rabbi was Liebman Adler, who occupied the position from 1861 to 1882, except for four years. Rabbi Adler was a good leader, teacher, and preacher, using his native German, and he contributed numerous articles to Jewish journals. He was a strong antislavery proponent and a supporter of the Union.

# MY LAST WILL

I desire that there be no haste in my interment. If there are no signs of decomposition sooner, the funeral should not be until forty-eight hours after my death.

If the physician who treated me should find it desirable in the interest of science to hold a post-mortem examination, I would like that he be not interfered with.

My coffin shall not cost more than $7.

No flowers.

My funeral to be directly from the place of demise to the cemetery.

Dear Hannah: In view of your delicate health, I desire that you remain at home and not join the funeral if the weather is the least inclement.

Not more than three days' mourning in domestic retirement.

I justly value the *Kaddish* of my sons and daughters, but I do so only if you, after the expiration of the year of mourning, do not omit attendance at the synagogue without necessity.

If financial conditions permit, each of my married children should join a Jewish congregation, the fittest being the Kehilath Anshe Ma'ariv.

Those children who do not live too distant should, if the weather permits, and if it can be done without disturbing their own domestic relations, gather every Friday evening around the mother.

My children, hold together! In this let no sacrifice be too great to assist each other and to uphold brotherly and sisterly sentiment. Each deed of love you do to one another would be balm to my soul. The example of eleven children of one father who stand together in love and trust would be to his grave a better decoration than the most magnificent wreath of flowers, which I willingly decline, but leave to your judgment. The small savings which I leave will come to you only after the death of the mother.

I know you; I may trust that you will not meet in an unfilial way about possession and disposition. The heritage which is already yours is a good name and as good an education as I could afford to give. It does not look as if any one of you had a disposition to grow rich. Do not be worried by it. Remain strictly honest, truthful, industrious and frugal. Do not speculate. No blessing rests upon it even if it be successful. Throw your whole energy into the pursuance of the calling you have chosen. Serve the Lord and keep him always before you; toward men be amiable, accommodating and modest, and you will fare well even without riches. My last word to you is: Honor your mother. Help her bear her dreary widowhood. Leave her undisturbed in the use of the small estate, and assist if there should be want.

Farewell, wife and children.

But one more word, children. I know well you could not, if you would, practice Judaism according to my views and as I practiced it. But remain Jews and live as Jews in the best manner of your time, not only for yourself, but also where it is meant to further the whole.

LIEBMAN ADLER.

---

Sinai's rabbi was Dr. I. Chronic, who had been brought from Germany. Although he was an eminent scholar, "his sermons were so weighty that few in his audience or in the community were able to appreciate them."[22] His sermons were always in German. Dr. Chronic was one of the first Reform rabbis in the country to advocate the replacement of the traditional Jewish Sabbath by Sunday services, although this change was not instituted during his tenure. He was successful, though, despite severe congregational opposition, in having Sinai contract with Rosehill Cemetery in 1867 for a section of its ground – the first time a Jewish congregation had burials in a non-Jewish cemetery. Dr. Chronic established the first Jewish publication in Chicago, *Zeichen der Zeit* (Signs of the Times), which appeared monthly in German.

Indicative of the Jewish community's growing numbers and affluence, a group of prominent Jews – many Concordia Club members disgruntled over some political issues – in 1869 organized the Standard Club, mainly as a social and recreational gathering place. Later it also became active in civic and communal affairs and supported many worthy causes.[23] The first club met downtown; then it relocated to Michigan Avenue and Thirteenth Street in 1870. In 1889 it moved into its own building at Twenty-fourth Street and Michigan Avenue, closer to the German-Jewish population, and still later (1926) settled in its present downtown home at 320 Plymouth Court. Earliest members included

*The last will of Liebman Adler (1812–92), scholarly author and the distinguished rabbi of Kehilath Anshe Maariv for almost twenty years.*

*(From Meites, ed., History of the Jews of Chicago.)*

many individuals who were or would become successful: Dankmar Adler, architect; Judge Philip Stein; Julius Rosenthal, lawyer; Nelson Morris, meat packer; Elias, Michael, and Henry Greenebaum, bankers; Abraham Kohn, city clerk; Simon Florsheim, Charles Schwab, Bernard Kuppenheimer, Emanuel Mandel, David Witkowski, Edward Rubovits, Joseph Rosenberg, and Charles Kozminski, manufacturers and merchants.

## THE GREAT CHICAGO FIRE AND ITS AFTERMATH

On the eve of the Great Chicago Fire, the city was a bustling community of great contrasts, described as follows:

> In the autumn of 1871, Chicago was a city of 334,000, partly a metropolis and partly a frontier town, six miles long and three miles wide . . . It was known by various nicknames: Gem of the Prairie, Garden City, Queen City. And some considered it one of the wickedest cities in the land. No one thought to call it the Matchbox, with its thousands of wooden structures, wooden sidewalks and heavy streets paved with wooden blocks.
>
> Chicago was divided into three divisions by its river, which was spanned by a dozen wooden bridges and which forked half a mile west of the lake, one branch running northwest and the other south. Nestling between the lake and the southern branch was the South Division, where the city's extremes of wealth and squalor were represented, the elegant houses along Michigan Avenue contrasting with the hovels of Conley's Patch and Healy Slough and Kilgubbin, the principal business establishments balanced by ramshackle barns and storage sheds. Between the north branch and the lake was the North Division, primarily an area of upper middle-class and wealthy homes, although along the river stood grain elevators, the Chicago and Northwestern Railroad depot, the McCormick Reaper Works, the wholesale meat market and laborers' dwellings. To the west of the river's fork was the West Division, comprising industrial plants, hundreds of frame houses occupied by workers' families and a small, handsome residential area around Union Park.[24]

The Jewish population at that time was an estimated four thousand. In contrast to the two small synagogues that existed about twenty years earlier, there were now ten congregations,[25] some housed in imposing buildings. The growing prosperity and commercial organization of the Jews were reflected in the many philanthropic, social, fraternal, and cultural organizations that had evolved.

The Jewish community was largely concentrated in an area of about half a square mile bounded by Van Buren Street on the north, Polk Street on the south, Clark Street on the east, and the river on the west. A few German Jews lived slightly south of this area. A small number of Jews lived north of the river, where the North Chicago Hebrew Congregation was located, and some lived west of the river, where there were the Zion Congregation and the newly organized (1870) B'nai Abraham Congregation at Halsted and Fourteenth Street, the latter composed mainly of German-speaking Bohemian Jews.

An 1870 city business directory shows that people believed to be Jews were

TABLE I. *Leading Occupations among Jews, 1870*

| Occupation | Number Reporting |
| --- | --- |
| Dry goods | 80 |
| Cigar and tobacco | 66 |
| Clothing | 59 |
| Boots and shoes | 43 |
| Distillers and saloons | 34 |
| Tailors | 32 |
| Meat markets | 22 |
| Furniture | 17 |
| Variety stores | 16 |
| Furriers | 15 |
| Jewelers | 13 |
| Physicians | 11 |
| Commissioned merchants | 11 |
| Bakers | 11 |
| Barbers | 11 |
| Flour and feed | 11 |
| Dressmakers | 10 |
| Hardware | 10 |
| Carpenters | 9 |
| Lawyers | 9 |
| Secondhand stores | 8 |
| Architects | 7 |
| Books | 7 |
| Real estate | 7 |
| Upholstery | 6 |
| Boardinghouses | 6 |
| Crockery | 6 |
| Druggists | 6 |
| Livery stables | 6 |
| Vinegar | 5 |
| Bankers | 5 |
| Dentist | 5 |
| Blacksmiths | 5 |

Source: *Edwards 13th Annual Directory of the Inhabitants, In-corporated Companies, and Manufacturing Establishments of the City of Chicago Embracing a Complete Business Directory for 1870* (Chicago, 1870), as classified by Michael Charney in 1974 at Hebrew Union College.

engaged in almost fifty different occupations at the time (table 1). A high percentage of Jews were merchants in either the retail or wholesale trade, with smaller numbers being professionals or skilled craftsmen.

People crowding west across the Randolph Street bridge in an effort to flee the approaching flames of the Chicago Fire of 1871. The Lake Street bridge is on the left.

(From an engraving in the October 28, 1871, issue of *Harper's Weekly*. Courtesy of the Chicago Historical Society.)

After an unusually long period of drought, what came to be known as the Great Chicago Fire started on the evening of October 8, 1871, in Mrs. O'Leary's barn at 558 DeKoven Street, just southwest of the major Jewish settlement in Chicago. That night happened to be the Jewish holiday of Simchat Torah, the festival of the rejoicing of the law, a celebration of merriment in which the congregants dance in their synagogues with the Torah scrolls. This is probably one of the reasons that some of the scrolls were saved from the fire.

Because the wind was blowing from the southwest, the fire leaped over the wooden bridges and ships in the river and engulfed today's downtown area. The flames raced northward for another two days, destroying almost everything in their path. When the fire was finally out, virtually everything in an area bounded approximately by Taylor Street (1000 South) to Fullerton Avenue (2400 North) and from Halsted Street (800 West) to the lake had been destroyed. The fire took more than 250 lives; consumed 17,000 homes, leaving one-third of the city's population homeless; and created a property loss reaching nearly $200 million.[26]

The Jewish community of Chicago was particularly hard hit by the fire as so many people had maintained homes and businesses in the downtown area. Some five hundred Jewish families were left homeless, and five of the city's seven

synagogue buildings were destroyed, as were four B'nai B'rith lodges. Ironically, a new synagogue, Beth El, had been organized on the eve of the fire.

The following article about the fire appeared in *The Israelite*.

DOMESTIC RECORD.

Chicago, Ill – The synagogues destroyed are first, North side Hebrew Congregation; 2. Fifth Avenue Congregation; 3. Sinai Congregation; 4. Benai Shalom Congregation; and 5. Beth Hamidrash Haggadol's. Benai Berith Lodges losing their furniture are: Ramah No. 33, Maurice Mayer No. 105, Jonashan No. 130, and Sovereignty No. 148, besides the District Grand Lodge No. 6. The lodge rooms, furniture of I. O. K. B. L. also were destroyed. The greatest calamity is the burning of the Jewish hospital with thirteen inmates. It is reported that thirteen of the poor patients fell victims to the conflagration. Besides them, it is reported, that many Israelites, especially young and daring men, perished in the flames, numbers and names not yet ascertained. 500 Jewish families, 300 among them destitute, have lost their homes, business places and employment. In fact the Jewish community in proportion suffers most by the loss of the public institutions, and places of business. The only relief committee fully organized to receive and distribute charity, is the Benai Berith committee, consisting of, with head quarters at 111 West Washington Street: Dr. Felsenthal, Pres.; J. Lederer, Treas.; K. Hexter, Sec'y.; L. J. Unna, B. H. Seligman, J. Ohnstein and A. P. Levi, Trustees. All communications, funds, packages, etc., should be directed to J. Lederer, Esq., 111 West Washington Street for the B. B. Relief Committee. This committee will work in conjunction with the Hebrew Relief Association, and the other benevo-

The ruins of the Simon and Strauss store on Lake Street, one of the many Jewish businesses destroyed by the Chicago Fire.
(From Meites, ed., *History of the Jews of Chicago*.)

lent associations of the city. Money is the main thing to be sent; clothing, bedding and provisions will be welcome to alleviate suffering, but money is the main thing needed. We appeal to each and to all, to give special aid to the above committee. It ought to be done at once and liberally. Let none be too late. All prominent Jewish firms of the city have lost their places of business, and many also their homes; so that the rich like the poor heavily feels the agony of the moment, and all need encouragement.[27]

The B'nai B'rith members immediately organized a relief committee, with J. L. Gatzert in charge, and sent out a national appeal for relief aid. Donations soon came pouring in from many parts of the nation and even from overseas. The United Hebrew Relief Association also raised money and the two organizations worked to help alleviate the suffering of the fire victims. After the fire the *Chicago Times* noted with approval that "not one (Jew) has been sent to ask for the aid of the general or special relief committee of the Gentiles."[28] Additionally, the Standard Club of Thirteenth Street and Michigan Avenue was used by General Philip Sheridan as his headquarters when martial law was declared after the fire.

The fire cast a pall on the future of Chicago. A New Orleans newspaper predicted that "Chicago will never be like the Carthage of old. Its glory will be of the past, not of the present, while its hopes once so bright and cloudless will be to the end marred and blackened by the smoke of its fiery fate." Other editorialists reflecting on Chicago's notorious reputation for gambling, brothels, and saloons felt that the fire might be deserved retribution: "Again the fire of heaven has fallen on Sodom and Gomorrah!"

This feeling of despair, however, was not shared by Chicagoans. The day after the fire Joseph Medill's *Chicago Tribune*, operating in an improvised plant in an unburned area, editorialized: "CHEER UP! In the midst of a calamity without parallel in the world's history, looking upon the ashes of thirty years' accumulations, the people of this once beautiful city have resolved that CHICAGO SHALL RISE AGAIN!" And Deacon Bross, one of Chicago's greatest boosters and a former lieutenant governor, declared:

> I tell you, within five years Chicago's business houses will be rebuilt, and by the year 1900 the new Chicago will boast a population of a million souls. You ask me why? Because I know the Northwest and the vast resources of the broad acres. I know that the location of Chicago makes her the center of this wealthy region and the market for all its products.
>
> What Chicago has been in the past, she must become in the future – and a hundredfold more! She has only to wait a few short years for the sure development of her manifest destiny.[29]

Determined Chicagoans, who had already built a settlement on a marshland, immediately started to rebuild their city, and in a few years visitors to Chicago found few signs of the disastrous fire of 1871. The Mandel brothers, who had set up a temporary store at Twenty-second Street and Michigan, moved back downtown. Henry Greenebaum obtained capital for mortgages on buildings, Nelson Morris expanded his packing house, and Moses Bensinger expanded his line of products at his J. M. Brunswick and Company.

Unfortunately, in 1874 Chicago experienced another fire on the near South Side, which threatened to be as disastrous as the first. Careful dynamiting, however, prevented the fire's progress, but not before KAM (which had escaped the 1871 fire) and Congregation Ohave Sholom Mariampol were destroyed and the Russian-Polish Jewish community, which had been only slightly hurt in the 1871 blaze, sustained major damage.

An appeal was launched by the United Hebrew Relief Association to raise funds for the victims of the most recent fire – the Russian-Polish Jews whose generally dire economic straits were compounded by the disaster. This time there was only limited response to the plea, partly because of the heavy financial drain exacted by the first fire and partly because many of the German Jews felt that the Russian-Polish Jews had not contributed their share of relief funds after the earlier fire and had taken more than their share. Furthermore, the cultural, religious, and economic differences of the newer Russian-Polish Jewish immigrants were abhorrent to many of the more affluent German Jews. While the German Jews had been mainly cityfolk, the Eastern European Jews were mainly from very small communities and had not been influenced by the reforms of the French Revolution, as had the German Jews. The respected Rabbi Liebman Adler was asked to help raise funds and to try to dispel the narrow sectionalism among the Jewish groups in Chicago. His message read as follows and had the desired effect:

> Scarce two decades have elapsed since all the Israelites of this city were living as in the bonds of one family circle. Each knew the other. All worshipped harmoniously in one temple and shared others' woes and joys.

How great is the change! Thousands scattered over a space of thirty miles, in hundreds of streets, divided by pecuniary, intellectual and social distinctions and differences. Separation, division, dissolution, estrangement, repeated and continual, are the words which characterize the history of our brothers in faith until now. Dissolved in the mass of our population, we are losing the consciousness of homogeneity and the strength gained for each individual by concerted action.

Let us also consider the oft-heard complaint that Poles and Russians absorb a disproportional large share of the means of this Association.

Brothers and Sisters: Are these poor ones less to be pitied, are they less poor, are they less Israelites because Poland or Russia is the land in which they first saw the light, or rather the darkness of this world? The poor of those countries are doubly poor. These unfortunates came to us from a country which is the European headquarters for barbarism, ignorance, and uncleanliness. In these countries, thousands of Israelites are densely crowded into small towns and villages, and they become singular and peculiar in their customs, manners, and ideas. In conferring charity, it is the duty of the Israelite first to look to the needs and then to the deserts of the recipient.[30]

The fires that so damaged the Chicago Jewish community also provided some opportunities. After KAM and Sinai congregations both had their synagogues destroyed, serious talks ensued about a possible merger. The plan faltered, however, over the issue of Sunday services.[31] Sinai had already instituted such services in lieu of Saturday services; the congregation sought to be more in harmony with the general community, and Saturday attendance was limited since many of its members worked on that day. KAM was opposed to Sunday services, and Sinai was facetiously labeled as the most religious Jewish congregation in Chicago because it was closed even on the Sabbath.

With the failure of the merger talks, each congregation moved out of the downtown area and located on the near South Side, to which the German-speaking Jewish community had started moving in large numbers after the Chicago Fire and as the downtown business community expanded. They initially progressed one or two miles south along such streets as Indiana, Wabash, and Michigan; later they were to move farther south into the Grand Boulevard, Washington Park, and Kenwood–Hyde Park communities, and still later, into South Shore. Also after the fire, a small number of Jews moved north of the river and for a while there was a Jewish community in what is now the Old Town area around Division and Wells streets. There, toward the end of the last century, within blocks of each other were three synagogues, Anshe Emet, Emanuel Congregation, and Temple Sholom. These synagogues later moved further north near the lake, where they are now the largest synagogues in the Lakeview-Edgewater area.

On the South Side in 1875, KAM moved into a former church building at Twenty-sixth Street and Indiana Avenue. The following year Sinai completed building its temple at Twenty-first Street and Indiana Avenue, whose architects included Dankmar Adler and Louis Sullivan.

Interior of Sinai Temple, designed by Louis Sullivan and Dankmar Adler. The congregation occupied the building from 1876 to 1912, when it moved to Forty-sixth and Grand Boulevard (now Dr. Martin Luther King Drive.)
(Courtesy of Chicago Sinai Congregation.)

In 1880 Sinai Congregation obtained the services of the dynamic Dr. Emil G. Hirsch as its rabbi, a position he held until his death in 1923. Born in 1852 in Luxembourg, where his father was chief rabbi, he came to the United States in 1866. After marrying Matilda Einhorn, the daughter of the well-known Reform rabbi David Einhorn, he assumed the pulpit of Sinai Congregation and soon won national recognition as an author, scholar, orator, civic leader, and strong advocate of Reform Judaism.[32] Five years later Sinai had become the largest Jewish congregation in Chicago. Hirsch was a prominent member and president of the Chicago Rabbinical Association (now the Chicago Board of Rabbis), which was founded in 1873 as an organization where communal, scholarly, and general Jewish matters could be discussed and where fellowship and cooperative efforts could be developed.

Rabbi Hirsch helped to bring about or solidify numerous radical reforms in his congregation, some very controversial, such as the temporary elimination of the traditional ark. Additionally, Hebrew readings were curtailed and services were held on Sunday instead of on Saturday. He defended his revolutionary concept of Judaism by writing numerous articles in Reform journals and by delivering forceful convincing sermons. He generally opposed Jewish nationalism and Zionism and in the World War I period was accused of being sympathetic to the Germans. His range of communal and scholarly activities was extensive and included being instrumental in organizing the Associated Jewish Charities, editing the *Reform Advocate,* serving as president of the Chicago Library Board, promoting vocational education, arbitrating labor disputes, and being one of the original faculty members of the University of Chicago, where he taught rabbinic literature and philosophy. (His grandson, Edward Levi, later served as president of the same university.)

Although believed to be the highest-paid clergyman of any denomination during the period he served (his congregation included such wealthy businessmen and contributors as Julius Rosenwald, Joseph Schaffner, Marcus Marx, B. Kuppenheimer, Siegmund Florsheim, and Max and Harry Hart), Hirsch had a strong commitment to social justice and fought for welfare reforms, slum clearance, women's rights, and the rights of organized labor. Dr. Hirsch died in 1923 and his funeral was attended by six thousand people. He was succeeded at Sinai Congregation by the well-known and respected Rabbi Louis L. Mann, who served there for more than three decades.

As the devastating effects of the fires faded into the past, many Jews, through hard work, began to gain a measure of affluence. Some had started out as virtually penniless backpacker peddlers who then became small store owners living above or behind the store. Large retail operations such as Mandel Brothers, L. Klein, M. L. Rothschild, Alden's, and Spiegel's emerged from modest beginnings to be followed decades later by other retailers such as Goldblatts, Morris B. Sachs, O'Connor and Goldberg, and Polk Brothers. From similarly modest beginnings there emerged major manufacturing concerns such as Hart, Schaffner and Marx, B. Kuppenheimer, Florsheim Shoe Company, Brunswick-Balke-Callender Company, Nelson Morris and Company, Albert Pick and Company, and Inland Steel, as well as such financial houses as A. G. Becker, Greenebaum Bank and Trust Company, Foreman National Bank, S. W. Straus and Company, and Silverman's Bank. Lazarus Silverman, a financial expert and the founder of the latter bank, is credited with helping to promulgate the Species Resumption Act of 1875, which helped stabilize U.S. currency after the Civil War.[33]

One person who achieved an especially eminent position in the business community and in communal and philanthropic works was Julius Rosenwald (1862–1932). The son of German immigrants, he became president and chairman of the board of Sears, Roebuck and Company and played a major role in the company's development and success. Throughout his life, Rosenwald felt a deep compassion and responsibility toward those in need and contributed unstintingly to Jewish and other social and civic causes. His philanthropy pro-

Dr. Emil G. Hirsch (1852–1923), nationally known rabbi of Sinai Congregation from 1880 until his death. (Courtesy of Sinai Congregation.)

vided for the erection of thousands of schools and YMCA-YWCA's for African Americans in the rural South, as well as model housing in Chicago. He contributed to the University of Chicago and founded the Museum of Science and Industry. He was very active in and served as an officer of numerous organizations, including a number of terms as president of the Associated Jewish Charities of Chicago. He gave significant amounts of money to help worthy Jewish causes locally, nationally, and overseas. He held that his funds should stimulate activity and not merely do things for people, and that every gift should be spent within a generation. He shunned lasting endowments or the naming of his contributions in his honor. Julius Rosenwald's philosophy of giving was stated in a speech he once made as president of the Associated Jewish Charities of Chicago:

Shall we devote the few precious days of our existence only to buying and selling, only to comparing sales with the sales of the same day the year before, only to shuffling our feet in the dance, only to matching little picture cards so as to group together three jacks or aces or kings, only to seek pleasures and fight taxes, and when the end comes to leave as little taxable an estate as possible as the final triumph and achievement of our lives? Surely there is something better and finer in life, something that dignifies it and stamps it with at least some little touch of the divine.

My friends, it is unselfish effort, helpfulness to others that ennobles life, not because of what it does for others but more what it does for ourselves.

*Julius Rosenwald (1862–1932), the son of German immigrants, became president and chairman of the board of Sears Roebuck and Company. He was very involved with and supportive of numerous Jewish and other community causes.*
(Courtesy of the Jewish Federation of Metropolitan Chicago.)

In this spirit we should give not grudgingly, not niggardly, but gladly, generously, eagerly, lovingly, joyfully, indeed with the supremest pleasure that life can furnish.[34]

### BUILDING SOUTH SIDE INSTITUTIONS

As their financial status improved, the German-speaking Jews and their families migrated farther south into newly developing prime residential areas. As they moved, so did their major synagogues. Sinai Congregation moved in 1912 to Forty-sixth Street and King Drive, where its facilities included a gymnasium, swimming pool, and social center. There was also a very active recreational and educational program for its over one thousand members and also for nonmembers. Its acclaimed lecture series attracted people from throughout the city. In 1950 it relocated to eastern Hyde Park near the lake. Similarly, KAM in 1891 occupied a beautiful temple at Thirty-third and Indiana Avenue designed by Louis Sullivan and his partner, Dankmar Adler (whose father, Liebman Adler, had been rabbi of the congregation). In 1920 it moved to Fiftieth and Drexel Boulevard where for many years Jacob J. Weinstein was the well-known rabbi. It is now part of KAM Isaiah Israel at 1100 Hyde Park Boulevard – its seventh home since it was founded in 1847. Comparably, B'nai Sholom after the fire moved to Michigan Avenue and Sixteenth Street; then in 1890 to Indiana and Twenty-sixth Street (the former KAM building); in 1906 to Forty-fourth and

This Kehilath Anshe Maariv (KAM) sanctuary at Thirty-third and Indiana Avenue was built at a cost of $110,000 and dedicated in 1891. The landmark building was designed by Louis Sullivan and Dankmar Adler. (Photo by Irving Cutler.)

St. Lawrence Avenue; in 1914 to Fifty-third and Michigan Avenue; and then in 1924 to 1100 Hyde Park Boulevard, where it too is now part of KAM Isaiah Israel. In joining together again, the two congregations came full circle, since B'nai Sholom had been formed in 1852 by members who broke away from KAM.

In addition to religious institutions, the Jews of the South Side built a variety of facilities to take care of the sick, poor, orphaned, and aged. These institutions included Michael Reese Hospital, dedicated in 1881. It was built mainly with money left by Michael Reese, who had died a bachelor in 1878 at the age of sixty-three. He had made his money out west and was never a resident of Chicago. However, most of his relatives, including six sisters and their families, lived in the city and were very favorably disposed to building a Jewish-sponsored hospital that would replace the one that had burned in 1871. His family used some of the money left to them plus some additional funds that they contributed or raised to build the hospital, which initially contained sixty beds. Today, in the same locale, it is one of the largest hospitals in the city, with a thousand beds, and it has been a pioneer in research. It was partially supported by the Jewish Federation[35] but, as it was from the beginning, it is open to all races and religions, as was its nursing school, which was established in 1890. The hospital was recently sold to a private hospital company.

Another major facility, the Drexel Home (Home for Aged Jews, as it was originally called), was opened in 1893 at Sixty-second Street and Drexel Avenue. Its construction was made possible by a generous gift of $50,000 from Abraham Slimmer, a cattle merchant and financier from Waverly, Iowa, an enigmatic individual who lived very frugally but contributed generously to a number of Chicago Jewish institutions. Most of the Drexel Home's residents, especially in its early years, were German Jews. Also located at Sixty-second Street and Drexel Avenue, from 1899 until it closed in 1942, was the highly rated Chicago Home for Jewish Orphans, which had also received a substantial amount of money from Slimmer.

The German Jews were also generous donors to numerous non-Jewish institutions, including the University of Chicago. Aid to the university goes back to the beginnings of the school in 1892 in Hyde Park. Its opening was threatened because of financial difficulties. An appeal for help brought a quick response from the Jewish community. A meeting was hurriedly organized at the Standard Club by Rabbis Bernhard Felsenthal and Emil G. Hirsch to which all Standard Club members were invited and at which $28,350 was raised. Dr. Goodspeed, secretary of the university, thanked the Standard Club members in a letter: "I am reminded that a year ago, when we were in utmost danger of failing in our efforts to secure the establishment of the University of Chicago, the club came to our relief. The subscriptions your committee handed me aggregated $28,350, and enabled me to meet the conditions imposed upon us and thus secure the establishment of the university."[36] Aid to the university continued through the years, and as late as the 1920s the University of Chicago was listed as a recipient of annual funds from Jewish charities.[37] Many of the university's facilities have also been funded by Jewish contributors.

Efforts were also made by the Reform and similar-thinking groups to set up an educational program under native leadership that would instill a knowledge and love of Judaism in the growing number of Jewish youth. The Jewish Educational Society was organized in 1876, and its aims were expressed in the following appeal:

Israelites of Chicago:

What have you done for preserving our faith and transmitting the noble bequest of ages to posterity? True, you have in the different parts of this city formed congregations and erected beautiful houses of worship, redounding to the honor of the God of our Fathers. You have ministers preaching to you every Sabbath and Festival Day well accredited by the surrounding world. You have Sabbath schools and teachers, besides, to imbue the youth with all elements of Jewish religion and history. But are you satisfied that thereby you have done all in your power to maintain the religion of our Fathers in its pristine glory and purity? True, you have raised your children as Jews, but do you believe that they, after having attended the Sabbath school up to the time of their confirmation, will be able to expound and to defend Judaism before the world? Or do you know of any one of them desirous of pursuing the study of Jewish lore and history, in order to know what Judaism is, and what it has accomplished in its wonderful march? And suppose there are such people, what opportunities have they of studying Hebrew and acquiring the knowledge indispensable for a thorough understanding of Judaism? Where are the schools from which you expect your future rabbis and teachers and well-read laymen to come? The latter can certainly not be imported from the old country for the purpose of upholding our Jewish institutions.

Indeed, indifference and dissension, ignorance and shallowness have long enough eaten the very marrow and root of our sacred inheritance. Compare the zeal and devotion, the generosity and sympathy manifested in Christian churches by young and old, with the indolence and lethargy which have estranged the young, particularly to our holy cause, so as to make every attempt of enlisting their interest fail at the very outset. Christian mission societies send forth their soul-hunting agents to ensnare Jewish young men and tear them away from the breast of their religion, while the Jewish community, for want of religious education and protection, leaves them to spiritual starvation.[38]

The writer then went on to appeal for the establishment of a Jewish high school and eventually a Jewish theological seminary. However, the reasoned call did not arouse the various, often divergent, elements in the community to action. More successful was the Zion Literary Society, founded in 1877, at Zion Temple. It provided well-attended weekly educational and musical programs, published a weekly newspaper, and provided a means for the older generation to preserve its culture while expanding its horizons in the New World.

# 2

# The Second Wave

## The Eastern European Jews

### HISTORICAL BACKGROUND

In the late 1880s about half of the world's ten million Jews lived in Eastern Europe, predominantly in the Russian Empire, with others living in Romania and parts of the Austro-Hungarian Empire. Between 1880 and 1925 over two million Jews left Eastern Europe, going mainly to American cities. In time, 80 percent of the Jewish population of Chicago consisted of such emigrants and their descendants.

These Jews came to America from an area even less hospitable to them than the states from which the German Jews had come. The Russian Empire was backward, autocratic, steeped in medievalism, a land where serfs were held in bondage until 1861 and where enlightened ideas of Western Europe were slow and late in penetrating. The Russian government's policy toward the Jews changed with every new ruler, but with few exceptions it was restrictive, harsh, often brutal, sometimes confusing and contradictory, with the Jews often being blamed for national calamities.

For the most part, the Jews had not come to Russia; rather, Russia had come to them, through a series of annexations. There were few Jews in Russia until the expansion of the Russian Empire into Poland, Lithuania, Latvia, and Ukraine in the seventeenth and eighteenth centuries. Prior to that, a small number of Jews had come from the area to the south, living in the Causcasus and around the shores of the Black Sea. In the Grand Duchy of Muscovy, the nucleus of the later Russian Empire, Jews were not tolerated, nor were most foreigners. The sixteenth-century czar Ivan the Terrible, after conquering the city of Polotsk in Belorussia, ordered the generals to "baptize the Jews who consent to baptism, and drown the rest in Polot River."[1] There, in 1563, three hundred Jews who refused to accept baptism were in fact drowned. It is small wonder that the Jewish blessing for the czar became "God keep the Czar – away from us."

The Jews were periodically expelled from Russia. In 1741, the Empress Elizabeth Petrovna decreed that

> from our whole Empire, both from the Great Russian and little Russian cities, villages, and hamlets, all Jews of the male and female sex, of whatever calling and dignity they may be, shall, at the publication of this our ukase, be immediately deported with all their property abroad, and shall henceforward, under no pretext, be admitted into our Empire for any purpose; unless they shall be willing to accept the Christian religion of the Greek persuasion. Such [Jews], having been baptised, shall be allowed to live in our Empire, but they shall not be permitted to go outside the country.[2]

The annexation by the Russians of large areas on their western borders brought into the empire substantial numbers of Jews, totaling about a million, from Poland and other lands – Jews who had lived in those areas for many centuries. Although some Jewish traders had been in Poland and Lithuania much earlier and some settlers had come from the Tatar invasion of the Black Sea region, the Jews had first started settling in those regions in large numbers between the twelfth and fifteenth centuries, coinciding with the Crusades and the period of the Black Death, events that had led to the massacres of thousands of Jews. Most of the Jewish settlers fled from the German areas and from Bohemia. Later they were joined by much smaller numbers of Jews fleeing the Spanish Inquisition of 1492.

The Jews differed markedly from the largely Slavic peasant population of the region. The Jews were small-town and city dwellers and were usually skilled craftsmen and merchants. They were welcomed and protected by Polish kings because they were experienced in trade and financial matters and could help build up a backward kingdom that had been ravaged by invaders from the east. In 1569, Poland and Lithuania united in a kingdom that stretched from the Baltic to the Black Sea. Jews played a role in colonizing parts of the country, including spreading out to the southeast into the Ukraine. They were active in local and international trade, in tax and rent collecting, and in the industries dealing with hides, timber, salt mining, and alcoholic beverages. They were often resented by the poor, illiterate peasants and by church authorities for their occupations and for their religion.

The Jews flourished in the relative economic and religious freedom and the self-government that they enjoyed in the kingdom during the fifteenth and sixteenth centuries. The Jewish Council of Four Lands (provinces) functioned almost as a Jewish parliament and was allowed to exercise religious, economic, and political control over the Jews. Jewish communities usually had their own internal governing organization (*kehillah*) and a religious-civil court (*bet din*). A Cracow rabbi wrote, "If it could only stay this way until the Messiah's arrival!" However, this peaceful existence began to change as economic competitors, including German gentile merchants who had moved into the area, and the clergy, who objected to the Jewish faith, pressured the Polish kings to restrict the Jews' economic activities and circumscribe the places where they might live and do business. In 1648 the Cossack and Ukrainian peasant rebellions, led by Chmielnicki, were disastrous for the Jews. In the next decade an estimated one-fourth to one-third of Poland's Jewish population was killed; over seven hundred communities were wiped out during this period of chaos and anarchy. A letter from a ravaged area reported: "They slaughtered eight hundred noblemen together with their wives and children as well as seven hundred Jews, also with their wives and children. Some were cut to pieces, others were ordered to dig graves into which Jewish women and children were thrown and buried alive. Jews were given rifles and ordered to kill each other."[3] The prolonged Cossack wars left most of the surviving Jews in poverty.

In the latter part of the eighteenth century, Poland was partitioned among Austria, Prussia, and Russia. Of the nearly 1,000,000 Polish Jews, Prussia inherited about 150,000, Austria 250,000, mainly in Galicia, and Russia well over 500,000 plus thousands of Polish Jews who were quickly expelled from Prussia.

In 1791, the Russian government established the Pale of Settlement for its newly acquired Jewish population. The Pale restricted Jewish residence to certain western parts of the Russian Empire, essentially eastern Poland, Lithuania, Belorussia, Ukraine, Bessarabia, and Crimea – areas where Jews had been living and adjacent areas to the southeast that the Russians were trying to colonize. Jewish merchants were prohibited from trading in the inner provinces of Russia although permission to live outside the Pale was granted to certain limited groups of professionals, skilled artisans, and businessmen, often subject to the arbitrary decision of the local governor. At times Jews were ordered out of certain segments of the Pale, and in 1882 a decree excluded Jews from rural areas inside the Pale. Many of the remaining rights that Jews had had under the Poles were taken away by the Russians. Between the Congress of Vienna (1815) and World War I more than one thousand decrees regulating Jewish economic, religious, educational, communal, tax, property, and military status were enacted.

Prussia and Austria also limited the areas of settlement of the Jews, but they were more liberal in their treatment of them. These countries too had a policy where a small number of rich or assimilated Jews useful to the government were given favorable economic treatment and entree to certain residential areas while the lives of the masses of poor Jews were very restricted. In Romania, as in Russia, discrimination against Jews was written into law; also as in Russia, the government often promoted violence against the Jews. Romania classified Jews

*(Opposite page) Jewish Eastern Europe, 1835–1917: The Pale of Settlement. This was the territory where most Jews were required to live in Czarist Russia. It generally consisted of twenty-five provinces in Eastern Poland, Lithuania, Belorussia, Ukraine, Bessarabia, and Crimea, although the boundaries changed through the years. The 1897 census showed about 5,000,000 (94 percent) of the Jews of Russia living in the Pale, almost all in villages, towns, and cities. They comprised 11.6 percent of the total Pale population but 36.9 percent of the urban population. The Pale was abolished in 1917. (Map by Irving Cutler and Joseph Kubal.)*

as foreigners; in effect the Jews there were a people without a country. The Jews had suffered little hardship during the period of Turkish rule in Romania and had been for the most part the middle class and often the intelligentsia of the country; but an independent, nationalistic Romania turned out to be very oppressive toward its Jews. Thus, in the nineteenth century, while restrictions against Jews in Western Europe were being eliminated, new ones were being imposed in Eastern Europe.

### SHTETL LIFE

The Eastern European Jews lived mainly in a town or village known as a *shtetl* or, in the plural, *shtetlach*. In the restrictive environment of Eastern Europe,

A scene in the shtetl of Ushitza, Ukraine. The woman barely visible in the center window is said to have been the mother of the famous cantor Mordechai Hirshman. (Courtesy of the YIVO Institute for Jewish Research.)

the Jews through the centuries developed a unique, close-knit, sociocultural community life in the shtetl. The inhabitants of the shtetl were bound together "by firm spiritual ties, by a common language, and by a sense of destiny that often meant a sharing of martyrdom; the Jews of Eastern Europe were a kind of nation yet without recognized nationhood. Theirs was both a community and a society; internally a community, a ragged kingdom of the spirit, and externally a society, impoverished and imperiled."[4]

The shtetlach of Eastern Europe had much in common although there were slight variations in the life of the Jewish population, often depending on whether the shtetl was in the east or west or was in the Ukraine, Belorussia, Poland, Lithuania, Romania, or various subdivisions in the Austro-Hungarian Empire. These differences could be in the Yiddish dialect spoken, superstitions, the religious rituals, or even in the seasoning of the Sabbath gefilte fish – with sugar or pepper.[5] But the shtetlach, in common, consisted mainly of poor, religious folk, steeped in tradition, superstitious, somewhat earthy, usually resisting secularism and dreaming of the Messiah who would return them to the Holy Land. They lived precariously in fear of drunken hooliganism, marauding Cossacks, or oppression by government and church officials.

The life of the shtetl revolved around the synagogue, the home, and the marketplace. The Orthodox way of life was very demanding. It provided a strict code of laws, 613 *mitzvot,* or obligations of the devout Jew, which governed much of daily life. Ethical values, dietary regulations, religious beliefs, and social duties were included in this code of laws.[6] The highest values of

the shtetl were achieved through *Yiddishkeit* (Jewishness) and *menshlikhkeit* (human decency).

Social roles were clearly defined, with the most honored position held by men learned in the Holy Books. Women would become breadwinners so that the husbands would have time to study and lead a life of piety, as this was the way to understand God, a living force in their lives. The best match of a bridegroom for a daughter was usually considered to be a *yeshivah* scholar who would bring *yichus,* or family status and pride.

Each shtetl, depending on its size, usually had at least one synagogue, *mikvah* (ritual bath), *cheder* (Hebrew school), house of study, bathhouse, and Jewish cemetery. Scattered throughout Eastern Europe, usually in the larger communities, were yeshivahs, institutions of higher learning where the Talmud was the major source of study. Bright students would leave their homes at a young age for distant communities to study at the yeshivah, an undertaking considered to be most honorable.

The synagogue was the center of the Jewish community life, a place of prayer, learning, and assemblage. In the smaller communities it was usually a wooden structure. The sharp social division of the shtetl was reflected in the seating arrangement in the synagogue, with the most esteemed, the men of learning, sitting closest to the eastern wall where the Ark with the Holy Scrolls was located. Next came the *balebatim,* or men of substance and good standing, followed by the *proste Yidn,* or common Jews. Farthest from the eastern wall were the beggars and needy strangers who were cared for by the extensive social service organizations of the Jewish community.

The home, often containing an extended family, was, in theory and from a religious viewpoint, patriarchal in structure, but in practice it was frequently dominated by the mother. The climax of each week was the joy of the Sabbath with its special holiness and ceremonies, when the best in dress and food was brought forth. On the Sabbath the whole town took on a different character.

In 1841, Dr. Max Lilienthal, a German Jewish scholar, visited Vilna, one of the largest Jewish communities in the Russian Pale, and described a Friday night, the eve of Sabbath, after synagogue services:

When I reentered the streets all was still and quiet. For the first time in my life I had an idea of a Sabbath as celebrated by our ancestors in the holy land in times of yore. Heaven and earth, moon and stars, houses and streets, all preached: "It is the Sabbath, the day consecrated by the Lord." All the stores were closed; no cart was moving in the street; a holy tranquility reigned anywhere. The men excepted, who returned from the service, no person was to be seen in the wide and empty streets. The high five-story houses were illuminated from the deep cellar to the garret rooms. It was as if the whole city had put on its holiday attire to receive in a dignified manner the heavenly bride of the Sabbath. I stood full of amazement in the midst of this spectacle, sunk in deep revery, disturbed only now and then by a "Good Shabbos" addressed to me by the men who passed by and quietly disappeared into their different homes.

I followed some of them, and through the cleft of a window shutter looked into the front room anxious to observe how the Sabbath was celebrated in the circle of these families.

How clean, how tidy looked the room! The floor, neatly scrubbed, strewn with sand; the walls were adorned with many lighted candlesticks; in the middle of the room stood a large table covered with snow white linen on which were several pairs of chalos (Sabbath-bread) and a bottle of wine with several silver cups. In one nook of the room in a large leather armchair sat the grandmother . . . . ; she played with a little grandson sitting on her lap. The mother . . . . sat with folded arms engaged in a quiet conversation with one of her daughters-in-law. All were nicely dressed. . . . They waited for their husbands, and none would dare to disturb the holy peace of the Sabbath by loud conversation before the men had returned with the sweet and charming greeting of a "Good Shabbos." . . .

I again looked through the windows into the rooms where many men were singing their zemirot (Sabbath songs), or engaged in a friendly conversation either with the members of their families or with some visitors. All had a different appearance – the gloomy, care-worn faces had disappeared; everybody seemed reconciled with his God and the troubles of life; the mitigating hand of religion had laid its balm upon the wounded hearts; the agonies of the past and the care of the future seemed to be forgotten. . . .

But soon the lights began to be extinguished. While passing several houses I perceived wife and children already asleep, but the men still sitting over a Hebrew book, enjoying the study of a commentary of a chapter read on the following morning. Half an hour more and Vilna, that beehive of Jews, being quiet and still, I returned to my hotel really delighted with the spectacle I had observed for the first time, and with the holiness with which the Sabbath is still kept among our coreligionists in Russia.[7]

Each home was an integral part of the larger Jewish community, which shared in the joys and sorrows of the family. Help was available during periods of crisis brought on by riots, fires, cholera epidemics, or economic need. The spirit of the shtetl is depicted in the following account by a shtetl dweller:

> There was a little boy my age who lived in the shtetl. He was an orphan. . . . Just his father was dead and his mother wasn't a strong woman and she couldn't take care of him very well. They were very poor and I remember how that boy used to walk around in those cold winter nights with torn boots. So he comes to the market on one of these busy days and he goes over to one of the stands where a man is selling these heavy boots that we used to wear in the shtetl. They were called "shtivl." The man has a small shack which he calls a store and he has dozens of boots hanging from the wall and over the doorway. So the orphan stole a pair of boots. All of a sudden the storekeeper rushes out of the store into the market and starts yelling "a ganef, a ganef," "a thief, a thief!" And people start rushing from all sides and the policeman comes and naturally they find the orphan boy who stole the pair of shoes, and the boy doesn't deny it. They return the pair of boots and the policeman is ready to take the boy to jail.
>
> All the Jews stand around and the women weep and cry, "What are we going to do, how can we let the police take away a Jewish boy? We have to do something about it," and so on. So one fat market woman who is selling some sort of beygl, picks up one of her dozen skirts – you know, they wore two or three skirts, one on top of the other to keep warm, and the money was kept in a pocket sewn into the last skirt so nobody should steal it. She takes out some money and offers it to the storekeeper and so on until a collection is taken up and about $2.00 is collected. The policeman puts his hand in the back and the money is slipped into his hand and he lets the boy go. This the policeman always expected. Whenever he is called in to an affair like that he knows that he will be bribed to let the "criminal" go.
>
> When the policeman goes away, then the real fireworks begin. The people start yelling that if the community took care of the boy, he wouldn't have to steal a pair of shoes. But the rich people are all too busy giving money to those who don't really need it instead of taking care of the orphans and the widows. So a committee goes up to speak to the big shots in the community. And the gabai begins to apologize that he didn't know that the widow was so poor and if somebody had only told him he would have seen to it that she and her family had enough to eat and to wear. And from that incident, the boy was always decked out in good clothes, and they always had food in the house. Now, I think, that could only happen in the shtetl.[8]

Although there was a hierarchy of non-Jewish government officials in most shtetlach, including the powerful chief of police and the constable, the Jews, through their own community council, administered their community and religious affairs. These included support of the major religious institutions as well as such organizations as burial, nursing, and loan associations, and sometimes a guesthouse and a poorhouse. Larger towns had public kitchens, free dispensaries, funds for assisting poor brides, and provision for Passover needs. A major source of funding for these activities was a tax on kosher meat.

Market day in Kremenits in eastern Poland. Almost half of the population of the community was Jewish. (Courtesy of the YIVO Institute for Jewish Research.)

The marketplace was the major source of livelihood for the Jewish community. It served the town and the surrounding rural area. Here the Jews as middlemen, tailors, shoemakers, dairymen, blacksmiths, bakers, tinsmiths, carpenters, fishmongers, butchers, draymen, and tavern keepers came in contact with the peasants of the surrounding areas and by means of trade tried to eke out enough to provide for Sabbath and holiday meals and the other necessities of life. The symbiotic relationship with the peasants in the marketplace was generally friendly, often involving much bargaining in their dealings in the Jewish stores and stalls around the marketplace, where the peasants would shop after selling their produce.

In the following account, a shtetl and its marketplace are depicted as

a jumble of wooden houses clustered higgledy-piggledy about a market-place . . . as crowded as a slum. . . . The streets . . . are as tortuous as a Talmudic argument. They are bent into question marks and folded into parentheses. They run into culs-de-sac like a theory arrested by a fact; they ooze off into lanes, alleys, back yards. . . . [At the center is] the market-place, with its shops, booths, tables, stands, butchers' blocks. Hither came daily, except during the winter, the peasants and peasant women from many miles around, bringing their live-stock and vegetables, their fish and hides, their wagon-loads of grain, melons, parsley, radishes and garlic. They buy, in exchange, the city produce which the Jews import, dry goods, hats, shoes, boots, lamps, oil, spades, mattocks, and shirts. The tumult of the market-place . . . is one of the wonders of the world.[9]

The shtetl was not isolated from the outside world. It was often located along the highways that brought a variety of travelers, including merchants, itinerant ministers, and entertainers. Traveling in and out of the shtetl were storekeepers going to the larger cities to buy merchandise, and yeshivah boys. Later, contacts with the outside world were often augmented by proximity to railroads and by the spread of newspapers, books, and the mail system. The winds of change began to affect the people of the shtetl, but unlike the peasants in the surrounding area, they maintained a high traditional educational level while learning also about the outside world.

These contacts with the outside allowed for the slow infusion of new ideas and movements into the shtetl, often leading to internal discord. One such conflict developed with the spread of Hasidism from its roots in Poland in the 1700s. This religious and social movement with mystical-revivalist overtones was started by Israel Ben Eliezer (the Baal Shem Tov – Master of the Good Name) and stressed the joy of being a Jew through an outward demonstrative emotional response. It embraced ecstatic prayer, song, and dance; miracles; optimism, enthusiasm, compassion; and strong personal loyalty to the "Tzaddik," the charismatic spiritual leader. It was a type of revolt of the "unlearned" against the strict rule of the seemingly pedantic rabbis. The humble Jew was as worthy as the most learned Talmudic scholar, and the deepest reverence for God could best be expressed through emotional prayer. Hasidism spread rapidly in Eastern Europe, where in time it was accepted by large numbers of Jews for whom it provided an emotional escape from their ever-threatening, explosive political and economic situation and from excessive religious concern with legalism and rationalism.[10]

Hasidism was met by strong, often bitter opposition from the traditionalists and the upper classes, and from Talmudic scholars who regarded it as heretical. One of its strongest opponents was the great scholar Rabbi Eliyah, the Vilna Gaon. In time both sides modified extremes in their positions and reached a type of accommodation, especially when both were threatened by a new movement, the Haskalah, or Enlightenment.

The Haskalah movement had its roots in the general European "enlightenment" movement of the eighteenth century. It took hold first among the Jews of western and central Europe and by the end of the century was penetrating into the Jewish communities of Eastern Europe. It encouraged Jews who had been steeped largely in religious studies and confined by the limitations of the ghetto, with its rigid, multiplicity of laws and customs sometimes tinged with myths and superstitions, to open themselves up to Western culture. It advocated the modernizing and westernizing of the Jewish religion and customs. Such changes, it was felt, would also lead to greater acceptance of the Jews by their neighbors, a dream that too often proved elusive. Out of the movement evolved a new type of Jewish school and literature, often in Hebrew, that included political, social, and economic ideas of the Western world.

With the onset of the industrial revolution in the latter part of the nineteenth century, many Jews moved into the slums of the larger cities. By 1897 more than half of the Jewish population of five million in czarist Russia was concentrated in the large cities, with a total of about a half million living in Warsaw, Lodz, and Odessa. Large numbers of Jews also moved to Grodno, Kovno, Berdichev, Vilna, Lublin, Bialystok, Minsk, and Kiev. They began to be employed in ever-larger numbers in manufacturing, many in the needle trades or tobacco factories. Some were employed in home workshops, others in larger factories, with a few becoming wealthy (see table 2).[11]

TABLE 2. *Jewish Occupational Groupings*

| Occupation | Percentage |
|---|---|
| Agricultural pursuits | 2.9 |
| Professional service | 5.0 |
| Domestic and personal service | 19.4 |
| Trade and transportation | 34.8 |
| Manufacturing and mechanical pursuits | 37.9 |

Source: 1897 Russian census.

A high literacy rate among urban Jews contributed to their employability. Most men, but less than half the women, were literate, especially in Hebrew and Yiddish – a higher percentage than that of the general Russian population. And, despite the many problems confronting Jews, their numbers grew rapidly in the Russian Empire – from less than two million in 1820 to over five million by the end of the century. They then constituted half of the world's Jewish population. In 1897, in their area of greatest concentration, Jews constituted 14 percent of the population of Poland. They comprised about one-third of the population of the two largest Polish cities, Warsaw and Lodz.

The influence of the Haskalah movement in secularizing many Jews, especially the young, paved the way for other new movements among the Jews in Eastern Europe. These included Zionism, the modern movement calling for the return to a Jewish national home in Israel; and the Bund (alliance), the Jewish workers movement, which was strongly Yiddishist, socialistic, and idealistic, a group that fought for civil rights but opposed Zionism. Both organizations, moreover, pushed the concept of self-defense for the Jew. Government despotism had helped radicalize some of the Jews, a small number of whom became revolutionaries.

Increasing secularization, the development of some modern industry, limited emancipation, and the rise of newer Jewish leaders apart from those of wealth or religious influence brought change and created problems in the Jewish communities of the shtetl and the cities. While these factors induced some migration, the mass exodus of Jews out of Eastern Europe was triggered largely by government restrictions, by the scarcity of economic opportunities and jobs for the rapidly expanding Jewish population, and especially by a series of devas-

Klezmorim, *traditional Yiddish folk musicians in Rohatyn (Retin) in Stanslawow province, Poland, 1912.* (Courtesy of the YIVO Institute for Jewish Research.)

tating *pogroms* (organized massacres of Jews). Brutal despotism, killings, and Jewish migration were frequently encouraged by the government, which was confounded by the stubbornness and unwillingness of increasing numbers of Jews to assimilate. Europe was amazed that Russia, which had developed a distinguished intelligentsia, could deliberately pursue such a relentless policy of butchery against the Jews.[12]

In the Austro-Hungarian Empire, Jews were often caught in the middle of the nationalistic conflicts. No matter which side they favored, the Jews usually ended up losers. But for half a century they were protected by the benevolent rule of Emperor Franz Josef. Fate, however, was never kind to Russian Jewry. Where there had been very few Jews before, by the nineteenth century there were millions and the numbers were growing rapidly. The government seemed to follow a policy outlined by one of its high officials as the only solution to the Jewish problem in Russia: one-third of the Jews should emigrate, one-third should become Christianized, and one-third should perish.[13]

One approach to this solution was the military draft. Nicholas I wrote in a confidential memorandum that "the chief benefit to be derived from the drafting of Jews is the certainty that it will move them most effectively to change their religion."[14] At the age of eighteen, a specified number of Jews were drafted for twenty-five years of military service. Sometimes they would be taken at the age of twelve for six years of additional preparatory training. To escape this prolonged and harsh military service many draft-age youths fled into the forest, mutilated themselves, or used other subterfuges. To fill the military quotas, "Khappers" (kidnappers) were used to snatch youths from their homes or off the street and transport them to the eastern provinces of Siberia. The Hebrew writer I. L. Levin, who saw such a transport start on its long eastward journey, described the scene he remembered from his youth:

Near a house stood a large and high wagon, to which a pair of horses were harnessed. Soldiers brought out children from the house, one after the other, and deposited them in the wagon. Soon it was packed to capacity. Children were sitting or lying on top of each other like herring in a barrel. Fathers, mothers, and relatives stood around. A person who has not seen the agonizing parting of parents from their little children and who has not heard their helpless lamentations that penetrate to heaven does not know real tragedy. One father gives his boy a little book of Psalms. Another hands his son phylacteries. From all sides are heard admonitions: "Remain a Jew; no matter what happens, hold fast to Jewishness!" Mothers wring their hands, the hopeless tears never stop, moans of agony and cries of despair resound.[15]

Alexander Herzen, a Russian intellectual and historian, described a convoy of conscripted Jewish children in the mid-1830s:

> "You see, they have collected a crowd of cursed little Jewish boys of eight or nine years old" [a Russian officer tells Herzen in a village in the province of Vyatka]. ". . . they just die off like flies. A Jew boy, you know, is such a frail, weakly creature . . . . he is not used to tramping in the mud for ten hours a day and eating Biscuit . . . being among strangers, no father nor mother nor petting; well, they cough and cough until they cough themselves into their graves."
>
> . . . . it was one of the most awful sights I have ever seen, those poor, poor children! Boys of twelve or thirteen might somehow have survived it, but little fellows of eight and ten . . .
>
> Pale, exhausted, with frightened faces, they stood in thick, clumsy, soldiers' overcoats, with stand-up collars, fixing helpless, pitiful eyes on the garrison soldiers who were roughly getting them into ranks. . . . And these sick children without care of kindness, exposed to the icy wind that blows unobstructed from the Arctic Ocean, were going to their graves.[16]

Under the somewhat more enlightened reign of Alexander II (1855–81), Jews enjoyed a respite from the usually harsh treatment and began to participate more in the intellectual and cultural life of Russia. But the assassination of the czar in 1881 was a major turning point in the history of the Jews of Russia. Some Russians suggested that Jewish revolutionaries were somehow connected to the assassination. What had appeared to be a gradual movement toward emancipation of the Russian Jews was reversed by the restrictive May Laws, which prohibited Jews from living in villages, confining them to towns, and severely limited the number of Jewish students in higher education. There followed hundreds of pogroms, the systematic eviction of Jews from Moscow, and the notorious Beilis blood libel charges of 1911 in which Menahem Beilis was accused of the ritual murder of a boy in Kiev.

The prejudice of the ages was unleashed on the Jews, possibly to cover the ineptness and corruption of the government, which was a prime instigator of the pogroms. Jews were accused of breaking cathedral crosses, ritual murder, enslaving peasants, destroying a portrait of the czar, espionage, contributing to peasant drunkenness, raising prices, crowding Christians off sidewalks, and other bizarre charges. On one occasion pogroms broke out simultaneously in three hundred or more cities and shtetlach.

The pogrom in the Pale community of Shpola in 1897 was reported in a toned-down version, omitting the deaths and barbarity, by the Russian newspaper *Novoye Vremya* as follows:

> At three o'clock in the afternoon an immense crowd of peasants rushed into our town, and wrecked completely the stores, homes, and warehouses belonging exclusively to the Jews. A large number of rich business places and small stores, as well as hundreds of houses, were demolished by the crowd, which acted, one might say, with elemental passion, dooming to destruction everything that fell into its hands. The town of Shpola, which is celebrated for its flourishing trade and its comparative prosperity, now presents the picture of a city which has been ravaged by a hostile army. Lines of old women and children may be seen moving (into the town) to carry home with them the property of the "Zhyds." Of essential importance is the fact that these disorders were undoubtedly prearranged. The local Jews knew of the impending disaster four days before it took place; they spoke about it to the local police chief, but the latter assured them that "nothing is going to happen."[17]

The Kishinev pogrom of 1903 resulted in the death of about fifty Jews and the severe torturing and wounding of six hundred more. The massacre brought protests from representatives of many countries throughout the world, including the Congress and president of the United States, and prompted the following letter from the great Russian writer Leo Tolstoy:

> My opinion concerning the Kishinev crime is the result also of my religious convictions. Upon the receipt of the first news which was published in the papers, not yet knowing all the appalling details which were communicated subsequently, I fully realized the horror of what had taken place, and experienced simultaneously a burning feeling of pity for the innocent victims of the cruelty of the populace, amazement at the bestiality of all these so-called Christians, revulsion at all these so-called cultured people who instigated the mob and sympathized with its actions. But I felt a particular horror for the principal culprit, our Government with its clergy which fosters in the people bestial sentiments and fanaticism, with its horde of murderous officials. The crime committed at Kishinev is nothing but a direct consequence of that propaganda of falsehood and violence which is conducted by the Russian Government with such energy.[18]

Chaim Nachman Bialik, the great Hebrew poet, wrote "In the City of Slaughter" after visiting Kishinev. The poem helped inspire many Jews to the cause of Zionism and the need for self-defense.

Added to the pogroms was the economic plight of the Jews. The governor of Bessarabia, a Russian area that was experiencing an influx of rural Jews, commented:

*Jews wrapped in their prayer shawls about to be buried after being killed during a pogrom in Russian Ukraine, 1919.*

(Irving Cutler Collection.)

The observer is struck by the number of Jewish signs in Bessarabian towns. The houses along second-rate and even back streets are occupied in unbroken succession by stores, big and small, shops of watch-makers, shoe-makers, locksmiths, tinsmiths, tailors, carpenters, and so on. All these workers are huddled together in nooks and lanes amidst shocking poverty. They toil hard for a living so scanty that a rusty herring and a slice of onion is considered the tip-top of luxury and prosperity. There are scores of watch-makers in small towns where the townsfolk, as a rule, have no watches. It is hard to understand where all these artisans, frequently making up seventy-five percent of the total population of a city or town, get their orders and patrons. Competition cuts down their earnings to the limit of bare subsistence on so minute a scale as to call in question the theory of wages.[19]

It was such conditions and events that started the mass migration of two million Jews from Russia during the four decades after the assassination of Alexander II in 1881. Their destination was the golden land that everyone was talking about. Mary Antin reminisced about her youth in Plotsk, Russia:

"America" was in everybody's mouth. Businessmen talked of it over their accounts; the market women made up their quarrels that they might discuss it from stall to stall; people who had relatives in the famous land went around reading their letters for the enlightenment of less fortunate folks, the one letter-carrier

A Jew praying on a boat
en route to America.
(Courtesy of the American
Jewish Historical Society.)

informed the public how many letters arrived from America, and who were the
recipients; children played at emigrating. . . . A few persons – they were a dress-
maker's daughter, and a merchant with his two sons – who had returned from
America after a long visit, happened to be endowed with extraordinary imagi-
nation (a faculty closely related to their knowledge of their old countrymen's
ignorance), and their descriptions of life across the ocean, given daily, for some
months, to eager audiences, surpassed anything in the Arabian Nights.[20]

Soon the migration became a mass exodus, and the shtetlach and cities of
Eastern Europe began to empty of Jews. World War I hastened the decline of
the shtetl, and the Holocaust of World War II completed the extinction. But
in those fateful years millions made it to freedom and opportunity, including
the "proste Yidn" and the "Balabatim," Hasidim and secularists, Bundists and
Zionists, yeshivah students and firebrand radicals, Litvaks and Galitzianer – interspersed occasionally with a Marc Chagall, Artur Rubinstein, Jascha Heifetz,
Chaim Weizmann, David Ben Gurion, Golda Meir, and such chroniclers of the
shtetl as Isaac Bashevis Singer and Sholom Aleichem.

The two million Eastern European Jews who migrated to America between 1881 and 1924 constituted one of the greatest mass migrations the world had ever witnessed. Their coming would greatly alter the established American Jewish community as well as leave an imprint on American culture.

Like other immigrants, the Jews who came to America were overwhelmingly young, but the Jewish migration included a greater percentage of family groups, urban dwellers, people of skills and some education, and permanent settlers than that of other European groups. An immigrant of 1882, Dr. George Price, described in his diary how the masses of Eastern European immigrants probably felt about leaving their homeland, despite some feelings of nostalgia for their birthplace: "Sympathy for Russia? How ironical it sounds! Am I not despised? Am I not urged to leave? Do I not hear the word Zhid [Jew] constantly? Can I even think that someone considers me a human being capable of thinking and feeling like the others? Do I not rise daily with the fear lest the hungry mob attack me. . . . It is impossible . . . that a Jew should regret leaving Russia."[21]

The reasons for leaving Eastern Europe were similar to but even more pronounced than in the case of the German Jewish migration. Fortunately for the much poorer Eastern European Jews, there was sometimes help available in the immigration process through the facilities of various organizations, especially HIAS, the Hebrew Immigrant Aid Society, which opened an office in Chicago in 1888 and whose president for about twenty-five years was Adolph Copeland.

While most of the Eastern European Jewish immigrants settled in the large cities of the eastern seaboard where they had landed, many continued westward to Chicago, where they may have had relatives and friends and where economic opportunities were considered especially good. The Chicago into which they started pouring in the 1880s was to double in general population in one decade to over a million people by 1890 – with about 80 percent of those being either immigrants or the children of immigrants. It was a city of opportunity but also of labor unrest that culminated in the bloody Haymarket Riot of 1886 and the Pullman Strike of 1894. In addition to its transportation and commercial importance as a major handler of grain, cattle, and lumber, Chicago was increasingly becoming a major center of diversified manufacturing. The bustling, burgeoning city of contrasts was described in 1896 by George W. Stevens, an English journalist:

> . . . Chicago! Chicago, queen and guttersnipe of cities, cynosure and cesspool of the world! Not if I had a hundred tongues, every one shouting a different language in a different key, could I do justice to her splendid chaos. The most beautiful and the most squalid, girdled with a twofold zone of parks and slums; where the keen air from the lake and prairie is ever in the nostrils, and the stench of foul smoke is never out of the throat; the great port a thousand miles from the sea; the great mart which gathers up with one hand the corn and cattle of the West and deals out with the other the

PURCHASER'S MEMORANDUM

# M. GINSBURG & SON
## RAILROAD AND STEAMSHIP
## TICKET OFFICE

635 W. TWELFTH STREET

Between Jefferson and Desplaines Sts.

CHICAGO

No. 10276      Date Sept 8 1913

Received of N Miller

($_____) _____ Dollars

(Balance, $ 63.95 65.20 ) _____ Dollars

On Account of Passage Jan Brela

Class III

From Krakau

To Chicago

Via _____

Adult One
Child._____
Inf._____
Age _____

M. GINSBURG & SON

Subject to European and American Immigration Laws. Passage not to be furnished until paid in full. Good for one year. Cancellation refunded less commission and cancellation fees, and after cancellation is confirmed from abroad and on return of this receipt and coupon. The above amount is paid for transportation only.

merchandise of the East; widely and generously planned with streets of twenty miles, where it is not safe to walk at night; where women ride straddlewise, and millionaires dine at midday on the Sabbath; the chosen seat of public spirit and municipal boodle, or cut-throat commerce and munificent patronage of arts; the most American of American cities, and yet the most mongrel; the second American city of the globe . . . the first and only veritable Babel of the age; all of which twenty-five years ago next Friday was a heap of smoking ashes. Where in all the world can words be found for this miracle of paradox and incongruity?[22]

The Yiddish-speaking Eastern European Jews who flocked into Chicago were poor and, although usually learned in Hebraic studies, had not generally had the opportunity for much secular education. On arrival they consequently

*An Eastern European Jewish immigrant settlement in the Maxwell Street area, around Twelfth and Jefferson streets, 1906.*

(Courtesy of the Chicago Historical Society.)

crowded into one of the poorest parts of the city – an area just southwest of downtown, near the railroad stations where they had disembarked and where rent was cheap and housing poor. It was a district that had previously been occupied by communities of German, Bohemian, and Irish gentiles. This habitat of the Jews on the Near West Side initially became known as the "Poor Jews Quarter" and somewhat later as the Maxwell Street area.

The Eastern European Jews moved southward along Canal and Jefferson streets, westward to Halsted Street, and then farther westward as new immigrants increased the congestion. By 1910, the Russian-Polish Jews occupied an area that stretched, in the shadow of the Loop, from south of Taylor Street to the railroad tracks at about Sixteenth Street, and from Canal Street westward to Damen Avenue. The more prosperous Eastern European Jews had moved to the western fringe of the area especially around Ashland Avenue. Bohemian Jews lived on the southwest fringe of the area. The focal point of the community was around the intersection of Halsted and Maxwell streets, where on adjacent blocks the population was 90 percent Jewish.

Between 1880 and 1910 an estimated fifty-five thousand Eastern European immigrants crowded into this area. Here for almost half a century the Jews lived in a teeming, transplanted Eastern European shtetl atmosphere that they had recreated. The security of the temporary, transitional culture within the Maxwell Street community, with its myriad familiar Jewish institutions and traditions, served to ease the pain of accommodation into the New World, even though the ghettolike settlement was itself a small and limited world.

For some, however, there was initial disappointment and difficulty in adjustment to the New World. Maxwell Street did not have the legendary streets paved with gold about which the new arrivals had dreamed. Earning a livelihood was difficult and living conditions were poor. But more shocking to many of the deeply religious Jews from the small European communities were the changed values they found among parts of the established Chicago Jewish community. Many of the partially assimilated prosperous German Jews in the city, like the gentiles, used Sunday as their major day of worship, had organs to supply music during services, and condoned men's and women's sitting together in their temples. These changes and others were made easy by the very freedom that the immigrants had sought. Yet one immigrant wrote in his autobiography: "When I first put my feet on the soil of Chicago I was so disgusted that I wished I had stayed at home in Russia. I left the Old Country because you couldn't be a Jew over there and still live, but I would rather be dead than be the kind of German Jew that brings the Jewish name into disgrace by being a goy. That's what hurts! They parade around as Jews, and down deep in their hearts they are worse than *goyim,* they are *meshumeds* (apostates)."[23]

Adjustment to the hurried and unfriendly atmosphere of the big city was often difficult for immigrants from small shtetlach where life had been slow paced and where everyone knew each other. Articles in such Chicago Yiddish newspapers as the *Daily Jewish Courier,* the voice of Orthodox Jewry, reflected these feelings (as reported by S. J. Pomrenze):

The "hurry up" spirit of the city overwhelmed him at first. The strangeness of the city left him lonely; and the longing to return "home" increased. "What kind of memories could the immigrant fleeing from a land of persecution have?" asked a *Courier* writer. Why was it that anything reminding the immigrant of the old home, like a pouch of tobacco, tea, or a European utensil brought forth a sigh and a tear? How could one compare the little village with the straw-bedecked houses and its crooked streets of dirt with the great American cities where noise, turmoil, hustle and bustle reigned, he quoted older immigrants querying the "greenhorn." Furthermore how could one help but scoff at the longing of the immigrant for his old home where here in a city like Chicago he found himself in the center of a civilization that was prepared to offer him everything with a broad hand? The writer answered these questions in a typical Jewish manner. When one digs a little deeper, he says with a Talmudical flourish of his hand, he will see that there were certain values in the little town that are still lacking in the big city. In a small town everybody was friendly and knew everybody else. In the big city the houses are "cold" inside, no matter how much better built, and how superior in other ways they may be to the little cottages. Moreover the social recognition given to men of learning and of honorable ancestry was lacking in the city.[24]

Nevertheless, many of the immigrants scrimped and saved to bring over their Eastern European relatives.

The immigrant's early experience in earning a living was often difficult. Bernard Horwich, a Lithuanian Jewish immigrant who arrived in Chicago in 1880 as a youth of seventeen, was directed from the railroad station to the Near West Side, where the "greenhorns" were to be found. At the time, he had no inkling that Jews lived in other parts of the city. He started out selling stationery on the streets and through the years went on to become president of two banks and one of the most prominent Jewish leaders of his time in community, charitable, European relief, and Zionist organizations. He also held various public offices, including election commissioner of Cook County. In later life he recalled the hardship encountered by Chicago's Eastern European Jews at the time of his arrival:

> Jews were treated on the streets in a most abhorrent and shameful manner, stones being thrown at them and their beards being pulled by street thugs. Most earned their living peddling from house to house. They carried packs on their backs consisting of notions and light dry goods, and it was not an unusual sight to see hundreds of them who lived in the Canal Street district, in the early morning spreading throughout the city. There was hardly a streetcar where there were not to be found some Jewish peddlers with their packs riding to and from their business. Peddling junk and vegetables, and selling various articles on street corners also engaged numbers of our people. Being out on the streets most of the time in these obnoxious occupations, and ignorant of the English language, they were subjected to ridicule, annoyance and attacks of all kinds.[25]

Periodically, some of the attacks resulted in deaths. In 1899 after a Jewish peddler was killed, nearly five hundred people attended a protest meeting at Porges Hall at Jefferson and Maxwell streets and organized the Hebrew-American Protective Association of Chicago.[26] And in 1905 after the killings of a rabbi and a peddler, Mayor Harrison took action: "'Jew-baiting in Chicago must cease. . . . The Mayor sent notices to the police magistrates throughout the city that hereafter they are to show no leniency to hoodlums who attack peddlers, and he suggested a remedy for the evil the heaviest fines permitted by law or assignment of the cases to the Grand Jury for investigation.'"[27]

But life within the Near West Side Maxwell Street community was safer and familiar. The community contained most of the trappings of a European shtetl, including the open-market bazaar. It had kosher meat markets, chicken stores, groceries, matzoh bakeries, dry-goods stores, tailor and seamstress shops, bathhouses, peddlers' stables, sweatshops, and second-hand stores, many identified by their Yiddish signs. For street snacks in the winter there were hot sweet potatoes and roasted chestnuts; buttered corn in the fall; ice cream and ices in the summer; and hot dog sandwiches all year round.

There were midwives, *shadchans* (marriage arrangers), *mohels* (for circumcisions), *shochets* (ritual meat slaughterers), and sacramental wine dealers. The rich and varied religious and cultural life included synagogues, Hebrew schools, the offices of Yiddish newspapers, Hebrew- and Yiddish-speaking literary societies, and Yiddish theaters. Yiddish was the language of the streets and the homes and was used in shopping, labor anthems, lullabies, and political debates.

Even the dress of the Jewish populace was that of the Eastern European ghetto. Bearded Jewish men wearing long black coats (*kapotes*), boots, and Russian caps or wide-brimmed hats were a common sight, as were shawled women.

A reporter described the ghetto of the Near West Side in the *Chicago Tribune* of July 19, 1891, as follows:

> On the West Side, in a district bounded by Sixteenth Street on the south and Polk Street on the north and the Chicago River and Halsted Street on the east and west, one can walk the streets for blocks and see none but Semitic features and hear nothing but the Hebrew patois of Russian Poland. In this restricted boundary, in narrow streets, ill-ventilated tenements and rickety cottages, there is a population of from 15,000 to 16,000 Russian Jews. . . . Every Jew in this quarter who can speak a word of English is engaged in business of some sort. The favorite occupation, probably on account of the small capital required, is fruit and vegetable peddling. Here, also, is the home of the Jewish street merchants, the rag and junk peddler, and the "glass puddin" man. . . . The principal streets in the quarter are lined with stores of every description. Trades with which Jews are not usually associated such as saloonkeeping, shaving and hair cutting, and blacksmithing, have their representatives and Hebrew signs. . . . In a room of a small cottage forty small boys all with hats on sit crowded into a space 10 x 10 feet in size, presided over by a stout middle-aged man with a long, curling, matted beard, who also retains his hat, a battered rusty derby of ancient style. All the old or middle-aged men in the quarter affect this peculiar head gear. . . . The younger generation of men are more progressive and having been born in this country are patriotic and want to be known as Americans and not Russians. . . . Everyone is looking for a bargain and everyone has something to sell. The home life seems to be full of content and easygoing unconcern for what the outside world thinks.[28]

Professor Charles Zeublin in 1895 compared the Chicago Jewish ghetto, where the great majority of Chicago Jews lived, with other ethnic communities:

> The physical characteristics of the ghetto do not differ materially from the surrounding districts. The streets may be a trifle narrower; the alleys are no filthier. There is only one saloon to ten in the other districts. . . . The race differences are subtle; they are not too apparent to the casual observer. It is the religious distinction which one notices; the synagogues; the Talmud schools; the "kosher" signs on the meat Markets. . . . Among the dwelling-houses of the ghetto are found the three types which curse the Chicago workingman – the small, low, one or two story "pioneer" wooden shanty, erected probably before the street was graded, and hence several feet below the street level; the brick tenement of three or four stories, with insufficient light, and drainage, no bath, built to obtain the highest possible rent for the

smallest cubic space; and the third type, the deadly rear tenement, with no light in the front, and with the frightful odors of the dirty alley in the rear, too often the workshop of the "sweater," as well as the home of an excessive population. On the narrow pavement of the narrow street in front is found the omnipresent garbage-box, with full measure, pressed down and running over. In all but the severest weather the streets swarm with children day and night. On bright days groups of adults join the multitude especially on Saturday and Sunday, or on the Jewish holidays. In bad weather the steaming windows show the over-crowded rooms within. A morning walk impresses one with the density of the population, but an evening visit reveals a hive.[29]

Missing from most of the ghetto were adequate plumbing, bathtubs, trees, grass, or recreational facilities. Density was made even worse by subdivision of apartments and because many of the ghetto families took in boarders or lodgers, predominantly single people, to help defray expenses. Boarders' rent started at a dollar a week and usually included coffee or tea in the morning, with other home-cooked meals being extra. About 25 percent of the families rented to "lodgers" or "boarders." The "hot bed" system, where the same bed would be used by a baker during the day and a butcher at night, so prevalent in other ethnic communities, did not prevail in Maxwell Street. There were no hotels or cheap lodging houses available in the neighborhood. To supplement the father's meager income, the wife and children often had to go to work. Yet despite these conditions, the rates of crime, death, disease, and illegitimacy in the Jewish ghetto were lower than those of most immigrant concentrations.

Rather limited statistical data may give a clue as to the diseases that afflicted the Jews of the crowded Maxwell Street area (see table 3). A 1991 study compared about one thousand cases in each of two hospitals, one having largely Eastern European Jewish patients and the other almost completely non-Jewish. Neither hospital accepted patients suffering from tuberculosis. The incidence of major disease for Jews was lower in diseases associated with alcohol,

TABLE 3. *Major Diseases Reported by Two Hospitals*

| Disease | Jewish Hospital | Non-Jewish Hospital |
| --- | --- | --- |
| Pneumonia | 41 | 24 |
| Rheumatism | 47 | 20 |
| Hernia | 56 | 29 |
| Neurasthenia | 39 | 17 |
| Diabetes | 5 | 3 |
| Delirium tremens | 1 | 36 |
| Morphinism | 1 | 5 |
| Syphilis | 4 | 18 |

Source: Charles Bernheimer, *The Russian Jew in the United States* (1905), p. 328.

Summary of relief disbursements from May 1, 1900, to April 30, 1901, by the United Hebrew Charities of Chicago.

(From *Reports to the Jewish Charities of Chicago*, 1901.)

## RELIEF DEPARTMENT.
### MAY 1, 1900—APRIL 30, 1901.
#### CASES AND PERSONS ASSISTED.

| | Residents | | | | Transients | | | Total of Cases Assisted | Total of Persons |
|---|---|---|---|---|---|---|---|---|---|
| | Parties Assisted | Adults | Children | New-comers | Parties Assisted | Adults | Children | | |
| May..... | 172 | 274 | 556 | 14 | 12 | 12 | 10 | 184 | 830 |
| June..... | 152 | 251 | 488 | 14 | 16 | 16 | 4 | 168 | 739 |
| July..... | 195 | 192 | 352 | 5 | 2 | 5 | ...... | 197 | 544 |
| August... | 230 | 233 | 440 | 4 | 3 | 3 | ...... | 233 | 673 |
| September | 178 | 243 | 537 | ...... | 10 | 7 | 3 | 188 | 780 |
| October.. | 245 | 373 | 660 | ...... | 5 | 5 | ...... | 250 | 1033 |
| November | 327 | 520 | 731 | 6 | 10 | 10 | ...... | 337 | 1251 |
| December | 285 | 459 | 812 | ...... | 9 | ..... | ...... | 294 | 1271 |
| January .. | 269 | 422 | 750 | 8 | 21 | 6 | 3 | 290 | 1172 |
| February.. | 259 | 400 | 740 | 11 | 9 | 9 | ...... | 260 | 1140 |
| March.... | 244 | 375 | 667 | 9 | 9 | ...... | ...... | 253 | 1042 |
| April..... | 160 | 235 | 423 | 2 | 11 | 2 | 3 | 171 | 658 |
| | 2716 | 3977 | 7156 | 73 | 117 | 75 | 23 | 2825 | 11133 |

### NATIVITY OF RECIPIENTS.

| | |
|---|---|
| American | 50 |
| Russian | 2,161 |
| German | 225 |
| Bohemian | 60 |
| Galician | 101 |
| Hungarian | 110 |
| Roumanian | 97 |
| English | 11 |
| Turkish | 1 |
| Swedish | 1 |
| Egyptian | 1 |
| Polish | 7 |
| Total | 2,825 |

### MODE OF ASSISTING.

| | |
|---|---|
| Cash | 1,965 |
| Assisted in kind | 427 |
| Cash and kind | 188 |
| Transportation | 184 |
| Surgical and optical aid | 58 |
| Sewing machines | 3 |
| Total | 2,825 |

### CAUSES OF DISTRESS.

| | |
|---|---|
| Widows with dependent children | 514 |
| Old age and debility | 347 |
| Sickness or death | 488 |
| Insanity | 43 |
| Lack of work | 355 |
| Insufficiency of earnings | 549 |
| Imprisonment of husbands | 4 |
| Temporary absence of husbands | 153 |
| Wilful desertion | 312 |
| Shiftlessness | 57 |
| Conflagration | 2 |
| Explosion | 1 |
| Total | 2,825 |

drugs, or promiscuous sexual behavior but higher in major illnesses such as pneumonia and nervous disorders.[30]

Several surveys around the turn of the century showed that over 90 percent of the people had no opportunity to bathe in their own homes. However, there were at least six large private bathhouses scattered throughout the community. These were used regularly by much of the populace, usually for a fee ranging from fifteen to twenty-five cents. In a few bathhouses, schmaltz herring, black bread, and seltzer water were available at an extra charge, and men on weekends would linger and sweat in their version of a country club. While children were limited in their play space by the lack of suitable facilities and by crowded and dirty alleys and streets, many made it over to Stanford Park – a small patch of ground filled with many activities, which opened in the area in 1910 – or to larger institutions such as Hull-House and the Chicago Hebrew Institute or smaller places such as Marcy Center, the Maxwell Street Settlement, and the Henry Booth House. The outward appearance often belied a life of high standards:

> Walking through the streets of the neighborhood one is shocked by the dirt and disorder. But it is the aesthetic and not the moral sense which is outraged. The district is not really a slum. Evidence of education, morality and intelligence are found in abundance. With the exception of incorrigible boys and petty gamblers, there is no vicious element. Temperance rules supreme. Soda water is sold at the grocery stores at two cents a bottle and at the stand for one cent a glass. This in summer and weak tea in winter are the national drinks of the Russian Jewish populace. No neighborhood in our city, with the exception of Prohibition districts, shows so few saloons to the number of population.[31]

Those few from the Maxwell Street ghetto who strayed into the criminal element were infamous more for the use of their heads than for the use of guns. Jake "Greasy Thumb" Guzik was a gambler, bootlegger, and financial overseer for the Capone gang. Joseph "Yellow Kid" Weil was also a product of the ghetto who became nationally recognized as one of the slickest and most innovative confidence men of his day. He served four prison terms and ran through a number of fortunes before his death in a convalescent home in 1976 at the age of one hundred. He was buried in a pauper's grave. The tough Maxwell Street area, however, also produced a few Jewish gangsters who were active during the Prohibition era.

The tough environment of the ghetto also produced a number of pugilists. Jackie Fields, whose father had a kosher butcher shop on Maxwell Street, became an Olympic champion and later held the world's welterweight boxing title. Barney Ross, whose parents had a small grocery store on Jefferson Street, became the lightweight and welterweight boxing champion of the world and later a hero in the battle of Guadalcanal. Still later he won another victory over a drug addiction he acquired while fighting off malaria on the island. Kingfish Levinsky, whose family had a fresh-fish stand at Maxwell and Halsted streets, was a top heavyweight contender, fighting a number of world champions. One of his managers was his sister, "Leapin'" Lena, who was also very strong, having carried many a barrel of herring at the fishstand.

### EARNING A LIVING

To earn a living, Eastern European Jewish immigrants worked in a variety of occupations. Although they were especially concentrated in the sweatshops of the clothing industry and in cigar-making factories, others became peddlers,

A garment industry sweat-shop in 1902 where child labor, long hours, low wages, and unhealthy working conditions prevailed.
(Courtesy of the Amalgamated Clothing Workers of America.)

butchers, bakers, tailors, barbers, small merchants, and artisans of every variety. Through hard work, diligence, and business acumen some rose from the most menial jobs to become successful entrepreneurs.

By far the largest employer of the Jewish men, women, and children was the garment industry, which was concentrated in the southern part of downtown (*shmatte* row) southward into the Maxwell Street area, where some worked in crowded shops above the storefronts. Most of the garment facilities were small ones where workers toiled long hours for low pay under abhorrent physical conditions. These "sweatshops" employed numerous women and children as well as men as helpers, operators, pressers, cutters, and tailors. Much of the work was piecework, often seasonal, and frequently supplemented by work done at home. Twelve- and thirteen-hour days, six days a week, were not unusual. Children eleven or twelve years of age were frequently employed.

When the workers were still "greenhorns," early attempts at organization and protest were limited and usually not very successful. In 1886, during the period of the bloody Haymarket Riot, thousands of Jews marched from the ghetto toward downtown to protest the intolerable sweatshop conditions. They were stopped at the Van Buren Street bridge by club-swinging police who beat and routed the marchers. In 1910, a prolonged and bitter strike in the garment industry, involving forty-five thousand workers, mainly Jewish, resulted in improved conditions for the garment workers.

Many of the immigrant Jews started out as peddlers, some carrying their merchandise, others using a horse and wagon that they could rent for a few dollars a day. There were a variety of peddlers, some specializing in a single field. There were junk peddlers who would collect items such as rags, sacks, clothing, metal, bottles, and furniture. There were dry-goods peddlers who would sell house-to-house, often going to small communities and rural areas. There were also a large number of fruit and vegetable peddlers who would arise before dawn, make their purchases at the wholesale produce market, and then hawk their produce all day in the alleys and streets of the many ethnic communities. A 1900 survey showed that there were about four thousand Jewish fruit, rag, and scrap-iron peddlers.[32]

Just as some of the garment workers opened their own shops, many of the peddlers opened small stores – grocery, fruit, candy, dry goods, and clothing – as they gained experience, some fluency in the English language, and a little money (often borrowed). Some in time became wholesalers in their field.

As one observer noted, "A Jew would rather earn five dollars a week doing business for himself than ten dollars a week working for someone else."[33] Probably for no other immigrant group did economic conditions change more rapidly than among the Jews, who in a relatively short period would often move from worker to manufacturer, retailer, or wholesaler.

### MAXWELL STREET MARKETING

Many earned their living as small merchants in the Maxwell Street area itself. Here was created the bazaarlike atmosphere of an Eastern European shtetl market, complete with open stands, live chickens, and lively haggling. The sights, sounds, and smells of the Maxwell Street market were familiar to both Jews and gentiles from Eastern Europe. The immigrants shopped in the area regularly to meet their everyday needs and sometimes to do a bit of socializing and reminiscing.

The great outdoor market was filled with people from dawn till past dark. Jewish merchants matched wits not only with other Jews but also with Poles, Lithuanians, Galicians, Russians, Bohemians, and others who felt much more at ease in the familiar ghetto market than in department stores. In turn, the multilingual Jewish merchants (some could speak a half dozen or more languages) knew the needs, tastes, and prejudices of their customers. The market was permeated with

the smell of garlic and of cheeses, the aroma of onions, apples, and oranges, and the shouts and curses of sellers and buyers fill the air. Anything can be bought and sold on Maxwell Street. On one stand, piled high, are odd sizes of shoes long out of style; on another are copper kettles for brewing beer; on a third are second-hand pants; and one merchant even sells odd, broken pieces of spectacles, watches, and jewelry, together with pocket knives and household tools salvaged from the collections of junk peddlers. Everything has value on Maxwell Street, but the price is not fixed. It is the fixing of the price around which turns the whole plot of the drama enacted daily at the

perpetual bazaar of Maxwell Street. . . . The sellers know how to ask ten times
the amount that their wares will eventually sell for, and the buyers know how
to offer a twentieth.[34]

The Maxwell Street area was probably best known to the general public
because of its unique, colorful marketing activity with an international flavor,
but the area actually had three distinct commercial streets, Twelfth Street,
Halsted Street, and Maxwell Street, each with a different selling approach.

Although Twelfth Street (today's Roosevelt Road) always had some retail
business, it served mainly as a street of wholesalers and jobbers. Here the Maxwell Street merchants would get some of their goods, as would small dry-goods
store owners from all over the city and the surrounding area. The once numerous customer peddlers would buy their merchandise on Twelfth Street and then
peddle it in the homes of various ethnic groups – usually on credit, a service
not readily available in those days. Every week or so the peddler would come
to collect an installment payment, deliver previously purchased goods, and

The intersection of Halsted and Fourteenth streets, 1906, with the L. Klein department store on the northeast corner.
(Courtesy of the Chicago Historical Society.)

display some new merchandise. Also on Twelfth Street, just west of Halsted Street, was Gold's Restaurant, a favorite meetingplace for the elite and for the crowd coming in after attending the Yiddish theater.

Halsted Street was a very busy transportation and shopping street with a mixture of basically one-price stores. It had some decorum in selling, and some of its merchants were graduates of the type of selling typical of the Maxwell-Jefferson street area. Halsted Street was anchored by two large fulltime department stores: the Twelfth Street Store on the corner of Twelfth and Halsted and L. Klein on the corner of Fourteenth and Halsted. At 1214 South Halsted Street was the original home of Vienna Sausage. Also on the street was the Bremmer Cookie Factory, the home offices of Yiddish newspapers, a number of nickelodeons, and the popular Nathan's Ice Cream Parlor.

The street that gave the area its name and reputation was Maxwell Street, although the pushcarts and stands of that thoroughfare had their origin on Jefferson Street. The open market started on Jefferson Street in the 1880s with Jewish peddlers and their two-wheeled pushcarts catering to the growing Eastern European Jewish population in the area. A large local clientele from the dense population that developed after the Chicago Fire, low operating expenses, and the ability to move about freely allowed the open market to flourish. On the street one could also get a *shiffcart* – a ticket for a steamship line – or

*Packing matzoh in boxes at the Wittenberg Matzoh Company at 1326 South Jefferson Street in the Maxwell Street area, 1937.*
(Courtesy of Mildred Wittenberg Mallin.)

save at the Schiff bank, or be clothed at Phillipson's, a firm that also supplied the numerous custom peddlers.

By the early 1900s Jefferson Street, with its electric trolley line, had become so crowded that buyers and sellers spilled over into Maxwell Street. In 1912 the city council passed an ordinance recognizing the Maxwell Street market and applying rules that included a fee for pushcarts of ten cents a day (later raised to seventeen cents). The fee was collected by a market master, a political appointee often accused through the years of shakedowns and accepting bribes to grant better locations – a practice not unfamiliar in czarist Russia. At its peak, the Maxwell Street market stretched some six blocks from Clinton Street westward to Sangamon Street, and the area contained over two thousand vendors selling from stores, stalls, pushcarts, wagons, and boxes. Along Maxwell Street were the stores, on the sidewalks were stands where some store merchandise was usually displayed, and on the street itself were the pushcarts. There was always an early morning

scramble by pushcart merchants for the best street locations, occasionally resulting in fighting that led to intervention by police and the market master.

Although the basic food, clothing, and household commodities were the most
important products sold on the street, anything and everything was sold there.
Most of it, by far, was new merchandise – some even of very good quality, which
later attracted affluent buyers. But on the stands, especially those of the week-
end-only merchants, could be found piles of clothing, rusty nails, used tooth-
brushes, shoes and shoelaces, used carpeting from Pullman sleeping cars, used
plumbing fixtures, coffins, bicycle parts, and even jinx-removing incense.

There was very little stolen merchandise sold on the street, although this was
sometimes the whispered implication so that the customer would think he was
getting a real buy. In the 1920s, sales were believed to have totaled between one
and two million dollars a month on Maxwell and Jefferson alone; and the entire Roosevelt-Halsted-Maxwell Street area probably ranked third in sales in the
city, after downtown and Sixty-third and Halsted streets.

Bargaining was an accepted and expected part of retailing. Both the merchant and the frequent customer knew the rules of the game. There was often
high-pressure selling and such ploys as the merchant's saying, "I'll give you a
special price since you are my first customer of the day and it's good luck to
break the ice." Sometimes, however, a store would have many first customers
of the day. Customers were often shrewd bargainers themselves and would shop
from store to store looking for the best buy. Generally most customers did get
good bargains because of the merchants' low overhead and because the merchants often obtained samples, odd-lot merchandise from auctions, or merchandise from overstocked manufacturers and wholesalers at low cost.

Another part of the market was the puller – a man who would stand in front
of the store and either verbally or physically persuade or practically drag people into the store. Their motto seemed to be that the "customer is always held
tight." Later when the pullers joined a clothing workers' union, they became
known as solicitors.

Maxwell Street had its weekly shopping cycle. Food was an important item,
as evidenced by the many groceries, produce stands, and eating places. Hot dog
stands were on almost every corner. Shopping during the week was mainly by
neighborhood people – Thursday was the big day for chicken and Friday for
fish sales to the Jewish women preparing for the Sabbath meals.

On weekends, when the street did about 70 percent of its business (50 percent on Sundays alone), as many as seventy thousand people would crowd into
a few blocks, among them a large influx of other ethnic groups, blacks, and
others, including some people from out of the city who were often there just
out of curiosity to visit what was often referred to as "Jewtown." Initially most
of Maxwell Street closed on Saturday, the Jewish Sabbath; merchants did a huge
business on Sunday when most of the Christian establishments were closed. In
time, however, in order to earn a living and remain competitive, and as the
influence of strict Old World traditions waned, more and more Jews kept their
shops open on Saturday. Only on the High Holy Days did street shopping
completely close down. As one veteran Jewish street-merchant complained:

*Vendors in the Maxwell Street area about 1906. A kosher butcher shop, with its Yiddish sign above it, is to the left.*
(Courtesy of the Chicago Historical Society.)

"Things aren't as they used to be around here fifteen years ago. We had a better class of Jews then. Everybody was gone on Shabboth. But now everybody is after the money, and you got to get out of business or stay here every day, because Saturday is one of our busiest days."[35]

Some of the stores on Maxwell Street became quite large. Machevich, which specialized in railroad salvage goods, employed about one hundred people. Louis Gabels Clothing was one of the largest retailers of men's and women's clothing in the city. Robinson's Department Store employed about fifty people and handled high-quality merchandise, including Oriental rugs, imported lamps, Dresden china, and valuable mah jongg sets. Joseph Robinson, the proprietor, helped many worthy Jewish causes and, in later years, helped to finance passage to America for many Eastern European Jews, most of whom were Holocaust survivors. In Chicago he was one of the advocates for the establishment of Jewish parochial schools.

Maxwell Street shopping continued to flourish even after the Jewish residents started to leave the area around 1910 and were being replaced by Mexicans and blacks. But beginning in the late 1950s the street began to decline and became barely a two-block skeleton of its former self. Blacks, Latinos, and some Asians became the major vendors and customers. Still, on Sundays the area was a sizable and busy flea market, filling the large vacant expanses, an important cultural transition for many who were new to Chicago but used to the Old World and Third World ways of marketing. The decline of the street was accelerated by the demolition caused by the building of the Dan Ryan Expressway on the eastern fringe and the construction of the campus of the University of Illinois at Chicago to the west and the northwest. Urban renewal has leveled most of the surrounding area but rebuilding is still pending. The university is anxious to clean up the area and is expanding its facilities. But, as one veteran street vendor said, "You would be lucky to live as long as Maxwell Street has been dying." Nevertheless, in the summer of 1994, despite strong opposition, the city closed and bulldozed most of what was left of the market and the land was sold to the university. A smaller Sunday-only market was opened almost a half mile to the east, but one without the sounds, smell, or more than century-old history of the Maxwell Street market.

From meager origins in small facilities on Maxwell Street, larger businesses such as Vienna Sausage, Keeshin, Meystel, Karolls Clothing, Chernin's Shoes, Morrie Mages Sporting Goods, Fluky's (which started as a sidewalk hot dog stand that used water from the city fire hydrant it encircled), and many others emerged. And living throughout the city and the suburbs are thousands of sons and daughters, grandchildren and great grandchildren – generally well educated and prosperous – whose successes can often be traced to the hard work and long hours, perseverance and *chutzpah* of their Eastern European ancestors who settled in the Maxwell Street area, to quote a merchant, "where they cheated you fair."

### MAXWELL STREET INSTITUTIONS

In 1881–82, when the Eastern European Jews first arrived in large numbers, a special temporary committee, the Russian Refugee Aid Committee, was established to try to find shelter and employment for the immigrants. Later, many of the established Jewish agencies came to their aid and a number of new and much-needed major institutions were established in the Maxwell Street ghetto area. These were usually funded by the German Jews, who by then were relatively well off financially. However, there was also a strong tradition of helping one another among the newly arrived immigrants.

The poor Russian Jew teaches us the highest type of charity. There is always room in the smallest tenement – though there be but two beds with seven occupants – for the neighboring family that is temporarily homeless; there is always a crust of bread, dry though it be, for the hungry one who needs it. A little coal can be cheerfully spared – though there be but a bucketful – if the children nearby are suffering from the cold. How gladly the proud possessor of a bonnet ties the precious object upon the head of her less fortunate sister when the latter finds it necessary to leave the neighborhood for some special purpose. Not the bonnet alone, but very often dress and wrap are loaned with equal readiness. How many a woman, the mother of a large family of little ones, goes into another home where sickness has entered, and nurses the suffering one back to health. How earnestly she goes about the work, preparing the necessary articles of diet, ministering to the needs of the little one doing in that strange home what she does in her own, even to the wielding of the scrub brush for the Sabbath cleaning! It is this beautiful spirit of sharing himself and what belongs to him that constitutes the greatest charm of the Russian Jew.[36]

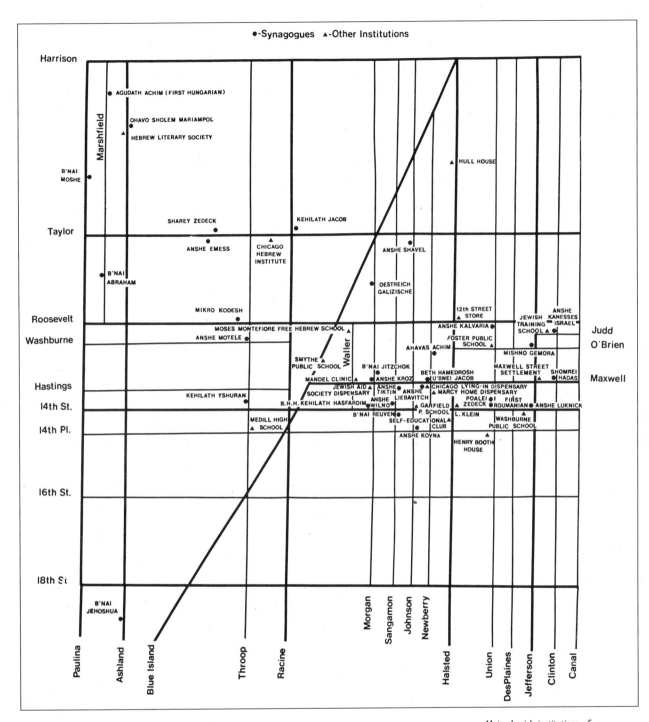

●-Synagogues ▲-Other Institutions

*Major Jewish institutions of the Maxwell Street area, 1910. The area then contained Chicago's largest Jewish community.*
*(Map by Irving Cutler.)*

A number of organizations were set up to aid the poor, often in conjunction with congregations. They included the Society for the Free Burial of the Dead; Bread for the Hungry Society; Sheltering Home, for transients and newcomers; the Women's Loan, and the Women's Society, the latter providing clothing for poor boys in school. Money was often raised gradually through contributions of a nickel and up. Many of the families kept *pushkas,* or contribution containers, as a handy means of making periodic contributions to worthwhile causes. There was also aid provided by the umbrella charitable organization, the Associated Jewish Charities.

The dominant institution of the area by far was the synagogue, just as in

*Anshe Sholom Synagogue at Ashland Boulevard and Polk Street, c. 1920. The congregation moved into its new Ashland Boulevard home in 1910, remaining until 1926 when it moved to Polk and Independence Boulevard in Lawndale. Its rabbi for a number of decades was the distinguished Rabbi Saul Silber. This Ashland Boulevard building is now a Greek church.*

*(From Meites, ed.,* History of the Jews of Chicago.)

the Old Country. The synagogue not only provided for the spiritual and social needs of the immigrant, but it also supplied a variety of auxiliary services such as Hebrew schools, health funds, charitable aid, burial arrangements, and loan funds. For example, many an immigrant was given a hundred-dollar loan to buy a pushcart and potatoes and onions, with repayment at two dollars a week.

Scattered throughout the Near West Side Maxwell Street area were more than forty synagogues, for the Orthodox synagogues had to be within walking distance of their members' homes. Most were small, usually with fewer than a hundred members. Many of them were small *shtiebl* (house) synagogues; in other cases, congregations met in rented halls or rooms above stores. A few, such as the Romanian synagogue at Fourteenth and Union streets, had once been churches. In time some beautiful large synagogues were built, such as Anshe Kanesses Israel (known as the Russische Shul) on Clinton and Judd streets (1884) and Ohave Sholom Mariampol (later Anshe Sholom). The latter was first located at Canal and Liberty, later at Ashland Boulevard and Polk streets (1910), in the more desirable part of the community toward the fringe of the Maxwell Street area and away from the main part of the ghetto at Maxwell and Halsted streets.

The synagogues were usually founded by groups of immigrants from the same community or region in Eastern Europe. Thus there evolved the Motele, Kalvaria, Suvalk, Tiktin, Odesser, Russische, Romanian, Pavalitcher, Warsaw,

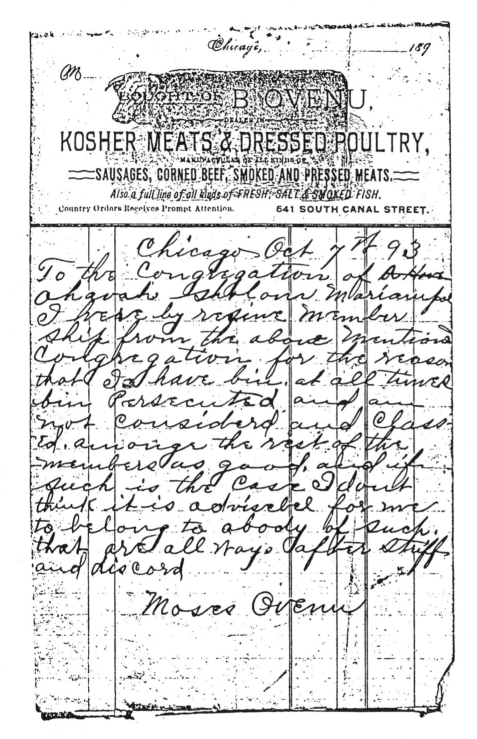

BOUGHT OF B OVENU,
DEALER IN

KOSHER MEATS & DRESSED POULTRY,
MANUFACTURER OF ALL KINDS OF
SAUSAGES, CORNED BEEF, SMOKED AND PRESSED MEATS.
Also a full line of all kinds of FRESH, SALT & SMOKED FISH.
Country Orders Receive Prompt Attention.     541 SOUTH CANAL STREET.

Chicago Oct 7th 93
To the Congregation of Ahva
Ahvah Sholom Mariampol
I here by resine member
ship from the above mentiond
Conghregation for the reason
that I have bin at all times
bin Persecuted and am
not considerd and Class-
ed amonge the rest of the
members as good and if
such is the case I dont
think it is advisebel for me
to belong to a body of such
that are all ways after stuff
and discord

Moses Ovenu

*A century ago, like today, there were disgruntled synagogue members, as shown by this 1893 letter of resignation given to Ahavah Sholom Mariampol by a member who felt unwanted and persecuted.*
(Courtesy of the Chicago Jewish Archives.)

Wilno, Kovne, and Austro-Galizien synagogues, all named after European locations. A few synagogues were founded by men who worked in the same occupation, for example, the laundrymen or the carpenters, or in some cases were
organized along particularized philosophic precepts, such as Lubavitcher, Hasidic, and Sephardic.

While the German Jews espoused new ideas in religious matters, most of the
Eastern European Jews wanted to continue the old Orthodox traditions. The
Orthodox were devoted to the Torah and its study, to daily attendance at the
synagogue if at all possible, and to strict observance of the Sabbath, religious

holidays, and the dietary and other laws as set forth in the Code of Jewish Religious Law and Practice (the *Shulchan Aruch*). The Eastern European Jews, with their strict Orthodox ways, did not feel at home in the atmosphere of German Reform congregations, where the rituals were different and where men and women could sit together, the men without skullcaps (*yarmulkes*). Nor did the German Jews make them feel overly welcome.

The Eastern European Jews found it important to belong to a synagogue; membership was an essential part of their faith and also a means for their children to obtain religious instruction, as this 1905 account reveals:

They know that the public school will attend to their secular education, so out of their scant earnings they pay synagogues and Talmud Torah (religious school) dues. The synagogue plays a very important part in the daily life of the Orthodox Russian Jew, for his life and religion are so closely interwoven that public divine worship is to him a duty and a pleasure. The synagogue is the religious and social center around which the activity of the community revolves and it has now become, since the formation of the auxiliary loan societies, a distributing agency for its various philanthropies where "personal service" is not a fad, but has always been recognized in dealing with the unfortunate. Small wonder is it that the orthodox Russian Jew clings to his synagogue. It is open not only "from early morn to dewey eve," but far into the night, and in some cases the doors are never closed. Daily worship begins early, so that the laboring man can attend services and yet be in time for his work. There are morning, afternoon, and evening services – seldom attended by women. Often the peddler's cart can be seen standing near the entrance while the owner is at prayer within. On Sabbaths and holy days services are always well attended by men and women, the latter occupying a gallery set apart for their use.

The older Jews, especially, found intellectual and spiritual sustenance in the synagogue:

Connected with the synagogue is the beth hamedrash, or house of learning, where students of religious literature are always welcome, and Bible and Talmud are studied and discussed. Many take advantage of the opportunity thus afforded, and form study circles or meet for devotional reading. There is much to attract and hold the older generation, who are continually receiving accessions from abroad, and in their lives the synagogue means much, if not all worth striving for.

The beginning of a congregation is generally a minyan or gathering of at least ten men for divine worship. This is held in rented quarters. As soon as a sufficient number of members are gained they resolve to form an organization and when funds are forthcoming a house of worship bought or built.

But with the younger Jews of the area, there were already problems, and the acculturation pressures were strong:

Expense is not spared in making the exercises interesting to the older people, but little is done to attract the younger generation. The beautiful He-

brew language, which they do not understand, is used exclusively in the services. And when there is a sermon it is in Yiddish, and rather tedious and
uninteresting for young people, who are almost starving for that religious
food which would satisfy the heart and mind.[37]

To further education that would satisfy the heart and mind of the young, a
Talmud Torah Hebrew School was established in 1883. The following year,
during the centennial celebration of the birthday of the great Jewish philanthropist and leader Sir Moses Montefiore, public-spirited Jews raised money for
a new and larger school building. A number of gentiles, including Marshall
Field, Lyman Gage, John Farwell, and William Kerfoot, contributed to the fund.
In 1889 the school moved into a large building on Judd and Clinton streets and
was known as the Moses Montefiore Hebrew Free School. The Religious School
Work Committee of the Council of Jewish Women in 1902 reported as follows:

> The largest religious school in this city is the Moses Montefiore Hebrew
> Free School which now occupies two buildings . . . with an attendance of over
> a thousand boys daily after public school hours. Here Hebrew reading, gram-
> mar and translation, Biblical history and Talmud are taught in the Yiddish
> language. . . . The condition of the rooms and the ventilation are not always
> what could be desired. This large school is supported by the Orthodox con-
> gregations which have no schools of their own and by private subscriptions.
> The children whose parents can afford it pay five or ten cents per week for
> tuition and are furnished with books free of charge.[38]

The school was also financed by the sporadic collection of voluntary contributions at births, funerals, weddings, and various social events. Later several branch

Talmud Torahs were established and the schools reached a total enrollment of about eighteen hundred students.[39]

Even those youngsters who obtained a Talmud Torah education, usually taught in the manner of the shtetl schools, found it hard to understand or appreciate the Old World beliefs and way of life of their parents. While in the circumscribed, somewhat autocratic Hebrew School they were learning in Yiddish and Hebrew about Abraham, Isaac, and Jacob, in the more open public schools they were speaking the English of their native land and were learning about Washington, Jefferson, and Lincoln. As Israel Zangwill said: "While there is always a difference between the old and the new generations, the difference between the Jewish immigrant and his American child is that of ten generations."[40] While in many cases the children followed the way of their parents, with some modification, there were many who felt estranged and even ashamed of the shtetl aura of their immigrant parents. In addition to the culture clash, the older generation often was so busy trying to eke out a living that they lacked the necessary time to devote to their children.

Along with the larger Talmud Torahs there were numerous *chedorim*, or private Hebrew classes, to be found on almost every block in the Maxwell Street area. It was reported that there were thirty *chedorim* as early as 1881.[41] The character of the school, whether progressive or old fashioned, depended on the individual instructor. Many taught in a manner similar to that of the Old Country. But in time, especially in the Talmud Torahs, efforts were made to broaden the education program, which often had consisted solely of the study of prayer books. There were also many private *melamdim* (teachers) who also usually helped prepare the boys for their Bar Mitzvah.

For the younger Jews, public education became the important means for acculturation and Americanization and also a means to move upward socially and economically, often away from the world of their parents. There were eight elementary schools in or on the fringes of the Maxwell Street area, which the Jewish students attended. Around the turn of the century, in two of these schools, Smythe and Foster, the student population was over 80 percent Jewish, and at Garfield and Washburne schools the student body was over 90 percent Jewish.

Only a small percentage of the students went on to high school. Instead, many went off to work at the age of thirteen or fourteen. Some went to work at twelve and never finished grammar school. There were also those who had been born in Eastern Europe and who dropped out of school in America because they were often years older than their classmates.

The two public high schools attended by students in the Maxwell Street area were Medill, in the heart of the neighborhood around Fourteenth Place and Throop Street, and, to a lesser extent, the more distant English High and Manual Training School. From high school some young people went on to nearby Lewis Institute at Madison and Robey (Damen) or, after 1913, to Crane Junior College at Jackson and Oakley. A few went to the University of Chicago, usually on scholarship, where they found many South Side German Jews enrolled, and some went on to professional medical schools, including the

The Jewish Training School, one of the first vocational schools in the country, opened in 1890 with 1,100 students.
(Courtesy of the Jewish Federation of Metropolitan Chicago.)

College of Physicians and Surgeons, Rush Medical College, and lesser-known medical schools such as Bennet or Harvey (a college having night sessions). A number went to the John Marshall Law School or other law schools scattered about the city, often attending at night. These students formed the nucleus of a professional class of Eastern European background.

Side by side with the public grade and high schools was the Jewish Training School, which opened in 1890 in a fine brick building on Judd Street (Twelfth Place), between Jefferson and Clinton streets. Sinai Temple members, probably in an effort to Americanize the Eastern European Jews more speedily, played a dominant role in founding the school. The school's first classes were located temporarily in a building adjacent to Sinai Temple, and the school's board met at the temple.[42] Formation of the school was a pioneering effort based on the philosophy that the manual trades should supplement commerce among the Jewish vocations. German Jews, the chief donors for the school, felt that it was better "to have among their brethren more mechanics and fewer peddlers," a reversal

*Jewish Training School class, c. 1920.*

(Courtesy of the Jewish Federation of Metropolitan Chicago.)

of the Old Country roles that had been fostered by government restriction.[43] The school offered area children, aged four to fifteen, an eleven-year grammar and vocational course that would provide them with trade and handicraft skills, domestic skills (especially for the girls), and the three R's for everyone.

An early promoter of the school was Dr. Emil G. Hirsch, rabbi of Sinai Temple, and there were substantial early financial contributions by Leon, Simon, and Emanuel Mandel and others. The school was one of the first vocational schools in the country and was nonsectarian, although the overwhelming majority of students were Jewish. There were no tuition fees. Capacity at the school was 800, but twice that number applied for admission when the school first opened, and 1,100 were finally admitted. Eventually the school had over 1,200 full-time students.

The school gave the underprivileged children of Eastern European Jews a chance for achievement. At the school's first graduation, Dr. Hirsch made the following comment: "It is to be regretted that they made a mistake in the selection of their parents. It would have been wiser to have chosen Chicago parents, perhaps those on Michigan Avenue. However, this cannot be altered any more and they will have to make the best of it, combatting prejudice by superior knowledge and just behavior. They as Jews were not entitled to achieve less than others, but it should be their earnest endeavor to supersede others by their attainments and by their moral action."[44]

Its first principal, Professor Gabriel Bamberger, had been born and educated in Germany and was an outstanding teacher and scholar. In 1883 he established the Workingman's School of New York and afterwards headed the Jew-

A dance class at the Jewish Training School, c. 1915. (Courtesy of the Jewish Federation of Metropolitan Chicago.)

ish Training School in Chicago, from its inception until his death in 1909. He introduced the most advanced methods and techniques into the school's curriculum, including some emphasis on physical development. The school also offered night classes for adults in the English language and American history, as well as in the vocational subjects. The school was successful and many of its graduates became prominent in the civic, professional, and commercial life of the city. Its graduates included Max Shulman, the Zionist leader, Alderman Jacob Arvey, and U.S. District Judge Abraham Lincoln Marovitz.

In 1921, after over three decades of outstanding service to the largely immigrant community, the Jewish Training School closed. The Jewish population had been moving out of the area and, additionally, the public schools were now offering practically every course that had been taught there. Well over half a century after the school closed, its loyal alumni were still holding annual reunions.

Various organizations were formed in the ghetto to fulfill the strong desire of the immigrants for self-improvement. One of these was the Self-Educational Club, whose leaders were of the same economic and social class as the beneficiaries. The club started in the drugstore of Leo Porges, which was a meeting place for area intellectuals, and later it occupied facilities on Halsted Street south of Fourteenth Street. It brought in well-known speakers, including the attorney Clarence Darrow and William Rainey Harper, president of the University of Chicago, and it also had a Sunday concert program. The club served as an Americanization catalyst without the "uplift" being imposed from above.[45]

An organization whose roots go back to 1883 is the Hebrew Literary Society

*Hull-House on South Halsted Street near Maxwell Street, 1910. Only a small remnant of this pioneering social service complex was preserved when the campus of the University of Illinois at Chicago occupied the site.* (Courtesy of the Chicago Historical Society.)

(*Schochrei Sfath Ever*), founded to help foster the Hebrew language and literature. It opened a library at Canal and Polk streets that contained a sizable collection of Hebrew books and later occupied a building on Johnson (now Peoria) Street north of Twelfth Street. Still later the society was located at 810 South Ashland. Among those supporting the organization were Rabbis Felsenthal, Anixter, Alperstram, and Eliassof, the journalists Leon Zolotkoff and M. Ph. Ginzburg, the community leader Bernard Horwich, and the Zionist leaders Meyer Abrams and Max Shulman. Its fine library and lectures helped make it an important intellectual and spiritual center of Chicago Jewry.

A major concern of the Orthodox Jews were disputes arising over *kashrut* (kosher practices), which eventually came under rabbinical supervision. The Va'ad Ha'rabonim (Board of Rabbis) was organized to handle various disputes that arose in the Jewish community. It consisted of prominent Orthodox rabbis, including Rabbis Abraham Cardon, Ephraim Epstein, M. Anixter, Louis Kaplan, Yehudah Gordon, Azriel Epstein, and Eleazer Muskin. They met regularly in public session every Monday and Thursday, when Jews from all parts

of the city would come for ritual inquiries and to settle business, family, marital, and neighbor disputes. Attempts to establish a chief rabbi of Chicago were never successful. Later in 1937, the Chicago Rabbinical Council (CRC) was established to handle questions and problems and to render certain services especially for the Orthodox community.

Hull-House, at 800 South Halsted Street, was important in helping to educate and Americanize the Eastern European Jews of the Maxwell Street area. Jane Addams, who founded the pioneering social settlement center in 1889, fought for better conditions for the various ethnic groups of the area and helped them adjust to their environment. Hull-House grew until it became a complex of thirteen buildings, and it offered a great variety of activities. Often more than half of the membership of the classes, lectures, and clubs at Hull-House was Jewish, but some Eastern European Jews stayed away for fear that there would be an attempt to convert them, although Hull-House was never a religious institution. Eager for the learning that had been denied them in czarist Russia, the Jews were especially attracted to those offerings that dealt with English literature, social studies, dramatics, and music and seemed least interested in the manual training and art studies. Among those who benefited from attendance at Hull-House were Sidney Hillman, Benny Goodman, Studs Terkel, and Arthur Goldberg. Although Jane Addams came from a wealthy background, she had great empathy with the immigrants of the area and through the years pushed for better health, sanitation, and labor laws. Before she died in 1935 she established an office in Hull-House whose major purpose was to bring over German Jewish refugees from the Nazis.

The forerunner of today's much-used Jewish community centers, the Chicago Hebrew Institute (CHI), started in the Maxwell Street area in 1903 in a run-down, $55-a-month rented building on Blue Island Avenue near Twelfth Street (Roosevelt Road). It contained classrooms, a library, an assembly hall, a gymnasium, baths, and parlors. In 1908 a six-acre tract of land with buildings and beautiful gardens, located nearby at Taylor and Lytle streets, was acquired from a convent through the generous financial aid of Julius Rosenwald and others. Though badly damaged by a fire in 1910, it was rebuilt and the institute soon became a vital part of the community by providing a wide range of educational, social, recreational, and physical-education programs for both the young and adults. The institute contained playgrounds, classrooms, clubrooms, assembly halls, gymnasiums, a library, and a synagogue. It was a vehicle for Americanization of the immigrants, teaching them the language, culture, and manner of the new country while at the same time preserving Jewish traditions. One of its founders, the attorney Nathan Kaplan, spoke of its purposes as follows: "The younger generation speaking English and mixing with English-speaking people loses its interest in things Jewish, and the older people speaking nothing but their native language live always in a foreign atmosphere. We

*A fleet of chartered streetcars on Taylor Street loading people for the Chicago Hebrew Institute's annual picnic, 1922.*
(Courtesy of the Jewish Community Centers of Chicago and the Chicago Historical Society.)

*(Opposite page, top) Boys in boxing poses in front of Chicago Hebrew Institute, c. 1915.*
(Courtesy of the Chicago Historical Society.)

*(Opposite page, bottom) The Chicago Hebrew Institute Orchestra, one of many cultural activities at the facility, c. 1919.*
(Courtesy of the Jewish Community Centers and the Chicago Historical Society.)

# CLUBS AND SOCIETIES:

Athena Club—
Sunday afternoon (1st and 3d), 3:00 P. M.
Carlisle Athletic Club—
Wednesday evening, 7:30 P. M.
C. H. I. Alumni Association—
Sunday Evening (2nd and 4th), 3:00 P. M.
C. H. I. Band—
Monday evening, 7:30 P. M.
C. H. I. Leaders' Club—
Tuesday evening (1st), 8:00 P .M.
C. H. I. Musical Club—
Saturday, 7:00 P. M.
C. H. I. Sunshine Girls—
Section "A"—Saturday afternoon, 5:00 P. M.
Section "B"—Sunday afternoon, 3:00 P. M.
C. H. I. War Service Club—
Tuesday evening, 7:30 P. M.
Chicago Hebrew Oratorio Society—
Sunday afternoon, 4:00 P. M.
Wednesday evening, 7:30 P. M.
Club Council—
Sunday evening (3d), 8:00 P. M.
Comus Fellowship Club—
Sunday afternoon (2d and 4th), 2:30 P. M.
Corona Court—
Sunday afternoon (2nd), 2:30 P .M.
Fidelity Social and Educational Club—
Saturday evening (1st and 3rd), 7:00 P. M.
Flora Rebecca Lodge 152—
Monday evening, 8:00 P. M.
Girls' Sewing Club—
Thursday evening (2nd and 4th), 6:00 P. M.
Halevi Social and Educational Club—
Saturday evening, 7:00 P. M.
Hatchiah Society—
Saturday evening (1st and 3rd) 8:00 P. M.
High School Study Circle—
Sunday afternoon, 4:00 P. M.
Independent Friendship Club—
Sunday afternoon, 3:00 P. M.
Independent Ladies' Auxiliary—
Tuesday evening (2nd), 8:00 P. M.
Independent Social Club—
Saturday evening (2d and 4th), 8:00 P. M.
Institute Women's Club—
Tuesday afternoon (2nd and 4th), 3:00 P. M.
"I Will" Degree Staff Social—
Thursday evening (2nd and 4th), 8:00 P. M.
Jewish Festival Club—
Sunday afternoon, 4:00 P. M.
Jewish Literary and Dramatic Society—
Tuesday evening, 8:00 P. M.
Jewish National Workers' Alliance—
Sunday afternoon, 3:00 P. M.
Branch 105—
Monday evening (2nd and 4th), 8:00 P. M.
Jewish Singing Society—
Wednesday evening, 8:00 P. M.
Jewish Socialist Singing Society—
Tuesday evening, 8:00 P. M..
Junior Social Club—
Saturday evening, 7:00 P. M.
Kohriner Young People's Ass'n.—
Sunday afternoon (1st and 3rd), 3:00 P. M.

Ladies' Auxiliary War Sufferers—
Tuesday evening (1st and 3rd), 8:00 P. M.
Loyal Social Club—
Monday evening (1st and 3rd), 8:00 P. M.
Maccabees' Women's Club—
Monday evening (1st and 3rd), 8:00 P. M.
Maccabees' Federated Committee—
Monday evening (2nd and 4th), 8:00 P. M.
Nature Study Club—
Sunday afternoon (1st and 3rd), 3:00 P. M.
New Citizens' League—
Sunday afternoon, 3:00 P. M.
New Americans' Educational and Social Club—
Sunday afternoon (2nd and 4th), 4:30 P. M.
Optimo Club—
Sunday afternoon, 3:00 P. M.
Paramount Fellowship—
Sunday evening (1st and 3rd), 8:00 P. M.
Players' Club—
Mon., Wed., and Thurs. evenings, 8:00 P. M.
Sunday evening (2nd), 8:00 P. M.
Poale Zion, Br. 1—
Saturday evening, 8:00 P. M.
Branch 5—
Saturday evening (2nd and 4th), 7:30 P. M.
Post Biblical Class—
Saturday Afternoon, 5:00 P. M.
Practical Club—
Wednesday afternoon, 4:00 P. M.
Progressive Doers Club—
Sunday evening, 8:00 P. M.
Rogers Social Club—
Saturday evening, 8:00 P. M.
Social and Educational Club—
Sunday evening (1st and 3rd).
Trestiner Relief Society—
Sunday evening (2d and 4th), 8:00 P. M.
United Social Club—
Sunday afternoon, 3:00 P. M.
Unity Club—
Tuesday afternoon, 4:00 P. M.
Wide Awake Girls—
Saturday evening, 7:30 P. M.
Y. G. E. Society of the Y. P. S. C.—
Sunday evening, 7:30 P. M.
Young Hebrew Educational Club—
Tuesday evening, 7:30 P. M.
Young Judea Leaders—
(2nd and 4th), 8:00 P. M.
Young Maccabees—(12 sections).
Saturday afternoon, 2:00 P. M.
Sunday morning, 10:00 A. M.
Saturday evening, 7:30 P. M.
Sunday evening, 6:00 P. M.
Sunday afternoon, 2:00 P .M.
Thursday evening, 7:00 P. M.
Young Men's Hebrew Association—
Thursday evening, 7:00 P. M.
Young Peoples' Progressive Club—
Sunday evening, 7:30 P. M.
Zion Buds—
Sunday afternoon (1st and 3rd), 3:00 P. M.

## —————CALENDAR OF SPECIAL AFFAIRS—————

SUNDAYS
2:00 P. M.  C. H. I. Symphony Concert, Assembly Hall, Adm. Bldg.
2:00 P. M.  Gym. Social, Small Gym., Gymnasium Bldg.
8:00 P. M.  Players Club Performance, (Second Sunday),
    Assembly Hall, Adm. Bldg.
8:00 P. M.  Club Council Meeting (Third Sunday),
    Reception Room, Adm. Bldg.
TUESDAYS
8:00 P. M.  Adult Dancing Class, Reception Room, Adm. Bldg.
8:00 P. M.  Club Leaders' Club Meeting (First Tuesday),
    Association Room, Adm. Bldg.
7:30 P. M.  C. H. I. Service Club, Assembly Hall, Adm. Bldg.
THURSDAYS
8:00 P. M.  Young Men's Hebrew Association, Club Room, Adm. Bldg.
SATURDAYS
9:00 P. M.  Adult Service, Assembly Hall, Adm. Bldg.
2:00 P. M.  Children's Services, Assembly Hall, Adm. Bldg.
4:00 P. M.  Sabbath School Teachers' Study Circle, Room 24, Adm. Bldg.
8:00 P. M.  Dancing Class, Social Hall, Adm. Bldg.
8:00 P. M.  Social Dance, Assembly Hall, Adm. Bldg.

*Pages from Chicago Hebrew Institute monthly publication listing the numerous groups and activities at the institute, 1917.*

*(Courtesy of the Jewish Community Centers of Chicago.)*

Sunday, December 2, 1917.
7:30 P. M.  C. H. I. Literary and Dramatic Club Performance, Assembly Hall, Adm. Bldg.
Sunday, December 9, 1917.
8:00 P. M.  Players' Club Performance, Assembly Hall, Adm. Bldg.
7:00 P. M.  Young Maccabees Chanukah Celebration, Social Hall, Adm. Bldg.

Thursday, December 13, 1917.
8:00 P. M.  Concert by Students of Hebrew Oratorio Society, Assembly Hall, Adm. Bldg.
Sunday, December 16, 1917.
7:00 P. M.  C. H. I. Chanukah Celebration, Assembly Hall, Adm. Bldg.
Sunday, December 23, 1917.
8:00 P. M.  Recital by Mr. Price, Reception Room, Adm. Bldg.

# Chicago Hebrew Institute Observer

Published Monthly by the
### CHICAGO HEBREW INSTITUTE
1258 West Taylor Street

PHILIP L. SEMAN
Editor.

Subscription. 50 Cents per Annum in
Advance. Single Copies Five Cents.

Telephones:
Haymarket 6400—6401

VOLUME 6.     DECEMBER and JANUARY     NUMBER 1—2
1917    1918

## "Looping the Loop".

Someone has said that "You can always appeal to the Jewish heart, and if that is found wanting, you can appeal to the Jewish intelligence, and finally you can appeal to the Jewish sense of humor."

It was to the Jewish intelligence that several groups of the directorate to the Chicago Hebrew Institute undertook to appeal when they dispersed themselves within the Loop for the purpose of soliciting memberships to the Institute.

It was not a campaign for charity; it was not an appeal to the Jewish heart Per Se; but it was a direct statement made to the Jewish business men in the Loop as to what the Chicago Hebrew Institute is doing. The response was none the less generous, coming from the heart because of the lucid dictation of the mind.

The business man is not frequently credited with a deep insight into the value of social work. The Committees as they made their way from office to office and from loft to loft, found that the level-headed business man readily distinguishes between preventitive work and charity, between education and distribution of alms.

In the presence of need the provident business man would preferably give to the potentially successful youth in the making, by virtue of his receiving an education, as readily as he would give to the actually poor individual whose possibilities of success have been lost because it is too late for him now to become educated and self supporting.

So one by one the wholesale houses, the business offices, and sample rooms were taken into the ranks of the Chicago Hebrew Institute membership, which aims at prevention rather than cure.

In less than fifteen hours, five or six groups of trios have gathered in over $4,000.00 to defray the deficit of $20,000.00 incurred by the Institute during the last three or four years. This goes to show that if similar campaigns were instituted annually, the institution would not report a deficit at the end of the year. But, since the deficit already exists, it seems that the best way to meet it would be for such members of the Board who feel inclined, to take off a half day once a month during the coming winter, so that by the end of the winter activities, which are the most expensive, the President in his annual report will not have to make the usual plea for additional funds to pay debts with, but rather to spur on his hearers to encourage the work because of its worth to the community.

There are but few in this great city who know what the Chicago Hebrew Institute is actually doing in every branch of its endeavors. The Institute does not cater to the poor only. It does not enlighten or educate only the ignorant. It can be truthfully said that every one who enters its portals, remaining in its precincts for even a short period, leaves the Institute with some knowledge of things that he didn't know before.

hope the Institute will give both an opportunity to meet on common ground and so, while making the Orthodox tolerant and the younger element better fitted to sympathize, preserve all that is best in the race and its faith."[46]

Under the long-term and able guidance of Jacob M. Loeb, the organization's president, and the very competent and innovative general director, Philip L. Seman, who served for thirty-two years, the Chicago Hebrew Institute became one of the most successful community centers in the nation. It was also noteworthy in that more than half of its total expenditures were covered by revenues obtained through its activities.

The institute's constructive programs offered something for almost everyone in a period when people's activities were generally limited to the neighborhood. In addition to Camp CHI (Chicago Hebrew Institute), a summer camp founded in 1921 for youngsters, it had a milk station for the poor, lectures, festivals for all occasions, picnics, dances, concerts, motion pictures, gardening, an orchestra, theatrical performances, art, swimming and other sports, and a broad range of classes – from Hebrew to housekeeping, and from citizenship to typing. It trained people for the trades as well as for social work. It had an accredited evening high school, one of the largest libraries in the city, some fifty different clubs, and even a champion wrestling team. It also established a branch on the Northwest Side. In 1926, after twenty-two years of serving the community, the institute moved with the Jewish populace to Lawndale after being renamed the Jewish People's Institute (JPI).

### THE *LANDSMANSHAFTEN*

A very important part of the lives of a large number of the city's Eastern European Jews were the *landsmanshaften* or *vereinen*. These were benevolent societies, formed predominantly by Yiddish-speaking immigrants from the same shtetl or group of shtetlach or regions of Eastern Europe. These organizations were probably the most spontaneous in character and the most frequent representative of the masses of any of the institutions of the Eastern European Jews; furthermore, they were established by the immigrants themselves. They were broadly based, taking in the rich and the poor, people of diverse religious and political views, but all of them people steeped in *Yiddishkeit.*

Most of the *landsmanshaften* were formed by men; some had women's auxiliaries. All were havens of help, safety, and security in the new alien world. They would often help by providing the rail and ship tickets, jobs, and places to live for their townsmen, as well as matchmaking opportunities. They served as the clearinghouses for all kinds of information. They sponsored picnics, theater benefits, holiday celebrations, and banquets. One *verein* was initially organized to raise twenty-five dollars for a *landsman* peddler so that he could replace his horse, which had died.

An estimated hundred thousand Chicago Jews belonged to the *landsmanshaften* through the years. Most of the organizations were formed by immigrants from the small communities of Eastern Europe, usually not by those from the larger cities or by those from Germany. The German Jews had some national fraternal organizations of their own that specialized in self-help, sports, cultural activities, and other pursuits.

Initially some *landsmanshaften* were social or family groups but many were religious, centering around the synagogue. Later they became largely unaffiliated and secular, serving as social clubs, loan associations, agencies for the sick and unemployed, mutual aid and burial societies, places to meet old friends and reminisce about *di alte heym* (the old-world home), and channels for aiding those who had been left behind. Despite the hardships and persecution the immigrants had experienced in their shtetlach of wooden shanties and muddy roads, they felt a certain affection for these communities, a fondness that grew greater as bitter memories mellowed and faded.

The *landsmanshaften* meetings were usually held monthly in a rented hall or a synagogue. Few outsiders attended. Yiddish was spoken and kosher refreshments of wine, schnapps, herring, chopped liver, and sweets were served after the meeting. Unlike in many other Jewish organizations, there was limited involvement in issues on the local or national political scene and no united *landsmanshaften* voice in these areas.

> Rickety yet durable, the landsmanshaften satisfied many needs. A member could assuage his nostalgia for the old country by listening to reports at the meetings from newly arrived immigrants or those who had gone back for a visit. He could share in the deeply rooted Jewish tradition of communal self-help, which in practice might mean sending money back home for Passover matzos or to repair the *shul.* The society would provide help for unemployed members, usually in confidential ways, and once the wives started their ladies' auxiliary, this task was often turned over to them, as appropriate to their superior sense of delicacy.[47]

Many of the *landsmanshaften* were organized during the early decades of the century, although some were older. From 1870 to 1970 there were about seven hundred such organizations in Chicago. In their constitutions, besides details of the organizational structure, there were often provisions that the books be kept in Yiddish, that the name of the hometown should always be part of their official name, that if a member married a gentile he would be stricken from the rolls, and that no sick benefits be given to anyone who had contracted an immoral disease.[48]

Some of the immigrants, especially those from the large Eastern European communities or those with more of a secular background, chose to bypass the *landsmanshaften,* fearing that such involvement would hinder their Americanization. These immigrants instead often became members of unions, radical organizations, or Zionist groups.

During the World War I and World War II periods, *landsmanshaften* were especially active in trying to aid their overseas *landsleit* with money, food, and clothing; persistent effort enabled them to bring many to America. There were still about 600 Chicago *landsmanshaften,* totaling 40,000 members, during World War II. They ranged in size from 25 to 600 members. When the Holocaust wiped out virtually all of the Jewish communities of Eastern Europe, and with them millions of relatives and friends whom the groups had tried to aid, the organizations then redirected their efforts to aiding Israel and other mainly Jewish needs. However, as the immigrant population began to diminish, the *landsmanshaften* declined rapidly in membership, and one by one they disappeared. Today there are only about three dozen still functioning.

One of the aims of the *landsmanshaften* members was to transmit an awareness of their origins to the younger generation. But their American offspring, with little knowledge or feeling for the shtetlach of their forebears, never joined the organizations in any significant numbers. For them the Old World was superseded by the more promising New World, although they continued to feel the *landsmanshaften* influence. Today, vestiges of the once-numerous *vereinen* are evident primarily in the *landsmanshaften* plots dotting Waldheim Cemetery in Forest Park[49] and in hundreds of *yizkor bikher* (memorial books), compiled by the *landsmanshaften* after the Holocaust, of the shtetlach that had been decimated.

There were also some seventy-five Jewish fraternal lodges in the Maxwell Street area, over two-thirds belonging either to the Independent Order of B'rith Abraham or to the Independent Western Star Order. Among the attractions of these orders were the life insurance and other services they offered. The lodges would also have occasional parties or balls to raise money for sick members or the impoverished family of a deceased member.

*Landsmanshaften*-like organizations were also formed by some of the small Sephardic Jewish groups that settled in Chicago. Sephardic Jews – those who originated in the Mediterranean area and in Southwest Asia – differed in background, language, and religious practices from the Ashkenazi Jews. The Sephardic Jews from Turkey and the Balkans spoke Ladino (a mixture of Spanish and Hebrew dialect), those from Syria spoke Arabic, and those from Persia (Iran) and the Caucasus region of Russia spoke Aramaic. Although the Sephardim counted for less than 4 percent of Chicago's Jewish population, a number of their synagogues were established in major Jewish areas, including Maxwell Street, Lawndale and, later, neighborhoods to the north.[50]

### THE YIDDISH THEATER

In addition to the entertainment and recreational facilities for adults at Hull-House and the Chicago Hebrew Institute, the Yiddish theater was a favorite form of enjoyment for the Eastern European Jews. The audience identified closely with the actors, with the joys and sorrows they expressed as they reminisced about the Old Country in a familiar language. In the early Yiddish theater, actors frequently ad-libbed or were helped by prompters, often upstaging each other and changing scenes they did not like. The audience would shout at the villains between bites of herring and black bread. The productions were more than mere entertainment; they usually reflected Jewish culture. Some of the first plays were melodramatic, tear-evoking performances that mixed deep emotion with religious and nationalistic fervor. Many dealt with the miseries of the immigrant's life while being nostalgic about the shtetl. Other shows dealt with the problem of a nice Jewish boy meeting a nice gentile girl (or vice versa). In contrast were the somewhat bawdy, lusty comedies and romantic musicals.

The first Yiddish theater company in Chicago was established in 1887 by the eighteen-year-old Boris Thomashefsky in a small rented theater on Twelfth Street. It later moved into a dance hall at 716 West De Koven Street. Thomashefsky's first popular production was *Blood Libel,* a play he wrote that was set in Russia and concerned the rumor that Jews used Christian blood to make their matzos.

In time there were a number of Yiddish theaters in the Maxwell Street area. The first of the major large Yiddish theaters was the Metropolitan at Twelfth and Jefferson streets. It opened in the early 1890s. After it was condemned as being unsafe, the People's Music Hall nearby on Twelfth Street was used for a while, and other Yiddish theaters – the Standard, the Empire, and the Haymarket – were established just to the north around Madison and Halsted. There was also a small Yiddish theater on Twelfth Street just east of Halsted, the Weisenfreund Pavilion Theater. There, a young boy, Muni Weisenfreund, played many different roles in his father's theater, sometimes appearing in as many as ten different stage shows a day. After more than a decade of acting in Chicago he joined the Yiddish theater in New York, later appearing in Broadway plays. In 1928 he went to Hollywood as Paul Muni. He was a noted and popular character actor who won an Academy Award for his performance in the movie *The Life of Louis Pasteur.*

In the period before World War I, there were also ten Yiddish vaudeville houses operating in the Maxwell Street area, "nickel shows" that offered variety entertainment. Just after the war, in 1919, the largest of the legitimate Yiddish theaters in the area opened on Blue Island Avenue near Roosevelt Road, in a building that formerly housed the power facility of the West Chicago Street Railway Company. Founded by Elias Glickman, a Russian-born Jewish actor and director, Glickman's Palace Theater flourished as the major Yiddish theater of the city. It was finally forced to close in 1931, a victim of the Depression and increased competition from newer Yiddish theaters in Lawndale, Humboldt Park, and Logan Square, where the Jewish population had been moving. An excellent nonprofessional group was founded in 1910 by a group of young immigrants. The long-lasting Yiddishe Dramatishe Gesellschaft performed classic and contemporary plays and for decades was housed at the Jewish People's Institute.

From simple and crude beginnings, through the years the Yiddish theater attained a high level of professionalism and sophistication. Plays were performed based on the writings of great Yiddish literary figures such as Sholem Aleichem, Mendele Mocher Seforim, Isaac Leib Peretz, Sholem Asch, I. J. Singer, Peretz Hirschbein, and others. Other productions showcased the works of playwrights and composers such as Jacob Gordon, Sholom Secunda, Abraham Goldfadden, David Pinski, and H. Leivick. Translations of plays by well-known non-Jewish writers such as Gorky, Chekkov, Tolstoy, Dostoyevski, Schiller, Molière, Wilde, and even Shakespeare were performed, including the latter's *Der Yiddisher Kain-ag Lear.* Popular Yiddish classics frequently performed included *The Dybbuk,*

The largest of many Yiddish theaters in the Maxwell Street area was the Glickman Palace Theater at Roosevelt Road and Blue Island Avenue, which operated from 1919 to 1931. The poster is for the 1925–26 season when an outstanding Yiddish acting group, the Vilna Troupe from Vilna, Lithuania, performed. Their plays that year were Day and Night, Hard to Be a Jew, and The Green Fields. (Courtesy of the American Jewish Historical Society.)

*Der Goilem, Mirele Efros, Die Greene Felder, Shulamith,* and *Yoshe Kalb.* Songs that have become part of the Jewish folk music include "Mein Yiddische Mame," "Roszhinkes mit Mandlen," "A Brevele fun de Mama," and "Bei Mir Bist du Schein."

Many of the best Yiddish actors and actresses from New York and Europe performed frequently in Chicago's Yiddish theaters. They included Jacob Adler, Celia Adler, Boris Thomashevsky, Molly Picon, Pesachke Burstein, Michael Michalesko, Ludwig Satz, Menashe Skulnik, Jacob Ben Ami, Aaron Lebedeff, and Maurice Schwartz. Schwartz was once a Chicago newsboy who spent his

(Opposite page) Paul Muni (1895–1967), famed stage and screen actor, began life as Muni Weisenfreund in the Maxwell Street area. (Irving Cutler Collection.)

theater apprenticeship years in the city. Some of the Yiddish performers were often as flamboyant as the colorful characters they portrayed on the stage. Decades later, perhaps buoyed by the legacy of Yiddish theater humor, a number of Chicago-born Americanized Jewish comedians who were also social critics – for example, Shelley Berman, Morey Amsterdam, Allan Sherman, Jerry Lester, and Jackie Leonard – won national recognition. And no one could forget the comedian from Waukegan, the perennial thirty-nine year old, Jack Benny, who as a youth played the fiddle, later one of his trademarks.

## RELATIONS BETWEEN GERMAN JEWS AND EASTERN EUROPEAN JEWS

The German Jews had arrived early in Chicago and at a more opportune time than did the Eastern European Jews. But by 1900 they were already outnumbered 50,000 to 20,000 by the latter group, and the character of the Jewish community had changed.

The coming of large numbers of Eastern European Jews upset the more affluent and established German Jews, who were by then living comfortably in the Golden Ghetto of the South Side and already partially assimilated into the American milieu. A number had become wealthy, held prominent social positions, and were leaders in the insurance, banking, real estate, and brokerage fields. They were embarrassed by the Old World ways, beliefs, demeanor, language, and dress of their poor coreligionists who were pouring into the Maxwell Street area and recreating a European ghetto. The poverty of the Eastern European Jews was more desperate than the German Jewish poverty had ever been, their piety much more intense than German Jewish piety, their irreligion more defiant, their radicalism more extreme, their support of Zionism much more fervent.[51] The German Jews feared that the "different," visibly alien Eastern European Jews might set off anti-Semitism, which the older settlers felt they had largely managed to defuse. The German Jews living mostly on the South Side or in smaller numbers on the North Side were physically removed from the Jews of the Near West Side ghetto, and they felt even further removed from them culturally and economically. They felt that they had gained recognition for themselves among their Christian neighbors as persons rather than as Jews; however, with the influx of the Eastern European Jews they were apprehensive that the amicable atmosphere that existed might drastically change.

Bernard Horwich, who arrived in Chicago from Eastern Europe in 1880, later recalled the early relationship of German and Eastern European Jews:

> The relationship between the Russian and Polish Jews and the German Jews was anything but amicable. The latter group, with their background of German culture, speaking the German language, engaged in more worldly and sophisticated business enterprises, and practicing Reformed Judaism, were looked upon as Germans rather than as Jews. The Russian and Polish Jews maintained that the reformed religious ideas of the German Jews made them

really "substitute" or "second-hand" Jews, and that their Rabbis were almost like Christian ministers. Some even asserted that they regarded the Christian ministers more highly than the Reformed rabbis, since the former were believers and preached their religion truthfully and faithfully, while the latter tried to deny their Judaism, so as to ingratiate themselves with the non-Jews.

The Russian and Polish Jews, having come from countries where oppression took the place of education, were considered "half-civilized." Very few of them could read or write English, and since there was as yet no Yiddish paper here, they received their information from their children of school age, who could understand a little of what was in the newspapers. The majority knew only what little Hebrew they had learned in the "cheders." . . .

The attitude of the German Jews towards their Russian and Polish brothers was one of superiority and unpleasant pity. They tolerated them only because they were Jews, and one would often hear the German Jews bewailing their fate – that they, Americanized businessmen, had to be classed in the same category with the poor, ignorant, ragged Jewish peddlers on the other side of the river, on Canal Street.[52]

Jane Addams, at a meeting of Jewish leaders at Hull-House in 1902, stated, "It seems to be that there is more ill feeling between Reform and Orthodox Jews than there is between Jews and Gentiles."[53]

The German Jews realized that they had to help the Eastern European Jews out of sympathy for their plight as well as for self-protective reasons. They had to take care of their own so that all would not be subject to disapproval; they also had to hasten the Americanization of their Eastern European brethren.

As one of their newspapers wrote:

Inasmuch, however, as they are here, they must be put to some use. On the other hand, it is to be assumed that at least the second if not the first generations, may become sufficiently Americanized to be tolerable, which in the case of the intelligent German Jewish immigrant, has been accomplished within a few years of his arrival. But take it all in all, what must be done for *unsere leite* (our people), will prove a very difficult task in cultural labor, and it would indeed be desirable if they would stay away altogether. We have enough and sufficient Polish Jews in the United States and will thank the powers that be in Europe, to not send us any more.[54]

The German Jews consequently embarked on an extensive program of financing and running a number of educational, health, and social-service institutions, mostly in the Maxwell Street area. These proved very helpful to the poorer Eastern European immigrants. Socially, the German Jews kept apart from the newer immigrants, living separately and maintaining their own clubs, synagogues, fraternal organizations, and community centers, at which the Eastern European Jews were not welcomed. Later, as the Eastern European Jews progressed, they built a parallel set of their own institutions, such as a hospital, old peoples' homes, charities, and orphanages. Although the distinction between the two groups was gradually blurred, for decades the social distance between the groups remained great. The German Jews, for example,

did not wish to have these Jews too close to them. These Russians were all right – of that they were quite certain – but, like the southern Negro, they had to keep their place. All sorts of philanthropic enterprises were undertaken in their behalf, but in the management of these enterprises the beneficiaries were given no voice. Charity balls by the debutantes of the German-Jewish elite in behalf of the wretched West Side Jews were held at the splendid clubs of the German Jews, which by this time had increased to four, and charitably inclined young Jewish men and ladies-bountiful spent their leisure hours in alleviating the hardships of the Jewish slum dwellers.

But the Russians did not take altogether willingly to the American ways of dispensing *zdoko* (charity). They were accustomed to assisting one another in the Old Country in much more informal style. The Jewish communities they had known in Russia were self-sufficient large families. These German Jews of the "societies" asked all sorts of embarrassing questions before they dispensed their financial and other aid. They made investigations and kept records. Most of all, they did not understand – they did not know – their own people; in fact, they were only halfway Jews; they did not even understand *mama loshon* (the mother-tongue), or Yiddish.[55]

Not all of the German Jews, of course, held a negative view of the Eastern European Jews. Many did not, especially such leaders as Dr. Emil G. Hirsch, who wrote somewhat prophetically in 1905:

The study of the future of the Russian Jew in the United States is of vital importance, because on his success or failure depends the very fate of Judaism itself in this land. Numerically, even now the dominant factor in America Jewry, the Russian Jew will at no remote day also assert the leadership in all movements expressive of his race and religion. It is the Russian Jew who will mold the character of the Synagogue and its ambition in the western world. In measure as he will rise socially, intellectually, morally and spiritually will the standing of Judaism and the influence of the Jew be accorded distinction and recognition. . . . And yet he [the German Jew] refuses to accept the decree which will relegate him to the second rank, for he effects in wealth, culture, education and liberalism over his Russian brother of late arrival. Yet, even in these aspects the Russian Jew is fast crowding him. . .[56]

At times the Russian-Polish Jews contemptuously resented the paternalistic, condescending attitude of their more worldly German Jewish brethren and the stigma of sometimes being called *schnorrers* (beggars), but they accepted their help because ghetto life was difficult and living conditions deplorable. In addition to establishing the Chicago Hebrew Institute and the Jewish Training School in the Maxwell Street area, the German Jews were instrumental in the establishment of other area institutions that offered aid. One of these was the West Side Dispensary (later the Mandel Clinic), whose large donors included Babette Mandel, a grandniece of Michael Reese. The dispensary was a modern

The Chicago Lying-In
Hospital (Chicago Maternity
Center), 1904.
(Courtesy of the Sentinel.)

facility at Maxwell and Morgan streets that provided free medical care and medicine for poor immigrants. Other such institutions included the Maxwell Street Settlement, on Maxwell Street east of Jefferson Street, established to "uplift" the culture of the populace by means of classes and clubs. It was modeled somewhat on Jane Addams's highly successful Hull-House. The Chicago Lying-In Dispensary and Hospital (Chicago Maternity Center), established in 1895 at Maxwell Street and Newberry, provided free prenatal and obstetrical care and was founded and supervised by one of the world's leading obstetricians, Dr. Joseph De Lee (1869–1942). In later decades it was run by one of his very able students, Dr. Beatrice Tucker.

The 1905 annual report of the director of the Associated Jewish Charities, an organization (founded in 1900) supported mainly by Reform Jews, listed its fourteen beneficiaries, most of which were involved in aiding Eastern European Jews: United Hebrew Charities for Relief; United Hebrew Charities for Michael Reese Hospital; United Hebrew Charities for West Side Dispensary; Home for Jewish Aged and Infirm; Chicago Home for Jewish Orphans; Jewish Training School of Chicago; Home for Jewish Friendless and Working Girls; Chicago Lying-In Hospital and Dispensary; Maxwell Street Settlement; Bureau of Personal Service; Cleveland Orphan Asylum; National Jewish Hospital for Consumptives, Denver, Colorado; Council of Jewish Women (Summer School Work); and Woman's Loan Association.

The Bureau of Personal Service, organized in 1897 in the Maxwell Street area, performed social services for the community and brought into closer cooperation the neighborhood philanthropic agencies. Its major early leader was Hannah Greenebaum Solomon. Among other programs, the Bureau of Personal Service supplied relief in emergency cases, worked with delinquents, and ran a

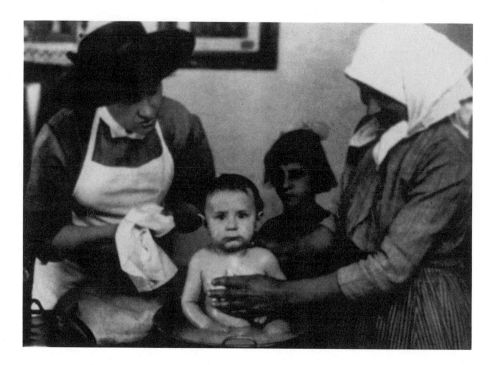

A nurse's visit to an immigrant family house in the Maxwell Street area about 1910.

(Irving Cutler Collection.)

work program for women. A familiar marital problem occasionally developed: a young man would marry a young woman in his native Eastern European village, have several children, and then leave for America, where he hoped to better his lot and send for his wife and children. In most cases he followed through; however, once he was in the New World, changes began to take place. The young man, often under the prodding of his more Americanized relatives, shaved his beard and earlocks, switched to American clothes, learned some English, and adopted American customs. When his wife finally arrived, after years of hardship and struggle in raising the family alone, he was sometimes appalled by the appearance and customs of his "greenhorn" wife. The end result was sometimes divorce or even abandonment.[57]

### MAXWELL STREET LEGACY

In time, through hard work and persistence, and with the aid of the various community organizations, including the Federated Orthodox Jewish Charities formed in 1912 by Eastern European Jews themselves, the Russian and Polish Jews generally began to adapt to and become part of their new environment in Chicago. They even helped elect a colorful but controversial saloonkeeper-politician, Emanuel "Manny" Abrahams, to represent their area, first, in the state legislature, and then, in the city council. Abrahams suffered a fatal heart attack immediately after successfully leading the fight to allow peddlers to continue shouting their products and services.[58]

By 1910, with improvement in their economic status, the encroachment of the railroad and industry, and the influx of blacks, many of the Jews started to move out of the run-down Maxwell Street area to better areas. They first moved westward toward Ashland, next to Robey (Damen) Street, and then, leapfrogging some three miles straight west from the Maxwell Street area, into Lawndale.

דער מושב זקנים בית

ORTHODOX HOME FOR THE AGED

דער סאנסומפּטיווס האספּיטאל

MAIMONIDES HOSPITAL

דער בית מחסה ליתומים

MARKS NATHAN ORPHAN HOME

# Federated Orthodox Jewish Charities

## THE CENTRAL ADMINISTRATION BLDG.

### 1020 S. WOOD STREET

#### TeL! SEELEY 919

**Officers:**
JULIUS ROSENWALD, HON. PRES.
JAMES DAVIS PRESIDENT
SAMUEL PHILLIPSON, VICE PRES.
A. D. LASKER VICE PRES.
BENJAMIN J. SCHIFF, TREASURER
MAX SHULMAN, SEC'Y.

SAMUEL LEFF EXEC. SEC'Y.

**Directors:**
PHILIP D. BLOCK
JOSEPH BLONDER
ISADORE COHEN
AREL DAVIS
SAMUEL DEUTCH
RABBI E. EPSTEIN
HARRY EPSTEIN
ISADORE FERGUSON

JUDGE H. M. FISHER
SAMUEL GINSBURG
B HORWICH
MOSES KREEGER
ADOLPH KURZ
J. A. LASSERS
H. R. MISCH
HERMAN MOLNER

A. PINK
THOMAS PISER
A. S. ROE
M. RUBIN
CHAS SHAFFNER
RABBI S. SILBER
MORRIS TOWER
AUGUST TURNER
GEO. WINSBERG

CHICAGO          Oct 17, 1915

The Federated Orthodox Jewish Charities is the central organization through which all that the community contributes for orthodox charitable purposes is economically collected, administrated and distributed among the following organizations:

Orthodox Home for the Aged
Marks Nathan Orphan Home
Maimonides Hospital
Jewish Consumptive Relief Society
Federated Relief Society
Four Free Hebrew Schools
Hebrew High School
Northwest Free Burial Society
Shelter House for Poor Strangers.

### Annual Budget

| | |
|---|---|
| Marks Nathan Orphan Home | $36,000. |
| Home for the Aged | 24,000. |
| Maimonides Hospital | 24,000. |
| Consumptives Relief Society | 10,000. |
| Federated Relief Society | 10,000. |
| Four Free Hebrew Schools | 14,500. |
| Hebrew High School | 4,500. |
| Free Burial Society | 1,000. |
| Shelter House | 3,600. |
| Administration | 9,000. |
| **Total** | **$136,600.** |

### The Work of the Federated and its Institutions.

Provides shelter, food, clothing and education for 250 orphan boys and girls.

Cares for over 120 old and feeble men and women amidst pleasant and pious surroundings.

Gives free medical treatment to the poor who seek to preserve the dietary laws when sick as well as when healthy.

Furnishes food, clothing and other relief to over 250 consumptive families.

Visits poor families in their homes and gives relief.

Instructs over 1500 children in the Jewish religion in various quarters of the city.

Gives higher courses in the Talmud for advanced pupils.

Attends to the burial of the poor in Jewish cemeteries.

Maintains a home to feed and lodge transient poor.

My dear Mr. Bressler,

The local conference of Jewish Social Workers contemplate a survey of normal industrial conditions among our Chicago Jewish people. We have unanimously hit upon you as the one man of our group who could make practical suggestions as to the method best to pursue. Also references where to find any publications that would throw some light on our specific problem, especially Industrial Removal reports.

We would appreciate any assistance rendered as we realize we are pioneering. Our job becomes easier with the enlistment of more workers.

With kind regard, I am
Yours very truly,
Samuel Leff

*Correspondence of the Federated Orthodox Jewish Charities, 1915, listing officers, services, and budget.*
*(Courtesy of the Chicago Jewish Archives.)*

Public-school enrollment figures show that the decrease in Jewish enrollment in the Maxwell Street area schools from 1914 to 1923 was about 60 percent.[59] By the 1930s the Jewish population had declined markedly, having dispersed north, south, and, mainly, west. Some older Jews lingered in the area a while longer, and most neighborhood businesses were still run by Jews into the 1960s. Today, however, there are few Jewish businesses left there, mostly on Halsted Street. Through the years some of the Jewish vendors got rich and some stayed poor, but they all managed to feed their families.

Urban demolition has left few remnants of the area's Jewish past – a few faded signs, the hot dog stand that once spawned Fluky's. Gone are such landmarks as the Twelfth Street and L. Klein stores, Gold's Restaurant, the Chicago Maternity Center, the *Daily Jewish Courier*, Turner Brothers Clothing, Robinson's, Machevich, and Gabels department stores, and Nate's Delicatessen, which was once owned by a black man who spoke Yiddish. Of the over forty synagogue buildings, two remain – one now a Greek church and the other a black church.

Ironically, in an otherwise solidly Orthodox neighborhood, Temple B'nai Jehoshua, the last surviving synagogue in the area (it closed in 1965) was a Reform congregation. This sole non-Orthodox congregation at 19th and Ashland Avenue, on the fringe of the Maxwell Street area, was organized by Bohemian Jews who wished to live near their small stores on 18th and 22nd streets in the Gentile Bohemian neighborhood of Pilsen. Like German Jews, Bohemians often favored Reform Judaism. Among the members of B'nai Jehoshua were the Bohemian Jewish immigrants Judge Joseph Sabath (1870–1956), and his brother, Congressman Adolph Sabath (1866–1952), who served in the U.S. House of Representatives for twenty-three consecutive terms, the second-longest continuous service of any U.S. congressman. Also members were the family that owned the chain of Leader Department Stores, which catered to Eastern European neighborhoods and sold, among other items, thousands of *perinas* (comforters) annually to their largely Bohemian and Polish customers. In 1965, B'nai Jehoshua merged with Congregation Beth Elohim of Glenview. The proceeds from the sale of its building on Ashland Avenue helped pay for the new site of the merged congregations.[60]

Among the legacies of the area are the myriads of Eastern European Jews and their children who surmounted the handicaps of the crowded ghetto in the New World, many becoming well known.

Joseph Goldberg was one of these immigrants. He came to America from Russia and eventually landed on Maxwell Street. He bought a blind horse, the only horse he could afford. He became a fruit-and-vegetable peddler; his son, Arthur, would serve in President Kennedy's cabinet and become a Supreme Court Justice of the United States.

Samuel Paley became a cigar maker in America, as did Max Guzik. Samuel's son William, born in the back room of the modest family cigar store near Maxwell Street, was founder, president and chairman of the board of the Columbia Broadcasting System. Mr. Guzik's son Jake, known as "Greasy Thumb," became the brains behind the Capone gang and, when he died in 1956, was among the top three on the FBI's list of public enemies.

Eastern European immigrants David Goodman and Abraham Rickover took jobs in Chicago as tailors. Their sons were Benny Goodman and Admiral Hyman G. Rickover.

The father of Barney Ross, onetime world lightweight boxing champion, and the father of Barney Balaban, the late president of Paramount Pictures, each owned a tiny grocery store in the Maxwell Street area.

Paul Muni's father owned a Yiddish theater near Maxwell Street, Jack Ruby's father was a carpenter there.

John Keeshin, once the greatest trucking magnate in America, is the son of a man who owned a chicken store on Maxwell Street, as did the father of Jackie Fields, former welterweight champion of the world. The father of Federal Court Judge Abraham Lincoln Marovitz owned a candy store near Maxwell Street.

Colonel Jacob Arvey, once a nationally prominent political power broker, was the son of a Maxwell Street peddler.[61]

Others who had roots in the Maxwell Street area were the author Meyer Levin, the businessman Morrie Mages, Judge Robert Cherry, and Judge Benjamin Schwartz. Saul Alinsky also grew up in the area and was to become a nationally known community organizer and social activist. His book *Reveille for Radicals* was used as the bible by community organizers throughout the nation. Alinsky taught poor communities how to organize to muster public opinion and challenge entrenched leadership.

Maxwell Street figured in a period that saw many profound changes in the Chicago Jewish community. Help from the German Jewish community was being replaced by self-help. Secular agencies eventually took over many of the social services from the synagogue; economic advancement and diversity increased; important changes took place in the quality of Jewish education; and many older religious, cultural, and social practices began to disappear. While members of the older generation generally kept to their Old World ways and their children sometimes followed, some members of the younger generation were rapidly adopting the ways of the New World, and their grandchildren were to become almost fully acculturated. Throughout recent centuries, the Jews had often adapted to the culture of the country in which they lived.

In 1925, as the Maxwell Street Jewish community was declining, the *Chicago Chronicle* quoted and commented on a speech by Rabbi Saul Silber of Congregation Anshe Sholom decrying the state of the younger generation in regard to Judaism:

"What will become of our children? Do we want them to grow up pinochle players and poker sharks, or do we want them to grow up men and women who have an understanding of the problems of life, who know the history of their ancestors, who are proud Jews, and who will be a credit to us? Our children are running away from us because we have nothing to hold them with, to make them worthy of their Jewish heritage. Orthodox Judaism is on the decline and will soon disappear entirely unless we do our duty toward maintaining its traditions."

Well spoken, Rabbi Silber. It is unfortunate that the Jewish population has the moving spirit and neighborhoods change practically overnight. First it was Douglas and Independence Boulevards, then the North Shore district, then Rogers Park; now it is Wilmette, Winnetka, and Glencoe, etc. These newly rich want to be "swell," and to be "swell" is to run away from Jews and Judaism – that's the modern curse.[62]

# 3

# Through the World Wars

## Expanding Communal Activity

With its customary audacity, the city that had been almost destroyed by the Great Fire of 1871 hosted the great World's Columbian Exposition of 1893, erecting the fairgrounds on what seemed to be an impossible sandy lakeshore site in the recently annexed Hyde Park–Woodlawn area. Chicago's population at that time had risen to almost 1.5 million, of whom about seventy thousand were Jewish.

The majority of the Jews in the city at the time of the fair, about fifty thousand, were the recently arrived Eastern European Jews, concentrated largely around Maxwell Street and increasing very rapidly in numbers. They lived in a crowded "Jewtown" that resembled in many ways the shtetlach from which so many had come. Less than a third of the Jewish population, about twenty thousand, consisted òf the original German-speaking Jewish settlers and their descendants. These German

Jews, living mainly on the South Side, were generally well established, quite Americanized, and accepted by the non-Jewish population.

The more Americanized Jewish community strongly supported the fair by purchasing its capital stock, serving in its administrative management, and participating in its major events. By taking part in the fair, a number of important Jewish organizations evolved, as did strong local leadership and cooperative elements among the city's Jews. The fair also brought the rapidly rising city of Chicago to the attention of Jews throughout Europe.

The event at the fair that most interested the Jewish community was the World's Parliament of Religions. Representatives of all world faiths were invited to attend and present papers or be discussants on a variety of themes, including the current state of religion and of their particular religion. In this non-discriminatory atmosphere, which would have been unheard of in Europe, Jewish leaders such as Dr. Emil G. Hirsch, Rabbi A. J. Messing, Dr. Bernhard Felsenthal, Dr. Joseph Stolz, Dr. Kaufmann Kohler, Dr. Isaac Mayer Wise, Professor Gabriel Bamberger, Henrietta Szold, Hannah Greenebaum Solomon, and others actively participated in the parliament events, which included three sessions on Judaism.

An integral part of these proceedings was the four-day Jewish Denominational Congress, presided over by Dr. Hirsch. It included numerous scholarly papers on Judaism. The congress was followed by the four-day Jewish Women's Congress led by Hannah Greenebaum Solomon, whose family were prominent Chicago Jews of German background. It was the first national gathering of Jewish women and it had a large attendance. Papers dealt with topics such as Jewish women and religion, women in the workforce, and religion in the home. The final session included a paper entitled "Organization," by Sadie American, a social worker and a native Chicagoan, who made an impassioned plea for the formation of a Jewish women's organization. She stated: "Not again may we have together so many women from all parts of our country drawn hither for the purpose of representing Judaism at its best. Let us form an organization whose object shall be spreading the understanding of and devotion to the highest type of Judaism, in whose service shall be put every faculty of our being."[1] Immediately thereafter, what later became one of the nation's leading Jewish organizations, the National Council of Jewish Women, was founded, with Hannah Greenebaum Solomon as president and Sadie American as secretary. Most of its early members were of German Jewish descent. The NCJW is dedicated to the furtherance of human welfare in the Jewish and general community through education, service, and social action. The Chicago section was the founding section; today there are over 100,000 members nationally. Through the years the group has aided immigrants and refugees; provided job placement services; created educational opportunities both at home and abroad (including in Israel); aided the young, old, and handicapped in a variety of ways; and fought for beneficial social legislation. Hannah Greenebaum Solomon went on to serve as president of the NCJW for twelve years and was also founder and longtime president of the Bureau of Personal Service, which provided social services for the immigrants. She was a prominent civic reformer and friend

and collaborator of Jane Addams and one who worked hard to preserve and promote Judaism in the face of a trend toward assimilation.

The chairman of the exposition's Committee on the Congress of Religions, Dr. Barrows, lauded the Jewish community for its help with the fair: "I do not forget, I am glad to remember, that devout Jews, lovers of humanity, have cooperated with us in this Parliament; that these men and women representing the most wonderful of all races and the most persistent of all religions, who have come with good cause to appreciate the spiritual freedom of the United States of America; that these friends . . . have zealously and powerfully cooperated in this work."[2]

The importance of the World's Parliament of Religion and its related events was summarized in a speech by Dr. Hirsch: "We are glad of this opportunity to invite the world to the secrets of our faith and the ultimate tendency of our hopes. And we shall be glad when men have heard us, they shall say: Why, you Jews are not different from us; you are men as we are; your hopes are our hopes; your beliefs are our beliefs. And why should the world not say this? Have we not all one Father? Has not one God created us all?"[3]

## THROUGH THE WORLD WAR I PERIOD

In 1898, five years after the closing of the World's Columbian Exposition in Chicago, which had commemorated the arrival of Columbus in the New World, the United States found itself at war with the patron of Christopher Columbus, Spain. President McKinley called for a volunteer army to aid the regular army, and many Chicago Jews answered the call – in sharp contrast to the Jews in czarist Russia who hid out, fled the country, and even sometimes mutilated themselves in order to avoid a military service that discriminated against and mistreated them.

Later, in 1914 during the American military landings at Vera Cruz, Mexico, the first American to be killed was eighteen-year-old U.S. marine Samuel Meisenberg, a European-born Jewish immigrant from the Near West Side ghetto of Chicago who had been employed as a machine operator at Hart, Schaffner, and Marx. His death brought forth a series of tributes, ranging from remarks by Secretary of State Josephus Daniels to recognition in the *Chicago Tribune,* in addition to praise from the saddened but proud Jewish community. Samuel Meisenberg was buried with military honors at Waldheim Cemetery and a tall marble shaft was erected as a monument over his grave. He was awarded the Order of the Purple Heart some seventy-three years after his death.

By 1900 the Jewish community of Chicago was well represented organizationally. There were 60 lodges, 50 congregations, 39 charitable societies, 2 mutual benefit associations, a technical school, a training school for nurses, a Sabbath teachers' association, a Hebrew Literary Society, and a rabbinical association.[4] There were also 13 loan associations, 4 Zionist groups, 11 social clubs, and numerous other organizations. In 1916 at the Sherman Hotel, delegates from some 250 of these Jewish organizations and also from other parts of the Midwest attended an "American Jewish Congress" organized by Jacob G. Grossberg and his associates. After early organizational and policy bickering and rivalry at the convention, discussion of Jewish problems and policies showed that these diverse and sometimes fractious groups could meet together fairly harmoniously.

Except during World War I, the number of these organizations grew as the Jewish immigrant population continued to increase rapidly, until immigration to the United States was curtailed in the 1920s. One who stood watch over the immigration and social welfare laws for decades in Congress was Adolph J. Sabath. He was a Bohemian Jewish immigrant who worked his way through law school and then held a number of city government positions until elected to Congress in 1906 from the heavily Bohemian southwest side of Chicago. He was reelected repeatedly to the House of Representatives, where he had a liberal voting record, and served as chairman of the powerful House Rules Committee.

In 1908, two years after Sabath's election, the Russian Jewish immigrant community was thrown into a state of apprehension and fear by a tragic event. A young Russian Jew named Harry Auerbuch appeared early one morning at the home of Chicago Chief of Police George Shippy, for an unknown reason. Auerbuch was shot to death when the chief suspected that he was an anarchist assassin, although there was no subsequent evidence to link the unarmed Jewish boy with anarchism or any other plot. The boy's sister insisted he knew nothing about political matters. The Chicago police, however, turned their wrath on the Russian Jewish community in an effort to uncover an anarchist

Adolph J. Sabath (1860–1952) served in the U.S. House of Representatives for twenty-three terms. (Courtesy of the Chicago Historical Society.)

plot and justify the killing. Jewish homes, printing offices, and restaurants in the Maxwell Street district were searched for papers and photographs of revolutionaries, and friends and relatives of Auerbuch were mercilessly interrogated. The Auerbuch affair brought back memories of Russian police methods, and fear arose – largely unwarranted – of the possible deportation of immigrant Russian radicals back to Russia.[5] Much of the press, after initial knee-jerk condemnation of Auerbuch, later adopted a more skeptical attitude toward Chief Shippy's account of the incident, and most reprinted a translation of the *Daily Jewish Courier*'s editorial headlined "Wanted an Emil Zola." Shippy later was a mental patient in a sanitarium, where he died.

World War I witnessed heavy Jewish involvement. Almost twenty thousand Chicago Jews took part, serving in virtually every branch of the United States armed forces. Over a hundred were killed in action and many more were wounded. Many Jewish soldiers served with distinction, and nearly a hundred were decorated for bravery. They garnered awards that included the Congressional Medal of Honor, given to Sergeant Sydney G. Gumpertz; numerous Distinguished Service Cross citations; and honors given by the British and French governments. Hundreds served as officers; many served as doctors in the medical corps. Two Chicago Jews attained the rank of general. One was Abel Davis, who came to Chicago from Lithuania and, as a teenager, fought in the Spanish-American War. He commanded the 132d U.S. Infantry of Illinois throughout World War I, including during the historic Battle of Verdun. Chicago-born General Milton J. Foreman commanded the 122d Field Artillery

עקסטרא · עקסטרא

שיקאגא פראטעסט געגען צזאר

WOMEN RIOT
AT RITUAL
TRIAL IN
KIEV

MILITANT
SAYS U. S.
SLAPPED
ENGLAND

*A special edition of the Chicago American in Yiddish, October 20, 1913, reporting on the massive rally of an estimated 25,000 people downtown the previous day that denounced the Russian government for its trial of an obscure Jewish worker, Mendel Beilis, who was accused of ritual murder of a Russian boy to provide the human blood alleged to be necessary for Passover services. The headline reads "Chicago protests against Czar." Among the speakers at the rally were Jane Addams, Reverend Father O'Callaghan, Booker T. Washington, and Dr. Emil G. Hirsch. After a worldwide protest, Beilis was acquitted.*
(From Meites, ed., *History of the Jews of Chicago.*)

through numerous battles in France. Both men were highly decorated for bravery. Before the war Abel had served in the state legislature and as Cook County recorder of deeds; after the war he became very active in Chicago Jewish communal affairs, headed many war relief and charitable drives, and served as a vice president of the Chicago Title and Trust Company. Foreman served as an alderman in Chicago and also as the state and the national commander of the American Legion.

A World War I war hero who received the French Croix de Guerre was Samuel "Nails" Morton, who was raised in the Maxwell Street neighborhood. By the time the war ended he had risen from the rank of private to first lieutenant. However, after the war he pursued a career that brought him both infamy and plaudits. He became a tough member of the underworld, engaging in gambling and bootlegging, and was accused a number of times of murders but was never convicted. He associated with big-time Jewish and non-Jewish gangsters of Chicago. But he also was considered a kind of hero by many Jews because he vigorously and successfully defended them during sporadic attacks by neighboring gangs. He died in 1923 at the age of twenty-nine after a fall from a horse while riding in Lincoln Park with his gangster friend Dion O'Banion. His funeral was attended by an estimated five thousand people, including government officials, military comrades, underworld figures, and Jewish mourners. The funeral procession was two miles long. In revenge for the death of his good friend, O'Banion is believed to have had the horse "bumped off."[6]

During the war some Chicago Jewish men joined the Jewish Legion, organized by the British for the purpose of freeing Palestine from Turkish rule. The organization was inspired by the Balfour Declaration of November 2, 1917, which was issued by the British government. The Balfour Declaration said that the Britons viewed "with favour the establishment in Palestine of a national home for the Jewish people, and will use their best endeavors to facilitate the

*During the World War I period Chicago Jewish women were active in worthwhile communal causes sponsored by the Chicago Hebrew Institute Service Club.*
(Courtesy the Jewish Federation of Metropolitan Chicago.)

achievement of this object." There were 212 Chicagoans who joined other Jews from numerous nations in the Jewish Legion, and some saw service in and around Palestine.

While many of the Jewish men were away fighting overseas, the Jewish community at home rallied to support the war effort. Those who remained in Chicago worked in defense plants, bought Liberty Bonds, participated in conservation efforts, held patriotic demonstrations, and looked after the physical, spiritual, and social welfare of servicemen through the newly organized Jewish Welfare Board and also the Red Mogen David (Red Shield of David), which concentrated on helping the members of the Jewish Legion and their families.

Several Chicago Jews held significant governmental positions during World War I. Julius Rosenwald, in addition to his numerous relief activities, was appointed by President Wilson to chair the Committee on Supplies of the Council of National Defense and also was sent on a special mission to France by the Secretary of War. Judge Julian W. Mack, well known for his leadership in welfare work, in the Zionist movement, and for espousing a liberal immigration policy, was on a number of important government boards during the war. He drafted measures providing for the compensation of the families of the men in the service and for the establishment of standards for the reasonable treatment of conscientious objectors. In 1906 he had been a founder and vice president of the American Jewish Committee, which aimed to ensure the civil and religious rights of Jews throughout the world and to secure equal economic, social, and educational opportunity for them.

### RELIEF FOR EASTERN EUROPE AND PALESTINE

One of the mightiest efforts of the Chicago Jewish community during the war was the raising of millions of dollars for overseas war relief. While money was raised for a variety of needs, the effort was especially concentrated in help-ing the Jews of Central and Eastern Europe who were caught in the war zone between invading and retreating armies. Pillaging and pogroms added to the hunger, homelessness, and epidemics that plagued the large numbers of Jew-ish inhabitants of the region. The hardships continued and sometimes even intensified after the war ended, as rampant nationalism, civil wars, political persecution, economic boycotts, and outright anti-Semitism plagued Jews in Europe. Chicago Jews frequently protested against the treatment of their broth-ers abroad by marching and demonstrating downtown and on the city's west and northwest sides. They also fought hard to keep the United States from curtailing the flow of Jewish immigrants from Europe.

Late in 1914, shortly after a national Jewish relief organization had been es-tablished, a number of dedicated Chicago Jews organized the Chicago Jewish Relief Committee for War Sufferers with Dr. Hirsch as chairman. Especially active on this committee, which was dominated by Reform Jews, were Max Adler, A. G. Becker, Abel Davis, Albert D. Lasker, Judge Henry Horner, Toby Rubovitz, George Dick, Julius Rosenwald, Charles Ruebens, Jacob K. Loeb, and Adolph Kraus. Kraus previously had tried to convince the Russian czarist gov-ernment to ameliorate the conditions of the Russian Jews. For almost a decade the relief committee served as the nucleus for the raising of millions of dollars, mostly for the aid of the Eastern European Jews. In a short time two major affiliated committees, with auxiliaries, were organized to solicit funds from specific constituencies. An Orthodox group, the West Side and Northwest Auxiliaries was led by Bernard Horwich, Max Shulman, Samuel Phillipson, Hyman L. Meites, Judge Harry Fisher, and Samuel Jacob Rosenblatt. A labor group known as the People's Relief Committee was composed of delegates of a number of labor unions and a few radical organizations.

As word of the plight of the Eastern European Jews spread, and as the efficien-cy of the fund-raising campaigns improved each year, larger and larger sums were raised under such slogans as "Share," "Suppose You Were Starving," and "Life-Saving Expedition." Jacob M. Loeb, chairman of the campaign commit-tee, introduced the highly successful Foodless Banquet on December 7, 1921, at the Drake Hotel when eight hundred relief-campaign workers arrived for dinner. Loeb admonished them as follows: "For so many to dine in this place would mean an expenditure of thirty-five hundred dollars, which would be unwarrantable extravagance, and in the face of starving Europe, a wasteful crime. Thirty-five hundred dollars will help to feed the starving, clothe the naked, and heal the sick. What right have we to spend on ourselves funds which have been collected for them? So that this money might be saved for them, you are brought here to this foodless banquet."[7]

On one occasion Julius Rosenwald contributed a million dollars, and a few days later President Wilson sent him the following telegram:

To Julius Rosenwald, Chicago
    Your contribution of one million dollars to the Ten Million Dollar Fund for the Relief of Jewish War Sufferers serves democracy as well as humanity.

The Museum of Science and Industry, Chicago's most popular tourist attraction, was founded by Julius Rosenwald in 1933. Located in Jackson Park, it occupies the restored Fine Arts building of the World's Columbian Exposition of 1893. Its two thousand displays explain the principles of science and how they are applied in industry and everyday life. Rosenwald's brother-in-law, Max Adler, had founded the Adler Planetarium in 1930. (Courtesy of the Chicago Convention and Tourism Bureau.)

The Russian Revolution has opened the door of freedom to an oppressed people; but unless they are given life and strength and courage, the opportunity of centuries will avail them little. It is to America that these starving millions look for aid; and out of our prosperity, fruit of free institutions, should spring a vast and ennobling generosity. Your gift lays an obligation even while it furnishes inspiration.

Woodrow Wilson[8]

Julius Rosenwald not only gave but also taught others to give. Businesslike methods of fund raising were developed and a series of successful drives was launched. The generous Chicago Jewish response for the aid of their brethren in Eastern Europe was buoyed by contributions from non-Jews. General Charles G. Dawes, Victor F. Lawson, Cyrus H. McCormick, Robert R. McCormick, Martin A. Ryerson, and William Wrigley not only contributed generously but also solicited contributions from others.

Much of the relief money was distributed in Europe by the Joint Distribution Committee. Bernard Horwich and Judge Henry Fisher were sent to Eastern Europe by the "Joint" to help organize and report on the relief efforts, and Judge Hugo Pam, also of Chicago, was sent to Europe as a representative of the Hebrew Immigrant Aid and Sheltering Society (HIAS).

Bernard Horwich (1861–1949), an immigrant from Russia, rose from a humble street peddler to assume presidency of two banks, becoming one of the most indefatigable and prominent Jewish community leaders. He held high offices in the Zionist movement and in numerous charitable and civic organizations, raised large sums of money for many causes, and also served in the Cook County government. One of the largest Chicago Jewish Community Centers is named after him.
(Courtesy of the Jewish Federation of Metropolitan Chicago.)

**The Chicago Jewish Committee for Palestinian Welfare**

invites you to its

**Members' Meeting**

to be held at the residence of

**Mrs. Julius Rosenwald, 4901 Ellis Avenue**

**Wednesday afternoon, December 10th, at 2 o'clock**

Program

Songs . . . Mme. Meta Schoenfeld Lustgarten
At the Piano . . . . Miss Sophie Ginsburg
Reconstruction in Europe and Palestine . Jane Addams

Guests 50 Cents each

An invitation for a meeting of the Chicago Jewish Committee for Palestinian Welfare at the home of the Julius Rosenwalds shortly after World War I, with Jane Addams as guest speaker. Mrs. Rosenwald was an officer of the organization for many years.
(Irving Cutler Collection.)

Bernard Horwich later wrote about the hardships he saw being endured by Jews in strife-torn Eastern Europe. On his way home he visited a Jewish refugee camp in Vienna where the people were living in a string of freight cars, with eighteen or twenty in each, and with very meager rations. In one he encountered a man, whose wife had died the day before, trying to teach the *kaddish* (prayer in memory of the dead) to his young son. Asked how he happened to be in this refugee camp, the man replied, in both sorrow and anger: "'While the great nations are dividing the world among themselves, they have forgotten us. First we were Austrians, then we were Poles. Now the Poles say that we belong to Slovakia, and Slovakia says that we belong to Poland. So we have to

# THE ALL-RUSSIAN JEWISH PUBLIC COMMITTEE
### For the Relief of War and Pogrom Sufferers
#### 110 WEST 40th STREET, NEW YORK CITY

Nọ 6177

| Purchaser's Receipt | Food Draft Receipt |
|---|---|

Date.................. Sept.1/22  5992
.......................192..

Received from M.......Henry Rothman............the sum of....ten dollars.($.10.-..)

(Address—Street) ........1236 So. Turner Ave.,........

(Town and State)........Chicago, Ill.............

Representing the value of food deliverable for above amount, in accordance with arrangement detailed on back thereof, and which is hereby made a part of this receipt.

Foodstuffs to be delivered to:

Моисей Стражник

Андреевская ул.,№9,кв.7

г. Киев.

THE ALL-RUSSIAN JEWISH PUBLIC COMMITTEE
Bureau of the Representative in U.S.A. and Canada

per-------------------------------

THE ALL-RUSSIAN JEWISH PUBLIC COMMITTEE will deliver to the designated beneficiary in Russia, for each $10., paid to its American Bureau, the following foodstuffs:

|  |  |  |  |
|---|---|---|---|
| 50 | lbs. | of | White Flour |
| 20 | " | " | Rice |
| 10 | " | " | Grits |
| 10 | " | " | Sugar |
| 10 | " | " | Fat (Beef or Crisco) |
| 3 | " | " | Kosher Corn Beef (or 5 cans of Salmon) |
| 3 | " | " | Cocoa |
| 5 | " | " | Soap |
| 10 tins | of | | Condensed Sweet Milk |

120 lbs.

In addition, for each 120 lbs. of foodstuffs delivered to the designated beneficiary in Russia, the ALL-RUSSIAN JEWISH PUBLIC COMMITTEE will assign 40 lbs. of foodstuffs for general relief.

If at the end of 90 days after receipt of advise the local Committee in Russia is unable to locate the beneficiary, it will notify the American Bureau, and the original $10.00 will be refunded to the donor.

The delivery of foodstuffs in Ukraine and White Russia will be made through the branches of the ALL-RUSSIAN JEWISH PUBLIC COMMITTEE. In places where there are no branches of the Committee, delivery will be made through the post office or any other available service, but only upon the written consent of the beneficiary.

*A receipt (1922) for a ten-dollar contribution by a Chicago Jew to the All-Russian Jewish Public Committee for the delivery of the listed foodstuffs and soap to relatives in Russia. (Irving Cutler Collection.)*

live here and wait until your great president and the other leaders of the world decide what is to become of us.'"[9]

A committee to aid the Jews of Palestine was organized even before the formation of the Chicago committee to assist the Eastern European Jews. The Palestine Fund Committee was organized in 1914 with Max Shulman as president. Prominent members of the committee included Orthodox rabbis Abraham Cardon, Ephraim Epstein, Ezriel Epstein, and Saul Silber, and other Chicago Jews such as M. Ph. Ginzburg, Hyman Meites, Samuel Phillipson, and Bernard and Harris Horwich. Money was collected largely through appeals in the synagogues, but transferring the funds to war-torn Palestine was difficult until Congressman Adolph J. Sabath arranged to have the Standard Oil Company transmit the money without charge through its Middle East office.[10]

It was soon found, however, that food supplies were of more value than money and a "Bread for Palestine" campaign started under the leadership of Max Shulman. Merchants and housewives brought their food packages, large and small, to synagogues for collection and eventual shipment to Palestine on a United States government-supplied ship.

As they did for Eastern European relief, the disparate Jewish groups of the city collaborated on help for Palestine. Dr. Emil G. Hirsch, although opposed to political Zionism, pleaded for such aid from Sinai Congregation, where Louis D. Brandeis and Julius Rosenwald also made appeals, with Rosenwald proposing that individuals pledge to give funds at regularly stated intervals.

### THE GROWTH OF ZIONISM

The monetary and supply aid for Palestine and the volunteers for Palestine were manifestations of the growing Zionist movement in Chicago. The movement had started gaining strength with the publication of Dr. Theodore Herzl's persuasive and influential *Der Judenstaat* in 1896, which outlined the goals of political Zionism and the creation of a Jewish state in Palestine.

Several years before Herzl convened the First Zionist Congress in Basel, Switzerland, in 1897, a well-known Chicago Methodist evangelist, Reverend William E. Blackstone, had begun advocating the establishment of a homeland for Jews in Palestine. The Jews would thus be removed from the vagaries and brutality of the Russian empire, the millennium could then come with the fulfillment of the Christian prophecy, and the Jews could be converted. For more than three decades Reverend Blackstone persisted in his efforts to establish a Jewish homeland in Palestine. He held countless meetings and conferences with prominent Jewish and gentile leaders, met with government officials, and prepared petitions, including the Blackstone Memorial petition. Directed to the president of the United States in 1891, the petition was signed by over four hundred leading Americans, both Jews and non-Jews, including J. P. Morgan, John D. Rockefeller, William McKinley, Chicago businessmen such as Emanuel Mandel, Potter Palmer, Philip Armour, and John Shedd, and numerous rabbis and Christian clergymen. Although Jews recoiled at Blackstone's advocacy of conversion, he also received much Jewish support for his idea and "his efforts undoubtedly helped to prepare public opinion in America to be receptive to the idea of a Jewish homeland."[11]

The first organized Zionist group in America was established in Chicago in 1895, mainly by members of the Hebrew Literary Society, which was located in the Maxwell Street area. Called the Chicago Zion Society, its founders were Leon Zolotkoff, Bernard and Harris Horwich, and Dr. Bernhard Felsenthal. Dr. Felsenthal was one of the first Reform rabbis to become a Zionist. Bernard Horwich was the organization's first president. One of the group's first acts was to raise money to send a delegate, the scholarly and multilingual journalist Leon Zolotkoff, to the First Zionist Congress in Basel. Zolot-koff is believed to have been the only American at the congress. Shortly there-after, the organization was changed to a fraternal society known as the Knights of Zion and in a year it had ten branches or "Gates" (from the Hebrew *Sha-ar,* for gate or entrance into Zion). It soon covered the Midwest with its societ-ies. Associated with the organization were a number of picturesque military units that marched in parades under the Zionist flag, kept order at meetings, and protected the dignity of Jews.

The Knights of Zion arranged for the memorial to Theodore Herzl when he died in 1904. His death brought great anguish to the nationalists. The Sun-day after his funeral all businesses in Jewish areas were closed and the store-fronts draped in crepe. A procession led by a band carrying black-draped in-struments wound its way through the Jewish throngs in the Maxwell Street area. Leading the mourners were the executive committee of the Knights of Zion and the venerable Dr. Felsenthal. Eulogies were given by Harris Horwich and Leon Zolotkoff.

The Zionist movement had its main strength on the west and northwest sides of the city among the Yiddish-speaking Eastern European Jews, some of whose kinsmen had already settled in Palestine. But there was far from unanimous support for the Zionist movement in its early stages. Opposition came from some extreme Orthodox circles who were convinced that only when the Mes-siah came would Jews return to their homeland and that there was little reli-gion in Herzl's Zionist movement. Most Orthodox rabbis, however, were sym-pathetic to the Zionist movement, as was the Yiddish *Daily Jewish Courier* published by M. Ph. Ginsberg. Most Reform Jews, including South Side Re-form rabbis and the pro-Reform Anglo-Jewish press, were opposed to the Zi-onist movement for a variety of reasons. These included the belief that the Jews were a religious group and not a nationality, that they were American citizens and the United States was their home, and that striving for a Jewish state might appear to be disloyal and unpatriotic and give more strength to anti-Semitic elements. As late as 1918, Julian W. Mack, a Cook County and U.S. judge and a noted Zionist leader, stated again and again that there is absolutely no in-compatibility between Americanism and Zionism.

Some thought the idea of a Jewish state was presumptuous and unrealistic. Occasionally, pro-Zionist groups confronted opposition and had difficulty collecting funds or using the facilities not only of temples but even of some Orthodox synagogues. Consequently many meetings were held in secular Maxwell Street halls, especially at Porges Hall on Maxwell and Jefferson streets.

Despite opposition, the dedicated local Zionists vigorously publicized and advocated their cause independent of the national Zionist organization. The Knights of Zion did not join the larger group until 1912, even then retaining autonomy in the ten midwestern states until 1918. Max Shulman and Nathan D. Kaplan joined the founders of the Knights of Zion in actively supporting the organization, each serving as its head. Technically, today's Zionist Organi-zation of Chicago is the descendant of the Knights of Zion.

A number of external events gave the Chicago Zionist movement great impetus. These included the Russian Kishinev Massacre of 1913; the plight of Jews caught in the fighting between the German and Russian armies in World War I; the Allies' capture of Jerusalem in 1917; and the Balfour Declaration of the same year, which called for the establishment in Palestine of a national home for the Jewish people, thereby giving official sanction to the Zionist goal. In 1919 Judge Julian W. Mack presided over the national convention of the Zionist Organization of America held in Chicago's Auditorium Theater. Most prominent Chicago Zionists were among the seven hundred delegates, as were many national Zionist leaders, including Justice Louis Brandeis, Dr. Stephen Wise, Louis Lipsky, Henrietta Szold, and Dr. Felix Frankfurter. It was a convention in which the various Zionist factions worked hard together to improve the growing American Zionist movement.

As the need for a Jewish state became more evident, an increasing number of Jews, buoyed by increased hope for its achievement and especially by the Balfour Declaration, rallied to the Zionist cause and formed numerous and varied Zionist organizations, including labor, religious, secular, and women's groups. By 1924 it was estimated that the overall Zionist movement in Chicago had almost seven thousand members. An ambitious attempt was made in that year to establish in Palestine a sister city, named "Chicago." The plan failed for lack of adequate funding, but many of the its zealous leaders continued working hard in behalf of the reconstruction and development of the Holy Land. Similarly, a plan by the Chicago Achooza Palestine Land and Development Company to establish a settlement in the lower Galilee at Sarona proved unsuccessful after struggling from about 1913 until 1928.

One of the earliest of the other major Zionist organizations was the Poale Zion, established in 1905 in Chicago as a party embodying socialist labor philosophy. It was the precursor of the current Labor Zionist Alliance. After some initial internal dissension regarding the relative merits of Palestine or Uganda as the logical homeland for the Jews of the world, the organization emerged as one of the most active supporters for a Jewish homeland in Palestine. As part of the Labor Zionist movement, it raised money, exerted public pressure for a Jewish homeland, and carried out educational programs, including the establishment of Yiddish Folks Shulen (schools) to give children fundamental training in Yiddish, Hebrew, Jewish history, and Zionism. The organization took an active part in the formation of the Jewish Legion in World War I and sent settlers to the cooperatives in Palestine. For many years it was headquartered in Lawndale in the National Socialist Institute at 3322 Douglas Boulevard (known as the "Institute"), owned in common with the Jewish National Workers' Alliance. As the neighborhood changed, it later moved to the Dr. Dolnick Center on California Avenue in West Rogers Park.

In addition to the Poale Zion, other active Zionist organizations developed under the aegis of Labor Zionists. These included Pioneer Women, organized in America by Golda Meir. Now named Na'amat USA, the group maintains a variety of social services, educational, agricultural, and recreational centers in Israel. The Farband, a workingmen's educational, fraternal, and insurance organization originally called the Jewish National Workers Alliance, also merged

# HABONIM

WE KNOW HOW OUR BOY AND GIRL SPEND THEIR TIME !

They spend it in a progressive Jewish environment.

They learn about Jewish life and culture.

They are inspired by Labor Palestine, the Chalutzim.

They enjoy Jewish songs and folk dances.

They celebrate Jewish national holidays.

They become acquainted with social and economic problems.

They develop their bodies and minds.

### THEY BELONG TO HABONIM

the most advanced and appealing organization for Jewish boys and girls. Habonim has been admired by scores of educators, community center workers, and other leaders of youth as a vital, constructive force in Jewish life.

IF you want your child to love the finest and best in Jewish life;

IF you want your child to grow up to be an intelligent and active Jew;

IF you want your child to have a balanced cultural and physical life —

### BRING YOUR CHILD TO US.

HABONIM is an organization for boys and girls between the ages of 10 and 18. HABONIM carries on many activities such as discussions; celebrations; camping; Zionist work; etc. HABONIM publihes the outstanding children's magazine, HABONEH.

### EVERY JEWISH CHILD HAS A PLACE IN HABONIM.

### WHAT DOES YOUR CHILD READ ?

If you found a stimulating, educating, entertaining magazine for JEWISH CHILDREN could you afford not to place it in the hands of your boy and girl ?

# HABONEH

(The Builder)

### A MONTHLY MAGAZINE FOR THE GROWING JEWISH BOY AND GIRL IN AMERICA

In the language of children and youth, "HABONEH" tells the story of Pioneering Palestine; of world Jews; of Jewish folk lore.

Only $1.00 a year. (Published Monthly except July and August).

### For further information, inquire:

## HABONIM 3322 Douglas Boulevard

A recruitment circular for Habonim, the youth group of the Labor Zionists, c. 1940. (Courtesy of the Chicago Jewish Archives.)

into the Labor Zionist Alliance. A Labor Zionist youth group, Habonim, met for many years at the "Institute" building on Douglas Boulevard, where young people held serious discussions on Zionism and Jewish history, sang Hebrew songs, and participated in Jewish folk dances. Many members attended the Habonim summer camps, and some eventually settled in Israel.

The Chicago chapter of Hadassah, the women's Zionist organization of America, was established in 1913 after Henrietta Szold's visit that year. The founder of the national Hadassah organization, Szold came to Chicago and spoke at the Chicago Hebrew Institute about Hadassah and its work for Palestine, emphasizing its promotion of health agencies, including the establishment of a major hospital there. Hadassah later expanded greatly and currently has some forty chapters in and around Chicago. Its program now also includes Youth Aliyah (an immigration program of youth to Israel), vocational training, and reclaiming of land in Israel. From 1921 to 1930 the dynamic president of the Chicago chapter of Hadassah was Pearl Franklin, an attorney and teacher who had come to Chicago from Huntington, Indiana, where hers was the only Jewish family. She was succeeded in the Hadassah presidency by the very active Zionist Bertha Berkman. Other early and prominent presidents included Mrs. Harry M. Fisher and Bertha Read Rissman.

The Mizrachi, the Orthodox wing of the Zionist organization (the Religious Zionists of Chicago), was also established in Chicago in 1913. Its aim was expressed in its motto, "The Land of Israel for the people of Israel according to the Torah of Israel." It worked hard for the development of an Israel that was religiously observant by furthering religious education, organizing summer camps and youth groups such as Bnei Akiva, and by supplying funds and volunteers for settlement in Israel. In 1951 it merged with the religious pioneering and labor movement Hapoel Hamizrachi. Like the Poale Zion, its headquarters followed the Jewish population from Maxwell Street to Independence Boulevard in Lawndale and then later to California Avenue in West Rogers Park. Among the Mizrachi leaders through the years were Rabbis Saul Silber, Eleazer Muskin, Ephraim Epstein, Menachem Sacks, Leonard Mishkin, and Aaron Rine.[12] Connected with the movement is AMIT Women (formerly American Mizrachi Women), which is involved in many religious, educational, and social service programs in Israel.

Numerous other organizations arose to help various aspects of the Zionist movement, especially as certain major world events made the fulfillment of what at first seemed just a dream appear more plausible. The Jewish National Fund, one of whose leaders for many years was William Jay Robinson, raised money for the acquisition, development, and afforestation of land in Palestine. Established Jewish organizations showed increased interest in helping Palestine and new ones arose. These included youth groups; *aliyah* organizations; groups supporting medical, social service, cultural, and educational facilities; political action groups; and religious organizations. Fund raising, education, and political support were important facets of these organizations.

Aid to Palestine was just one accomplishment of these organizations. Another was to make both the Jewish and non-Jewish public aware of the aims of Zionism, nationally and locally. In 1915, due mainly to the efforts of Harry A. Lipsky, a member of the Chicago Board of Education, the new school at the junction of Douglas and Independence boulevards in the heart of Lawndale was named after Theodore Herzl, the great Zionist leader. The school subsequently served as the place for many major meetings and rallies of the Jews of the surrounding area.

As was the case in the World's Columbian Exposition of 1893, Chicago's Century of Progress World's Fair in 1933 provided the occasion for a great rally of the Jews of Chicago.[13] Coinciding with Jewish Day at the fair, a great pageant produced by Meyer Weisgal, the executive director of Zionist activities in the Midwest, and chaired by Judge Harry Fisher, a very active Zionist who had been an emissary to Europe and Palestine, attracted a capacity crowd of 125,000 people to Soldier Field. A cast of 6,000 Jewish singers, dancers, and actors took part in a production called "The Romance of a People," written mainly by Rabbi Solomon Goldman and depicting the highlights of Jewish history from the beginning until the return of the pioneers to their homeland. The guest speaker was Chaim Weizmann, who in 1948 became the first president of the State of Israel. The fair also featured a Jewish exhibit in the Hall of Religion. Financed by various individuals and organizations of the Chicago Jewish community, the exhibit was organized by Rabbis Louis Mann and Gerson Levi. By means of murals, slides, and various articles, Jewish contributions and contributors to progress were featured.[14]

The year 1933 also marked the establishment of the first Women's American ORT group in Chicago. The organization founded in Russia in 1880 as the Society for Rehabilitation and Training has become an international organization for the promotion of skilled trades and agriculture among Jews. It operates in thirty countries and has its largest program in Israel. The organization has grown in the Chicago area to almost fifty chapters today, totaling over five thousand women.

## FURTHER COMMUNAL DEVELOPMENT AFTER WORLD WAR I

The post–World War I period witnessed the continued movement of the Jewish population and institutions out of the Maxwell Street area. They relocated mainly into Lawndale, but also into communities to the north and northwest, and to a much lesser extent to the south side. With the decline of the Jewish population in the Maxwell Street area, one by one the neighborhood institutions that had served the immigrant community so well began to close. In 1919, the Maxwell Street Settlement closed, followed by the Helen Day Nursery in 1920 and the Jewish Training School in 1921. Most of the area's approximately forty-five synagogues moved into the Lawndale district.

While Maxwell Street declined as a Jewish community, Jewish synagogues and other institutions were rising in several other parts of the city where the Jewish population was growing. For example, a half dozen of what were to become major synagogues were organized on the north and northwest sides of the city in the five-year span from 1917 to 1922. These included Temple Beth Israel and Congregation Beth Itzchok in Albany Park; B'nai Zion, Agudas Achim North Shore, and Temple Mizpah in the Uptown–Rogers Park area; and Shaare Zedek in Logan Square.

Hundreds of Jewish institutions were financed and built during the early decades of the twentieth century by a largely poor immigrant population. Incidents of fraud, such as is implied by the following letter to a recalcitrant member of Congregation B'nai Bezalel, in Hyde Park, were extremely rare:

Chicago, December 11, 1922

Dear Sir:

At the last regular meeting, Dec. 3, 1922 of the Congregation B'nai Bezalel a resolution was passed directing the secretary to notify you for the *Last Time,* to appear at the meeting of the Board of Directors on Thursday, December 14, 1922, at 8:15 P.M. to be held at 6141 Drexel Ave., Chicago, Illinois to make accounting of all moneys collected by you for and in behalf of the Congregation. The Congregation has been extremely lenient and indulgent with you in the past and its kindness has not been appreciated by you. You are therefore notified that unless you appear at the meeting of the Board of Directors on December 14, 1922 at 8:15 P.M. at 6141 Drexel Ave. and there make a full and accurate accounting of all moneys received by you for and in the name of the Congregation B'nai Bezalel, proper and legal action will be taken against you.

If you wish to avoid expense, inconvenience, and the exposure and disgrace which will necessarily follow you will appear before the Board of Directors as directed by the resolution.

Yours truly,
M. L. Roman
Secretary

H. Primstein
President
S. B. Bransky
Chairman of the
Board of Directors[15]

Organizations other than synagogues were also founded during the post–World War I period. These included the Northwest Fellowship Club, established as a social and cultural club in Wicker Park with its own clubhouse in a large former residence at 2020 Pierce Avenue. Nearby, in 1917, at 1441 Wicker Park Avenue, the Daughters of Zion Jewish Day Nursery and Infant Home was established, with Mrs. L. C. Rieger its prime founder and first president. Mrs. Rieger, an immigrant from Austria, became interested in the project when she saw a Jewish mother and her two children leaving a non-Jewish nursery and making the sign of the cross. The mother explained that she had to work and that there was no other place to leave the children. A few years after its founding, the nursery moved into a large, modern building at California and Hirsch avenues, opposite Humboldt Park. The new building had capacity for five hundred children. Another group established the Douglas Park Day Nursery in the Lawndale area in 1919. It eventually located opposite Douglas Park at 1424 South Albany Avenue, where an average of forty children were cared for daily.[16]

The Covenant Club was established in the midst of Chicago's downtown in 1917. Founded by B'nai B'rith members, many of them businessmen, as a private social, recreational, and cultural club, in the 1920s it built an eleven-story structure at 10 North Dearborn, a location that served its members until the building was sold in 1986 and the club disbanded. Through the years it engaged in many worthy communal activities. Unlike the Standard Club, which was organized largely by German Jews, the membership of the Covenant Club was composed mainly of Jews of Eastern European descent. The club's membership peaked at twelve hundred in the late 1940s but was down to six hundred when it sold its building because it could no longer cover its expenses. In its prime it had hosted such dignitaries as Albert Einstein and Eleanor Roosevelt.

In 1918, after more than three quarters of a century of Jewish presence in Chicago, a number of leading Jews, headed by Russian-born Hyman L. Meites (1879–1944), a printer and publisher very active in Jewish movements and one of the city's earliest Zionists, formed the Jewish Historical Society of Illinois. The society's stated purpose was to collect and preserve historic data, mark with tablets Jewish historic places of interest, publish articles on the history of the Jews of the area, and encourage the study of Jewish history. Its early presidents included Julius Rosenwald and Dr. Emil G. Hirsch. One of the society's major accomplishments was the publication in 1924 of the comprehensive and monumental *History of the Jews of Chicago,* edited by Meites, which strongly emphasized the important individuals, organizations, and institutions of the Jewish community as well as its history. The society also dedicated a memorial tablet in 1918 on the old post office building at Clark Street and Jackson Boulevard to commemorate the site of the first Jewish house of worship (1851) in Illinois. During a dedication ceremony attended by many noted Jews and non-Jews, one of the speakers, Dr. Joseph Stolz, rabbi of Isaiah Temple, made the following statements:

These men and women (the Jewish pioneers) made good in their new settlement. They founded homes, gave their children the advantage of a good education, practiced industry, thrift, economy, established commercial and industrial houses, organized charities, and not least of all, erected houses of worship for the cultivation of the spirit. . . .

In proof and testimony of this, the Jewish Historical Society of Illinois has, by the grace of our Government, placed a bronze tablet upon one of the pillars of this majestic Federal Building.

Let the non-Jews who pass along this busy thoroughfare learn from it, that already in the days of their smallest beginnings and when the struggle for existence was hardest, the pioneer Jews of Chicago realized that "man cannot live by bread alone, but by what cometh from the mouth of the Lord." Let those who bear the honored names of our pioneer builders read the inscription on this tablet, and from generation to generation rejoice in this pious act of their forebears, realizing that it imposes upon them the responsibility to take upon themselves the burdens their ancestors so willingly and lovingly assumed, when they laid the foundations of our Jewish communal life upon the bedrock of religion, it being the divine law that "instead of thy fathers shall be thy sons."

Yes, let this Jewish community which, within the three score years and ten spent in Chicago by the man who unveiled the tablet, has grown from a handful to a quarter of a million; let this great Jewish community, enriched by the spiritual contribution of immigrants from every part of the world, be inspired by the deed immortalized by the tablet to realize, as did our first settlers, that a people without vision must perish, a people without faith cannot accomplish great things, a people without reverence for its own past builds without a secure foundation.[17]

The Jewish community in which there was the greatest amount of institutional construction in the post–World War I period was Lawndale. In addition to the dozens of new synagogues built there, a number of other major institutional buildings were constructed. During the 1920s such established Lawndale institutions as Mount Sinai Hospital, the Douglas Park Day Nursery, the Marks Nathan Jewish Orphan Home, and the Orthodox Jewish Home for the Aged were joined by the Beth Hamedrash L'Torah (Hebrew Theological College) and the Jewish People's Institute.

In addition to their own endowments and fund raising, support for many of these institutions came from two citywide charities of Chicago: the Associated Jewish Charities, which was supported mainly by the Reform Jews, and the Federated Orthodox Jewish Charities, which was supported primarily by the Eastern European Orthodox Jews. Despite some skepticism, especially by the smaller Orthodox organizations, the two charities merged in 1923 under the leadership and eventually the presidency of the indefatigable Julius Rosenwald, becoming the Jewish Charities of Chicago. The merger was planned to eliminate duplication of effort and to create a more efficient and all-encompassing single communal fund-raising organization. The fusion of the two organizations, it was believed, would also bring about better understanding among the various major groups that were often at odds – the Reform and the Orthodox, the German and the Eastern European Jews, and the West Side and South Side Jews.

By 1930 the united group embraced 26 organizations, had 9,500 subscribers, and was collecting $1.5 million a year. These funds helped support two homes for the aged with a total of 200 residents, two hospitals, two orphanages accommodating almost 500 children, two dispensaries that treated 20,000 annually, a home-finding society caring for 325 children, a tuberculosis sanitarium caring for or supervising 1,200 patients annually, and a number of Jewish schools. The money also funded a social-service bureau that provided legal aid; help for wayward boys and girls; industrial workshops for the handicapped; assistance for the poor, the sick, the unemployed, and transients; and help for those with a variety of family problems.[18]

The budget of the Jewish Charities of Chicago for 1934,[19] during the heart of the Depression, was as follows:

I. Requirements for 1934

| | |
|---|---|
| Aid Association for Incurable Orthodox Jews | $ 8,875.00 |
| Board of Jewish Education | 86,580.00 |
| Chicago Home for Jewish Orphans | 28,882.00 |
| Hebrew Sheltering Home | 6,256.00 |

| | |
|---|---|
| Home for Aged Jews | 11,782.00 |
| Jewish Children's Welfare Society | 6,855.00 |
| Jewish Free Employment Bureau | 21,091.00 |
| Jewish Home Finding Society | 173,310.00 |
| Jewish Social Service Bureau (including Industrial Workshops and Northwest Center) | 436,069.00 |
| Marks Nathan Jewish Orphan Home | 64,831.00 |
| Michael Reese Hospital | 154,061.00 |
| Mandel Clinic | 54,688.00 |
| Mount Sinai Hospital and Dispensary | 27,641.00 |
| Orthodox Jewish Home for the Aged | 34,266.00 |
| The Winfield Sanatorium | 54,759.00 |
| Woman's Loan Association | 2,975.00 |
| Special Budgetary Reserve | 100,000.00 |
| Subventions | 11,050.00 |
| Administration Office Expense | 45,342.00 |
| Net Requirements of The Jewish Charities | $1,329,293.00 |

Because of different degrees of *kashrut* observance, separate orphanage, hospital, and home for the aged facilities were maintained by the Orthodox even after there was a unified charity organization. In 1950 the name of the Jewish Charities of Chicago was changed to the Jewish Federation of Metropolitan Chicago to reflect the new concept that social welfare services are important to all people, not just the needy and disadvantaged, and also that the Jewish community had dispersed beyond the Chicago city limits.

The Chicago Jewish community had grown very rapidly during the early decades of this century and by 1930, numbering almost 300,000, was very active and highly organized as evidenced by its 84 Orthodox, 13 Reform, and 7 Conservative congregations. There were 3 rabbinical associations, the theological seminary, a Jewish People's Institute with an annual attendance of one million, the Conference of Jewish Women's Organizations with 86 affiliates with a total membership of 35,000,[20] and a school program that had grown steadily in the 1920s while Alexander Dushkin headed the Jewish Education Committee (incorporated as the Board of Jewish Education in 1926) of the Jewish Charities of Chicago. In 1930 there were 90 schools where 15,000 – 28 percent – of eligible Jewish youth attended. The students were about equally divided between weekday and Sunday schools, with Orthodox youths being taught mainly in the daily afternoon Hebrew school or the Yeshivah, Conservative youths in weekly and Sunday schools, and the Reform in Sunday School only. Almost one-third of the students attending daily Hebrew school were girls, while slightly over one-half of the Sunday School students were girls.[21]

Central Hebrew High School was established in 1924 and was soon housed in the Jewish People's Institute in Lawndale. In 1929 the school established a branch in the Humboldt Park area and in 1933 founded one in Albany Park. The College of Jewish Studies was organized in 1924 to train Sunday and Sab-

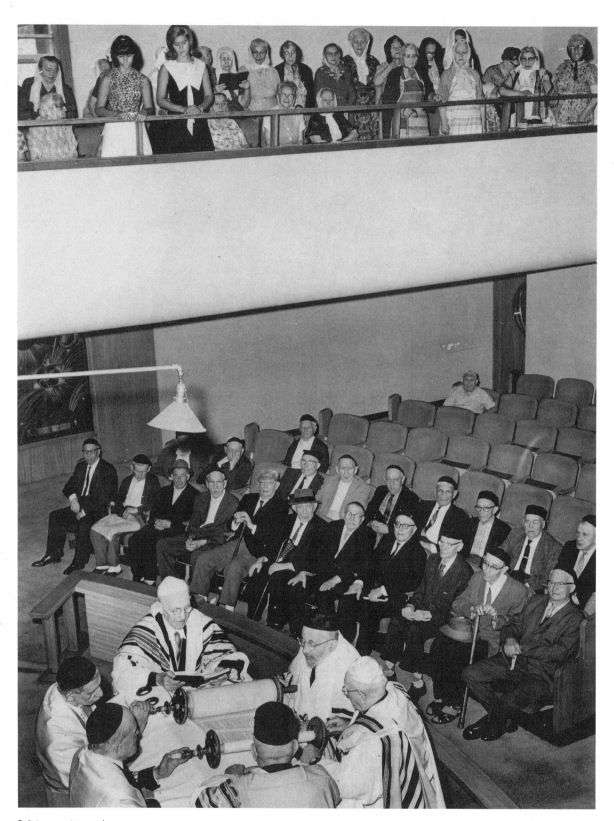

*Religious services at the Orthodox Jewish Home for the Aged, with the sexes seated separately, 1964.*
(Courtesy of the Jewish Federation of Metropolitan Chicago.)

bath school teachers as well as club leaders, and to allow young adults to continue their Jewish education. It later opened a Hebrew Teachers Training Department, developed a graduate program, and had a summer camp in Buchanan, Michigan. The college was housed for many years in the Board of Jewish Education building at 72 East Eleventh Street. Now known as the Spertus In-

Three young Chicago girl athletes at Camp CHI in 1921, a summer vacation camp established by the Chicago Hebrew Institute. Through the years numerous Jewish summer camps were established by various Zionist, religious, political, and community youth organizations.

(Courtesy of the Jewish Federation of Metropolitan Chicago.)

stitute of Jewish Studies, it is a fully accredited liberal arts institution located at 618 South Michigan Avenue.

In the 1930s, during the depths of the Depression, the Associated Talmud Torahs of Chicago was established as the central agency to assist and supervise the Orthodox schools that were not part of the Board of Jewish Education. For over forty years Rabbi Menachem B. Sacks, the agency's executive director, and Rabbi Leonard C. Mishkin, the educational director, skillfully guided the Orthodox schools as neighborhoods changed. The organization now serves about a dozen grade and high schools.

The general progress of the Jewish community nationwide in the 1920s was frequently marred by anti-Semitism. In addition to the usual anti-Semitic individuals and small groups, many of whom had carried their hatred over from Europe, there were also two major home-grown sources of hatred and sinister accusations against the Jews. One was the Ku Klux Klan, the secret society that had spread from the South into the Midwest with its anti-black, anti-Catholic, and anti-Semitic policies. After gaining strength in the early twenties, a postwar period of some intolerance, the Klan rapidly declined in the thirties. The other major source of anti-Semitism was Henry Ford, the successful and wealthy automobile manufacturer. Through his newspaper the *Dearborn Independent* he launched a vicious campaign of vilification and denigration of the Jews based on his ignorant acceptance of the infamous fabrication and forgery, "The Protocols of the Elders of Zion," which purported to reveal a secret Jewish plan to overthrow Christian

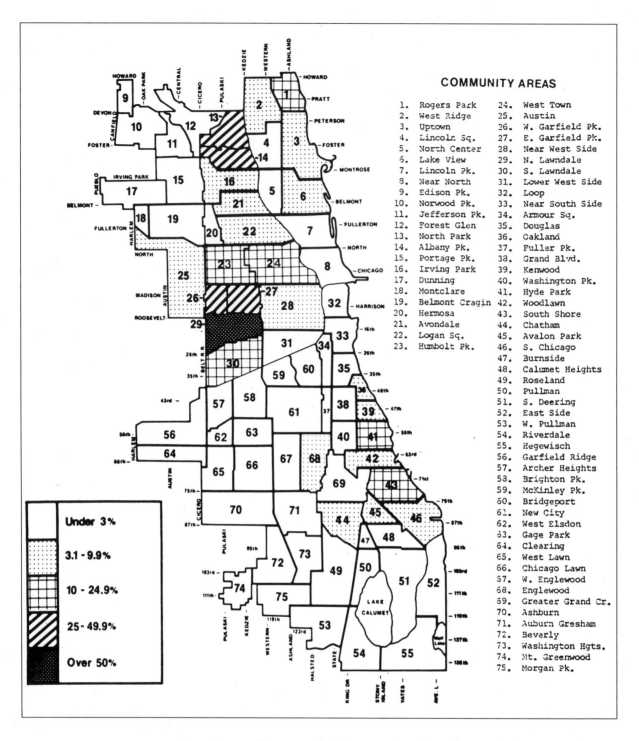

## COMMUNITY AREAS

| | | | |
|---|---|---|---|
| 1. | Rogers Park | 24. | West Town |
| 2. | West Ridge | 25. | Austin |
| 3. | Uptown | 26. | W. Garfield Pk. |
| 4. | Lincoln Sq. | 27. | E. Garfield Pk. |
| 5. | North Center | 28. | Near West Side |
| 6. | Lake View | 29. | N. Lawndale |
| 7. | Lincoln Pk. | 30. | S. Lawndale |
| 8. | Near North | 31. | Lower West Side |
| 9. | Edison Pk. | 32. | Loop |
| 10. | Norwood Pk. | 33. | Near South Side |
| 11. | Jefferson Pk. | 34. | Armour Sq. |
| 12. | Forest Glen | 35. | Douglas |
| 13. | North Park | 36. | Oakland |
| 14. | Albany Pk. | 37. | Fuller Pk. |
| 15. | Portage Pk. | 38. | Grand Blvd. |
| 16. | Irving Park | 39. | Kenwood |
| 17. | Dunning | 40. | Washington Pk. |
| 18. | Montclare | 41. | Hyde Park |
| 19. | Belmont Cragin | 42. | Woodlawn |
| 20. | Hermosa | 43. | South Shore |
| 21. | Avondale | 44. | Chatham |
| 22. | Logan Sq. | 45. | Avalon Park |
| 23. | Humbolt Pk. | 46. | S. Chicago |
| | | 47. | Burnside |
| | | 48. | Calumet Heights |
| | | 49. | Roseland |
| | | 50. | Pullman |
| | | 51. | S. Deering |
| | | 52. | East Side |
| | | 53. | W. Pullman |
| | | 54. | Riverdale |
| | | 55. | Hegewisch |
| | | 56. | Garfield Ridge |
| | | 57. | Archer Heights |
| | | 58. | Brighton Pk. |
| | | 59. | McKinley Pk. |
| | | 60. | Bridgeport |
| | | 61. | New City |
| | | 62. | West Elsdon |
| | | 63. | Gage Park |
| | | 64. | Clearing |
| | | 65. | West Lawn |
| | | 66. | Chicago Lawn |
| | | 67. | W. Englewood |
| | | 68. | Englewood |
| | | 69. | Greater Grand Cr. |
| | | 70. | Ashburn |
| | | 71. | Auburn Gresham |
| | | 72. | Beverly |
| | | 73. | Washington Hgts. |
| | | 74. | Mt. Greenwood |
| | | 75. | Morgan Pk. |

Under 3%

3.1 - 9.9%

10 - 24.9%

25 - 49.9%

Over 50%

society. Later, after court decisions, and perhaps some enlightenment, he was forced to apologize for his articles.

In Chicago, this anti-Semitism was fought by organizations such as the Anti-Defamation League of B'nai B'rith, which had been founded in Chicago in 1913 chiefly through the efforts of Sigmund Livingston, a Chicago lawyer and B'nai B'rith president. The ADL was organized to fight anti-Semitism and to protect Jews and others from discrimination and bigotry in education, employment, and housing. It presently also tries to improve intergroup relations and understanding and fights for civil rights reforms. Through the years, and especially after the Holocaust, anti-Semitism became less prevalent and more covert, although it still exists. College student quotas, restricted housing and resorts, and job discrimination have substantially declined, due in part to the activities of the Anti-Defamation League, which was headed very effectively for a number of decades in the Chicago area by A. Abbott Rosen.

A number of non-Jews, many of them well-known figures such as Jane Addams and Clarence Darrow, strongly denounced anti-Jewish propaganda, and in 1921 four hundred Protestant ministers meeting in Chicago raised their voices in condemnation of both Ford and the Klan and called upon their members to join them in fighting bigotry. Such efforts evidently brought results, as Hyman L. Meites then noted: "Chicago, happily, showed little susceptibility to the anti-Semitic virus, and the relations between the Jewish and gentile communities were, as they had ever been, most friendly. Though symptoms of infection were to be seen in certain quarters, these were isolated cases and the rare exception."[22]

Anti-Semitic propaganda did not impede the efforts of Jews to achieve public office. Among the Jewish judges elected during the 1920s were Henry Horner, Harry Fisher, Hugo Friend, Samuel Heller, Joseph W. Shulman, Max Luster, and Michael Feinberg. Congressman Adolph J. Sabath was repeatedly reelected, as was Jacob M. Arvey, alderman of the Twenty-fourth Ward. Important appointments included Albert D. Lasker as head of the United States Shipping Board and also Morris Eller, a powerful but notorious ward committeeman with alleged gang connections, as city collector.

## DECADES OF TRAGEDY AND TRIUMPH: THE 1930S AND 1940S

By the start of the 1930s, Jews, like the rest of the populace, were beginning to feel the effects of the Great Depression. They were also increasingly worried about their children, who were rapidly becoming Americanized, often losing their loyalty to ancient values and traditions. Statements had appeared in the Jewish press of the 1920s contending that "every Jew who goes to the university is lost to Judaism" and "we are keeping alive more than one half of the Jews of the world. But . . . the greatest need of all is the education of the children of the Jews of the United States." Other articles reported that "the movement of Jews to Christian Science is the greatest defection we have had in centuries. Never in the last five centuries have as many Jews been converted to another religion of any kind as in the last 25 years to Christian Science." While these statements appeared overly alarmist, the problem of keeping Jewish youth involved in Judaism remained a major challenge through the ensuing decades.[23]

A more tragic and fatal development of the 1930s was the rise of Hitler and his Nazi party in Germany. As early as 1923 the Jewish press had pinpointed the danger with headlines such as "Hitler Wants Jews Held as Hostages."[24] Almost weekly, the Jewish press had also been reporting acts of anti-Semitism in Eastern Europe. Many of the incidents, frequently resulting in deaths, took place in Poland or Romania. At the same time, Judaism was rapidly collapsing in the Soviet Union under the rule of the communists.

*(Opposite page) The Jewish population of Chicago, 1931, by community areas; based on population data of Jewish Charities of Chicago. The population was estimated at almost 300,000. The Jewish population was divided by communities as follows: 110,000 in the Lawndale–Garfield Park area; 35,000 in West Town–Humboldt Park–Logan Square; 28,000 in Kenwood–Hyde Park–Woodlawn–South Shore; 27,000 in Albany Park–North Park; 27,000 in Lakeview–Uptown–Rogers Park; smaller numbers lived in Englewood, Austin, South Chicago, Roseland, Chicago Lawn, and other communities. About 45 percent of the Jewish population was foreign born, with 78 percent coming from the former Russian empire, 18 percent from Central Europe, 2 percent from northwestern and Western Europe, and 2 percent from the Mediterranean and Middle Eastern areas.* (Courtesy of the Jewish Charities of Chicago.)

As Hitler came to power in Germany in 1933, spewing his hatred of the Jews, the Chicago Jewish community began to take steps to help the beleaguered German Jews just as for decades they had been helping the Eastern European Jews. The National Council of Jewish Women opened an office in Jane Addams's Hull-House with the main purpose of trying to rescue Jews from Nazi Germany. ORT extended its vocational and retraining programs to help Jewish refugees from Nazi Germany. Special funds were raised to aid European Jews. Of those who came to Chicago from the German parts of Europe, quite a few became successful in business and the professions, including Dr. Rolf A. Weil, president of Roosevelt University. A number became well-known rabbis, such as Herman Schaalman of Temple Emanuel, Karl Weiner of Temple Judea, Ernst Lorge of Temple Beth Israel, and William Frankel of Am Israel.

The American Jewish Congress, active on the world Jewish scene and in social legislation promoting and protecting the rights of Jews, established its first permanent branch in Chicago in 1934 and immediately helped push an anti-Nazi boycott in the city in conjunction with the newly organized Jewish Labor Committee, which later also became very active in the antidiscrimination and civil rights movements. The Chicago Jewish community gave its support to the boycott, although there were those who felt strongly it would be counterproductive. The boycott was effective in that German exports to the United States dropped almost in half. But the boycott did not stop inflammatory radio broadcasts or the torrent of Nazi propaganda literature that was pouring into the United States, fueling the activities of local anti-Semites and helping to enlarge such groups as the German-American Bund, the Silver Shirts, and the followers of Father Coughlin, the pro-Nazi radio priest of Detroit.

The unfolding disaster in Germany caused Jewish organizations to overcome their petty bickering and rivalry and work for the common cause of rescue. The need for a Jewish homeland in Palestine became increasingly evident, even to those opposed to Zionism, as German Jewish refugees were turned away from country after country. The United States refused to make any significant changes in its immigration quota laws despite the desperation of the refugees and the pleas of major U.S. Jewish groups. Virtually every Jewish organization embarked on programs of help. It has been noted that "Chicago became a beehive of activity. HIAS, ORT, YIVO, National Council of Jewish Women, Landsmanschaften, Farband, Mizrachi, B'nai B'rith, Labor Zionists, American Jewish Congress, and the Jewish Charities of Chicago. Every branch and splinter of the Zionist Organization plunged into the work from the very young to the aged."[25]

Rabbi Solomon Goldman (1893–1953) of Anshe Emet Congregation was chosen to lead the Zionist movement in 1938, to succeed Rabbi Stephen S. Wise as president of the Zionist Organization of America. He was the organization's first president who did not come from New York. Russian-born Rabbi Goldman was a recognized scholar, communal leader, innovator (he organized Chicago's first modern Jewish day school), orator, and author of a number of books, including studies of the Bible. Years later Max Bressler, a totally committed and tireless worker for Zionism, was also to serve as president of the Zionist Orga-

One of Chicago's most beloved rabbis was Solomon Goldman, Conservative rabbi of Anshe Emet Synagogue for almost a quarter of a century. He is seated here with Zionist leader Rabbi Stephen S. Wise of New York (left) and Professor Albert Einstein (right).
(Courtesy of the Jewish Federation of Metropolitan Chicago.)

nization of America. Bressler also became president of the Zionist Organization of Chicago and of the Jewish National Fund of America.

While busy protesting against Hitler and fighting the increasing anti-Semitism at home, the Jews were engulfed by the Great Depression of the 1930s. Compared with prosperous 1929, 1933 saw Chicago's employment in manufacturing cut in half; payrolls were down almost 75 percent, home foreclosures were up fivefold, and over 160 banks had closed. Like others, many Jews lost their homes when they were unable to make mortgage payments. Anxiety and despair overtook the jobless as careers and hopes were shattered. The Jews pulled through by prudent economies and hard work; men who had once been employed in better jobs sometimes spent long hours peddling with horse and wagon up and down alleys and streets. There were evictions and even suicides, although much help was supplied by the government and by the relief agencies of the Jewish community. Many Jews were aided by the Jewish Charities of Chicago, whose able and innovative executive director from 1930 to 1966 was Samuel A. Goldsmith. Eventually, the defense boom of the late 1930s and early 1940s helped turn the economy upward, and employment conditions improved greatly.

A bright spot during the Great Depression was the election in 1932 of Judge Henry Horner (1878–1940), the first Jewish governor of Illinois. More than three decades earlier, in 1900, another Jewish judge, Samuel Alschuler (1859–1939) had been defeated in his bid for the same office. Every four years from 1914 through 1930, Horner had been elected as judge of the Cook County Probate Court, a position he served with distinction. In 1930 he led the county Democratic ticket. With a 1932 gubernatorial campaign theme of "With Horner we'll turn the corner," he easily was elected, garnering the vast majority of Jewish votes.

Despite Governor Horner's four years of sound administration during the depths of the Depression, his independence and executive actions alienated the Cook County Democratic machine, led by the Chicago mayor, Ed Kelly, and even some of Horner's Jewish allies. Nevertheless, Herman Bundesen, the machine candidate, failed in his efforts to defeat Horner in the 1936 Democratic

אִיר מוזט זִיך רעגיסטרירען

דינסטיק,
מארטש
דעם 15טן

צו קענען
וואוטן פאר
האדוש

העברי האָרנער
פאר גאווערנער

זאגט אן אייערע פריינט צו רעגיסטרירן זיך

רעגיסטראציאנס טאג
דינסטאג, מארטש דעם 15טן

פאלס זיינען אפן פון 8 פרי ביז 9 אונט

*A campaign poster in Yiddish in 1932 for Henry Horner for governor.*
(Courtesy of the Jewish Federation of Metropolitan Chicago.)

primary election. The primary saw the more affluent, usually Republican German Jews of the South Side voting for Horner; the Eastern European Jews of the West Side, still often dependent on favors, aid, and jobs from the regular Democratic party organization led by Twenty-fourth Ward leader Jack Arvey, voted for Bundesen. But the West Side's Jews were not happy with their dilemma and one elderly Jew shouted at Jack Arvey, "You did a terrible thing to me today. A terrible thing. You made me vote against Henry Horner, our Henry Horner."[26] However, in the November 1936 general election, Henry Horner was overwhelmingly reelected, this time with very strong support from both the German and Eastern European Jews. He suffered a severe stroke in 1938 and

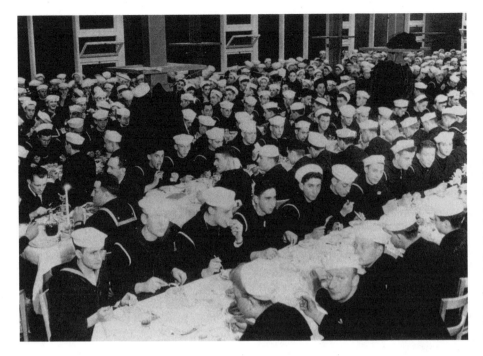

A Passover seder at the Great Lakes Naval Training Station at North Chicago, Illinois, during the middle of World War II, 1943. It was organized by Mrs. Jacob (Clarissa) Schwartz of Waukegan and Chaplain Julius Mark.
(Courtesy of the Jewish Federation of Metropolitan Chicago.)

he died in office in 1940. His collection of Lincoln memorabilia, more than six thousand items, was bequeathed by Horner to his native state.

Jack Arvey grew up on the Near West Side behind his parent's dairy store in an apartment without plumbing. He attended the Jewish Training School and later John Marshall Law School. As a politician he rose from Twenty-fourth Ward alderman to chairman of the Cook County Democratic Central Committee and Democratic national committeeman from Illinois. He became successful financially mainly through real estate investments, some controversial. His powerful position later was used to bring about the nomination and election of two distinguished liberals: Adlai Stevenson as governor and Paul Douglas as senator. He is believed to have used his position in 1948 to help convince President Truman to push for the creation and recognition of the state of Israel. Through the years Jack Arvey was involved in many Jewish causes both at home and abroad.

With the entrance of the United States into World War II following the attack on Pearl Harbor on December 7, 1941, many Jews went to work in defense plants or volunteered their services in war effort causes. Over 45,000 Chicago Jews joined the country's armed forces, a ratio of 11.1 percent of the Jewish population as against 10.6 percent for the total population of Chicago.[27] Almost 1,000 of those who served were killed in service, and another 1,400 were wounded. More than 2,100 Purple Hearts were awarded to Chicago Jews for wounds received in action during World War II and the Korean conflict. Numerous medals for distinguished service were also given.

Among Chicago Jews who received medals for distinguished service during World War II were Major General Julius Klein, who later became national commander of the Jewish War Veterans of the United States; Lieutenant General Samuel T. Lawton, Major General Robert M. Woodward, Lieutenant

The pageant We Shall Never Die *was performed to a capacity crowd at the Chicago Stadium on May 19, 1943. The pageant exposed the ongoing slaughter of Jews in Europe and called for remembrance and vengeance. The pageant was written by Ben Hecht with music by Kurt Weill and was narrated by John Garfield, Burgess Meredith, and Jacob Ben-Ami. It was sponsored by the Committee for a Jewish Army of Stateless and Palestinian Jews, which was founded by members of Irgun Zvai Leumi, a militant underground group in Palestine.*

(Courtesy of Janice Schurgin.)

Colonel Harry Lutz, Federal Judge Abraham Marovitz, Alderman Jack Arvey, Judge Harry Hershenson, and champion boxer Barney Ross. Dozens of local rabbis served during World War II or Korea in the chaplaincy, including Morton Berman, Charles Shulman, Earl E. Stone, Richard Hertz, Oscar Lifshutz, Samuel Volkman, Gunther Plaut, Norbert Rosenthal, David Cedarbaum, Lawrence Charney, Phillip Lipis, Joseph Miller, Ernst Lorge, Edgar Siskin, Paul Gordon, Arnold Wolf, Carson Goodman, Irving Tepper (killed in action in France), and Judah Nadich. Nadich rose in the army to become a special advisor on Jewish affairs to General Dwight D. Eisenhower.

After World War II Jewish servicemen and women returned rapidly to civilian life. Job barriers against employment of Jews were declining, although as late as 1953 a report issued by the Bureau on Jewish Employment Problems concerning over 2,000 white-collar job openings placed with commercial employment agencies showed that Jews were denied jobs in over 25 percent of them solely because of their religion. Comments on job orders included "this is a Gentile firm," "we want Christian girls," "Nordics only," "desperate but not desperate enough to hire Jews," "can't use Matzo-ball queens," and "a Jewish girl wouldn't be comfortable here." The same year, a study of some 3,700 Chicago business firms uncovered explicit statements of discriminatory policy in 27 percent of these companies. Although conditions were improving in response to the pressure of new laws and efforts made by Jewish agencies, discrimination remained especially severe in the fields of banking, insurance, and public utilities. An inheritance of discriminatory policies, especially prevalent in the past, was the overwhelming concentration of Jewish wage earners in Jewish-owned businesses or in government, or in welfare and civic agencies.[28]

Many veterans went to college under the GI Bill of Rights and became professionals. Relatively few joined the veterans' groups, even the Jewish War Veterans. One account observed, "Jews are not mass joiners of veteran organizations. The reason is clear. When the Jew fights for America, he 'fights like hell' as the record shows, but basically he hates war. Therefore, when it is ended, he finds other things to do. . . . The Jew does not boast about his military exploits. Seldom does a Jewish artist mold a war-like figure. Moses is known to us as a prophet, not as a military hero."[29]

Veterans, however, as well as other Jews, participated in many ways after World War II in aiding the Jews in Europe and Palestine and in working for an independent state of Israel. Many of the returning soldiers had been eyewitnesses to the concentration camps and gas chambers of the Nazis – the ghastly details of which were just becoming known to the general public after World War II.

The shocking revelations of the slaughter of 6,000,000 Jews in Europe gave added impetus to the Zionists' cause. British restrictions on Jewish immigration to Palestine provoked strong protests and demonstrations. In Chicago more than 100,000 people – Jews and non-Jews – marched along Michigan Avenue urging justice for the Jews in Palestine.

In autumn of 1947, the Jews of Chicago, as in the rest of the world, focused their attention on the United Nations as it ground toward a fateful decision on the future of Palestine. Jewish organizations that previously had shown no special interest in Zionism held rallies and demonstrations to impress upon the U.S. government the public's support of the United Nations' partition plan for Palestine. Jews listened anxiously to their radios as the world's nations voted on the plan, which ultimately received the necessary two-thirds votes on November 29, 1947.

It was time for rejoicing although everyone recognized the formidable task still ahead in realizing the dream of an independent Jewish state. On December 21, 1947, "to celebrate the fulfillment of 50 years of Zionist aspirations" (1897–1947), a great rally was held at the Civic Opera House. Dr. Emanuel Neumann, president of the Zionist Organization of America, spoke; Mischa Elman, the world famous violinist, played; Cantor Moses Silverman of Anshe Emet Synagogue sang; and a play entitled *The Seed and the Dream,* by Morton Wishengrad, based on the work and sacrifices of the early Zionists, was performed. Honored people were applauded: "the Horwich brothers, the Jerusalemsky sisters, the Shulman family, the Kaplans, the Isadore Turners, the Steinbergs, and the Zolotkoffs of Chicago."[30]

The long-awaited proclamation came on the fifth day of Iyar, May 14, 1948, when David Ben-Gurion announced the creation of the State of Israel. Two days

*An elderly Jew celebrating the establishment of the State of Israel at a rally on May 16, 1948, in Chicago Stadium.*

(Courtesy of the Chicago Tribune.)

later, on May 16, 1948, between fifty thousand and sixty thousand Jews and many non-Jews jammed the Chicago Stadium and massed outside, in the "Salute to the New Jewish Republic." "Mazel Tov," shouted the non-Jewish Bartley Crum, a member of the British parliament who had fought so hard for the creation of Israel, as cheers shook the rafters of the stadium. The cheers were joined by tears as the colors of the United States and for the first time the colors of the State of Israel were presented to the vast multitude, and thousands of voices breaking with sobs sang Hatikvah, the Israeli national anthem. Joy was unrestrained. An "old patriarch, who must have been in his 80s, and overcome with emotion, began to dance a Hasidic dance in the aisle, while tears ran down his cheeks."[31]

More significant than the celebration was the dedication of the Jews of Chicago to helping Israel in its struggle against the invasion of the armies of five Arab countries. Personnel, money, and arms were funneled into Israel. "Americans for Haganah," the fighting arm of Israel, was formed. The Combined Jewish Appeal was organized and the Israel bond drive was started. Among the prominent leaders of the Zionists in Chicago during this period and after were Max Bressler, Maxwell Abbell, Judge Harry Fisher, Rabbi Solomon Goldman, Rabbi David Polish, Philip Klutznick, Robert Adler, Dr. Paul Hurwitz, Dr. Mark Krug, Dr. Max Dolnick, and Frank Isaacs. The latter was to serve thirty-five years as executive director of the Zionist Organization of Chicago. Out of the tragedy of the Nazi era, a determined State of Israel survived and flourished.

While much effort was being devoted to assisting Israel, major changes were taking place within the Chicago Jewish community. By the 1950s the Eastern European immigrants were rapidly declining in numbers; their immediate offspring often lived in two worlds and had the values and traditions of both – those of their immigrant parents and those of America. The grandchildren became even more acculturated. They pursued American leisure and cultural

A jeep presented to Haganah, the Jewish self-defense force in Palestine, by a Jewish fraternal aid group during the 1940s. (Courtesy of the Jewish Federation of Metropolitan Chicago.)

activities, intermarried more, and followed the white middle-class movement out of the old neighborhoods toward the perimeter of the city and into the suburbs. The descendants of the immigrants had more education and more economic security than their forebears. Yet, in spite of these polarities, there usually lingered an ingrained Jewish feeling that manifested itself in any number of ways – in religion, support of Israel, foods, humor, attitudes, or friends.

# 4

# Moving Upward

## The Arts, Professions, and Commerce

### THE LITERARY FIELD

The Jews of Europe had been limited in their opportunities for advancement by various governmental decrees, lack of acceptance, and outright anti-Semitism, which often resulted in vocational restrictions and forced migrations. In America, the Jews took advantage of the generally open door for education and vocational opportunities and moved ahead rapidly in various fields, contributing significantly to the community.

Through the years, the Chicago literary scene was alive with a profusion of newspapers, periodicals, and books. Shortly after settlement in Chicago, the Jews began producing a variety of publications. They also formed literary clubs, which were among the earliest of the Jewish organizations.

Jewish publications in the early years could be divided into four broad categories. In succession, there appeared publications written especially for the German Jews, those directed mainly toward the Eastern European Jews, those written for the general Jewish population, and later those aimed at the general public. The publications not only frequently coincided with the prevalent native background of the Jewish population, but represented a broad spectrum of views ranging from Reform to Orthodox to agnostic and from capitalistic to socialistic to communistic.

Before the Great Fire of 1871 all literary writing in the Jewish community was in the German language. Among the most prolific writers of that period were three practicing rabbis, all natives of Germany: Dr. Bernhard Felsenthal, Dr. I. L. Chronic, and Dr. Liebman Adler. Their writings included pieces about the Reform movement, essays on Jewish education, literary reviews, interpretations of news events, and sermons. In Chicago the first significant publication of Jewish content was Dr. Felsenthal's popular brochure of 1859, *Kol Kore Bamidbar* (A Voice Calling in the Wilderness), which advocated Reform Judaism.

After the fire, most Jewish publications were written in English, Hebrew, or Yiddish.[1] Some were scholarly. The first German-Jewish English language periodical, the *Weekly Occident,* was started in 1873 and published until 1895. It covered items of specific interest to the Jews, including general news, social news, and the arts and sciences. It was essentially the voice of the Reform-oriented Jews of Germany and initially carried much news about the Jews of that country. It was followed through the years by numerous other Anglo-Jewish periodicals such as the *Chicago Israelite,* begun in 1884 as a local edition of Isaac Mayer Wise's *American Israelite,* and the *Reform Advocate,* started in 1891, both produced by the Bloch Publishing Company. The *Reform Advocate* was a weekly publication devoted to the interests of Reform Judaism but it also featured news articles, editorials, social notes, essays, and sermons of general Jewish interest. The periodical bore the imprint, high ideals, and powerful voice of Dr. Emil G. Hirsch, who served as its first editor for thirty-two years, from 1891 to 1923. He was succeeded by his son-in-law, Rabbi Gerson B. Levi. The *Reform Advocate* ceased publication in 1947. Among other Anglo-Jewish periodicals were the *Chicago Jewish Chronicle,* a weekly started in 1919 by Hyman L. Meites; the *Chicago Jewish Forum,* a scholarly quarterly founded in 1942 by Benjamin Weintraub; and the weekly *Press-Advocate,* published for a brief period after World War II.

Of all the early independent Anglo-Jewish periodicals in Chicago, only the *Sentinel* survives. It was founded in 1911 by Louis Berlin and Abraham L. Weber and has been published since 1943 by J. I. Fishbein. This weekly paper features local, national, and international news; social notes; often controversial, hard-hitting editorials; and articles of interest to the Jewish community. Unlike the *Reform Advocate,* whose appeal was greatest among those of German descent, the *Sentinel*'s focus has been on the wide spectrum of Chicago Jewry.

The monthly *JUF NEWS,* published by the Jewish Federation of Metropolitan Chicago, has the largest Anglo-Jewish circulation and is mailed free to most JUF contributors. It has developed into a substantial publication that features thought-provoking and informative articles on a variety of topics of Jewish interest, in addition to covering JUF activity and local news. Two newer publications include the biweekly general newspaper *Chicago Jewish Star* and the *Mid-*

*west Jewish Week,* the latter directed chiefly to the Orthodox community. An even newer general news publication, started late in 1994, is the *Chicago Jewish News,* whose editor/publisher is Joseph Aaron, former editor of the *JUF News.*

The influx of Eastern European Jews into Chicago that began in the 1870s soon prompted the establishment of Yiddish periodicals in the city. The earliest such publication was the weekly *Israelitsche Presse,* founded in 1877 by a Talmudic scholar, Nachman Dov Ettelson, a native of Suvalk, Russia. Although it contained a Hebrew section, which would broaden its appeal, it lasted only three years; Ettelson's later publication, the *Yiddische Press,* met the same fate. Early attempts at establishing Yiddish publications were hampered by Eastern European Jews' lack of familiarity with Yiddish secular literature; there were then very few such publications in the Russian Empire. However, as the Eastern European Jewish population in Chicago swelled, a number of Yiddish publications managed to gain a foothold. They served as the voice of the new immigrants who had crowded into the Near West and Northwest sides, in contrast to the German-Jewish and Anglo-Jewish press that largely served the earlier arrivals then living on the South Side and the North Side. Unlike the German-Jewish press, whose editors were often religious leaders, the Yiddish press was edited by a diverse group of union leaders, printers, business owners, and journalists.[2]

By 1893 there were two fiercely competing Chicago Yiddish daily newspapers, the *Chicago Yiddish Tageblatt,* the city's first Yiddish daily, and the *Daily Jewish Courier.* Both were the voice of Orthodox Jewry, with the *Tageblatt* inclining more toward labor. Among those especially involved in the establishment of the early Chicago Yiddish press were Leon Zolotkoff and M. Ph. Ginzburg, both immigrants from Russia.

Through the years dozens of Yiddish dailies, weeklies, and journals of almost every political and cultural persuasion were established. Despite the inclusion of writings by prominent Yiddish writers such as S. B. Komaiko, Dr. S. M.

Yiddish writers in Chicago, c. 1923, most of whom were active in the literary group known as Yung Chicago (Young Chicago) in the 1920s and 1930s, are shown on the occasion of a visit of the noted Yiddish poet and dramatist H. Leivick. Standing, left to right, Ben Sholem, Itzhok Elchonen Ronch, H. Leivick, Moishe Bogdansky, Mattes Deitch, and L. Gorelick. Seated, left to right, Boruch Goldhart, Isaac Plotner, and Pessie Hershfield. (Courtesy of Clare Pomerantz Greenberg.)

Melamed, James Bernard Loebner, Dr. A. Margolin, the poet Morris Rosenfeld, and others, many of whom were active in the literary groups known as "Yung Chicago" (Young Chicago), most of the publications were short-lived, including the *Tageblatt,* which ceased publication in 1896. Similarly, numerous publications in Hebrew, which often had a religious or Zionist orientation, were also of short duration, although many were of highest textual quality. Chicago Jewish publications also felt the competition from a number of New York Jewish newspapers that ranged in philosophy from the very Orthodox to the leftist *Der Morgen Freiheit.*

By 1920, and for several decades thereafter, two major Yiddish dailies served the Yiddish reading public: the *Daily Jewish Courier* and the popular *Jewish Daily Forward* of New York. The *Forward,* which began a Chicago edition in 1920, was unlike the Orthodox-oriented *Courier,* speaking more for the laboring, socialist-inclined immigrants, the unions, Workmen's Circle members, and secular Jews. At its peak it had a circulation of about fifteen thousand and was known for its warm, often argumentative style, which produced coverage that was frequently punctuated with razor-sharp wit and barbs. For many years it had an annual fund-raising ball, often at the Coliseum, which was usually attended by thousands. Both papers had great influence among the Jewish immigrants, presenting local and world news of Jewish interest, shaping political viewpoints, arbitrating domestic situations, promoting the establishment of

פאָרווערטס

Chicago, Sunday, July 26, 1936.

Kedzie Ave., at 13th St
Crawford 1600

1936 ,26 רושולאַ ,זונטאָג ,שיקאַגאָ

VICTOR I. LEVINSON
MANAGER

JACOB
SIEGEL
MANAGING
EDITOR
CHICAGO

EDITORIAL STAFF
LEFT to Right
M. TOLCHIN – S. ZAMO
J. SPIVAK – M. SESKIND
DR. Z. LORBER

The Jewish Daily Forward building at Kedzie Avenue and Thirteenth Street and the paper's managing and editorial staff, 1936. The Yiddish daily served largely as the voice of the Jewish laboring class from 1920 to 1953.

(Courtesy of the American Jewish Historical Society.)

needed institutions and charities, while at the same time giving a basic education in Americanization. The *Courier* always supported the Democratic candidates for office, while the *Forward* supported the Socialist candidates, even in 1924 when it followed the Socialist party by supporting the Progressive presidential candidate, LaFollette.

The most popular feature of the Yiddish press was the *Forward*'s "Bintel Brief" (a bundle of letters), letters to the editor. Every year thousands of immigrants would pour out their hearts in letters, often poorly written, seeking advice about personal problems and hoping for answers in the Bintel Brief column, which actually was a forerunner of the Ann Landers type of advice column. They wrote of the problems Jewish immigrants faced in adjusting to life in a country with unfamiliar religious and social customs, of generation gaps in the observance of these customs, and of marital and family conflict that often stemmed from life in the new environment. The correspondence also dealt with economic problems, the agonies of two World Wars, and festering political issues involving socialists, anarchists, and freethinkers. The letters ranged from the comic to the tragic, but usually dealt with poverty, desertion, loneliness, illness, homesickness, discrimination, and sweatshop exploitation. The themes changed somewhat with the passage of time, reflecting problems faced by the immigrants that were often brought on or compounded by tragic world events. Written by ordinary people, the letters gave a generally realistic picture of life.[3] Typical distressful letters included complaints about the daughter-in-law who did not keep a kosher home, a son who wanted to marry a gentile, a husband who had a mistress, a son who had a Christmas tree in his house, a wife who was deserted after helping her husband through medical school, and a husband who insisted on being buried next to his first wife.

In the 1930s, with immigration curtailed and the younger Jewish generations speaking little Yiddish and reading it even less, the circulation of the two Chicago Yiddish newspapers began to decline. In 1944, after a half century of existence, the *Daily Jewish Courier* ceased publication, followed in 1953 by the closing of the *Jewish Daily Forward*. Their demise was another step in the metamorphosis of the Jews from their Eastern European cultural heritage, which included a rich and expressive language, into the American scene.

With Americanization came Jewish participation in the broader American journalistic and literary fields. In the early decades of this century a number of Jews started working for Chicago's daily newspapers. Some were to gain prominence as journalists and a number went on to become recognized authors. Among the more prominent Jewish newspaper writers were Isaac Kahn Friedman, Ben Hecht, Edna Ferber, Meyer Levin, Herman Kogan, and Sydney J. Harris. Irv Kupcinet has been one of the city's more popular columnists for over fifty years. Gene Siskel and the late Sam Lesner achieved fame as movie critics, and Ann Landers (Eppie Lederer) is a widely read advice columnist, as is her twin sister, Abigail Van Buren. Herbert Block, known to millions as "Herblock," won two Pulitzer Prizes for his work as a powerful satirical political cartoonist. He was one of the first to expose the danger to the country posed by Senator Joseph McCarthy.

Mainly in this century, several hundred Chicago Jews have written what probably amounts to a few thousand titles. Benjamin Weintraub compiled a list of Chicago Jewish authors active during the half century from 1911 to 1961, pointing to more than two hundred such authors and almost a thousand titles.[4] The books include many scholarly treatises, general nonfiction, poetry, drama, short stories, and novels. Only New York City, America's literary capital, has produced a greater number of Jewish-American writers. Almost a fifth of the Chicago writers on Weintraub's list are academicians connected with the area's universities. They included Daniel Boorstin, Herman Finer, Milton Friedman, Louis Gottschalk, Melville Herskovits, Mark Krug, Edward Levi, Hans Morgenthau, Sol Tax, and Louis Wirth.

Many of the writers made significant contributions to literature, and a number received special national recognition for their work, especially some of the novelists. Among the earliest to be honored were Edna Ferber (1887–1968) and Ben Hecht (1893–1964). Both were brought up in small midwestern towns, arrived in Chicago in 1910, and started working for Chicago newspapers. Edna Ferber later wrote a number of popular novels and plays, many of which were made into movies. Among her best-known works are *Show Boat* (1926), *Cimarron* (1930), *Dinner at Eight* (1932), *Stage Door* (1936), *Saratoga Trunk* (1941), *Giant* (1952), and *So Big* (1924). Ferber was the first Jew to win a Pulitzer Prize for fiction, for *So Big*. Because she lived much of her later life in the East, few of her novels have a Chicago setting, and few of her main characters are Jewish, although her 1917 novel *Fanny Herself* is the story of a small-town Jewish girl and a family in many ways similar to her own.

*Meyer Levin (1905–81), prominent reporter and author, was born in the Maxwell Street area of Chicago.*

(Irving Cutler Collection.)

Ben Hecht first gained fame when he teamed up with Charles MacArthur to write the irreverent drama *The Front Page* (1928) about the tempestuous Chicago newspaper business. His novel *A Jew in Love* (1931) gave an unsympathetic portrayal of Jews. However, after the rise of Nazism, Hecht became a dedicated champion of an independent Jewish state and an ardent supporter of Irgun, the dissident underground organization. His *Guide for the Bedevilled* (1944) is a sharp protest of the persecution practiced against the Jews for so many centuries. His autobiography in 1954, *A Child of the Century*, was a best-seller. Hecht also wrote, produced, and directed for the motion picture industry. In addition, he wrote and produced a number of Jewish pageants that raised money for a Jewish state.

The West Side Eastern European immigrant neighborhoods of Chicago produced three notable novelists: Meyer Levin (1905–81), Albert Halper (1904–84), and Louis Zara (1910– ), each of whom created classics dealing with the people and communities they knew so well. Levin's masterpiece, *The Old Bunch* (1937), portrayed his generation of mainly Lawndale-area Jews, the children of immigrants, coming of age during the 1920s and the early Depression years, and has been called "the definitive Jewish growing up novel of its era."[5] His novel *Compulsion* (1950), about the murder of Bobby Franks by Leopold and Loeb, became a best-seller that was later dramatized and filmed. As a foreign correspondent for the *Chicago Daily News* Levin became acquainted with Palestine, wrote extensively and produced a number of films about the land, and later settled there. He died in Israel in 1981 at the age of seventy-five.

Albert Halper, who grew up poor on Chicago's crowded West Side, wrote about proletarian workers in such novels as *Union Square* (1933), *The Foundry* (1934), and *The Chute* (1937). His collection of short stories, *On the Shore* (1934), is about a young man remembering his youth in Chicago. Louis Zara, another product of Chicago's Eastern European Jewish neighborhood, completed in 1935 his first and most widely acclaimed novel, *Blessed Is the Man,* the story of the upward mobility of a Russian Jewish immigrant in the melting pot of Chicago set against the backdrop of the city's West Side. This was Zara's only novel that dealt with the Chicago Jewish scene. Like Ferber, Hecht, Levin, and Halper, Zara moved out of Chicago after some productive years in the city. Another writer, Leo Rosten, although born in Poland in 1908, spent his early life in Chicago before also leaving the city. While in Chicago he wrote the hilarious book *The Education of H\*Y\*M\*A\*N  K\*A\*P\*L\*A\*N* (1937), based on his experience of teaching English to an immigrant group in Chicago. In 1968 he wrote *The Joys of Yiddish,* which was a big success.

The post–World War II period produced a new group of talented writers, most of whom grew up on Chicago's Northwest Side, especially in the Humboldt Park–Logan Square region. The group included nonfiction writers such as the Chicago chronicler and journalist Herman Kogan (1914–89); the astute newspaper columnist Sydney J. Harris (1917–86), whose selected columns have been published in a number of volumes; and Studs Terkel, the renowned radio and television personality, whose books are based on taped interviews dealing with a cross section of individuals and their remembrances of periods of societal stress. His book *The Good War* (1984), dealing with recollections of the World War II period, received the Pulitzer Prize for general nonfiction.

Another writer from the Northwest Side was Isaac Rosenfeld (1918–56), poet and novelist. His only novel, the autobiographical *Passage from Home* (1946), showed great promise, but that potential was never fully realized. He ended his life at age thirty-eight in a shabby North Side room. Maxwell Bodenheim (1893–1954), also a poet and novelist, championed many unpopular causes, and his themes were as unconventional as his life. His writings include the poetry volume *Minna and Myself* (1918) and the novel *Naked on Roller Skates* (1931). He lived in poverty and met a tragic death at the hands of a deranged ex-convict. Sam Ross, also from the Northwest Side, wrote a number of novels dealing with Chicago Jews. They include *Someday, Boy* (1948) and *Windy City* (1970).

Saul Bellow, born in Quebec in 1915 and raised on Chicago's Northwest Side, has become one of the leading figures in American and world literature. Bellow received three National Book Awards, the Pulitzer Prize, and in 1976 the Nobel Price for literature. His novels include *The Adventures of Augie March* (1953), *Henderson the Rain King* (1959), *Herzog* (1964), *Mr. Sammler's Planet* (1970), and *Humboldt's Gift* (1975). Most of the main characters in his novels are Jewish and Chicagoans. But "Bellow is less concerned with immigrants or Jewish neighborhood life than he is with the minds of sensitive, educated people and the difficulties they have adjusting to the inevitable personal confrontations of life."[6] Bellow was on the faculty of the University of Chicago for over two decades.

*Canadian-born Saul Bellow was raised on Chicago's Northwest Side. An acclaimed American novelist, he has won three National Book Awards, the Pulitzer Prize, and in 1976 the Nobel Prize for literature.* (Courtesy of the Jewish Federation of Metropolitan Chicago.)

Nelson Algren (Nelson Abraham, 1909–81), who was half Jewish, wrote largely about the seamy side of the West Town area of the Northwest Side of Chicago where he lived for many years. Probably because of his stark realism in characterizing the downtrodden neighborhood and some of its earthy people, he never received much acclaim in Chicago. However, his novel *The Man with the Golden Arm* (1949), about the drug traffic in his Wicker Park neighborhood, won the first National Book Award for fiction and was made into a highly successful movie. His other books include *Never Come Morning* (1942) – which was briefly banned by the Chicago Public Library after some Polish-American citizens took offense at his description of certain Chicago neighborhoods – *The Neon Wilderness* (1947), *Chicago – City on the Make* (1951), and *A Walk on the Wild Side* (1956).

One of the best known of the young playwrights in Chicago is David Mamet, a former South Sider. Some of his successful plays include *The Duck Variations* (1972), *Sexual Perversity in Chicago* (1974), *American Buffalo* (1975), and *Glengarry Glen Ross* (1983). He also writes for the movies.

In a special category as a writer was Ben Aronin, who was for many years on the staff of Anshe Emet Synagogue and the College of Jewish Studies. He was author and director of many Jewish pageants, plays, and radio and television scripts. "Uncle Ben" was especially well known and beloved for his children's books and songs both in English and Hebrew. Also in a special category is Leonard Dubkin, a nature writer for the *Chicago Tribune* and the author of six books on nature including *My Secret Places* (1972).

Rabbi Meyer Waxman (1887–1969) was a scholar and prolific writer on the history of Jewish thought and literature. A professor for over two decades at the Hebrew Theological College in Chicago, his numerous publications include his monumental five-volume *History of Jewish Literature.*

ARTISTS

The commandment against producing "graven images," added to the material destruction that occurred during periodic outbursts against Jews, served to limit Jewish activity in representational painting and sculptures through the centuries, especially in very religious circles. In Chicago there was little significant Jewish activity in these fields until the 1920s. It was then that an exhibit at the Art Institute of Chicago of the biblical paintings of Abel Pan of the Bezalel School of Arts in Palestine was shown. The exhibit, described as an inspiration, "something beautiful stepped down to the stony structure of the Art Institute from the Bible,"[7] motivated the Jewish students of the Art Institute to organize the group called Around the Palette. This group, often aided by the Jewish Women's Art Club, sponsored exhibits, lectures, discussions, and debates at the Jewish People's Institute, at synagogues, and at other cultural institutions.[8] The artists met regularly until 1939, when internal dissension over the lack of a common program and perhaps divergent feelings about their Jewishness versus universality led to the breakup of the organization.

Of course, Jewish artists often reflected their multicultural backgrounds and Jewish traditions. Among those whose work was frequently based on Jewish history and tradition were Leon Garland, A. Raymond Katz, David Bekker, and Todros Geller. Geller (1889–1949), born in Ukraine, and a resident of Canada for a while, came to Chicago in 1918. He soon won recognition for his fine paintings, woodcuts, woodcarvings, and etchings. His work is imbued with Jewish tradition, often moralistic in implication, and frequently depicts the sorrow of the ghetto or the joy of a dancing Hasid. He was a leader in the field of synagogue and religious art. For many years he served as the head of the art department of the Jewish People's Institute. On Friday evenings his studio was the meeting place of Jewish artists and often there were discussions about the validity of a "Jewish art" steeped in the joys, sorrows, customs, and traditions of the Jewish people.

In the Depression years of the 1930s the United States Congress established the Federal Arts Project, a division of the Works Progress Administration, which gave employment to professional and novice artists. Dozens of Jewish Chicago artists were helped through the Depression, working in the program painting murals in public buildings, sculpting, teaching, or lecturing. Some of these works, especially in public buildings, have been "rediscovered" in recent years. Among the numerous Jewish artists in the program, many of whom are well known, were Emil Armin and William S. Schwartz. The Austrian-born Armin (1883–1971) was a modernist painter known especially for his depictions of landscapes, primitive peoples, flowers, and animals. William S. Schwartz's achievements in painting and lithography won him many awards and representation

Yiddle with the Fiddle *by
Todros Geller (1889–1949).*
(Courtesy of the Jewish Federa-
tion of Metropolitan Chicago.)

in many leading art facilities. He was one of the organizers in 1940 of the
American Jewish Arts Club, the successor of the Around the Palette group, and
Todros Geller was elected its first president. It carried out a program of cultural activities that included exhibitions, awards, lectures, and the issuing of a
comprehensive bulletin called "Brush Points." Its members included Jewish
painters, sculptors, printmakers, and art educators.

The roster of other Jewish artists, past and present – most belonging to the
American Jewish Arts Club – includes Louis Weiner, Henry Simon, Aaron Bohrod, William Jacobs, Lillian Desow-Fishbein, Ann Roman, Maurice Yochim,
Pearl Hirshfield, Jennie Siporin, Harry Mintz, Mitchell Siporin, Edward Mill-
man, Leon Golub, Seymour Rosofsky, Morris Topchevsky, Sadie Garland, Samuel Greenberg, Leo Segedin, Louise Dunn Yochim, Bacia Gordon, and Victor
Perlmutter. In the era of the Depression, war, and persecution, many of the
artists depicted the social ills, inequities, and despair of the period.

Aaron Bohrod, who grew up in Chicago, was an American realist painter
who won international recognition, as did Richard Florsheim, a versatile painter
and printmaker and a strong advocate of artists' rights who served as national
president of the Artists Equity Association. The sculptor Milton Horn, an east-
erner, resided in Chicago from 1949 until his death in 1995 and won widespread
acclaim for his works, which are found in many parts of the country. Often
emphasizing environmental and humanistic needs, his works can be seen in Chicago on a number of public, organizational, and synagogue buildings.

Sam Ostrowsky (1885–1946) was an immigrant from Russia who achieved
artistic success with his portraits, landscapes, and other paintings. Especially
outstanding were his stage designs for the Yiddish theater. He designed many
of the stage sets for Glickman's Palace Theater in Chicago and also for the Yid-

dish Art Theater in New York. Like many other Jewish artists, he found in America a receptive atmosphere for his talents.

There have been many Jewish benefactors of the arts. Their help ranged from financial contributions, such as those of Julius Rosenwald and others, to patronage by civic-minded collectors such as Max Epstein, Arnold Maremont, Leigh Block, Herman and Maurice Spertus, Lewis Manilow, Nathan Cummings, Joseph Shapiro, Barnet Hodes, Edwin Bergman, and others, who have made their collections available periodically for public viewing. Shapiro also founded the Museum of Contemporary Art.

## MUSIC

Jews have a long tradition in music composition and performance going back to biblical times. Though music was usually associated with their religious services, it has through the centuries also expressed their joys and sorrows, hopes and struggles. The earliest Jews in Chicago, the German Jews, came with a musical tradition of Bach, Beethoven, and Mozart as well as their religious prayer music. The Eastern European Jews, who arrived later, came with music derived from the realm of the synagogue cantors and of the *klezmorim,* small itinerant Jewish bands that entertained with folk music at weddings and social functions. In Chicago these Jewish musical traditions were carried on in modified form, and additional contributions were made by performers, composers, teachers, and patrons of music.

Among the earliest of the prominent Jewish musicians of Chicago was Carl Wolfsohn (1834–1907), a noted concert pianist and teacher. Born in Germany, he came to America in 1854 at the age of twenty and settled in Chicago shortly after the fire. He became a close friend of Theodore Thomas, the founder of what was to become the Chicago Symphony Orchestra. Wolfsohn contributed financially to the orchestra in its early years. In 1873 he founded the Beethoven Society, the largest choral group for mixed voices in Chicago. In addition to giving numerous choral concerts, the organization sponsored concerts by talented musicians and chamber music groups, all under Wolfsohn's direction. The society was later superseded by the Apollo Musical Club.

Wolfsohn was a great admirer of Beethoven and performed his music in many piano concerts. In 1896 Wolfsohn presented to the city a bust of Beethoven, which was placed in Lincoln Park; at the dedication, music was played by former members of the Beethoven Society, which by then was defunct.[9] As a teacher Wolfsohn taught many pianists who were later to receive widespread recognition, one of whom was Fanny Bloomfield-Zeisler.

Fanny Bloomfield-Zeisler (1863–1927) was born in Austria and emigrated with her parents to Chicago at the age of two. Her early musical training was in Chicago but because of her great talent, she was sent to Vienna to study piano. After successful performances in Europe, she began her concert career in the United States in 1893. She soon gained international acclaim as one of the world's greatest pianists. Another woman who was a star with the Chicago Opera for many years was Rosa Raisa (1893–1963), one of the great dramatic

*Fanny Bloomfield-Zeisler (1863–1927), one of the world's greatest pianists.* (Courtesy of the *Sentinel.*)

sopranos of her day. Born in Bialystok, Poland, she attracted enough attention as a child prodigy that the means were provided for her to study in Italy, and in 1913 she came to the opera in Chicago.

Contemporary with Wolfsohn and also born in Germany was Emil Liebling. A student of Franz Liszt, he arrived in Chicago in 1872 and soon became recognized as a brilliant pianist, an able composer of salon pieces, and a prolific writer, critic, and editor in his field.[10]

The tendency of many Jewish families to scrimp and save in order to provide for violin lessons for their children was strongly reinforced for Chicago families at the turn of the century when Mischa Elman, a Russian Jewish violin prodigy, visited the city. The fact that a young Jewish boy from Czarist Russia could gain worldwide fame meant that doors were opening for Jewish musicians, and this knowledge underscored many parents' determination to provide a musical education for their offspring. Through the years some very talented Jewish violinists, pianists, and music teachers emerged in Chicago. Many instrumentalists initially worked in one of the many movie theater orchestras or radio studio orchestras that were mushrooming in the early decades of the century. However, the employment of musicians was later hurt by the coming of the sound track in movies and good musical recordings for radio.

Among the earlier famed Chicago Jewish violinists were Simon Jacobsohn and his pupil Max Bendix, the latter the first concertmaster of the Chicago Symphony Orchestra. Later concertmasters of the orchestra included Harry

Weisbach, Jacques Gordon, Mischa Mischakoff, Alexander Zukovsky, and Sidney Harth. The principal violist with the symphony for decades was Milton Preves, and the principal cellist for twenty-six years was Frank Miller, both highly acclaimed musicians. Currently with the Chicago Symphony Orchestra – and also conducting suburban symphony orchestras – are Francis Akos, from Hungary, Samuel Magad, from Chicago's West Side, and Victor Aitay, a concentration camp survivor. About one-fourth of the string section of the Chicago Symphony Orchestra is now comprised of Jewish musicians. Elaine Skorodin, a fine Chicago Jewish violinist, has appeared as a violin soloist with prominent orchestras throughout the world.[11] Among pianists, Rosalyn Tureck is considered one of the greatest interpreters of Bach.

A number of talented Jewish conductors, although usually not Chicago natives, have led Chicago-area orchestras – primarily the Chicago Symphony Orchestra – for varying periods of time. These include Fritz Reiner, Sir George Solti, and Daniel Barenboim. Reiner, a Hungarian-born Jew, conducted the Chicago Symphony Orchestra with distinction from 1953 to 1963. Solti, also a Hungarian-born Jew, was the honored conductor of the Chicago Symphony Orchestra from 1969 until 1991, helping to mold it into one of the world's great symphony orchestras. His successor is the renowned Jewish pianist-conductor Daniel Barenboim.

Three notable Chicagoans who worked primarily in the field of popular music were Art Hodes, Mel Tormé, and Benny Goodman. Hodes (1904–93) was for many decades one of the top jazz pianists in America. Mel Tormé, from the South Shore community, has been called one of the country's "most venerable jazz oriented pop singers"; he has a reputation as a skilled craftsman and intuitive improviser.[12]

Benny Goodman (1909–86), the well-known clarinetist and band leader, was born in the Maxwell Street area. As a child he learned to play the clarinet in a music instruction program fostered by a synagogue and also at Hull-House. In 1933 he organized his own orchestra and soon became known as the "King of Swing." His was one of the first jazz ensembles where both white and black musicians played together. Goodman also made numerous appearances with symphony orchestras and chamber ensembles, and Bartók, Hindemith, and Copland each wrote clarinet music dedicated to him. He performed before royalty as well as in Carnegie Hall.

The cantor (*chazan*) has been an integral part of synagogue services since the days following the destruction of the Second Temple in Jerusalem. His voice leads the congregational prayer to God, and through the centuries pious men with beautiful voices have served in this position. Until recent decades most of the cantors in Chicago came from Europe. The more outstanding cantors were usually hired by the larger and more affluent Chicago synagogues for the High Holy Day services and for special occasions. Some of these world-famous cantors included Joseph (Yosele) Rosenblatt, Pierre Pinchik, Gershon Sirota, Zavel Kwartin, Moishe Oysher, David Roitman, Mordecai Hershman, and Moshe Koussevitsky, all of whom thrilled the capacity audiences with their beautiful ritual chants while linking the past with the present. Another favor-

Benny Goodman (1909–86) learned to play the clarinet at Hull-House and in a band at a Lawndale synagogue. (Courtesy of Benny Goodman.)

ite was Richard Tucker, who in addition to being a Metropolitan Opera star was a cantor. He conducted the services for the High Holy Days for many years at synagogues in Lawndale and Humboldt Park.

There were also a number of especially fine cantors who were permanently connected with various Chicago synagogues, such as Joseph Giblichman, Todros Greenberg (The Blind Cantor), Aaron Kritz, Tevele Cohen, A. Manovitz, Pavel Slavensky, Moses Silverman, and Joshua Lind. The cantorial voice was most appreciated in the Orthodox synagogues, just as it had been in the towns and shtetlach of Eastern Europe. For years, many of the Reform temples functioned without cantors, but that trend has been reversed. The late Max Janowski was a noted composer of Jewish music who for many years was the musical director at KAM Isaiah Israel Temple.

Music has had a number of Jewish patrons and organizers in Chicago. Louis Eckstein was a principal founder and patron of Ravinia Park, Chicagoland's outdoor summer concert park located in a picturesque Highland Park setting. Eddie Gordon served as executive director at Ravinia for many years and James Levine has been the musical conductor. Seymour Raven, a well-known newspaper music critic, for a number of years was also the general manager of the Chicago Symphony Orchestra. Max Adler, born in Elgin, Illinois, studied music in Berlin and later enjoyed a dual career, as a vice president of Sears Roebuck and Company and as a concert violinist. Adler maintained his interest in music throughout his life and helped many young men and women in their mu-

*The Adler Planetarium was established in 1930 by Max Adler, an executive at Sears Roebuck and Company who was also a concert violinist.* (Courtesy of the Adler Planetarium.)

sical careers, including Isaac Stern. For years in his South Side home on Greenwood Avenue there were weekly concerts devoted to chamber music and quartets. A true benefactor of the city, Adler gave Chicago its planetarium.

Many Jews served as private teachers of music and on the faculty of Chicago music schools, including Leopold Godowsky, the world-famous concert pianist; Herman Devries, a successful operatic singer and music critic; composer-conductor Leon Stein; the talented operatic singer and music critic Maurice Rosenfeld; and a leading baritone, Adolph Muhlman. Two men who have contributed to the cultural growth of Chicago are Harry Zelzer and Danny Newman. As president of Allied Arts Corporation, Zelzer was Chicago's leading impresario, bringing to the city some of the top musical talent of the world, including the Metropolitan Opera Company of New York and outstanding soloists. Newman is the dean of theatrical publicists and has been an executive with the Lyric Opera of Chicago since its inception in 1954 as well as being active with the Art Institute, the Goodman Theater, and the Yiddish Theater. His book *Subscribe Now,* a classic marketing text giving the principles of dynamic subscription promotion, is used in thirty-one countries. Also important in the entertainment field in Chicago were Barney Balaban and Sam Katz and their families. Balaban and Katz created a chain of deluxe movie and stage-show palaces that included most of the downtown and major neighborhood motion picture theaters. At its peak the chain included 125 theaters in Chicago and the Midwest. Barney Balaban later became president of Paramount Pictures and Sam Katz became a production executive at Metro-Goldwyn-Mayer in Hollywood. Adolph Zukor, once a furrier in Chicago, also headed Paramount Pictures at one time. Florenz Ziegfeld, from Chicago's West Side, started in the entertainment field during the World's Fair in Chicago in 1893 and later, in New York, became nationally known as the producer of the Ziegfeld Follies and other shows.

Chicago has had a number of excellent Jewish choral groups. They have usually been the product of efforts by dedicated leaders, many of whom volunteered their services or worked for very little money. Various organizations had people who joined to sing Yiddish folk songs, religious melodies, songs of workers, or Israeli tunes. Such choral groups included the Jewish People's Choral

*Three men who contributed to the cultural growth of Chicago Jewry (left to right): Hyman Resnick, director of the Halevy Choral Society for many years; Danny Newman, theatrical publicist and executive; and Ben Aronin, composer and author. Danny Newman's wife was the late Dina Halpern, a famous Yiddish stage actress.*
(Courtesy of the Jewish Federation of Metropolitan Chicago.)

Society, founded in 1914 by Jacob Shaefer; the Halevy Choral Society, directed for many years by Hyman Resnick; the Workmen's Circle Chorus; the B'nai B'rith choral group; the Jewish National Workers' Alliance Choral Society; the Freiheit Gezang Farein; the Hazomir Choral Society; and the Hashomer Hadatai Chorus of the religious Zionists.[13]

### SPORTS

In the open atmosphere of America, Jews competed freely in athletics and a few made it to the top, or nearly to the top, to the delight of their coreligionists. As in other immigrant groups, the winners became heroes to sports lovers and to their people, despite having strayed far from the vocations of their ancestors.

The most successful Jewish athletes in Chicago came out of the Maxwell Street milieu in an era when many trades and professions were still difficult for Jews to enter. Their greatest success at that time came in boxing, a survival skill they had to learn in the often rough and tumble crowded ghetto environment. They frequently had to defend themselves within their own neighborhood as well as against taunting gentile youths from adjacent areas. Their skill helped them counter the stereotype of the Eastern European Jew as someone fearful and weak.

One of the earliest of the successful boxers was Jackie Fields (Jacob Finkelstein, 1908–87), a product of the Maxwell Street area. In the 1924 Olympics in Paris, at age sixteen, he made history as the youngest boxer to win a gold medal. Five years later he won the world welterweight title.

Barney Ross (Barnet David Rasofsky, 1909–67), was also from Maxwell Street.

Barney Ross (1909–67) was a world boxing champion raised in the Maxwell Street area.

(Courtesy of the *Sentinel*.)

When Ross was fourteen his father was murdered in the family's grocery store during a robbery. After that, the boy quit school and worked at various odd jobs, including one as a messenger for Al Capone, whose headquarters were not far from Maxwell Street. Spurred on by the success of Jackie Fields, Ross began to box and hang around gyms. He soon became a Golden Gloves champion, turned pro, and in 1932 became the world's lightweight champion and world's junior welterweight champion, later also winning the welterweight title. In World War II he served heroically as a Marine on Guadalcanal, where he was wounded and where he contracted malaria as well as a drug habit that took years to cure. He is a member of the Boxing Hall of Fame and has been rated one of the best boxers Chicago has produced.

Another boxer, "Kingfish" Levinsky, got his nickname because he helped in his family fish store on Maxwell Street. A flashy fighter with a clownish nature, he came up against a number of top heavyweights, including Jack Dempsey, Max Baer, and Joe Louis, but never made it to the top. His lowest point came when he lasted less than one round with Joe Louis. There were other prominent Jewish boxers, almost all coming from the West Side. Harry Harris won the world bantamweight title; Joey Burman became world featherweight champion; and Ray Miller, Davey Day, Eddie Lander, and Milt Aron (the rabbi's son) were top contenders in their class. Ruffy Silverstein won much acclaim as a leading wrestler.

Abe Saperstein (right), founded the clowning, sharpshooting Harlem Globetrotters and coached the team for about forty years. On the left is Meadowlark Lemon, one of the stars of the allblack basketball team.
(Courtesy of the *Sentinel*.)

Jews were not as active in professional baseball and football in Chicago as they were in boxing. In baseball the standouts were Ken Holtzman of the Cubs, who pitched two no-hitters, and Steve Stone of both the Cubs and the Sox, who won the 1980 Cy Young Award. In football, All-American Lou Gordon was a standout lineman for both the Chicago Bears and Chicago Cardinals. Sid Luckman, the legendary Bears quarterback, and Marshall Goldberg, all-around halfback ace of the Cardinals, were non-natives but longtime residents, and each is in a football hall of fame.

Basketball was a sport in which many Chicago Jews did well. Probably the most prominent Jew involved in basketball was the five-foot-tall Abe Saperstein (1901–66), the immigrant son of a London tailor. He organized, nurtured, and for about forty years guided the clowning, sharp-shooting Harlem Globetrotters – originally from the confines of the Savoy Ballroom on the South Side – making them world goodwill ambassadors for basketball, for blacks, and for the United States. They played before British royalty and in packed Moscow stadiums, and they had audiences with popes. When they were organized in

1927 with only five players, Abe drove them around in a dilapidated car. To the delight of the crowds, shorty Abe would fill in when a player got hurt. Saperstein is a member of the Basketball Hall of Fame.

Many Jewish boys picked up their initial basketball skills playing in gyms at Jewish centers such as the Jewish People's Institute, American Boys' Commonwealth, Boys' Brotherhood Republic, or the Deborah Boys' Clubs. Some became prep and college stars and a few played in the professional leagues. The Marshall High School team of 1944–46, composed largely of Jewish players, won a record ninety-eight consecutive games. Among the Jewish Chicagoans who made it into the pro ranks were Irv Bemoras, "Hershey" Carl, "Red" Skurnick, Max Zaslofsky, and Mickey Rottner.[14]

Although Jews in Chicago today participate in most sports and although there are some very good players, few are stars at the professional level. There are no longer the striving, tough Jewish kids of Maxwell Street and the West Side who fought their way up the sports ladders as a route to economic success. They have been replaced by other impoverished newcomers to the city. With improved economic conditions and more opportunities in the professions, few Jews concentrate on athletics after high school. However, Jews continue to be active in Chicago sports on a different level. Jerry Reinsdorf, the cofounder and former chairman of the Balcor real estate syndicate, owns the Chicago Bulls basketball team, and he and Eddie Einhorn head the White Sox organization. In the field of soccer, Lee Stern will be remembered for his long, valiant, and ultimately losing struggle to make the Chicago Sting a successful franchise.

### HEALTH CARE

Medicine is a field in which Jews have been very active in Chicago, especially in this century. But Jews have shown a predilection toward medicine since biblical times. Starting in the Middle Ages, Jewish doctors, including Maimonides and others, were often chosen as court physicians despite the hostility of many rulers to the Jewish masses. Medical careers first attracted Chicago's German Jews, including sons of pioneer businessmen. As most of Chicago's early hospitals were run by religious groups, Jewish doctors encountered imposed restrictions and found hospital affiliation quite limited. They found employment, however, with the opening of the first Jewish hospital on the Near North Side at Schiller and La Salle streets in 1869. Although that hospital was destroyed in the 1871 fire, the subsequent opening of the sixty-bed Michael Reese Hospital on the Near South Side in 1881 offered Jewish doctors affiliation with what was to become one of the largest hospitals in the city, although its original staff was largely non-Jewish.

The hospital grew through the years as numerous facilities were added – a children's building, a nursing school (closed a few years ago), and a clinic. The original hospital building was replaced in 1907. Patients at the hospital were largely immigrants who had come from both Eastern and Western European countries. Occupational statistics for male patients in 1885 are given in table 4. Most of the women patients were simply listed as housewives. One woman later recalled her experience as a young patient at the hospital in 1902:

When I was a young girl we lived on the West Side of Chicago, in a neighborhood of Russian Jews, Bohemians and Italians. This was the turn of the century. At the age of twelve I came down with typhoid fever in the early part of the summer. I was brought to Michael Reese in a horse-drawn vehicle which might have been an ambulance but which was probably a patrol wagon. My parents could not easily have afforded the expense of an ambulance. I was very sick and compelled to stay at the hospital for two months. Schoolmates got the erroneous word that I had died.

We were in the midst of a typhoid epidemic at the time, and the wards were very crowded. Extra beds had been set up to accommodate the patients. Even so, the children's ward was full, and I was consequently put in with the adults. To keep my fever down, the doctors administered cold baths. A fence was placed around my bed, and this held a rubber sheet in place. Then buckets of ice water were poured over me. I managed to survive this treatment and started feeling better.[15]

In 1893, Michael Reese Hospital established the West Side Dispensary in the Maxwell Street area to serve the burgeoning immigrant population there, on an out-patient basis. First located next to the Jewish Training School at Judd (Twelfth Place) and Clinton streets, it moved in 1899 to larger quarters at Maxwell and Morgan streets. In 1901 more than 20,000 patients were treated and 23,000 prescriptions filled. Prescriptions were filled at a nominal fee of ten cents each "so as not to humiliate the people and to make them feel as though they were paying in part at least for the services rendered them."[16] To cope with a high incidence of children's diseases the dispensary program included the distribution of pasteurized bottled milk. A recorded 80,964 bottles were dispersed in 1906.[17]

Michael Reese Hospital became a pioneer in the development of pediatrics due largely to the work of two of its Jewish doctors, Isaac Abt and his student Julius Hess, who were trailblazers in the care of premature infants and in child nutrition. Dr. Abt (1867–1955), a native of Wilmington, Illinois, interned at

TABLE 4. *Occupational Statistics for Male Patients at Michael Reese Hospital, 1885*

| Occupation | Number Reporting |
|---|---|
| Peddlers | 38 |
| Laborers | 26 |
| Clerks | 17 |
| Merchants | 13 |
| Brewers | 10 |
| Tailors | 9 |

Source: Michael Reese Hospital Archives.

The original Michael Reese Hospital building opened in 1881 on the South Side of Chicago. It was built mainly with funds bequeathed by Michael Reese and his family.
(Courtesy of the Michael Reese Hospital.)

Michael Reese Hospital in the 1890s and then served as attending physician there until 1927. He helped bring the Sarah Morris Children's Hospital to Michael Reese. He was also a professor and chairman of the Department of Pediatrics at Northwestern University Medical School from 1909 to 1945. Dr. Abt was one of the first to define and promote the improvement of children's medicine through clinical investigation, technical innovation, teaching, editing and writing, and fighting tenaciously for the improvement of child care. An unfortunate quarrel over child care with Michael Reese administrators led to his resignation in 1927.

Dr. Julius Hess (1876–1957), from Ottawa, Illinois, also on the staff at Michael Reese for many years, developed an incubator for premature infants. He established the world's first nursery for premature infants there in 1922. He had become interested in the problem of such infants when he saw them exhibited as carnival curiosities at the World's Columbian Exposition in 1893. Like Dr. Abt he wrote a number of pioneering treatises in the field of children's diseases. Hess also held a number of public offices, among them advisor to the Children's Bureau of the U.S. Department of Labor. He served on the faculties of Northwestern University and the University of Illinois. Doctors Abt and Hess, through their curative undertakings and research, were responsible for saving the lives of countless children and are among the founders of American pediatrics.

Numerous other prominent Jewish doctors were connected with Michael Reese Hospital. The development of the first artificial shoulder and the establishment of the link between heart disease and cholesterol are just two of the many important research developments carried out there. The research on cho-

*Early incubator room at Michael Reese Hospital. The incubator for premature babies was developed at Michael Reese Hospital by Dr. Julius H. Hess around the beginning of this century.* (Courtesy of the Michael Reese Hospital.)

lesterol was conducted by Dr. Louis S. Katz (1897–1973), who was later honored with the presidency of the American Heart Association and the presidency of the American Physiological Society. Dr. Katz's colleagues in the research were Dr. Ruth Pick and Dr. Jeremiah Stamler. Dr. Stamler also conducted important epidemiologic studies on the importance of the environment on coronary diseases.

Michael Reese Hospital was founded as a project of the United Hebrew Relief Association more than a century ago; the association's current equivalent, the Jewish Federation of Metropolitan Chicago, contributed to the hospital's operating funds until the facility's recent sale to a private corporation. Thus, for more than a century, Jewish philanthropy shared certain responsibilities with the hospital's board of directors in the stewardship of its large staff of 750 doctors and huge complex of 28 buildings containing over 1,000 beds.[18]

Two years after Michael Reese Hospital established its West Side Dispensary in the Maxwell Street area, Dr. Joseph Bolivar De Lee (1869–1942) in 1895 started the Chicago Lying-In Dispensary and Hospital (Chicago Maternity Center) at Maxwell Street and Newberry Avenue. Dr. De Lee was to become a world-renowned obstetrician, the designer of over twenty medical instruments, the author of three standard textbooks in the field, and the force behind the Chicago Lying-In Hospital at the University of Chicago. He was a professor of obstetrics at Northwestern University and later at the University of Chicago and was one of the founders of the American College of Surgeons.

The second of the major general hospitals founded and supported by the Chicago Jewish community is Mount Sinai Hospital. While Michael Reese Hospital was founded largely by German Jews, Mount Sinai Hospital was es-

tablished primarily by Eastern European Jews who wanted a facility of their own. In 1910 a group met to plan a hospital that would follow Jewish religious practices, including kosher food preparation (which Michael Reese did not have), and where Jewish doctors, especially those of Eastern European descent – who often had difficulty finding places of employment in existing hospitals, including Michael Reese – would have a place to work. Additionally, a hospital was needed to serve the burgeoning West Side population, a large percentage of which was Jewish and Orthodox. The group, headed by Judge Harry M. Fisher, began the arduous task of obtaining funding. A site was purchased on California Avenue and Fifteenth Street opposite Douglas Park in Lawndale. Maimonides Hospital, as it was first called, was opened in 1912. The hospital soon experienced serious financial difficulties and in 1918, after being closed briefly, it was reorganized and renamed Mount Sinai Hospital.

Through the years Mount Sinai Hospital expanded its facilities a number of times to almost five hundred beds, fostered significant research, and, like Michael Reese, served the various peoples of the vicinity after the neighborhood became non-Jewish. It is still partially supported by the Jewish Federation of Metropolitan Chicago, although there is some opposition to supporting a hospital that now has relatively few Jewish patients and in which there is limited observance of Jewish traditions, although it does serve many newly arrived Russian as well as poor Jews. However, both Michael Reese Hospital and Mount Sinai Hospital have served as stabilizing factors in their neighbor-

Mount Sinai Hospital (originally called Maimonides Hospital) was opened in 1912 as a hospital that would follow Jewish religious practices and serve the burgeoning West Side Jewish population.
(Courtesy of Mount Sinai Hospital.)

hoods, as sources of employment, and as reflections of the Jewish commitment to reaching out and offering help. Both hospitals are aided by numerous auxiliaries that provide volunteers and some funding.

As at Michael Reese Hospital, the staff of Mount Sinai Hospital has included a number of very prominent Jewish doctors. Dr. Samuel Zakon, a noted dermatologist, was on the hospital staff for forty-five years. He was "an able clinician, admired teacher and a noted medical historian" with some eighty-five papers to his credit.[19] Also well known and on the hospital's medical staff for forty years was Dr. Israel Davidsohn, a European immigrant. Dr. Davidsohn contributed to the knowledge of the Rh factor and to the better diagnosis of infectious mononucleosis. His research was presented in some 160 papers and four books. He received thirteen major awards for his contributions to medicine. A colleague, Dr. Kurt Stern, carried out experiments that were later to help in the prevention of Rh hemolytic diseases in newborn children.

Located near Mount Sinai Hospital, the Schwab Rehabilitation Center was founded in 1912 as Rest Haven, a convalescent home for poor Jewish immigrant workers. It is now a large physical and rehabilitative medical center. It was originally housed in various South Side buildings and from 1928 to 1951 occupied the mansion that had belonged to Marshall Field, Jr., at 1919 Prairie Avenue. The center is now affiliated with Mount Sinai Hospital. From 1977 until 1991 the dynamic and innovative Ruth Rothstein was president and chief executive officer of both the Schwab Rehabilitation Center and Mount Sinai Hospital.

The Chicago Medical School has been strongly supported by Jewish medical circles since its founding in 1912 as a facility to accept qualified students on a nondiscriminatory basis and also to provide night classes in medicine for employed persons. Its founding helped compensate for covert quota systems for Jews at the area's private medical schools.[20] The first facility was located on the South Side of the city but in 1930 the school moved to 710 South Wolcott in what is now the city's major medical complex. In 1948, under the vigorous leadership of Dr. John J. Sheinin, it became fully accredited. In the 1960s the school moved to a modern eleven-story building at 2020 West Ogden. In 1967, the Chicago Medical School announced the establishment of the University of Health Sciences, thus becoming one of the first schools in the country committed to developing interlocking educational programs for physicians and related professionals. In the mid-1970s the university moved to a site adjacent to Downey Veteran's Administration Hospital in Lake County, Illinois. In 1994 the school was renamed the Herman M. Finch University of Health Sciences/ The Chicago Medical School to honor the person who for almost three decades, as chairman of the board and chief executive officer, has helped guide the school to its present successful position.

Among other Jewish doctors who made significant contributions to the advancement of their specialties, Dr. Theodore B. Sachs (1868–1916), a Russian-born Jewish immigrant, fought the scourge of tuberculosis, a disease that was especially prevalent among the poor immigrants living in crowded conditions. He played an important role in the establishment of the Municipal Tuberculosis Sanitarium and became its first supervising physician. Bearing in mind the high incidence of tuberculosis among Jews in the vicinity of Maxwell Street, Dr. Sachs later helped to establish the Winfield Tuberculosis Sanitarium located west on Roosevelt Road in Du Page County. Despite his long, devoted, and successful work at Municipal Tuberculosis Sanitarium, he encountered what he considered corrupt political influences and a grossly unfair undermining of his cherished project. In 1916, sensitive and emotionally exhausted, he took his own life. Dr. Emil G. Hirsch, in an editorial in the *Reform Advocate,* wrote that

> Dr. Sachs did not fit into the world of getters and grafters. His was a radically different philosophy of life. Service, not success, was his pole star. . . . the institutions created for the protection and the helping of the destitute, the feeble, the sick and the delinquents he believed should be closely dyked against the incoming of the ravenous and unscrupulous self-seekers and their retinue of petty grafters eager for the small pickings of the game. And to this insistence he fell a martyr.[21]

Dr. Otto Saphir (1896–1963), chief pathologist at Michael Reese Hospital and a noted medical author, helped organize and headed the Exiled Physicians Program. This program helped bring to this country talented medical personnel who were survivors of the Nazi Holocaust and helped them to become established in the United States.

Dr. Bernard Fantus (1874–1940) is noted for his work on blood preservation, which subsequently helped make possible the establishment of the world's first working blood bank, at Cook County Hospital.[22] The outpatient clinic at Cook County Hospital is named after him. For many years he chaired the American Medical Association's therapeutics committee.

Dr. Max Thorek was one of many noted surgeons in Chicago. He was an author, a photographer, and a founder of the International College of Surgeons.

Vienna-born and once a concentration camp inmate, Dr. Bruno Bettelheim

(1903–90) was a leading psychologist, psychiatrist, and educator at the University of Chicago for over three decades. Though sometimes controversial, he was known widely as an expert on the clinical treatment of children. He headed the university's Sonia Shankman Orthogenic School, a residential school devoted to the treatment and education of severely emotionally disturbed children. He was a pioneer in the treatment of the autistic child and wrote extensively about disturbed children and social problems.

Dr. Morris Fishbein (1889–1976), editor for twenty-five years of the *Journal of the American Medical Association,* an important voice of the profession, exerted great influence in American medicine. He was an authority on medical economics and wrote many books on medicine for the general public. In the field of public health, Dr. Samuel Andelman, who had forsaken a rabbinical career for medicine, served as Health Commissioner of Chicago.

Ben Reitman was an unusual, frequently outrageous, antiestablishment, social-activist medical doctor. His practice and his empathy were focused largely on radicals, hoboes, prostitutes, the homeless, and, sometimes, gangsters. Born to Russian immigrant parents in 1879, Dr. Reitman became acquainted at a young age with hoboes. He rode the rails with them, organized a branch of the Hobo College in Chicago, and became known as the "King of the Hoboes." His wide range of activities also included participation in numerous radical labor movements, editing the anarchist magazine *Mother Earth,* and, for some ten years, being an intimate associate of the dynamic anarchist Emma Goldman. A provocative speaker and author, he helped to establish the first venereal-disease clinic at the Cook County jail. Reitman reportedly died "more or less a Baptist in Chicago" in 1942.[23]

The medical profession in Chicago now includes a large number of Jewish doctors, in part because hospitals and schools are open to all who are qualified. In recent decades an estimated 20 percent of the doctors of the region were Jewish.[24] While a few of the recognized contributors have been noted, there were thousands of Jewish doctors who worked out of their small offices in most of the neighborhoods of the city, made house calls when needed, and followed the code of Maimonides in taking care of the sick – "the rich and the poor; the good and the bad; the friend and the foe." Similarly, thousands of Jewish dentists and pharmacists ministered to the needs of their clientele throughout the city's neighborhoods.

In addition to the medical facilities there was also an array of Jewish community facilities dedicated to taking care of the aged and the needy. Most of these were and continue to be partially supported with funds provided by the Jewish Federation of Metropolitan Chicago or its predecessors. The majority of these institutions had volunteer auxiliaries that raised needed funds. There were several homes for the Jewish aged. In 1893 the Home for Aged Jews (later the Drexel Home) was established in Woodlawn at 6140 South Drexel. It was used mainly by the Reform community. The Orthodox Jewish community in 1903 opened its own home, the Orthodox Jewish Home for the Aged, the Beth Moshav Z'Keinim (BMZ) at 1648 South Albany opposite Douglas Park. Abraham Slimmer, a Jewish philanthropist from Iowa, provided substantial seed

Abraham Slimmer (1835–1917) was born in Russia but spent most of his life in Waverly and Dubuque, Iowa, where he became wealthy as a cattle merchant and financier. Without any fanfare he contributed to numerous secular and Jewish causes. His contributions in Chicago helped make possible the establishment of the Drexel Home (Home for Aged Jews), the Orthodox Jewish Home for the Aged, and the forerunners of Mount Sinai Hospital and the Jewish Children's Bureau. (From Meites, ed., *History of the Jews of Chicago*.)

money for both projects. In 1930 a smaller second home for the Orthodox Jewish aged, the Jewish People's Convalescent Home, was established in Lawndale at 1518 South Albany, and in 1951 the Park View Home for the Aged was established at 1401 North California Avenue opposite Humboldt Park. Through the years these institutions modernized procedures in order to better serve the psychological and social needs of their residents.

As the neighborhoods on the South Side, the West Side, and the Northwest Side lost their Jewish population and changed, one by one these institutions closed. They were replaced by new structures either on the North Side of the city or in Skokie. Realizing the importance of looking after the welfare of the growing number of elderly Jews, the Jewish Federation of Metropolitan Chicago created an umbrella organization, the Council for Jewish Elderly, to continue the Jewish tradition of taking good care of the aged.

### BAR, BENCH, AND OTHER GOVERNMENT SERVICES

One of the most popular of professional pursuits among bright, studious, articulate Jews has been the legal profession. Law is a field in which the Jews have made important contributions, leading to their involvement and leadership in government, politics, organizations, public service advocacy, and civil rights and Jewish defense agencies.

Edward S. Salomon (later a Civil War general), Adolph Moses, and Julius Rosenthal were German immigrants who became the first prominent Jewish lawyers in Chicago, entering practice in the city in the 1850s and 1860s. They were also active in Jewish community affairs. Joseph Moses, the son of Adolph Moses, and James and Lessing Rosenthal, sons of Julius Rosenthal, also were well-known lawyers. The younger Moses served as president of the Chicago Bar Association in the 1920s. Lessing Rosenthal served as president of the Law Club of Chicago and the Civil Service Reform Association and was one of the key figures in a court case that helped preserve Chicago's beautiful lakefront.[25] James Rosenthal was a member of the Chicago Board of Education and was the first secretary of the Young Men's Hebrew Charity Association.

Of the thousands of Jewish lawyers who practiced through the years, some stand out largely because of their civic achievements. One such lawyer was Julian W. Mack (1866–1943). Born in San Francisco, he graduated in 1887 from the Harvard Law School where he was the founding editor of the *Harvard Law Review,* assisted by Louis Brandeis, another budding lawyer who was to become one of his closest friends. After settling in Chicago, Mack was quickly recognized as a brilliant jurist. He served in the Circuit Court, the Juvenile Court (which he helped to reform), the Illinois Appellate Court, and finally the U.S. Circuit Court of Appeals, to which he was appointed by President William Howard Taft. Judge Learned Hand called Julian Mack "one of the most distinguished judges of his time." He further quoted a fellow judge as saying that Judge Mack was "the ablest living American judge; and that too while Holmes, Brandeis and Cardozo were still on the bench. Whether that was extreme, it was certainly a tenable opinion."[26] Mack also served as a professor of law at the University of Chicago and Northwestern University and as president of the National Conference of Social workers. In World War I he was asked by President Wilson to formulate a policy regarding the rights of soldiers and conscientious objectors.

In addition to these many activities, Judge Mack had a deep and abiding interest in the welfare of the Jewish people and worked for many of their organizations. He was the first president of the American Jewish Congress (1917) and, despite his Reform background, became one of the leading Zionists in the country, serving as president of the Zionist Organization of America from 1918 to 1921. For him, loyalty to the ideals of America and to those of Judaism and Zionism were mutually strengthening. His credo was "we ask no more for the Jew than we ask for anyone else."

Adolph Kraus (1850–1928) came to America from a small town in Bohemia at the age of fifteen. He was to become a successful lawyer, civic leader, and man of action for Jewish causes. He served the city of Chicago as president of the Board of Education, corporation counsel, and president of the Civil Service Commission. He was active in the B'nai B'rith and became its international president in 1905, holding that position until 1925. Kraus helped to break down B'nai B'rith's restrictions against admitting Eastern Europeans to membership. He also helped to lift the organization to a higher cultural level and to establish its Anti-Defamation League.[27] He was among those instrumental in having the United States commercial treaty with Russia abrogated in 1911 because of that country's inhumane treatment of its Jews. Another of the numerous important positions he held for a number of years was that of editor of the *Chicago Times.*

Kraus was one of a number of distinguished members of the law firm of Kraus, Mayer, and Stein. One of the partners was Samuel Alschuler (1859–1939), who served as a member of the Illinois House of Representatives and ran a strong but unsuccessful race in 1900 for the governorship of Illinois. In 1915

*Adolph Kraus (1850–1928), an immigrant from Bohemia, became a very successful lawyer, civic leader, and leader for numerous Jewish causes.*

(Courtesy of B'nai B'rith.)

Alschuler was appointed by President Wilson as judge of the U.S. Circuit Court of Appeals. During World War I he was appointed labor arbitrator and ably handled a number of thorny labor disputes.

Levy Mayer (1858–1922), from the same firm, became one of the nation's leading corporation lawyers and had some of the country's largest businesses as his clients. He helped organize the Illinois Manufacturer's Association and other industrial groups. Mayer was one of the early officers of the Zion Literary Society, and his biography was written by the poet Edgar Lee Masters. Until 1960 the entire Northwestern University Law School was housed in Levy Mayer Hall. Mayer was one of a number of Jews who donated large sums to the university.

Another partner of Adolph Kraus – and a brother-in-law as well – was Phillip Stein (1844–1922), who in 1892 became the first Jew to be elected as judge in Chicago, later becoming a judge of the Appellate Court of Illinois. He also served as a member of the Board of Education.

The two Pam brothers, Max and Hugo, were both prominent Chicago attorneys although quite different in their interests. Max, the elder, became an influential corporation lawyer with clients ranging from U.S. Steel and International Harvester to "Bet-a-million" John W. Gates. A wealthy bachelor, he founded Notre Dame University's School of Journalism and also contributed generously to the Zionist cause. His brother, Hugo, was elected judge of the Superior Court of Cook County in 1911 and was reelected three times. He was a very active participant in many Jewish and non-Jewish organizations. He became a national leader in such organizations as the American Jewish Congress, the Jewish Agriculture Aid Society, and the Zionist organization. It was said that "his eloquence, oratorical powers and legal mind made him an outstanding personality at Zionist gatherings."[28] Although of German Jewish descent, he acquired a deep understanding of Eastern European Jews when he worked in the Maxwell Street Settlement.

An attorney who was particularly active in Chicago Jewish communal affairs was the Lithuanian-born Harry M. Fisher (1883–1958). A capmaker by day, he attended law school at night. In 1912 he was elected judge of the Municipal Court and served as a highly acclaimed and respected judge at various levels for nearly fifty years. Many of his decisions, including one on community libel and others on social reform, have become milestones in Illinois law. Fisher is also credited with initiating a number of important legislative acts that improved the court system. His numerous civic activities included being president of Maimonides Hospital (later Mount Sinai), serving as chairman of the Board of Jewish Education, and assuming leadership roles at the Chicago Hebrew Institute, the Orthodox Jewish Home for the Aged, the Jewish Charities of Chicago, and in Zionist organizations. After visiting Russia in 1920 he returned to lead a very successful drive for aid for the Eastern European Jewish survivors of World War I. For his tireless leadership efforts in so many causes he was held in the highest esteem by the Jewish community as the "immigrant boy who never forgot his heritage."

Lawyers, more than members of any other profession, have been involved in Illinois politics and government service. A number of men with legal backgrounds, such as Congressman Adolph J. Sabath, Alderman Jacob M. Arvey, and Governor Henry Horner, have already been noted. Another Jewish governor was Samuel Shapiro of Kankakee, the immigrant son of a bootmaker, who moved up from lieutenant governor to governor upon the resignation of Governor Otto Kerner. Shapiro lost in a subsequent election.

Others who went on to render notable public service include Arthur Goldberg (1908–90), one of eleven children of a Russian immigrant who was a fruit and vegetable peddler living in the Maxwell Street neighborhood. He became a labor lawyer working as general counsel for the Congress of Industrial Organizations (CIO) and the United Steelworkers of America. He later served as U.S. Secretary of Labor, U.S. Supreme Court justice, and United Nations ambassador. During World War II Goldberg was a department head in the Office of Strategic Services (OSS). He was also president of the American Jewish Congress. Goldberg was one of a number of prominent Jewish lawyers who represented labor interests. Others included Moses Salomon and Sigmund Ziesler, who both defended the accused in the Haymarket bomb case; Peter Sissman, a partner of famed liberal lawyer Clarence Darrow; and Leon M. Despres, who served for twenty years as the hardworking, independent alderman of the Fifth Ward, the conscience of the Chicago City Council. Despres was also a teacher of labor law and a member of the Chicago Plan Commission.

Marshall Korshak, also in labor law, has served as an officer or board member of numerous civic and philanthropic organizations as well as assistant state's

attorney of Cook County, state senator, Metropolitan Sanitary District trustee, director of revenue for city and state, and city collector.

Congressman Sidney Yates, the son of immigrants, has represented the North Side of Chicago in the U.S. House of Representatives since 1949, except for one term. A champion of the arts and of environmental protection, he also is credited with helping to make possible the Holocaust Museum in Washington. He has been an effective, liberal congressman, as was his equally liberal and distinguished colleague, Congressman Abner J. Mikva, who originally represented the city's South Side and had been a law partner of Arthur Goldberg. Mikva also served in the Illinois House of Representatives for five consecutive terms, earning several "Best Legislator" awards from the Independent Voters of Illinois. In 1979 he was appointed by President Carter to the United States Court of Appeals for the District of Columbia. He later served as an advisor to President Clinton. State senators Arthur Berman and Howard Carroll also effectively served in the Illinois State Legislature, each representing parts of Chicago's North Side for over twenty years.

Two Chicago attorneys, Seymour Simon and Abraham Lincoln Marovitz, held numerous important public positions before being elevated to high court positions. Simon served four terms as a Chicago alderman from the Northwest Side and then five years as president of the Cook County Board of Commissioners before being elected to the Illinois Appellate Court in 1974 and the Illinois Supreme Court in 1980. He had often clashed with the entrenched Cook County Democratic organization, but his reputation continued to provide electoral success.

*(Left) Arthur Goldberg (1908–1990) was raised in the Maxwell Street area, one of eleven children of a fruit and vegetable peddler. He became a noted labor lawyer, Secretary of Labor, United Nations Ambassador, and U.S. Supreme Court Justice.*
(Courtesy of the Chicago Historical Society.)

*(Right) Harry M. Fisher (1883–1951) arrived from Lithuania at the age of ten. While working as a capmaker, he attended law school at night. He served as a highly respected judge for almost half a century and was also exceedingly active in Jewish affairs.*
(Courtesy of the Jewish Federation of Metropolitan Chicago.)

Marovitz grew up in the Maxwell Street neighborhood. Reflecting on his childhood days, he has noted, "It was certainly from this rather unique background, and the mixture of characters who filled it, that I learned my liberal viewpoints . . . and I am a better man because of it." He has served as assistant state's attorney and was the first Jew to be elected to the state senate, where he became the Democratic leader. He was a Superior Court judge and chief justice of the criminal courts, and for many years served as the senior United States district judge. He served with the Marine Corps in World War II. Through the years he has been honored by numerous groups for his achievements and for his involvement in so many Jewish and non-Jewish organizations. He is also known for his extensive Lincoln memorabilia collection. He was a close friend of the late Mayor Richard J. Daley and administered the oath of office to him six times; he later swore in Daley's son, Richard M. Daley.

Edward Hirsch Levi, son and grandson of famous rabbis, is a distinguished educator as well as an attorney. He has been at the University of Chicago law school for many years, including serving as its dean. He was university president from 1968 to 1975, its first Jewish president. From 1975 to 1977 he served as President Gerald Ford's attorney general, one of many positions he has held with the federal government. Also holding a high federal government position, as chairman of the Federal Communications Commission under President John

F. Kennedy, was Newton Minow, who secured national attention with his description of television as "a vast wasteland."

Although Chicago Jews have held various governmental offices, there are many positions they have not yet filled. These include state's attorney for Cook County, U.S. district attorney for the area, Illinois attorney general or secretary of state, U.S. senator, or mayor of Chicago, although in recent decades Richard Friedman, William Singer, and Bernard Epton have made strong, but unsuccessful, runs for the latter office. Since World War II, as the Jewish population of Chicago has had a relative decline, and as Jews dispersed geographically and have become well established in business and the professions, their interest in political office and patronage has also declined as has some of their political clout, although in 1971 seven Jewish aldermen were elected to the Chicago City Council. Jews gain access to government now, however, more through business and social contacts and their own economic status. Although they have only a limited number of elected officials, there are many Jewish advisors to elected officials.

Chicago Jewish lawyers have been active in virtually all aspects of the law.

Included among the distinguished law professors are Wilbur G. Katz, Phillip Kurland, and Nathan Louis Nathanson. Judge Jacob M. Braude and Barnet Hodes, Chicago's corporation counsel for many years, have written law books for the general public. Elmer Gertz, Marshall Patner, and Alexander Polikoff, among others, have been active in civil liberties and public interest groups, and Patner and Polikoff have been involved with Business and Professional People for the Public Interest, an organization founded in 1969 with the aid of a Chicago Jewish businessman, Gordon Sherman.[29] Jewish lawyers who have been most active in politics and public affairs in recent decades are generally the children and grandchildren of the Eastern European immigrants and are usually liberal and Democratic. In contrast, earlier leaders had been largely of Central European descent and somewhat more conservative and Republican.

Until recent decades there were relatively few women lawyers in the country. The picture has changed dramatically, with women comprising almost one-third of all law school students. In the Chicago area a number of Jewish women have held important positions. In 1977 Esther Rothstein became the first woman president of the Chicago Bar Association, and Carole K. Bellows became the first woman president of the Illinois Bar Association. In 1983 Nina S. Appel was appointed dean of the Loyola University Law School and the following year Charlotte Adelman was made president of the Women's Bar Association of Illinois. In 1984 Ilana D. Rovner was appointed judge of the U.S. District Court for Northern Illinois.

It has been estimated that until 1950, about 85 percent of the Jewish lawyers worked for Jewish law firms. As discriminatory barriers were broken, more Jewish lawyers found positions with non-Jewish law firms and, conversely, more non-Jewish lawyers have become connected as partners and associates with firms that had been predominantly Jewish. It is estimated that of the 26,000 lawyers now in Cook County, about 5,000 are Jewish.[30] About 1,600 belong to the Decalogue Society of Lawyers, organized in 1934 to combat discrimination against Jewish lawyers and to protect their rights. It provides numerous professional and social services for its members and for law students. In addition to holding monthly forums, it grants awards to distinguished individuals, both Jewish and non-Jewish; funds scholarships; fosters adherence to the highest ethical principles; confronts anti-Semitism; and generally watches over Jewish interests.

Thousands of Jewish people have been active in public education in Chicago. They served mainly as teachers but many were also principals and district superintendents. There were even three Jewish presidents of the Chicago Board of Education, Adolph Kraus, who served from 1883 to 1886; Jacob M. Loeb, who was on the board from 1914 to 1917; and Sol Brandzel, who was president from 1983 to 1984. Curtiss Melnick, Edwin Lederer, and Harry Strassburg have been assistant superintendents of schools. Many Jewish teachers entered the system following World War II, after the political patronage system had been largely eliminated. Some, such as Lillian Herstein, who worked in the teachers' union, and Samuel Dolnick, who served in the principals' association, were leaders in teachers' and principals' organizations, and others, such as Joe Rosen, became activist community leaders. Due to changes in demographics, school conditions, and employment options, the number of Jews in the Chicago public school system has declined in recent years, some switching to suburban schools. For example, in 1980 there were almost a hundred Jewish school principals; today the number is estimated at about twenty-five.

## COMMERCE AND INDUSTRY

Once peddlers with packs on their backs, when they first came to Chicago about a century and a half ago, Jewish businessmen have emerged in modern times as major forces in Chicago's commerce and industry. As Chicago's population expanded rapidly, many hard-working Jewish business owners were able to grow with the city. Aided by Chicago's advantageous geographical location and its position as a transportation and resource center, and operating in an unfettered free-enterprise environment, they moved up from peddler to small store or crafts-shop owner. They built some of today's numerous Jewish-owned commercial and industrial concerns, many of which are now household names. These enterprises often have been further developed by generations of capable and interested offspring. Many of these individuals were also active community leaders working diligently for civic and charitable causes. Most of them attained their success as owners rather than as executives working for others. Until recently, high executive positions were not readily open to Jews, especially in certain industries. Jews frequently started businesses in "new" fields not already dominated by non-Jews, such as mail-order operations; the manufacture of automotive accessories, electrical components, and ready-to-wear clothing; or in radio broadcasting and the film industry.

Chicago Jews have been involved in a variety of businesses, one of the earliest of which was the clothing industry. It began in the 1840s when Jewish tailors set up business on Lake Street. Later, Jews were both the employers and employees in the clothing industry, which provided work for many thousands of Eastern European immigrants, some of whom had tailoring and capmaking skills from the old country. Many worked in small crowded shops, often taking home "piecework" to supplement their meager incomes. Some of these immigrants later established small shops of their own, sometimes becoming suppliers to the larger concerns.

The largest of the Jewish-founded clothing companies included B. Kuppenheimer and Company; Hart, Schaffner and Marx; Society Brands; and Oxxford Clothes Company. After Hart, Schaffner and Marx purchased many of its competitors, including Kuppenheimer and Society Brands, the present giant Hartmarx emerged. The company traces its beginnings to 1872 when Henry Hart and his younger brother Max opened a retail clothing store on State Street in Chicago. They were joined by Joseph Schaffner in 1887 and the firm gradually became predominantly a manufacturer of men's clothing. Later it also owned major retail stores and became a manufacturer of women's clothing. The company was involved in the long and bitter garment strike of 1910; since then, however, the labor relations of the company have been exemplary.

South Water Market, the city's major wholesale fruit and vegetable market, looking east on Fifteenth Street from Aberdeen Street, 1941. Jewish produce peddlers would load up their wagons and trucks there early in the morning and then proceed to the various ethnic communities to sell their produce. Today an estimated one-third of the wholesale merchants of the market are Jewish.
(Courtesy of the Chicago Historical Society.)

One of the nation's best-known brands of fine shoes, Florsheim, was founded by Siegmund Florsheim and other family members who had emigrated from Germany to Chicago in the mid-1800s. Today it is one of the largest shoe manufacturers in the country.

Retailing is a field in which Jews have been especially active and successful. Many of the largest department stores on State Street were founded or originally headed by Jews. These included Mandel Brothers; the Boston Store; Siegel, Cooper, and Company; Schlessinger and Mayer; Henry C. Lytton; Maurice L. Rothschild; Morris B. Sachs; and Goldblatt's. Mandel Brothers, founded in the 1850s, was run by the Mandel family for about a century, until it was bought out by Wieboldts. The Boston Store owed much of its success to the Cinderella story of Mollie Alpiner. While still a teenage clerk in the Boston Store, she met and subsequently married its owner, Charles Netcher. After his death in 1904 she owned and operated the store, which she relocated to State and Madison streets, until she sold it in 1946.

Goldblatt Brothers, eventually a ten-store chain, was founded by Nathan and Maurice Goldblatt in 1914 in a small store at 1617 West Chicago Avenue, and

catered to the working classes with lower prices. The expanding chain was run by the four Goldblatt brothers. In the 1930s, when it opened its downtown store, it was given the title of "America's fastest growing department store chain."[31] However, in the late 1970s, after over sixty years of growth, the chain started running into the financial difficulties overtaking department stores nationwide and eventually filed for bankruptcy. Maurice Goldblatt was a major contributor and fundraiser for a variety of medical facilities at the University of Chicago.

Outlying stores of importance included L. Klein, Klee Brothers, Leader, Franks, and Yondorff. Shoe chains were O'Connor and Goldberg, Cutlers, Maling Brothers, and Chernin's (still extant). Clothing chains included Sherman Shops, Karolls, Katz Hats, and Morris B. Sachs – the latter founded by a door-to-door dry goods peddler in Chicago's Back-of-the-Yards area. Sachs later gained fame for his sponsorship of an amateur hour on radio from 1934 to 1957 and served as city treasurer under Mayor Martin Kennelly.

Polk Brothers was started by eighteen-year-old Sol Polk in 1935 with a store on North Central Avenue. It was to grow into the city's largest appliance chain with stores throughout the Chicago region. Its executive staff eventually included Sol Polk's sister and four brothers. It was one of the first of the discounters, and during the 1950s and 1960s it was the largest retailer of brand-name appliances in the country. Sol Polk was the son of Romanian immigrants who had peddled irons and ironing boards door-to-door during the Depression. All of the stores had closed by the early 1990s.

Another merchant with a flair for salesmanship was Morrie Mages (1916–88), for many years "Chicago's Mr. Sporting Goods." Starting his career hawking goods from a pushcart in front of his Russian immigrant father's sporting goods store on Maxwell Street, Mages eventually became owner of a popular chain of sporting goods stores in Chicago and its suburbs.

The mail-order business included a number of Jewish businessmen. Foremost was Julius Rosenwald, who headed Sears, Roebuck and Company for many years and who instituted many of its major policies, such as store expansion, profit sharing, and money-back guarantees. Aldens, now closed, was for years one of the major companies in the mail-order business. It was founded in 1900 by Samuel B. Rosenthal to mail millinery supplies to "parlor milliners," women who made hats in their homes.[32] Spiegel, Inc., founded at the end of the Civil War as a small furniture company, eventually became one of the giants in the mail-order field, developing especially in this century under the leadership of Modie J. Spiegel.

Crate and Barrel is a rapidly growing contemporary housewares chain. It was founded by Gordon Segal and his wife, Carole, in Chicago and is still concentrated there, but its over fifty stores are now in other cities, including New York. Gordon Segal is very active in community affairs and philanthropic undertakings.

In the building and real estate field, a number of architects, engineers, and community developers have gained national prominence for their work in the Chicago area and elsewhere. Among the best known was Dankmar Adler (1844–1900), who was born in Germany and came to Chicago in 1858 where his father, Dr. Liebman Adler, became the distinguished rabbi of Kehilath Anshe Maariv Congregation. After serving in the Civil War, the younger Adler was in partnership for about fifteen years with Louis Sullivan in the firm of Adler and Sullivan. Their landmark Chicago buildings include the Auditorium, the Chicago Stock Exchange, and the Garrick Theater. Adler also designed the Standard Club, and Sinai, Zion, KAM, and Isaiah synagogue buildings. He was especially known for his knowledge of acoustics and his work on the engineering aspects of the steel-framed skyscraper.

Alfred S. Alschuler (1876–1940), another noted architect, began his work in the office of Dankmar Adler. He designed many industrial, commercial, and institutional buildings. Probably the best known of his commercial buildings is the London Guarantee Building (now 360 North Michigan Building) in downtown Chicago. He is also known for his synagogue structures, which in Chicago included Temple Isaiah (now KAM–Isaiah Israel), B'nai Sholom, Sinai Temple (on Grand Boulevard), what is now Anshe Emet, Am Echod in Waukegan, and an earlier home of North Shore Congregation Israel in Glencoe. The landmark KAM–Isaiah Israel Synagogue, of Byzantine-style architecture, features ornamental motifs similar to those on a second-century synagogue that was unearthed in Tiberias, Israel.

David Saul Klafter was a versatile Jewish architect who practiced for over a half century. He designed the first moving-picture theaters in the city and a number of synagogues, including Humboldt Boulevard Temple and B'nai Bezalel. Klafter served as the Cook County architect from 1941 to 1948.[33]

One of the best known and most innovative of current American architects is Bertrand Goldberg, whose two circular sixty-story Marina City Towers in downtown Chicago have become city landmarks. The Raymond M. Hilliard Center, a public housing project Goldberg designed, has also won awards. Goldberg is currently developing River City south of the Loop along the river, which contains numerous distinctive features using his trademark cylindrical-tower form. Another leading innovative architect is Stanley Tigerman, who is also one of the foremost architects concerned with urban renewal and low-income housing.

Jerrold Loebl and Norman Schlossman, of the architectural firm bearing their

names, helped design shopping centers such as Old Orchard and Oakbrook, worked on the design of cities such as Park Forest, and were the architects of hospital buildings at Weiss Memorial and Michael Reese hospitals. They also have been involved in designing some of Chicago's most distinctive synagogues, including Beth Hillel in Wilmette, West Suburban Temple Har Zion in River Forest, and Chicago's Temple Sholom, Emanuel Congregation, and the Chicago Loop Synagogue.

Abraham Epstein, an immigrant from Russia and an engineer by profession, in the 1920s started a firm that today is known as A. Epstein and Son International, Inc., one of the largest architectural firms in the country, with offices also in Europe and Israel. Abraham Epstein claimed "that he weathered the Great Depression with an assist from the stockyards fire of 1934 whose reconstruction he handled."[34] The company has built several thousand buildings throughout the world. Buildings in the Chicago area include those for Borg-Warner, the International Amphitheatre, Fansteel Metallurgical, Chicago Medical School, Rodfei Zedek Synagogue, and the Associates Center and the new United Airlines terminal at O'Hare Field. After Epstein's death in 1958, his sons, Raymond and Sidney, took over the firm.

Jacob Sensibar (1890–1968), a self-educated Russian immigrant who came to the United States in 1900, established what was to become one of the largest excavation firms in the country, the Construction Aggregates Corporation, which earned him the title of the "world's greatest earth mover." Among some

Part of the sanctuary of the Chicago Loop Synagogue, founded in 1929 and located at 16 South Clark Street. It serves people working in or visiting the downtown area as well as Jews who live in the surrounding areas. The present sanctuary, completed in 1958, is especially noted for its stained glass windows by Abraham Rattner and for work by the Israeli sculptor Henri Azaz, including the design of the Ark holding the scrolls of the Torah. Many of the Loop Synagogue's members also belong to neighborhood synagogues.

(Photo by Irving Cutler.)

of the projects he was involved with were leveling the sand dunes for the site of the huge U.S. Steel plant in Gary, Indiana; the development of the "Sensibar Sand Fill Method," in which ships suck up sand from water bottoms and pump it into landfills; the filling of the swamp where the Field Museum of Natural History now stands; building parts of Chicago's modern lakefront; and turning forty-four thousand acres of swampland around Lake Huleh in Israel into productive farmland.

Marvin Camras (1916–95), who grew up near Lawndale and for many years was connected with the Illinois Institute of Technology, was an ingenious inventor. Foremost among his inventions was his magnetic tape recorder, which revolutionized the recording field. He held about five hundred patents.

Included among the giants in the real estate field is Arthur Rubloff. Rubloff, until his death in 1986, was a major real estate developer, based in Chicago but with national and international enterprises. In Chicago he developed such places as Carl Sandburg Village and Evergreen Park Shopping Plaza and helped sponsor the Magnificent Mile development along North Michigan Avenue. He made major philanthropic contributions to such institutions as the Art Institute, the Chicago Historical Society, the University of Chicago, and Northwestern University, where in the 1980s he provided for the erection of the university's new law school.

Phillip Klutznick is also a major force in the real estate business. Klutznick's many activities and contributions in the local, national, and international

*Philip Klutznick, a prominent lawyer, community developer (Park Forest, Water Tower Place, suburban shopping centers), and Jewish leader, was born in Kansas City, Missouri, in 1907 but has been a long-time resident of Chicago.*

(Courtesy of the Jewish Federation of Metropolitan Chicago.)

spheres have made him one of the most respected people in the Chicago community. A lawyer, he was head of American Community Builders and of the Urban Investment and Development Company, which were pioneers in the development of the planned community of Park Forest, the multi-use Water Tower Place, suburban shopping malls, Dearborn Park, and numerous other properties. His government service and Jewish community leadership through the years have been unusual in their scope and success. He has served in the federal government under seven presidents,[35] including appointments as director of the Federal Housing Authority, delegate to the United Nations, and Secretary of Commerce. Klutznick's many activities in Jewish affairs include terms as international president of the B'nai B'rith, general chairman of the United Jewish Appeal, and president of the World Jewish Congress. He has been a major developer of real estate in Israel. A most thoughtful and courageous leader, he has not been averse to taking unpopular but sound positions.

Another lawyer who became successful in real estate was Maxwell Abbell (1902–57). He eventually established the nationwide Abbell Hotel chain. Besides his generous philanthropic works, he was also very active in local and national Jewish life, holding leadership positions in numerous Jewish organizations.

Jerrold Wexler, chairman of the board of Jupiter Industries, Inc., until his death in 1992, was active in developing that company's extensive real estate holdings, which include major hotels and residential facilities. His Outer Drive East apartment building was a pioneering venture in that district. Morris R.

DeWoskin was also prominent in the hotel industry, in both the United States and Latin America. Judd Malkin and Neil Bluhm have developed JMB Realty into one of the nation's largest real estate companies. Lawrence and Mark Levy in 1978 formed the Levy Organization. The company has major office-building holdings in Chicago and the suburbs. It also operates a number of popular restaurants in the city. Richard Melman is also making a name for himself in the restaurant business. Melman is president and founder of the Lettuce Entertain You Enterprises, Inc., which operates twenty-four distinctive and individualized restaurants, including the world-famous Pump Room.[36] Another popular Chicago restaurateur was Eli Schulman, whose famous cheesecake is now sold nationwide.

Jews have been active in the Chicago food business since 1842 when Henry Horner, the grandfather of the 1930s governor, opened his modest retail and wholesale grocery store at the corner of Randolph and Canal streets. Later he was instrumental in founding the Chicago Board of Trade. Nelson Morris (1834–1907), an immigrant from Germany, established Nelson Morris and Company, one of Chicago's major meat packers in the nineteenth century. The enterprise was later absorbed by Armour and Company. Through the years a number of food companies developed that began by catering primarily to the Jewish populace. These included several successful sausage companies such as Vienna, Kosher Star, Best Kosher, Sinai Kosher, and David Berg. Of these, the largest is the Vienna Sausage Company, which was started in the 1890s by two Jewish immigrants from Austria-Hungary, Samuel Ladany and Emil Richel. Their initial success came when they sold their "Old Country" sausage at the World's Columbian Exposition of 1893.

In recent decades the names of Charles Lubin and Nathan Cummings became important in the food industry. Lubin started as a baker's apprentice at age fourteen. Later, at his own bakery, he became very successful with his cheesecake, which he named after his daughter, Sara Lee. This success caused his business to grow so rapidly that it kept outgrowing its facilities. Lubin pioneered frozen baked goods, and there are now over two hundred frozen Sara Lee products sold nationwide. In 1956 his company was purchased by the food conglomerate Consolidated Foods, whose name was later changed to Sara Lee Corporation. Consolidated Foods had been founded by Nathan Cummings, who built it into one of the largest food-processing, distributing, and retailing companies in the food industry; it now includes Best Kosher and Sinai Kosher products. Sara Lee is important also in producing nonfood consumer products. Another major company, Pabst Brewing Company, was headed for forty years by Harris Perlstein as president or chairman, during which period he brought about many industry innovations.

The development of the Midwest required substantial financial backing, which was supplied by a variety of establishments. Jews were generally not included in the higher echelon of the major Chicago financial institutions. Their participation was mainly in smaller community banks, often in Jewish neighborhoods or in larger financial houses that they themselves had started. One of the earliest of these was the mortgage banking firm started in 1855 by the

Charles Lubin rose from being an apprentice baker at age fourteen to a major producer of Sara Lee bakery products, named after his daughter.
(Courtesy of the Sara Lee Corporation.)

Greenebaum brothers, Henry and Elias. It was to become one of the largest of its kind in the country and was subsequently headed by some of the Greenebaum children. An early bank founded by Jews was established by Gerhard Foreman in 1862, later known as the Foreman National Bank and the Foreman Trust and Savings Bank.

The Walter E. Heller Company, founded in 1919 by Walter E. Heller initially as an auto financing business, was to become one of the largest diversified financial firms in the country. Its president from 1974 until recently was Maynard Wishner, who is also an extremely active leader in the Chicago Jewish community. He recently served as president of the Jewish Federation of Metropolitan Chicago and currently heads the nationwide Council of Jewish Federations. Wishner, an aficionado of the Yiddish language and theater, was a part-time actor on the Yiddish stage in his youth.

A number of major brokerage firms were founded by Jews. One such firm was A. G. Becker and Company. Abraham G. Becker had previously been a junior partner in a bank that failed in the crash of 1893. He sacrificed his own money so that the depositors were repaid, widows and needy first. He went on to establish the brokerage firm bearing his name and served on the board of directors of a number of companies including Hart, Schaffner and Marx, and Westinghouse Electric.

The Chicago Board of Trade and the Chicago Mercantile Exchange have many Jewish members. Some of them have held the highest offices at both these exchanges. Leo Melamed, former head of the Chicago Mercantile Exchange, has been credited as the innovator of a number of its new financial instruments.

Prominent in the insurance field was Jacob M. Loeb, who was also exceedingly active in community affairs. His community activities included serving as president of the Jewish People's Institute, the Standard Club, and the Chicago Board of Education, where he vigorously fought against the prevailing graft and corruption.

There were a number of Jewish pioneers in new fields such as transportation and communication. Around the beginning of this century Max Epstein founded the General American Transportation Corporation, now GATX, one of the nation's largest lessors of transportation equipment. John Keeshin, a grade-school dropout, started out when he was a teenager with a horse and wagon in the Maxwell Street area and eventually developed the trucking company bearing his name. At one time it was the largest independent trucker in the country. The company grew at a time when trucking was an especially rough and bruising business, which Keeshin was able to handle. During World War II Keeshin and his truckers were called upon to help build the famous "Burma Road," which brought supplies to embattled China.[37]

Another transportation tycoon was John Hertz, who, in 1923, purchased the nation's first auto and truck rental company, which had been founded in Chicago by Walter L. Jacobs in 1918 with an initial inventory of twelve used Model-T Fords. In addition to his connection with the Hertz car rental system, John Hertz was active in the ownership and management of the Chicago Motor Coach Company, the Chicago Yellow Cab Company, Yellow Truck and Coach Manufacturing Company, and a number of New York City transit companies.

Ben W. Heineman, an attorney, served the state and federal governments in important positions, including being on the civil affairs staff of General Eisenhower during World War II. Later he became the chairman of the Chicago and Northwestern Railway and was largely responsible for turning around a faltering railroad and establishing an exemplary commuter service in the Chicago area. He was instrumental in transforming the railroad into a large conglomerate, Northwest Industries, where he was also chairman and chief executive officer.

Maxim M. Cohen, a maritime expert who served for many years as the general manager of the Chicago Regional Port District, was instrumental in the development of the Port of Chicago once the modern St. Lawrence Seaway was established. Harold M. Mayer, for many years a geography professor at the University of Chicago and a noted expert and consultant on transportation and urban planning, served on numerous government agencies and commissions.

He was the author of many articles and books on various aspects of Chicago transportation and development. Ira Bach was another prominent urban planner as well as an architect who served through five Chicago mayoral administrations as the director of various housing and planning agencies. He was involved in many of the important planning decisions affecting Chicago. Philip Hauser, for several decades a professor of sociology at the University of Chicago, was also involved in urban planning and was an expert on urban demographics. He also had served as the acting head of the U.S. Census Bureau.

A remarkable success story in the field of communications is that of William S. Paley (1901–90). His father, Samuel, was a cigarmaker in the Maxwell Street area, where William was born. The father later became a cigar tycoon with his La Palina brand cigar. William, after working a few years in his father's growing company, became interested in the fledgling radio business through his advertising work for his father's company. He was later to found the Columbia Broadcasting System and was its dynamic president or chairman of the board for over fifty years, being largely responsible for the network's growth.[38] In the field of media distribution, in 1893 Charles Levy founded a business, later developed further by his son, that was to become the Charles Levy Circulation Company, one of the largest distributors of books, magazines, and videocassettes in the country. Charles Levy started his business at the age of twenty after winning a horse and wagon in a raffle.

A number of other major American corporations have been founded or largely developed by Chicago Jewish families. Albert Pick in 1892 founded a company bearing his name that became a major supplier of restaurant and hotel equipment and supplies. His son, Albert Pick, Jr., later was part of a group that became the Pick Hotels Corporation. The Block family has been instrumental in the growth of the Inland Steel Company. A number of family members have served as president of the Chicago Association of Commerce and Industry and the Jewish Federation of Metropolitan Chicago and in numerous other civic and charitable groups. The Bensingers have been involved in the growth of what is now the Brunswick Corporation, a major producer of recreational equipment. Similarly, the Stone family has guided the Stone Container Company since its founding in 1926 by Joseph H. Stone. Today it is the world's largest producer of containerboard and kraft paper. The Gidwitz family led Helene Curtis Industries to its present rank as one of the largest cosmetics companies in the country and is active in civic affairs.

Two families, the Pritzkers and the Crowns, have established huge conglomerate empires. Both have roots in the Wicker Park section of Chicago. Their success has allowed them to make very substantial philanthropic contributions to numerous Chicago and national institutions and to Israel. Abram Nicholas Pritzker (1896–1986), the family patriarch, served as a navy chief petty officer in World War I and later received a law degree from Harvard. He helped accumulate and develop a very large, diversified group of companies that included the Hyatt Hotels, the Marmon Group, Hammond Organ, and *McCall's* magazine.[39] A few months before he died at age ninety he received the Israel Prime Minister's Medal.

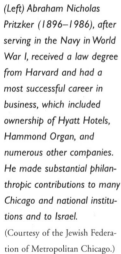

(Left) Abraham Nicholas Pritzker (1896–1986), after serving in the Navy in World War I, received a law degree from Harvard and had a most successful career in business, which included ownership of Hyatt Hotels, Hammond Organ, and numerous other companies. He made substantial philanthropic contributions to many Chicago and national institutions and to Israel.
(Courtesy of the Jewish Federation of Metropolitan Chicago.)

(Right) Henry Crown (1896–1990), prominent industrialist and philanthropist, in 1919 helped start Material Service Corporation, a building materials company, and through the years had other major industry investments. The Crown family has been a major source of funds for numerous philanthropic causes including being one of the largest contributors to local Jewish causes with special support for Jewish education.
(Courtesy of the Jewish Federation of Metropolitan Chicago.)

The industrial empire of the Crown family, of which Henry Crown (1896–1990) was the patriarch, started in 1919 when Henry and his brothers, Sol and Irving, started a building materials company, Material Service Corporation. Through the years Henry Crown acquired ownership of a number of buildings, including the Empire State Building, and also interests in a number of large concerns such as the Hilton Corporation, General Dynamics Corporation, and the Rock Island Railroad. He received numerous decorations for his service as a colonel in the Corps of Engineers in World War II.

Besides these very successful entrepreneurs, thousands of Jewish shopkeepers and craftsmen also contributed to the community, toiling long hours in their small food, drug, clothing, furniture, shoe, and dry goods stores to support their families and serve the neighbors they often knew so well. Their hard work in many cases allowed their more educated offspring to move into the higher ranks of the professions and industry. Today, however, small storekeepers, once a vital part of the livelihood of the Jewish community, are a vanishing breed, the victims of a rapidly changing society built around the automobile, the chain store, and the shopping mall.

### THE JEWISH LABOR MOVEMENT

Many thousands of the Eastern European Jews who poured into Chicago starting in the 1880s found work in the rapidly growing industries of the city, especially in the garment industry, where many were skilled laborers. As new

immigrants, they at first submitted to the exploitive "sweatshop" working conditions of that era. They contended with long hours, low pay, child labor, piecework at home, and abhorrent physical working conditions. In time, when they were no longer greenhorns, these workers – many of whom were imbued with values from their European populist, proletarian background – began to organize into unions whose members and leaders were largely Jewish. The unions vigorously fought the most unyielding employers by various means, including a number of bitter, prolonged strikes; and they generally helped bring about better conditions for the workers. A few of the Chicago-initiated unions became national in scope and models of progressiveness. In the clothing industry, labor leaders such as Sidney Hillman, Sam Smith, Bessie Abramowitz, Samuel Levin, Morris Bialis, Frank Rosenbaum, Jacob Potofsky, and others became national figures.

The Jews in the labor movement, unfettered by the restrictions and fears of the Old World, demonstrated a propensity for organization, sacrifice, and enlightened social thinking. As one Yiddish writer said about a major strike in the garment industry, "the 70,000 zeros became 70,000 fighters."[40]

The earliest Eastern European immigrants were often not employed in the clothing factories because of the strong hostility of the Irish and German women workers there to the "funny Jews," even though many of the factories were Jewish owned.[41] Instead, many of the Jews did piecework at home for the factories. In some cases, ten to fifteen people worked long hours in the home "sweatshop." By the 1890s, a demand for labor and a recognition of their skill and diligence enabled Jews to be employed in large numbers in the factories.

The Jewish labor movement in Chicago started in 1886, the landmark year in American labor history that saw the founding of the American Federation of Labor by Samuel Gompers, a Jewish immigrant from London. The movement's first major action in Chicago was calamitous. Labor unrest and social strife culminated in the city on May 4, 1886, in the disastrous Haymarket Riot, which resulted in the deaths of seven policemen and a number of McCormick Works strikers. The following day some four hundred immigrant cloakmakers, mainly Jewish, marched out of their Near West Side ghetto meeting-hall toward the Loop to protest intolerable living and working conditions. Unaware of the Haymarket events, they were met by police at the Van Buren Street bridge over the river. The marchers were beaten and clubbed and sent running back to the ghetto. The loosely knit union had received their "baptism by fire."[42]

Strikes called by the union were unsuccessful and the union floundered. In 1890 a new Chicago Cloak Makers Union received a state charter and became the city's first official Jewish union. Its success varied with conditions in the garment industry – an industry subject to severe seasonal fluctuations. However, the cloakmakers, with the help of Jane Addams and other socially conscious leaders, helped to achieve enactment of state labor legislation, which eliminated employment of children under the age of fourteen, prohibited women from working more than eight hours a day, and prevented the maintaining of a workshop and residence in common, some of the worst examples of the sweatshop. But there was little sustained continuity in the union.

Around the turn of the century, new attempts to organize the large number of Jewish immigrant workers employed mainly in the clothing industry were intermittent and not overly successful. A number of organizing attempts had been stymied by unyielding employers, many of whom were German or Hungarian Jews who had arrived in an earlier wave of immigration and who had already "made it." It was charged that the employers ruled imperiously over the "greenhorns" and profited richly from their labor. And although many of the employers made generous *tzedakah* contributions to Jewish philanthropies, the workers often felt that the contributions were made at their expense. One relatively ineffective early union was the United Garment Workers of America. However, from it, three major needle-trade unions emerged, each initially consisting of predominantly Jewish membership and leadership. The three are the Amalgamated Clothing Workers of America, the International Ladies Garment Workers' Union, and the United Hat, Cap, and Millinery Workers' Union. All three unions became well known for the progressive benefits they won for their members and for their social democratic philosophy.

The Amalgamated Clothing Workers of America, representing workers in the men's clothing industry, owes its beginning to the great garment strike of 1910 in Chicago, although the union was not officially established until 1914 when it parted from the United Garment Workers of America.[43] The 1910 strike was at first a spontaneous walkout started by sixteen women protesting dismal working conditions, long hours, and a cut in the piece rate for seaming pants. Compounding the protest against work and pay conditions was the seasonality of work, sometimes tyrannical foremen, and the lack of adequate employee-employer communication. Some equally discontented workers dropped their needles, left their benches and sewing machines, and poured out of the shops demanding better working conditions, recognition of the union, and collective bargaining. Soon forty thousand workers, 80 percent of them Jewish, were on strike against a number of manufacturers, including Hart, Schaffner and Marx, the large Jewish-owned men's clothing manufacturer. Ironically, the strike generally pitted the German Jewish factory owner against the largely Eastern European Jewish workforce. The bitter strike lasted seventeen weeks, during which two strikers were killed by strike breakers and many were injured, especially in altercations with the police. The strikers were encouraged and aided in their efforts by many Chicagoans, including Jane Addams, Ellen Gates Starr, Clarence Darrow, and Professor Charles E. Merriam of the University of Chicago, then a member of the city council. The strike against Hart, Schaffner and Marx was finally settled, with major issues sent to an arbitration committee to consider the workers' grievances and how to handle them in the future, when Joseph Schaffner became convinced that the strikers had been justified in their complaints. In a speech he stated:

> Careful study of the situation has led me to the belief that the fundamental cause of the strike was that the workers had no satisfactory channel through which minor grievances and petty tyrannies of underbosses . . . could be amicably adjusted.

The Hart, Schaffner and Marx men's clothing factory, 1930, where many of the immigrant Jews worked. (Courtesy of Hartmarx Corporation.)

Shortly before the strike was called I was so badly informed of the conditions that I called the attention of a friend to the satisfactory state of the employees. It was only a few days before the great strike of the Garment Workers broke out. When I found out later of the conditions that had prevailed, I concluded that the strike should have occurred much sooner.[44]

Two weeks later the other strikers went back to their jobs without obtaining the advantages gained by the Hart, Schaffner, and Marx workers. Other companies, affiliated with the Chicago Wholesale Clothiers Association, did not sign an agreement providing for a "preferential union shop," the forty-four-hour week, and arbitration machinery until 1919, after a number of additional bitter strikes. Shortly thereafter, the whole industry in the city was unionized and union membership rose to forty thousand. Because of his liberal view on labor, Joseph Schaffner was never forgiven by the other manufacturers and he was blackballed by one of their clubs.[45]

The major gains accrued from the strike were the establishment through the ensuing decades of amicable relations between the union and the industry and

the emergence of new, capable leadership among the garment workers. The coleaders of the strike were Sidney Hillman (1887–1946) and Bessie Abramowitz (1889–1970), who later became husband and wife. Hillman, an immigrant from Lithuania, went to work for Hart, Schaffner and Marx as an apprentice cutter. He later served for thirty years as president of the Amalgamated Clothing Workers of America and was one of the founders and a vice president of the Congress of Industrial Organizations. Hillman held high government positions under President Franklin D. Roosevelt and played a key role in the passage of labor legislation. Bessie Abramowitz served as a vice president of the Amalgamated Clothing Workers of America and was one of the foremost women activists in the labor movement.

Other Jewish strikers who became prominent labor leaders were Frank Rosenbaum, who later became secretary-treasurer of the union and a vice president of the CIO; Jacob Potofsky, who became the Amalgamated president in 1946 and also served as a vice president of the CIO; and Samuel Levin, who became a national union vice president and was very active both in the union and in civic affairs in Chicago. Levin was instrumental in the union's founding of the Amalgamated Trust and Savings Bank of Chicago in 1922, the first labor bank in the United States. Later he served as president of the Amalgamated insurance and social benefits programs. Sam Smith, from Moghiloff, Russia, as was Samuel Levin, was too young to participate in the 1910 strike, but he built a strong record of leadership in the union, including serving as international vice president, as well as involvement in the civic community. Sol Brandzel, an attorney and a more recent leader of the Amalgamated, has served on the governing board of the Chicago City Colleges, as president of the Chicago Board of Education, and as president of the midwest region of the American Jewish Congress.

*(Left) Bessie Abramovitz Hillman (1889–1970) was one of the leaders of the 1910 garment workers' strike in Chicago, when she was twenty-one. She became one of the foremost women activists in the labor movement and the wife of Sidney Hillman.*
(Courtesy of the Amalgamated Clothing Workers of America.)

*(Right) Sidney Hillman (1887–1946), a prominent progressive labor leader, was born in Lithuania. In Chicago he went to work for Hart, Schaffner and Marx and was a leader in the bitter garment workers' strike of 1910. Besides being a national labor leader, he also held a number of high government positions under President Franklin Roosevelt.*
(Courtesy of the Amalgamated Clothing Workers of America.)

Building on Van Buren Street in downtown Chicago which housed a number of companies in the garment industry, many Jewish-owned, 1979. Garment patterns are hanging in the second-floor windows.

(Photo by Irving Cutler.)

Workers in the women's clothing field were organized into a separate union, the International Ladies Garment Workers Union. Like the Amalgamated, the union was interested in providing educational, cultural, and social benefits for its members. It offered classes in English, citizenship, economics, and arts and crafts, as well as concerts by famous singers and musicians and lectures by prominent people. Workers received health, unemployment, and retirement benefits. An important leader of the union for decades was Morris Bialis, an immigrant from Tiktin, Poland. After heading the Chicago locals he became a vice president of the international union. He too found time to participate in various governmental activities and was appointed to a variety of governmental boards and commissions by Mayors Kelly and Daley, by Governors Horner and Stevenson, and by President Franklin D. Roosevelt.

The third and smallest of the "Big Three" in the needle trades was the United Hat, Cap, and Millinery Workers Union. Led by Sam Winn, an old-time cap-maker from Lithuania, the union was the first in the needle trades to achieve the forty-hour week for some of its workers. It pioneered, with management, product promotion campaigns and industry stabilization programs under which suicidal competitive practices were discouraged.[46] All of the needle-trades unions, after achieving union recognition and collective bargaining, developed a constructive and successful program of labor-management relations and industrial stability revolving around the arbitration of disputes.

In addition to the needle-trades unions, other unions comprised predominantly of Jewish members and leadership included the fur and leather work-

קלאוק מאכער דרעס און רעגען קוט מאכער לײדעס טײלערס

## דיא יניאן איז אין געפאר!

א מאססען מיטינג פון אלע אינטערנעשאנאל מעמבערס וועט אפגעהאל-
טען ווערען מאנטאג נאוועמבער דעם 15-טען, 1926, 8 אוהר אבענד אין לייבאר
ליסעאום, אגדען קארנער קעדזי עוועניוס.

שוועסטער און ברידער: —

עס איז פון דער גרעסטער וויכטיגקייט אז איהר זאלט אנוועזענד זײן בײ דיזען
מאססען פארזאמלונג וואו וויכטיגע פראגען וואס שטעלען אין געפאר דעם עקזיסטענץ
פון אונזער יוניאן באשפראכען ווערען.

שוועסטער און ברידער: —

עס האט גענומען לאנגע יאהרען פון שווערע ארבעט לײדען און נויט ביז אונזער
יוניאן איז אויפגעבױט געווארען צו זײן א ווירקזאמע וואפע געגען די אנדלונגען און
אטאקעס פון די באליבאטים.

ווילט איהר דערלאזען אז אונזער יוניאן זאל צובראכען ווערען?

אויב ניט קומט צום מאססען מיטינג.

מיט גרוס,

וו. דײלי, סעם לעדערמאן, מענדע פינבערג, דזש. האפמאן
פיליפ דייוידס

דזשאינט באארד דעלעגאטען

---

CLOAK, DRESS, RAIN COAT MAKERS AND LADIES TAILORS

# The Union is In Danger!

A MASS MEETING of all International members will be held ON
MONDAY EVENING, NOVEMBER 15th, 1926, 8 P. M. sharp, at the Labor
Lyceum, Ogden and Kedzie Avenues.

Sisters and Brothers, it is of the utmost importance that you be present
at this meeting.

Questions that is now up in our Union and that treatens the existance
of our Union will be discussed.

COME IN MASSES.                                        PROTECT YOUR UNION.

Brotherly yours.

W. DAYLY, SAM LEDERMAN, MANDY FINEBERG, J. HOFFMAN
and PHILIP DAVIDS

Joint Board Delegates

562

*A union poster, in English
and Yiddish, announcing a
mass meeting at the Work-
men's Circle Labor Lyceum,
1926.*

(Irving Cutler Collection.)

ers, the pocketbook and luggage workers, carpenters, bakers, cigar makers, fish
handlers, meat cutters, and *shochtem* (ritual slaughterers). Such unions were
confined to a limited number of industries where the workers were largely Jewish
immigrants. These local unions arose because members felt more accepted and
secure among their kinsmen, whereas in the general unions they may have experienced some hostility because of their religious and cultural differences and
because, as newly arrived immigrants, they often worked for lower wages.

Many of the Jewish labor leaders, especially those of Eastern European background, were inclined toward a socialist philosophy. The Jewish unions were
run for the most part democratically and also participated in and contributed

to many Jewish causes. They were also among the largest groups participating in the huge annual workers' May Day parades.

Jewish local unions fit in well in certain shops. In the cigar-making factory of Isaac Goldsmith, an Orthodox Jew, the "Sabbath was observed; and every pay-day was made a day of giving for the Jewish brethren in Palestine."[47]

The Jewish carpenters union was formed because the United Brotherhood of Carpentry and Joiners of America was unwilling to have Jews join its organization. In order to control the Jewish carpenters, however, it allowed for the chartering of a separate union, the Jewish Carpenters' Union, Local 504. Most of the Jewish carpenters initially came from the town of Motele in what is now Poland. In Chicago they formed their own synagogues, which they helped to construct.[48]

The United Hebrew Trades organization coordinated the work of Jewish trade unions. It served as an important force in helping to acclimate the immigrants to their new industrial jobs, in settling disputes between union members and between union officials, and in the 1920s in fighting against the attempted infiltration of communists into some of the unions.[49] In 1930 a factional fight developed within the United Hebrew Trades, leading to the formation of a new organization named the Federation of Jewish Trade Unions.

The Jewish trade unions affiliated with the new federation in the 1930s were:

Amalgamated Clothing Workers Union, Local 144
Bakers Union, Local 237
Capmakers Union, Local 5
Carpenters Union, Local 504
Cleaners and Dyers Union, Local 17742
Cantors Association, Local 19097
Egg Inspectors Union
Fish Handlers Union, Local 553
Fur Workers Union, Local 45
Hebrew Typographical Union, Local 903
Hebrew Waiters Union
Hebrew Butchers Union, Local 596
Hebrew Teachers Union
Hebrew Singers Union
I.L.G.W.U., Local 5
I.L.G.W.U., Local 18
I.L.G.W.U., Local 59
I.L.G.W.U., Local 100
Installment Canvassers Union
Meat Drivers and Helpers Union
Millinery Workers Union, Local 47
Millinery Workers Union, Local 52
Pocket Book Workers Union
Retail Food Clerks Union, Local 834
Shochtem Union, Local 598

Shoe Repairers Union
Sausage Workers Union, Local 485
Y. L. Peretz Writers Union, Local 17886

The *Jewish Daily Forward,* with its extensive Jewish immigrant readership, strongly backed and spoke for the Jewish trade unions. Its labor editor, Morris Seskind, a former cigarmaker, printed union news daily and was a tireless reporter and organizer for Jewish trade unions, which he felt were a means of lessening worker exploitation and bringing about economic justice.

The Chicago Labor College, organized in 1934, was a pioneer effort to help educate the workers further so that they could better participate in union and civic affairs. It was housed in a Loop office building and at its peak had a student body of several thousand, who were members of various local unions, and a staff of over twenty teachers. One of its teachers was a young lawyer, Leon Despres, who was to serve a number of terms as the respected alderman from the Hyde Park area.

Jews were also involved in non-Jewish labor unions. Among the most active was Lillian Herstein (1886–1983), a dynamic suffragist, teacher, and organizer of the Chicago Teachers Union and one of the founders of the American Civil Liberties Union. In 1937 Miss Herstein was appointed by President Roosevelt as the American representative to the International Labor Organization in Geneva, Switzerland. That same year *Life* magazine called her "the most important woman in the American Labor movement." Arthur Goldberg, who had an illustrious record of labor advocacy as counsel for various labor groups, including the CIO and the United Steel Workers of America, was one of Miss Herstein's students, as were Studs Terkel and Leon Uris.

In time, as most of the Jewish immigrants passed from the scene and were replaced in the workforce by more recent immigrant groups after World War II, the need for Jewish labor unions declined and one by one they disbanded. The children of the immigrants were no longer factory workers; many were in business or the professions. Some of the union activities have been assumed by the Jewish Labor Committee, which today "maintains the principle that the human rights of the Jews are best aided through the human rights of all."[50]

The legacy of the Jewish labor unions is not only the improvement in wages and working conditions won for their members, but also the morals, ethics, and principles of social caring by which they were governed – almost invariably without a hint of scandal. The outstanding leaders they produced carried these ethics to the national scene. The Chicago Jewish labor unions, in the uncertain era of the struggling immigrants, fostered courage, tenacity, and high ideals. However, the radicalism and revolutionary zeal that many of the Jewish laborers had displayed in Russia were not necessary in America, where there was much more freedom and opportunity. Instead of focusing solely on the traditional bread-and-butter issues, the unions reached out broadly to become centers of social and cultural life with educational programs, cooperative housing, social insurance, and Yiddishist activities. They also fought for dignity; one ten-day strike was called to make the boss agree "to speak to the girls as he would

אַגרימענט

בעקערי און קאנפעקשיאנערי ווארקערס יוניאן לאקאל 237.
שיקאגא, איל.

דיזער אַגרימענט איז געשלאסען צווישען דעם לאקאל 237 פון די בעקערס
און קאנפעקשיאנערי אַרבייטער אינטערנייַשאָנאל יוניאן און די מאסטער בעקערס
פון שיקאגא, איל.

יעדער אייגענטימער פון א בעקעריי וועמען דער לאקאל 237 גיט אַרויס
דעם יוניאן לייבעל פון דער בעקערס און קאנפעקשיאנערי אינטערנייַשאָנאל
יוניאן פון אמעריקא, איז פאַרפליכטעט נאכצוקומען פאלגענדע פונקטען:

.1 צו באַשעפטיגען נאר אַזעלכע אַרבייטער, וועלכע זיינען גוטשטעהענד
אין דער דערמאָנטער יוניאן, און צו באַקומען זייערע אַרבייטער דורך דעם
אפיס פון דעם יוניאן לאקאל 237.

.2 דער אייגענטימער פון א בעקער איז נים ניט ערלויבט צו האַלטען
ביי זיך קיין אַרבייטער אויף קעסט אדער וואהנונג.

.3 נים צו פארלאַנגען פון די וו צו מאן וועלכע עס איז אַרבייט אויסער-
האלב דעם שאפ.

### אַרבייטס שטונדען :

.4 א) צו אַרבעטען בלויז 6 טעג אין וואך און 8 שטונדען אין טאג.

.4 ב) אין גרויסע שעפער וואו עס זיינען פאראן סקיילערס און מאלדערס
זאל די אַרבעטם צייט זיין בלויז 6 טעג א וואך, מ'ל 7½ שטונדען א טאג.

.4 ג) נים צו אַרבעטען אין ערשטן מאי.

### ווירדושעס :

.5 דער מינימום רייט פון א וואר ווירדושעס פאר ברויט, קייקס און
ביינעל, זאל זיין ווי פאלגט:

| | |
|---|---|
| פארמאן | $81.00 |
| צווייטע האנט | $78.00 |
| דריטע האנט | $67.00 |

.6 יעדער ארויסחעלפער, וועלכער ווערט נעשיקט פאר א באס זאל קריגען
באצאלט: $14.00 בענטש מאן און $14.50 א טאן אלס פארמאן.

.7 אווערטיים זאל ערלויבט זיין נאר אין א נויטפאל, און זאל באצאלט
ווערן טיים און האלב.

.8 נאכט אַרבעט וואס ווערט געטאן צווישן 7 אוהר אווענט און 6
אוהר פריהמארגען, זאל געצאָלט ווערן לויט די רעגולע סקייל, ווי אין סעקשאן
5 און א עקסטרא באצאלונג פון 15 סענט פאר יעדער שטונדע.

.9 דער פארמאן, אדער דער שעף רעגולעגעט אדער דער ערשטער אַרבייטער,
זאל האבען די אויפזיכט איבער די לייבעלס און זאל זיין פאראנטווארטליך
פאר די צו די בעקערי און קאנפעקשיאנערי יוניאן לאקאל 237.

---

## Agreement
### OF BAKERY AND CONFECTIONERY WORKERS
### INTERNATIONAL UNION LOCAL NO. 237
#### OF CHICAGO, ILLINOIS

This agreement made and entered into this date, as signed below between Local 237 of the Bakery and Confectionery Workers' International Union of America and the Master Bakers of Chicago, Ill.

Every proprietor of the bakery to whom Local 237 issues the union label of the B. & C. W. I. U. of A. is obliged to observe the following conditions:

1st. To employ only such bakers as are in good standing in the mentioned Union, and to secure their employes through the office of Local Union No. 237.

2nd. Not to board or room any journeymen bakers.

3rd. Not to request from any baker worker to do any work outside the bakery.

#### WORKING CONDITIONS

4th. (a) To work six days a week, eight hours shall constitute a day's work.

4th. (b) In larger bakeries, where scalers and molders are used, 7½ hours shall be the regular working day and six days a week.

4th. (c) Not to work on the First of May.

#### WAGES

5th. The minimum rate of wages per week on bread, cakes, and baigel shall be as follows:

| | |
|---|---|
| Foreman | $81.00 and not less |
| Second Hand | 78.00 |
| Third Hand | 67.00 |

6th. Substitutes that work for a boss shall receive the following pay: Foreman $15.00 and Bench hands $14.00 per day.

7th. Overtime shall be allowed only in time of an emergency. Such overtime shall be compensated at the rate of time and one-half.

8th. Night work performed between the hours of 7 P. M. and 6 A. M., shall be paid for at the regular scale as in section 5 above plus extra compensation of 15 cents per hour.

---

*A labor agreement in English and in Yiddish, between the Jewish bakery workers and the bakery owners, spelling out working conditions and wages, c. 1940.*
*(Courtesy Richard W. Laner.)*

to his own daughters."[51] As Jewish editor J. C. Rich pointed out, in those early days "the Union was as holy an institution as the synagogue had been to their fathers. Only this kind of devotion could have carried them through the long and bitter strikes marked by hunger, cold and brutal assaults of police and hired thugs."[52]

In labor, as in commerce, the arts, and the professions, the Jews have been important contributors. However with increased Americanization, strong emphasis on education, the decline of certain industries, and ever-widening opportunities in many fields, the number of Jewish skilled and unskilled laborers decreased as increasing numbers of Jews qualified for more challenging and rewarding roles in other fields. The sharp decline of Jewish union workers also led to the decline of Jewish labor leaders, although many Jewish labor lawyers remain in the field.

# 5

# The Last Half-Century

## Changing Neighborhoods and Lifestyles

DECLINING DIVERSITY AND

SHARED CONCERNS

Just before the outbreak of World War II, the Jewish population of Chicago was approaching an estimated 300,000, or about 9 percent of Chicago's population. About 110,000 were then living in the greater Lawndale area, in the largest and most developed Jewish community that ever existed in Chicago. Most of the families had moved there earlier from the Maxwell Street area. There were also other areas of significant Jewish populations. These included those on the North Side – the Lakeview–Uptown–Rogers Park area (27,000); the Northwest Side – the West Town–Humboldt Park–Logan Square (35,000) and Albany Park–North Park areas (27,000); and on the South Side – the Kenwood–Hyde Park–Woodlawn–South Shore area (28,000). Smaller Jewish communities were situated in Austin (7,000), Englewood–Greater Grand Crossing (4,000), and Chatham–Avalon Park–South Chicago (3,000).[1] Small num-

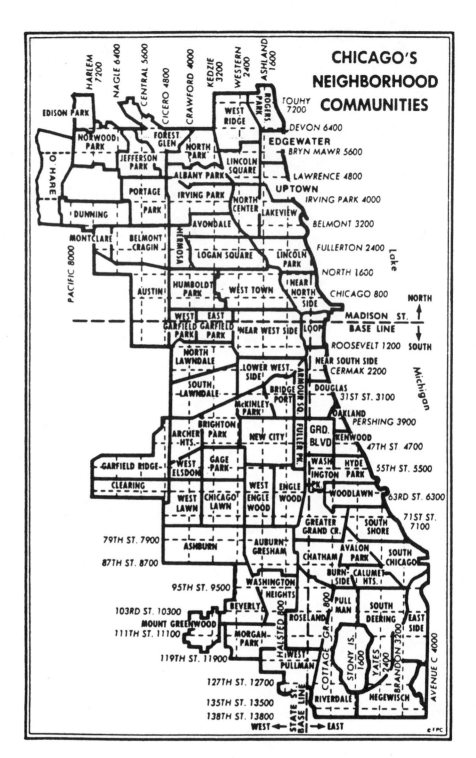

**CHICAGO'S NEIGHBORHOOD COMMUNITIES**

*Chicago's neighborhood communities. Only about ten of these seventy-seven communities – mainly north along the lake, on the far north side, and in the Hyde Park–Kenwood area – now have substantial numbers of Jews.*

(Adapted from M. S. Ratz and C. H. Wilson, *Exploring Chicago*, Follett Publishing Company, 1958.)

*(Opposite page) Synagogue distribution in Chicago, 1888, 1918, 1948, and 1978. The changing patterns reflect the changing residential locations of Chicagoland's Jewish population. Each dot represents one synagogue location.*

(Map by Joseph Kubal.)

bers of Jews also lived in Roseland, Chicago Lawn, and scattered sites on the Near North Side, the Southwest Side, and in other communities of the Northwest Side, as well as in the suburbs. Each of the Jewish neighborhoods of Chicago had distinct characteristics, but they were to decline or even disappear as Jewish neighborhoods in the next few decades.

Differences among neighborhoods and between Germans and Eastern Europeans were not the only distinctions among the Jews of the pre–World War II period. The Eastern European Jews were themselves divided into those who

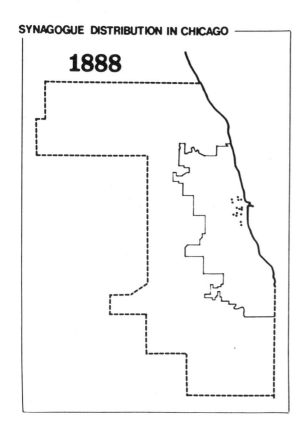

SYNAGOGUE DISTRIBUTION IN CHICAGO

**1888**

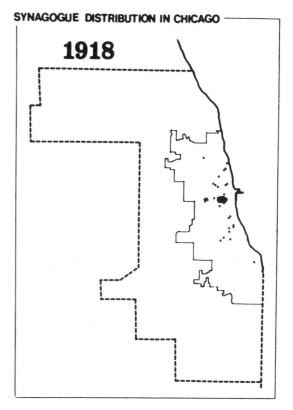

SYNAGOGUE DISTRIBUTION IN CHICAGO

**1918**

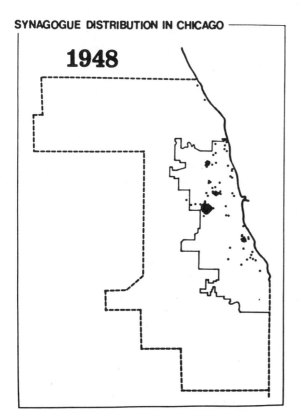

SYNAGOGUE DISTRIBUTION IN CHICAGO

**1948**

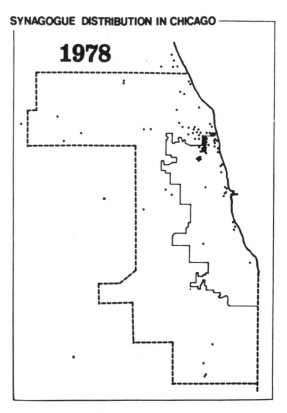

SYNAGOGUE DISTRIBUTION IN CHICAGO

**1978**

were from Lithuania, Poland, Ukraine, Bessarabia, Galicia, Latvia, and other
regions. Reflecting these different homelands, the Eastern Europeans differed
in such ways as the Yiddish dialect they spoke, their religious practices, their
seasoning of gefilte fish, and their cutting of farfel. There were even Yiddish

songs written about these differences, including one dealing with the Litvak (Lithuanian Jew) versus the Galitzianer (Galician Jew). Besides the German and Eastern European Jews, there were also several thousand Sephardic Jews from the Mediterranean and the Middle East. Today the Sephardim still maintain three congregations, one each in West Rogers Park, Evanston, and Skokie. While they are a majority in Israel, in Chicago they are a minority within a minority and have found it difficult not to be absorbed by the larger Ashkenaz Jewish community; many have married Ashkenazi Jews. However, in recent years there has been some immigration of Sephardic Jews from Israel, Egypt, and Iran who have become part of the Chicago Sephardic community. As a survival measure, some of the Sephardic synagogues, past and present, have restricted membership to Sephardic Jews. However, worshipping is open to all.

Jews in Chicago were also divided along major lines of observance and belief – Orthodox, Conservative, and Reform. There were additionally Traditional, Hasidic, Reconstructionist, and secular Jews, Zionists and anti-Zionists, radicals and conservatives, employees and employers, and aspiring assimilationists and ardent Yiddishists. Economically, the Jews of the South Side had the highest income, followed in order by those of the North Side, the Northwest Side, and the West Side.[2] Economic well-being correlated generally with distance from the city center, with notable exceptions. Religious observance ranged from the most Orthodox area, Lawndale, to the South Side, where Reform Judaism was the strongest in the city.

Many of the differences among the Jews stemmed from the Old World and declined as the large immigrant generations passed from the scene and were replaced by their more Americanized offspring in the latter half of this century. But despite some lingering diversity, the Jews were unified after World War II by the need to aid European Jewish refugees and by their strong concern for the security of the State of Israel. The independence of Israel in 1948 and the Sinai Campaign in 1956 mobilized a wide spectrum of Jewish support. The 1967 Six-Day War between Israel and five Arab nations had Jews in Chicago worried, tense, and glued to their radios and television sets until the war ended. That war inspired Chicago Jews to an unprecedented outpouring of money for Israel. Chicago ranked second only to New York in contributions, and donors included thirteen thousand families not normally on the Combined Jewish Appeal lists. Thousands also bought Israel bonds. Similar strong support for Israel totaling over sixty million dollars came from the Chicago Jewish community during the Yom Kippur War of 1973, when the surprise attack by Syria and Egypt caused initial setbacks but was turned into a decisive Israeli victory. Support for Israel was also manifested in other ways, such as by demonstrations, including one in which ten thousand Jews rallied outside of the Palmer House in 1970 to protest the visit of French President Pompidou to Chicago because of his country's Middle East policy.

Several other issues confronted the Chicago Jews in the post–World War II period. There were sporadic acts of vandalism and continual anti-Semitic propaganda by groups like the American Nazis and by such Black Muslim leaders as Louis Farrakhan. Despite Jews' active efforts through the years in helping the blacks and taking part in the civil rights movement, black-Jewish relations began to deteriorate. In the turbulent period of the Vietnam War many Jewish youths participated in the antiwar demonstrations, as they later did in the movement to free Soviet Jews. The Jewish community also faced vexing problems dealing with assimilation, alienation, intermarriage, education, and church-state separation.

In the post–World War II years, thousands of Jews, mainly the elderly, still lived in poverty, but as a whole the Jewish community prospered. Many shared their prosperity by contributing generously to Jewish and other causes, although critics sometimes charged that the chief Jewish contribution of some people was only "checkbook Judaism." But despite this criticism, as the decades rolled by, Chicago's Jewish community developed from meager beginnings to a highly organized, caring network of institutions serving various needs of Jews both at home and abroad. These institutions were supported by a relatively high percentage of the Jewish population who, in the 1980s, contributed about a half billion dollars to the Jewish United Fund. In 1976 on the occasion of the nation's bicentennial, Maynard Wishner, chairman of the Public Affairs Committee of the Jewish United Fund, wrote an article entitled "In Praise of Ourselves," which recounted a great achievement of American Jewish life.

Let's take a moment off from our fund raising, bond selling, card calling, priority setting, assimilation resisting, rally holding, petition gathering, anti-Semitism fighting, Jewish children educating, United Nations condemning, letter to the editor (and Congressman) writing, Jewish identifying, dinner honoring, Jewish establishment attacking, and advice to Israel giving, to *shep* a little *naches* from ourselves. It's our Bicentennial too – and look at what we have wrought.

We came with *pecklach* on our backs from *shtetlach* and *derfer* from Kasrilivke and Yehupetz and from "civilized" places too, like Berlin and Vienna. We were fragmented, subcultured, non-English speaking, frequently oddly dressed, most of us vocationally unskilled. We clustered together for warmth in fraternal associations and *landsmanschaften* with fellow townsmen sharing a common recollection of *der haim.*

But, ever since the very first one of us encountered a nasty Peter Stuyvesant, every succeeding one of us found someone else who had come before, and had us on his agenda of concern. And as soon as we got here, we were already concerned about those left behind, those that went elsewhere, and those who were still coming. . . .

So happy birthday, America! . . . . and *mazel tov* to us too![3]


THE SOUTH SIDE

The most affluent of the Jewish communities in Chicago in the pre–World War II period was in the Hyde Park–Kenwood area, with a growing spillover farther south into the South Shore community. Over 80 percent of the Jews of the South Side lived in these areas in the 1940s, and the Jewish population of

# MAJOR SOUTH SIDE JEWISH INSTITUTIONS - 1955

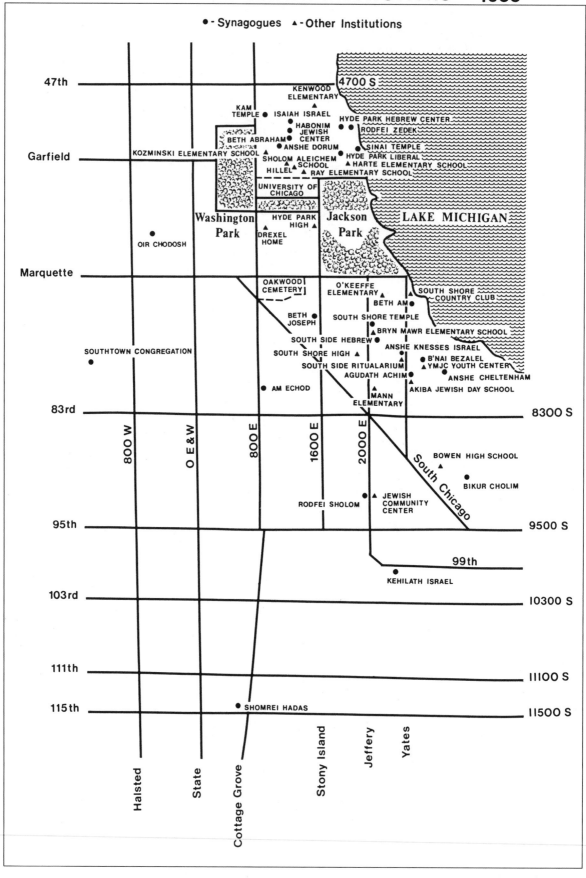

●-Synagogues  ▲-Other Institutions

these neighborhoods had increased over 50 percent from 1930 to 1946. Located near the lake with its beaches and parks, near the University of Chicago, and with good transportation to the Loop, especially via the Illinois Central Electric Railroad, these communities housed the bulk of the German Jewish community. Many of these people owned their own homes but most lived in large apartments or in the fine residential hotels near the lake. Some were the descendants of the first Jewish settlers in Chicago, were generally well established in business or the professions, and had through the years gradually moved southward into the Hyde Park–Kenwood communities. Some had come from communities directly to the west, Grand Boulevard and Washington Park – communities whose growth spurted with the coming of the South Side elevated line in 1892. In the latter two communities in particular, in the early decades of the century, there were imposing synagogues and Jewish residences arrayed along streets such as Indiana, Michigan, and Grand Boulevard (now Dr. Martin Luther King Jr. Drive), until the communities began changing racially. By 1930, blacks comprised over 90 percent of each of the two communities, whereas in 1920 they had numbered just 15 percent in Washington Park and 32 percent in Grand Boulevard.

The German Jews of the South Side were later joined by a minority of Eastern European Jews, who started trickling into the "Golden Ghetto" after World War I. The Jewish population of Hyde Park–Kenwood, about 13,000 in 1930, was also bolstered in the 1930s and 1940s by an influx of refugees from Nazi Germany. Some of these 12,000 to 15,000 German Jews had been helped by Chicago relatives to come to America. At first most of them settled on the South Side, especially in the Hyde Park area, where there were German Jews living. There they established social welfare agencies, such as the Self Help Home for the Aged, and religious institutions, among them Congregation Habónim and the Hyde Park Liberal Congregation, later to become Temple B'nai Yehuda. They opened Old World–style stores such as Bachenheimer's Delicatessen and Nachmann's Candies and Pastries along Fifty-third Street. In a relatively short time they integrated into American life and many became highly successful in their businesses and professions.

The main commercial streets of the Hyde Park area were Fifty-third, Fifty-fifth, and Fifty-seventh streets, which also served thousands of University of Chicago students. Interspersed among the bookstores, taverns, and theaters (such as the Compass Players, which spawned Second City and such stars as Elaine May, Mike Nichols, Shelley Berman, and David Steinberg) were a number of Jewish-owned bakeries, delicatessens, fish stores, and butcher shops. Near the lake were high-rise apartment hotels such as the Shoreland, Sherry, Del Prado, and the Windermeres (East and West). Further south opposite Jackson Park was the highly-rated Hyde Park High School, which most of the area's students attended after graduating from local elementary schools, which included Ray, Harte, Kenwood, and Kozminski. Hyde Park High School was actually in Woodlawn, which until the late 1940s had a small Jewish population.

The University of Chicago, with its broad range of classes, starting with nursery classes at the laboratory school, was an intellectual stimulus to the

*The Nathan Goldblatt Memorial Hospital is one of the numerous University of Chicago facilities funded by Jewish donors.*

(Courtesy of the University of Chicago.)

community. Typically, Jewish students, faculty, and staff at the university numbered over 2,000; Jewish students usually made up from 20 to 25 percent of the student body and Jewish faculty members comprised a somewhat higher percentage of the teaching staff. The university was a source of countless lectures, movies, plays, rallies, and social and athletic events, including ice skating in the winter on the Midway.

Many of the Jewish students would congregate at the Hillel Foundation

building on Woodlawn Avenue for religious services (Orthodox, Conservative, Reform, and a women's minyan), kosher meals, social interaction, Jewish causes, study, and discussion. Hillel also sponsored the annual great *Latke* versus *Hamentash* Debate at the University of Chicago. An exercise in parody that attracts some five hundred people, the debate was started in 1946 by Rabbi Maurice Pekarsky, the university's first Hillel director (serving 1944–62), and carried on by Rabbi Daniel Leifer, director at Hillel since 1964. People come to listen to a number of distinguished professors present satirical academic papers, often in relation to their disciplines, on the psychological, sociological, metaphysical, historical, economic, medical, and even religious relative virtues of the *Latke* and the *Hamentash,* gastronomical delights of Hanukkah and Purim, respectively. Usually one gentile professor also participates to add a "note of gentility" to the symposium.[4]

The University of Chicago has had numerous Jewish faculty members, some renowned in their field. Six have received the Nobel Prize: Albert Michaelson (1907, physics), the first American to be so honored in that field; Saul Bellow (1976, literature); Milton Friedman (1976, economics); Leon Lederman, from the university-managed Fermilab (1988, physics); Gary S. Becker (economics, 1992); and Robert W. Fogel (1993, economics).

Jews who made large financial contributions to the university have included Mandel, Rosenwald, Pick, Crown, Rubloff, Kersten, Klutznick, Epstein, Pritzker, Goldblatt, Regenstein, Cummings, Mitchell, and Kuppenheimer.

The German Jews who had moved to the South Side in an earlier period had advanced swiftly socially and economically and had established their own par-

Kehilath Anshe Maariv–
Isaiah Israel resulted from
the merger through the years
of a number of congrega-
tions, including the two
oldest in Chicago, KAM
(established 1847) and B'nai
Sholom (1852). Also part of
the merger were Temple
Israel (1894) and Temple
Isaiah (1895). This present
building at Hyde Park
Boulevard and Greenwood
Avenue was designed by
Alfred Alschuler in a modified
Byzantine style and was
dedicated in 1924.
(Photo by Irving Cutler.)

ticular institutions. As early as 1884 they had organized the Lakeside Club, a
social club that later moved into a palatial clubhouse at Forty-second Street and
Grand Boulevard. In 1893 the Drexel Home for the Aged was started at Sixty-
second Street and Drexel Avenue. In 1899 the Chicago Home for Jewish Orphans opened on the same block. The following year, the German Jewish community organized the Ravisloe Country Club in south suburban Homewood.
Its beautiful grounds and clubhouse made it the foremost Jewish club of its type
in the area, and it included among its members the most prominent and wealthiest Jewish families.

The Hirsch, Rosenwald, Adler, Florsheim, Schaffner, Mandel, Heineman,
Kestenbaum, Leopold, Loeb, Franks, and other prominent Jewish families lived
in the Hyde Park–Kenwood area during the early decades of the 1900s. Most
lived in Kenwood, which because of its stately homes and pastoral, suburban-
like surroundings was often referred to as the "Lake Forest of Chicago." The
Leopold, Loeb, and Frank families, all active in the community and philanthropic, were to become household names in the 1920s due to the notorious
"crime of compulsion" involving their sons; Richard Loeb, 17, and Nathan
Leopold, 18, murdered Robert Franks, 14.

The German Jews of Hyde Park–Kenwood and surrounding areas usually
belonged to one of the three large Reform temples in the vicinity – Temples
Sinai, Kehilath Anshe Maariv (KAM), and Isaiah Israel, where Rabbis Louis
Mann, Jacob Weinstein, and Morton Berman, respectively, were long-term
spiritual leaders. In the 1930s the rabbi at KAM was Joshua Loth Liebman, who
later became nationally famous through the great success of his book *Peace of
Mind.*

Sinai and KAM had followed the Jewish population southward from their
downtown sites. Isaiah Israel resulted from the merger of the two congregations,
Isaiah and Israel, whose synagogues had been built in the 1890s just a few blocks

*Rodfei Zedek Congregation was organized in 1874 in the stockyard area, where it was housed in a store. After a series of easterly moves, it reached its present location at 5200 Hyde Park Boulevard in 1950.*

(Photo by Irving Cutler.)

from each other in the Grand Boulevard area. In the 1920s they moved into Hyde Park. Social life in the Hyde Park area frequently centered around the synagogues. Meetings, ceremonies, and dances were also held in the large hotels near the lake. Outdoor activity often concentrated along the Midway, in Washington Park, or Jackson Park, especially at "The Point," a promontory at Fifty-fifth Street and the lake in Jackson Park.

By the end of World War II there were nine synagogues in the Hyde Park area. In addition to the large Reform temples, there were a number of smaller Orthodox synagogues and the large Conservative congregation, Rodfei Zedek. The latter had been founded in the stockyard area in 1874 and was moved into Hyde Park in 1925. Its rabbi for about a half century was Rabbi Ralph Simon.

Rodfei Zedek was one of the earliest Conservative congregations in Chicago. The Conservative movement started growing in the United States toward the end of the nineteenth century and, like the Reform, was formulated to adjust to contemporary conditions. The difference was that the Conservative movement maintained more of the traditional practices and spirit of historical Judaism than did the Reform movement. Conservative Judaism used more of the Hebrew language and adhered more fully to the traditional liturgy and religious holidays. It did, however, allow for some major changes from the Orthodox, including mixed seating of men and women during worship services, the confirmation of girls, the sermon and some prayers in English, and generally broader interpretation of the Codes of Jewish Law. It not only modified strict Orthodox practices but also was a reaction against the extreme changes that had been instituted by Reform Judaism. Many American-born children of Eastern European Jews were attracted to the Conservative philosophy because it reconciled some of the traditions of their youth with their acculturation in America.[5] Many of Chicago's Conservative synagogues, including Rodfei Zedek, start-

Students at the Sholem Aleichem School, 5558 South Greenwood Avenue in Hyde Park, 1947. The Yiddish folk school was established after Eastern European Jews started moving into the area, which for a number of decades had contained numerous German Jews. (Courtesy of Phyllis Goldman.)

ed out as Orthodox synagogues, as did some Reform synagogues. Like the other Jewish denominations, the Conservative movement in Chicago maintains a system of schools, a summer camp, and a variety of auxiliary organizations. It is generally considered the largest of the three major movements.

The Conservative and Orthodox synagogues that were later built in the Hyde Park–Kenwood area and the Sholom Aleichem School for children were signs that increasing numbers of Eastern European Jews were moving into the area. This change and the change in the racial composition of the Hyde Park–Kenwood area and adjacent communities after World War II were some of the reasons that the German Jews began to leave the area, moving further south or to the fashionable North Shore suburbs, where a few of the wealthier families had already established summer homes early in this century. This movement gained momentum when Julius Rosenwald bought an estate in Ravinia in 1912. He used it mainly as a summer home, but it became the core of a larger complex when homes were later built there for his son and daughter and their families.

The Jewish population of Hyde Park–Kenwood, numbering about 15,000 in 1950, started to decline rapidly in the late 1950s as the racial composition of the area began to change after the long-standing Cottage Grove Avenue boundary between blacks and whites was broken. Restrictive covenants by then were illegal. However, a determined effort by the community and the University of Chicago, backed by government subsidies, has stabilized and integrated the community racially, eliminated many of the rundown structures (many of which had been subdivided during the postwar housing shortage ), and replaced them

*The Drexel Home for the Aged opened in 1893 at Sixty-second Street and Drexel Avenue.*
(Photo by Irving Cutler.)

with new residential buildings. As a result, Hyde Park–Kenwood, unlike most other former Jewish neighborhoods, still contains a viable Jewish community. Estimated at about 7,000, the Jewish population is smaller than it had been and is concentrated largely in the eastern part near the lake. Some of the residents are former Hyde Parkers who lived for a period further south and have returned. The three remaining synagogues – KAM–Isaiah Israel, Sinai, and Rodfei Zedek – are among the most venerable in the city; the first two are the oldest in Chicago. Many of their members now live outside of the immediate area. The Jewish community, now composed mainly of elderly, lifelong residents and much younger people often connected with the university, helps support the three synagogues, the Akiba-Schechter Day School, two Jewish nursery schools, a small Jewish community center, and the very active B'nai B'rith Hillel Foundation at the university. However, one of these synagogues, the five-hundred-member Sinai, is planning to move into a newly constructed building on the Near North Side where many of its member now live.

The Drexel Home for the Aged at Drexel Avenue and Sixty-second Street, an important facility whose earliest residents were primarily German Jews, closed in 1981 and many of its latter-day residents were transferred to the new Lieberman Geriatric Health Centre in Skokie. At the time of its closing, the average age of its residents was eighty-seven, with forty-five of them over ninety years old.

Farther south, along the lake, the Chicago community of South Shore for almost half a century had a growing, cohesive Jewish population that reached about 20,000 in the 1950s, up from 11,000 in 1930. Eventually the majority were people of Eastern European descent. Rapid racial change started around 1960 when the Stony Island Avenue boundary between blacks and whites was broken. Community housing ranged from sections with fine single-family homes to areas with spacious three-story apartments, as well as the occasional tall apart-

*South Side Hebrew Congregation and its community house at Seventy-fourth and Chappel in the South Shore area. The congregation was organized in 1888 and was originally on State Street near Thirty-first Street. In a series of moves southward with the Jewish population, it relocated into South Shore, where it remained for over forty years, and then in 1970 moved to the Near North Side, where it is the Central Synagogue of South Side Hebrew Congregation.* (Photo by Irving Cutler.)

ment and residential hotel buildings nearer the lakefront. Parts of the broader area were known as Jackson Park Highlands and Windsor Park. Jackson Park Highlands, in the northern part of the community near the park, was an especially attractive residential area with stately, high-priced single-family homes.

When the Jewish population was at its highest there were about a dozen synagogues in the South Shore area, divided among Reform, Conservative, and Orthodox. There were also other institutions such as Jewish schools and community centers. Among the larger synagogues in the area were South Shore Temple (Reform) on Jeffery Boulevard (founded in 1922 as the area's first synagogue) and South Side Hebrew Congregation (Conservative) on Chappel Avenue, which moved from the Washington Park area. The major commercial street was Seventy-first Street, which had the Illinois Central tracks running down the center. A number of Jewish butcher shops, bakeries, and delicatessens flourished along that artery and, to a lesser extent, along Seventy-fifth and Seventy-ninth streets. Students chiefly attended the O'Keeffe, Bryn Mawr, Bradwell, Parkside, and Mann elementary schools and the highly ranked Hyde Park or South Shore high schools. South Shore had developed a type of infrastructure and range of activities that duplicated those found in most of the larger Jewish communities. Following the postwar influx of Jews, the intersection at Seventy-sixth and Phillips Avenue contained a large youth center sponsored by the Young Men's Jewish Council and two conservative synagogues, Congregation Habonim and Congregation B'nai Bezalel. The center (1954–72) housed many of the area's youth groups, which included numerous AZAs (B'nai B'rith youth organizations), and its amateur stage productions. One featured performer was Mandy Patinkin, who later achieved fame in Hollywood and in the theater. Patinkin later wrote that his career started at the youth center. His cousin, Sheldon Patinkin, is prominent in the entertainment field as a theatrical director and as one of the founders of Second City.

The initial Jewish population of South Shore was largely Reform or Conservative, as were most of the synagogues. However, starting about 1950, many Orthodox Jews of Eastern European descent began to move from Lawndale into South Shore. They established the Torah Synagogue, Anshe Kanesses Israel (the name of the giant Russische Shul in Lawndale), at Seventy-fifth and Yates Avenue. Soon there was the South Side's only *mikvah,* next door to the synagogue, and nearby was a Shomer Shabbos bakery, a Bnei Akiva youth group, an Akiba Day School – all supported by a viable Orthodox community that was largely concentrated in the area between Seventy-first and Seventy-ninth streets, from Jeffrey to Yates.

The South Shore community changed racially from less than 1 percent black in 1950 to about 70 percent black in 1970. Most of the Jews had left by the early 1970s, and only a few remain in the area, mainly in apartments near the lake or in the fine homes in the "Highlands" just south of Jackson Park. There are no synagogues left. A number of congregations relocated on the North Side of the city. The Orthodox were among the last to leave.

In South Chicago, the adjacent community to the south, where Jewish store owners and a small number of Jewish steelworkers once lived, Congregation Agudath Achim-Bikur Cholem continues to barely exist at 8927 South Houston, in what is now virtually an all-Mexican neighborhood. It has occupied the same building since 1902. It has the distinction of being the city's oldest synagogue building in continuous use. Until the 1950s, when ethnic and racial changes took place, the surrounding neighborhood still had a kosher meat market, a bakery, and Workmen's Circle organization. Today, Agudath Achim-Bikur Cholem is the only remaining synagogue in the quadrant of Chicago from approximately Fifty-fifth Street south and from Kedzie Avenue east. In recent decades it drew its very small and declining membership from a wide area of the city and outlying areas, including northwest Indiana. Since 1994 it has been sharing its building with a black Hebrew congregation that has a membership of about forty-five families. The few remaining members of the original congregation, unable to attain a minyan, attend the services of the black Hebrew congregation.

South Chicago was the site of one of the worst instances of anti-Semitism in Chicago history, at the time of the infamous trial of Mendel Beilis in Russia in 1913. Beilis had been accused of the "ritual" murder of a Russian boy to get blood to make matzos, and a similar rumor spread around Passover time among the largely Polish population in the "Bush" area of South Chicago. Jewish stores were boycotted and Jews feared to leave their homes. On one occasion horse-drawn fire engines came into the area and firefighters turned their hoses on a crowd of Poles to disperse them. Davy Miller, a tough fight referee from the West Side and a defender of mistreated Jews, finally dispelled the rumor about the alleged murder. He asked the parish priest of the Polish people to inquire from the pulpit if any of the parishioners' children were missing. There was no response to the question and calm returned to the neighborhood.[6]

For a time after World War II other small Jewish communities flourished south of South Shore, among them South Shore Gardens, Merrionette Man-

*Agudath Achim-Bikur Cholem, located in South Chicago near the steel mills, has been in this building since 1902, making it the oldest synagogue building in continuous use in the Chicago area. In the 1970s, Agudath Achim South Shore merged with Bikur Cholem. The synagogue continues barely to exist even though there are no longer any Jews in the community and the members come from distant areas. The building is now shared with a black Hebrew congregation.*

(Photo by Irving Cutler.)

or, Jeffery Manor, and South Shore Valley. Pill Hill, located on a limestone ridge within South Shore Valley, in an area bordered by Jeffery Boulevard and Stony Island Avenue and by Eighty-seventh and Ninety-third streets, got its name because many Jewish doctors lived in the area's fine, single-family homes. Near the center of Pill Hill, all four homes at the intersection of Ninety-second Street and Bennett Avenue were occupied by doctors. Many of the physicians who resided in Pill Hill were connected with the various medical facilities of the Calumet industrial district. Among the district's institutions were the Henry Hart Jewish Community Center and Congregation Rodfei Sholom. Jeffery Manor, a new but less affluent area of duplexes, small homes, and townhouses, was located south of Ninety-fifth Street and mainly east of Jeffery Boulevard. Serving mostly the young families of the area was Congregation Kehilath Israel at Ninety-ninth and Oglesby. Both Pill Hill and Jeffery Manor contained some of the first residential construction on the South Side after the housing shortage that followed World War II. Expectations that these communities might become stable Jewish neighborhoods were altered when the area's racial composition rapidly changed in the 1960s and later.

A small Jewish community numbering a few thousand existed in and around Englewood into the 1950s. Many of the Jewish inhabitants had businesses in the once-major shopping area around Sixty-third and Halsted streets and two of Englewood's synagogues, Oir Chodosh (Conservative) and B'nai Israel, "the Aberdeen Street Shul" (Orthodox), had been built near that major intersection. The Jews comprised barely an estimated 10 percent of the community's population but they were served by a number of kosher butcher shops, Jewish groceries, a kosher bakery, and a Talmud Torah. One of the larger stores was owned by Morris B. Sachs, a clothier, philanthropist, and city official. Another resident who later gained prominence was Herbert Brown, who left school at fourteen to help run the family hardware store after his father died. Brown went on to win the 1979 Nobel Prize in chemistry. Some five miles due south, a smaller Jewish community existed in Roseland and was served by the Shomre Hadas Congregation. Some of Roseland's Jewish residents had businesses around 111th Street and Michigan Avenue. The Roseland Jewish community dispersed several decades ago.

Chicago's southwest side never attained much of a Jewish population although there were scattered small Jewish enclaves consisting of the families of local business people. A few small synagogues were widely dispersed in the area but only one now remains, Lawn Manor Beth Jacob at 6601 South Kedzie Avenue near Marquette Park, in a largely Lithuanian neighborhood. Established in 1925, the congregation reached a membership of about four hundred in the 1950s and had eight classrooms in its religious school. Despite its absorbing Beth Jacob of the Scottsdale area further to the southwest in 1974 and serving a large city and suburban area, the congregation has declined in membership to about one hundred. It no longer has a religious school and the vast majority of its members are senior citizens. Membership dropped as Jews moved to the suburbs and as the racial composition of the neighborhoods changed, but Lawn Manor Beth Jacob's large synagogue building continues to be the meeting place of a number of Jewish organizations of the southwest side.

### LAWNDALE, THE LARGEST OF ALL

Whether they live today in Chicago or its suburbs, many Jews can trace their roots to the greater Lawndale area, for during much of the first half of the twentieth century, as many as 40 percent of the Jews of Chicago lived there.

The Jews had started moving to Lawndale in the first decade of this century. They came largely from around Maxwell Street and leapfrogged over the railroad and industrial area to settle some three miles to the west along the

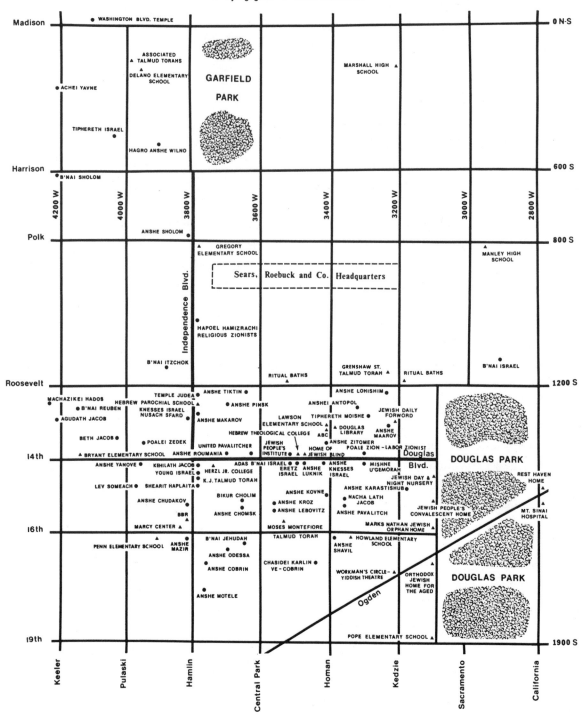

● – Synagogues   ▲ – Other Institutions

Madison ———— 0 N-S

● WASHINGTON BLVD. TEMPLE

ASSOCIATED
▲ TALMUD TORAHS
▲
DELANO ELEMENTARY
SCHOOL

GARFIELD
PARK

MARSHALL HIGH ▲
SCHOOL

● ACHEI YAVNE

TIPHERETH ISRAEL

●
HAGRO ANSHE WILNO

Harrison ———— 600 S

● B'NAI SHOLOM

4200 W    4000 W    3800 W    3600 W    3400 W    3200 W    3000 W    2800 W

Polk ———— 800 S

● ANSHE SHOLOM

▲ GREGORY
ELEMENTARY SCHOOL

MANLEY HIGH ▲
SCHOOL

Sears, Roebuck and Co. Headquarters

Independence Blvd.

HAPOEL HAMIZRACHI
RELIGIOUS ZIONISTS

● B'NAI ITZCHOK

GRENSHAW ST.
TALMUD TORAH    RITUAL BATHS    ● B'NAI ISRAEL

RITUAL BATHS
▲

Roosevelt ———— 1200 S

MACHAZIKEI HADOS ▲    TEMPLE JUDEA ▲    ● ANSHE TIKTIN    ●    ANSHE LOHISHIM ●
● B'NAI REUBEN    HEBREW PAROCHIAL SCHOOL ▲    ● ANSHE PINSK    ANSHEI ANTOPOL    JEWISH DAILY
● AGUDATH JACOB    KNESSES ISRAEL    FORWORD
NUSACH SFARD    ● ANSHE MAKAROV    LAWSON    TIPHERETH MOISHE ●    ●
ELEMENTARY SCHOOL ▲    ▲ DOUGLAS    ANSHE
BETH JACOB    HEBREW THEOLOGICAL COLLEGE    ABC    LIBRARY    MAAROV
● POALEI ZEDEK    UNITED PAVALITCHER    ● ANSHE ZITOMER
▲ BRYANT ELEMENTARY SCHOOL    ANSHE ROUMANIA ●    JEWISH    ▲ ▲ JEWISH BLIND    POALE ZION –LABOR ZIONIST
PEOPLE'S    HOME OF
14th    INSTITUTE ●    Douglas    Blvd.    DOUGLAS PARK

ANSHE YANOVE    ● ADAS B'NAI ISRAEL ● ●    ● ANSHE    ● MISHNE
KEHILATH JACOB ●    ERETZ ANSHE    KNESSES    U'GEMORAH
YOUNG ISRAEL ▲    ● HERZL JR. COLLEGE    ISRAEL LUKNIK    ISRAEL    JEWISH DAY &    REST HAVEN
K.J. TALMUD TORAH    ANSHE KARASTISHUB    NIGHT NURSERY    HOME
LEV SOMEACH ●    ● SHEARIT HAPLAITA    ● ANSHE KOVNE    ● NACHA LATH    JEWISH PEOPLE'S    MT. SINAI
ANSHE CHUDAKOV ●    BIKUR CHOLIM    ● ANSHE KROZ    JACOB    CONVALESCENT HOME    HOSPITAL
● BBR    ● ANSHE CHOMSK    ● ANSHE LEBOVITZ    ANSHE PAVALITCH
16th    MARCY CENTER ▲    ▲    MARKS NATHAN JEWISH
MOSES MONTEFIORE    ORPHAN HOME

▲    ● B'NAI JEHUDAH    ▲ HOWLAND ELEMENTARY
PENN ELEMENTARY SCHOOL    ANSHE    TALMUD TORAH    ANSHE    SCHOOL
MAZIR    ● ANSHE ODESSA    SHAVIL    DOUGLAS PARK
● ANSHE COBRIN    CHASIDEI KARLIN    WORKMAN'S CIRCLE – ▲    ORTHODOX
VE - COBRIN    YIDDISH THEATRE    JEWISH
HOME FOR
● ANSHE MOTELE    Ogden    THE AGED

POPE ELEMENTARY SCHOOL ▲

19th ———— 1900 S

Keeler    Pulaski    Hamlin    Central Park    Homan    Kedzie    Sacramento    California

*Major Jewish and other institutions in the greater Lawndale area, 1948.* (Map by Irving Cutler.)

Roosevelt Road axis. At first they met some opposition from the gentiles then living in Lawndale. Some of the German and Irish residents initially tried to stop the influx of Jews by refusing to rent to them. However, after a number of Jewish families had established themselves and more started buying the two-flat brick homes and building large three-story apartment buildings, the neighborhood began to change very rapidly. By 1920 it was predominantly Jewish, and 110,000 Jews lived there by 1930. Yiddish spoken in various dialects could then be heard throughout the community.

A residential block in Lawndale, Millard Avenue near Eighteenth Street, showing the type of two-flat buildings that were prevalent in the neighborhood.

(Photo by Irving Cutler.)

The Jews had at first moved primarily into the Chicago community of North Lawndale. Somewhat later, and to a much lesser extent, they spilled over into the adjacent communities to the north, East Garfield Park and West Garfield Park (the combined areas forming greater Lawndale). Greater Lawndale was a quiet, relatively new residential area with spacious streets and parks, encircled on its perimeter by the belt railroads. Unlike the Maxwell Street area, Lawndale had no crowded wooden firetraps, sweatshops, or pushcarts. Most of the brick and stone houses lining the streets had light and airy rooms, baths, front and back porches, and backyards bordered by alleys.

As Jews poured into this attractive area, the population of the North Lawndale area more than doubled between 1910 and 1930 and became one of the most densely populated communities in Chicago. By 1930, its proportion of foreign-born, chiefly Russian and Polish Jews was higher than that of any other Chicago community (about 45 percent). Its almost solid Jewish population led to the neighborhood being referred to as the "Chicago Jerusalem." However, the Orthodox Jews still living in the Maxwell Street ghetto sometimes disdainfully referred to greater Lawndale as "Deutschland" and its inhabitants as the "Maxwell Street Yankees of Douglas Park," because they saw in the newer Jewish neighborhood a relative "desertion of the old customs and religious beliefs, and the aspiration to emulate the German Jews with their 'goyishe' ways."[7]

The greater Lawndale area at its broadest delineation stretched approximately from California Avenue (2800 West) to Tripp Street (4232 West) and from Washington Boulevard (100 North) to Eighteenth Street.[8] The greatest Jewish

John Marshall High School at Kedzie Avenue and Adams Street in the late 1940s. It was the high school that the majority of the Jewish students of the Lawndale area attended.

(Photo by Sid Bass.)

concentration was in North Lawndale, south of Arthington Avenue, the street along which Sears Roebuck and Company had its half-mile-long complex of mail order, department store, and headquarter facilities. Many Jews worked there possibly because Julius Rosenwald had been the company's top executive for many years. There was also a small spin-off of Jewish population to the west in the Columbus Park–Austin area where some eight thousand Jews lived in the 1940s.

The Jewish people lived in Austin, mainly to the east and north of Columbus Park, essentially between 1915 and the late 1960s. They lived among Italian, Greek, Irish, and other ethnic groups. The community had three synagogues and the Rambam Day School, and along Madison Street and Central Avenue there were well-known stores serving the Jewish community, such as Randl's Delicatessen, Diamond Bakery, Mesirow Drugs, Fine's Kosher Meat Market, Sutker's Grocery, and Fox's Dry Goods Store. The students mainly attended Emmet Elementary School and Austin High School. The people living there were generally perceived to be more prosperous and perhaps somewhat "less Jewish" than those living in Lawndale.

In the central core of greater Lawndale, south of Roosevelt Road, the Howland, Penn, Lawson, Herzl, and Bryant public elementary schools each averaged about two thousand Jewish students, or more than 90 percent of each school's enrollment, by the 1930s. From these schools most of the students went on to Marshall High School, although a smaller number went to Manley, Harrison, Crane, Farragut, or Austin high schools. In the midst of Lawndale, at Thirteenth Street and Homan Avenue, was the busy Douglas Library, which served both students and adults. It was especially noted for its Yiddish and Hebrew collection, and for a short time a young woman named Golda Meir — later Israel's prime minister — served as one of the librarians at its previous storefront location nearby.

The heart of Lawndale was the L-shaped area formed by Douglas (1400 South) and Independence (3800 West) boulevards, parkways whose wide, grass-

covered median strip separated one-way roads. The boulevards were each about a mile long. Douglas Boulevard was terminated on the east by Douglas Park (which stretched from California to Albany avenues), and the boulevard intersected with Independence Boulevard on the west. Independence stretched from Douglas on the south to Garfield Park on the north (from Homan to Hamlin avenues). Both parks were beautifully landscaped with flower beds, lagoons, and woodlands. Each park had large fieldhouses, ballfields, boat rentals, and free band concerts on summer weekends. Additionally, Garfield Park also had a beautiful conservatory.

Many of the major Jewish community institutions were built along Douglas and Independence boulevards. They included about a dozen synagogues, many of imposing classical-style architecture and all but one of them Orthodox; the Hebrew Theological College (opened in 1922), whose Orthodox rab-

*Golda Meir, prominent Israeli leader, is welcomed to Chicago by Mayor Richard J. Daley in 1968. Mrs. Meir had resided for a short period in Chicago and worked as a librarian in the Douglas Library in Lawndale. In the background is Sol Goldstein (left), a leader of the Holocaust survivors, and James P. Rice (right), executive director of the Jewish Federation of Metropolitan Chicago.* (Courtesy of the Jewish Federation of Metropolitan Chicago.)

At the intersection of Douglas Boulevard and St. Louis Avenue in the heart of the Lawndale area were two major Jewish institutions. The Jewish People's Institute (left) was an important cultural, social, and recreational center of Chicago Jewry from 1926 to 1955. The Hebrew Theological College (right), which attracted students from many countries, was located in Lawndale from 1922 to 1956. The college now occupies a sixteen-acre site in Skokie.

(Photo by Sid Bass.)

binical students were from many countries; a large community center, the Jewish People's Institute (1926); a home for the Jewish blind (1944); and a number of other religious, Zionist, and cultural organizations. Douglas Boulevard was sometimes referred to as the "Lake Shore Drive of the West Side" or as that "swell street," as it was termed in Meyer Levin's novel about the area, *The Old Bunch.*

At the junction of Douglas and Independence boulevards at Independence Square was Theodore Herzl Junior College, which was opened in 1934 after the building had first served as a grade school. It had a large enrollment of Jewish students from the area. The junior college assisted in the educational and economic advancement of a whole generation of Jewish students. Its large auditorium was often the site of election-week political rallies, protest meetings denouncing the harsh treatment of Jews in some European countries, and rallies supporting a Jewish homeland in Palestine. Just to the west of Herzl was Kehilath Jacob Congregation, which had the largest Talmud Torah in the area. The synagogue had a band whose members included the young Benny Goodman. There were numerous other Hebrew schools on the two boulevards as well as on a number of side streets, among them Moses Montefiore Talmud Torah on St. Louis Avenue, south of Fifteenth Street, and the large Grenshaw Street Talmud Torah, just west of Kedzie Avenue near where the future admiral, Hyman Rickover (1900–1986), lived. As early as the 1920s the Grenshaw school had a daily attendance of about six hundred students.

Among the earliest and largest of the synagogues on Douglas Boulevard (near Homan Avenue) was Anshe Kanesses Israel Congregation (1913), known as the

Anshe Kanesses Israel
Congregation, the "Russische
Shul," was founded by
immigrants from Russia in
1875. For many years the
synagogue was located on
Twelfth Place and Clinton in
the Maxwell Street area. In
1913 the congregation
erected this building on
Douglas Boulevard near
Homan Avenue.
(From Meites, ed., History
of the Jews of Chicago.)

"Russische shul." Its fine architectural details, high arched roof, and two carved lions on the facade helped make it a Lawndale landmark. Like most of the approximately sixty synagogues in Lawndale, it had moved from the Maxwell Street area. Its seating capacity of thirty-five hundred was the largest in the city. Some of the best cantors in the world, including Moshe Koussevitsky, Yosele Rosenblatt, and Pierre Pinchik, were invited to conduct its High Holy Day services. It also had an excellent boys' choir. Many well-known and influential Eastern European Jews were congregation members. The synagogue remained open nearly around the clock so that scholars, usually devout elderly men who were often subsidized by the congregation, could continue their Judaic studies. It possessed thirty-five Torah scrolls. Rabbi Ephraim Epstein (1876–1960) served as the congregation's rabbi for almost half a century. He was a renowned Talmudic scholar who furthered the cause of Jewish education and helped rescue many Jews from Europe during the Nazi period.

Another of the large synagogues on Douglas Boulevard, near Millard Avenue, was the First Romanian Congregation. In 1926 its members gave Queen Marie of Romania a royal welcome when she visited the synagogue on her tour of the United States – even though many of them had fled her country because they could not tolerate its anti-Semitic policy.

Independence Boulevard was also home to a number of large synagogues and

*Rabbi Saul Silber (1881–1946), a founder of the Hebrew Theological College, was its president from 1922 until his death. He was the rabbi of the large Anshe Sholom Congregation for thirty-six years. He was very active in many Jewish organizations and was a leader in the Zionist movement.*
(Courtesy of Michele K. Vishny.)

a few smaller *shtiebl* congregations. Near the north end at Polk Street was the Anshe Sholem Congregation, built in the classical style. In 1926 the congregation had moved from its beautiful building on Polk and Ashland on the western fringe of the Maxwell Street area. For many years the members were led by the indefatigable Rabbi Saul Silber, well known also as a chief organizer and president of the Hebrew Theological College. Nearby on the boulevard was the large apartment complex known as Kessel Garden (Castle Garden), full of Jewish immigrants and named after one of the early places of immigrant debarkation in New York City. On Independence Boulevard near Roosevelt Road was Temple Judea, the only Reform temple in the heart of the greater Lawndale area, although a second Reform temple, Washington Boulevard Temple, on Washington Boulevard and Karlov Avenue, was on the northwest fringe of the area. Temple Judea had many innovative programs for youth groups and a popular lecture series; nevertheless it was looked upon suspiciously by many Orthodox Jews, who were skeptical of the Judaism of an institution that allowed such practices as the seating of men and women together, uncovered heads, and riding on the Sabbath; some even speculated that such an institution might be supported by Christian missionaries.

Almost directly across the boulevard from Temple Judea was another classical-style synagogue housing Knesses Israel Nusach Sfard, variously known as KINS or the "laundrymen's shul," because many of its founders were Jewish laundrymen. Just south of the synagogue was the "mansion" of Jack Arvey, the alderman. All along the boulevard, interspersed among the numerous public institutions, were well-kept, substantial three-story apartment buildings and two-story, two-family buildings.

On the Jewish High Holy Days, Douglas and Independence boulevards were crowded with people in holiday dress who promenaded or gathered in front of the numerous synagogues, the younger folks going from synagogue to synagogue visiting parents, grandparents, and friends and showing their presence. Almost everyone went to the synagogue at that time, and the older generation would not leave until the services were over. There was separate seating of men and women in the Orthodox synagogues, with the women usually sitting up in the balcony. Local automobile traffic virtually stopped. On the first day of Rosh Hashanah, over twenty-five thousand Jews would proceed to the Douglas Park lagoon to symbolically "cast off" their sins in the traditional *Tashlich* custom by emptying their pockets.

Other Jewish holidays also had their visible manifestations. On Sukkoth, the festival celebrating the completion of the harvest, hundreds of Jews could be seen proceeding to morning services with the *lulav* (palm branch) and *etrog* (citron fruit) in their hands. Many houses had the traditional holiday sukkah booths covered with boughs in the backyard. On the Hanukkah holiday, menorahs were lighted in most of the homes of the area, and on Passover the windows of every grocery store were loaded with boxes of matzos and other Passover products, including the filbert nuts that groups of children would roll on the sidewalks in a game of chance.

On the major Jewish Holy Days, contributions were solicited during the synagogue services, usually for certain ritual honors. The apocryphal story is told of the Twenty-fourth Ward politician who made the rounds of the major synagogues on every High Holy Day promising a contribution of the same $1,000. The amount of money he actually donated to each of the synagogues was questionable but he nevertheless had received the attention he desired.

Friday had special meaning for a great many Jewish families of the area. Starting at dawn, the housewife would be busy cooking and baking and later washing the floor, which was then covered with newspapers. In the evening came the lighting of the Sabbath candles, the synagogue services, and the festive Sabbath meal, which usually included wine, challah (braided bread), gefilte fish, chopped liver, chicken soup and matzo balls or noodles, chicken, prune compote, sponge cake, and seltzer from siphon bottles, all finished off with a glass of hot tea. In the more Orthodox homes the meal was usually followed by singing and religious discussions and sometimes by nostalgic and occasionally frightening memories of *der heim* (home in the Old Country). Afterward, Jewish teenagers exchanged "Good Sabbath" greetings on Douglas Boulevard and often gathered at Independence Square to meet, socialize, and sing. Others would attend the popular Friday night lectures at the young Orthodox movement's Adas B'nai Israel building across from the Jewish People's Institute.

On the side streets were about four dozen synagogues, all Orthodox, many of which bore the names of the communities in Russia, Poland, Lithuania, or Romania from which their founders had come. These included the Odesser,

Pavalitcher, Zitomer, Tiktin, Motele, Wilno, Pinsk, Kovne, Makarover, Chomsk, Karlin, and Cobrin synagogues. Some of the synagogues were founded by organized occupational groups; thus there evolved the laundryman's synagogue, the carpenter's synagogue, and, on Sawyer Avenue, the politician's synagogue to which many of the Twenty-fourth Ward political figures belonged. As late as 1944, greater Lawndale's sixty synagogues constituted about one-half of the synagogues of Chicago. The decorum in the Orthodox synagogues was very lax compared with that of the Reform or Conservative synagogues in other parts of the city. During prayer in the Orthodox synagogues, each man was more or less on his own – he prayed at his own personal pace and intensity of emotion often accompanied by gentle swaying (*shuckling*).

In the days before Social Security and Medicare, some of the synagogues or their auxiliaries, in addition to their religious functions, also provided for health, loan, welfare, and funeral-cemetery benefits. During the Great Depression of the 1930s when many people experienced unemployment and poverty, the Jewish tradition of taking care of their own continued. Families who had little themselves gave to others who had even less. Help also came from the Jewish Charities of Chicago, from government relief agencies, and even from the local political machine. Unemployment was so high that many young men who were unable to find work simply played cards all day. Many families, unable to make mortgage payments, lost their homes. Others were evicted from their apartments for nonpayment of rent and all of their belongings were often placed outside on the sidewalk. Suicide became a way out for the most despondent. People with businesses were often badly hurt financially. Business competition became heated and a barber who tried to eke out a living by charging only a quarter for a haircut had his windows smashed periodically and stink bombs thrown into his barbershop. But by prudent economizing, cooperation, aid from a variety of sources, and hard work, the Jewish community pulled through the hard years until the economy improved in the late 1930s.[9]

There was a major concentration of institutions other than synagogues in the eastern part of the community. The *Jewish Daily Forward* building was located on Kedzie Avenue and Thirteenth Street and in the days before radio became so universal in scope, crowds would gather on election night to watch the election results flash on an outside wall. At Kedzie and Ogden avenues was the large Douglas Park Auditorium building, which contained the educational and administrative facilities of the Workmen's Circle (Arbeiter Ring), the Yiddish-oriented fraternal organization established in Chicago in 1903, which ideologically had many similarities to the Eastern European Bund. At one time the Workmen's Circle had forty-three branches in Chicago and four children's schools. The organization's building was purchased in the early 1920s for $225,000 and its name changed to the Labor Lyceum. This reflected the group's major constituents, the laboring classes, for which the Workmen's Circle provided a variety of medical benefits; burial provisions; and cultural, political, and social programs, including Yiddish-oriented classes and camps for the children.

The Labor Lyceum served as the meeting place for many Jewish labor unions as well as a home for Chicago's last full-season Yiddish-speaking theater (1938–

Dina Halpern (1910–89), a renowned actress of the Yiddish theater in pre–World War II Poland, later settled in Chicago, where she starred in many Yiddish plays. Here she is shown as Portia in Shylock and His Daughter, 1948.
(Courtesy of Danny Newman.)

The Douglas Park Auditorium, located at Kedzie and Ogden avenues in Lawndale, was a multipurpose Jewish institutional building that housed the Workmen's Circle, Jewish labor unions, and the Yiddish Theater.
(Photo by Irving Cutler.)

51), the Douglas Park Theatre. Some of the top Yiddish stars performed there, including Aaron Lebedeff, Menasha Skulnik, Maurice Schwartz, Michael Michalesko, Pesache Burstein, Dina Halpern, Molly Picon, and Leon Fuchs. A younger performer named Bernard Schwartz went on to become a star in Hollywood under the name of Tony Curtis. Plays included adaptations of Shakespeare and Chekhov, Yiddish classics such as *Der Goilom* and *The Dybbuk* as well as comedies such as *Shmendrick from Lake Shore Drive*. The theater

A poster for one of the performances at the Douglas Park Theatre, which functioned continuously as a Yiddish theater from 1938 to 1951 in the Douglas Park Auditorium building in Lawndale.

(Courtesy of the American Jewish Historical Society.)

was supported by more than one hundred Jewish organizations that regularly purchased blocks of tickets on a "benefit" basis. In 1951, however, the Douglas Park Theatre closed, the result of the rapid change in the neighborhood's racial mix, a steadily declining number of Yiddish-speaking Jews, and the advent of newer means of entertainment and recreation. The theater's demise marked the end of the full-season Yiddish theater in Chicago, although through the years there were Yiddish theatricals performed sporadically in Chicago, some later using English almost as much as Yiddish.

Major Jewish institutions were aligned on both the east and west sides of Douglas Park. On the east side along California Avenue were the Rest Haven and Mount Sinai Hospital buildings. On the west side of the park along Alba-

ny Avenue (3100 West) was an imposing array of social service institutions supported by the Jewish community. These included the Douglas Park Day Nursery, established in 1919; the Jewish People's Convalescent Home (1932); the
Marks Nathan Orphan Home (1912) (whose residents at one time included,
among others, the young Elmer Gertz and Barney Ross); and the Orthodox
Jewish Home for the Aged (1903). These institutions received not only monetary support from the Jewish community, but also the donated skills and materials of individuals.

The impetus for the Marks Nathan Jewish Orphan Home was the bequest
of Marks Nathan for $15,000. Established in 1906 on the Northwest Side, the
building soon proved inadequate. In 1912 a larger, modern facility was dedicated on Albany Avenue opposite Douglas Park. It was equipped to handle three
hundred boys and girls, who were comfortably housed, dressed, well fed with
kosher meals, and educated in the public schools. The success of the institution can be gauged by the successful adjustment to adult life made by thousands of its former residents, some of whom became very prominent. The involvement of volunteers and the importance of donations are indicated in the
report of the home's annual meeting in 1920, in which thanks are expressed for
the "kindness of Mr. Sam Adelman for his donation of a suit of clothes for each
boy; to Mr. Emil Braude for the regular supply of eyeglasses for all the children; and to Mr. I. Schorr for making good all breakage of windows by the
boys."[10] Eventually, needs changed, as did the philosophy of child care, and the
Marks Nathan Home, as it had come to be known, closed in 1948.

Shopping in the greater Lawndale area was done almost wholly in the neighborhood in small Jewish-owned stores. There was a hierarchy of shopping areas ranging from the corner and mid-block mom-and-pop stores, to the shopping strips along Kedzie Avenue, Sixteenth Street, and parts of Ogden and
Crawford (Pulaski) avenues, to the major mile-long stretch along Roosevelt
Road from approximately Kedzie to Crawford avenues. Occasionally one would
venture a little further out of the neighborhood to Madison and Crawford

*The Graemere Hotel at Homan Avenue and Washington Boulevard (shown here in 1968), opposite Garfield Park, was used extensively by Jews, especially from the Lawndale–Garfield Park area, for weddings, honeymoons, Bar Mitzvahs, and a variety of meetings and social events.*
(Photo by Sigmund J. Osty, courtesy of the Chicago Historical Society.)

(Pulaski), where there were the large Goldblatts and Madigan stores and the two large Balaban and Katz movie palaces, the Marbro and the Paradise, with their statues and fountains. Further east, opposite Garfield Park, was the large, beautiful Graemere Hotel, which was used frequently by Jewish groups.

Before the advent of almost universal refrigeration and supermarkets, shopping was frequent and done at a variety of small, specialized stores, most within walking distance. One of the chores of the children was to go to the stores, sometimes several times a day, perhaps to fill up a bottle with vinegar that came from a barrel or to buy a pound of butter that was scooped out of a large wooden tub. Sometimes a half dozen trips were made to the shoe repair store over the course of many months to prolong the life of a single pair of shoes. A large number of the 425 kosher butcher shops found in Chicago in 1940 were located in Lawndale.

Located along Roosevelt Road were a half dozen movie theaters where performers such as the four Marx Brothers, Sophie Tucker, and a local boy named Benny Goodman appeared in person. Two of the theaters, the Independence (Gertlers) and the Lawndale, at one time served as Yiddish theaters. Also along Roosevelt Road were Rosenblum's and Goodman's Jewish bookstores, funeral chapels, restaurants (some specializing in Romanian and Hungarian dishes), delicatessens such as Carl's and Silverstein's, banquet cafes such as the Blue Inn and Cafe Royale, kosher sausage establishments such as Best and Lazar, groceries, fruit stores, butcher shops, fish stores (with elderly horseradish grinders and their machines on the sidewalk outside), ice cream parlors, furniture and clothing stores, bathhouses, three banks, meeting halls such as the Roosevelt, Liberty, Lawndale, and Culture Center, and headquarters of political organizations. Favorite hangouts especially for the younger people were Fluky's Hot

Dogs and Ye Olde Chocolate Shoppe. Above the stores were apartments; offices of doctors, dentists, and lawyers; the meeting halls where many of the numerous *landsmanschaften* organizations met; and also a few clubs where Yiddish or Hebrew was spoken. The restaurants were lively, informal community centers where news, rumors, and gossip were exchanged.

Roosevelt Road near Kedzie Avenue also had such well-known institutions as "Zookie the Bookie" Zuckerman, later ambushed and slain, and Davy Miller's pool hall–boxing gym–gambling-restaurant complex, which had originated on Maxwell Street. Frequently present in the gym were such boxers as Barney Ross, Davey Day, and "Kingfish" Levinsky. Many in the community frowned upon the toughs, gamblers, and occasional gangsters who hung around those facilities, even though these establishments served a purpose, in their way. It was clear that their patrons were a new breed who displayed a toughness that contradicted the long-held concept that the Jews were physically weak and passive. For example, the Davy Miller boys, including some gang members, took on the gentile youth gangs that harassed the yeshivah students or taunted the elderly long-bearded Jews. In the 1920s, the Miller boys also fought the young gentiles of Uptown for the right of Jews to use the new Clarendon Beach freely, just as in earlier days they had fought for the right of Jews to use Humboldt and Douglas parks. In later years, these Jewish youths battled members of the Nazi Bund. While gambling facilities were prevalent in Lawndale, especially in backrooms along Roosevelt Road – in such places as Putty's and the Lawndale Restaurant – taverns, even after the repeal of prohibition, were almost nonexistent.

*Sam's Fruit and Vegetable Store at 3509 West Sixteenth Street, shown here in 1937, was typical of the small "mom and pop" stores in Lawndale.*

(Courtesy of Rose Pollack.)

The Best Kosher Sausage Company facility in Lawndale at 3521 Roosevelt Road, next to the Central Park Theater, 1947. The window reflects the upstairs apartments across the street. Today the company's kosher products are found in thousands of stores and restaurants. The company was recently purchased by Sara Lee.

(Courtesy of Best Kosher Sausage Company.)

Headquartered on Roosevelt Road was the most powerful political machine in Chicago, the Twenty-fourth Ward Democratic Organization. In the 1936 presidential election Roosevelt received 26,112 votes to Landon's 974, and FDR called the ward "the number one ward in the Democratic Party." The brothers Michael and Moe Rosenberg were responsible for the early development of the ward organization. Moe Rosenberg once served a prison term for receiving stolen goods and was later indicted for income tax evasion but died before the trial started. The organization was carried to its strongest point by Jack Arvey, who became its alderman in 1923 at the age of twenty-eight and served as alderman until 1941. An influential and powerful politician, he later held a number of high positions in the local and state Democratic party.

The Twenty-fourth Ward Democratic Organization was a model of efficiency. Its sixty neighborhood precinct captains, almost all of them Jewish, were each responsible for a small section of the ward where they knew everyone and almost everything. They befriended the voters, helped them by supplying food, clothing, and coal to the needy, found patronage jobs for some, helped immigrants secure citizenship papers, and assisted people who had run afoul of the law or who needed traffic tickets fixed. In many cases they functioned almost as social workers. Each precinct captain belonged to at least one local religious, social, or fraternal organization, and in later years to the Donkey Club, an organization of Jewish precinct captains and their assistants. His was a year-round job, but he was especially visible among his neighbors before each election, when every home was visited, often more than once, to convince and plead with voters to go out and vote for the endorsed candidates. Much was at stake, often including the precinct captain's job with the government.

The ward organization helped citizens by staging picnics, parties, dances, athletic events, and other social activities. On election day, babysitters and transportation services were provided when necessary. The often-beholden voters turned out landslide majorities for the party machine, which sometimes garnered as much as 97 percent of the vote. Jack Arvey once said of the Twenty-fourth Ward that "the only ones who voted Republican were the Republican precinct captains, election judges and their families."[11] Most Chicago Jews had usually voted Republican until the late 1920s when especially the West Side and North Side Jews started voting Democratic; in 1924 they gave 28 percent of their vote to the Progressive and Socialist party candidate, Robert La Follette. In the 1936 presidential election in the Twenty-fourth Ward, which was almost wholly Eastern European Jewish, Roosevelt received 95.95 percent of the vote to Landon's 3.57 percent. In contrast, in the German Jewish South Side wards, which had been traditionally Republican, Roosevelt received 59.21 percent of the vote to Landon's 39.77 percent.[12]

The Lawndale community was alive with outdoor activity, especially in the warmer months. Through the alleys, which were sometimes littered with garbage, came a constant procession of peddlers in horse-drawn wagons, hawking their fruits and vegetables. Mingled among them were the milkman, the iceman, the garbage collector, and, periodically, the coal man. The streets and alleys were also traversed by the "ragsoline" (rags/old iron collector), the knife sharpener, the umbrella man, the "pop man" with his bottles of flavored soda pop and seltzer water, the newsboys shouting their "extras," and, for the children, the organ grinder and his monkey, the merry-go-round truck, and the pony-ride man with his ponies. Sometimes itinerant fiddlers would play Jewish melodies in the yards and the housewives would throw them a few coins wrapped in paper. Insurance collectors, telephone-box coin collectors, and *pushka* box collectors were regular visitors to the homes. Blaring sound trucks would occasionally cruise the streets advertising the movies at the local air-conditioned theater, or during election time reminding people to vote for the "outstanding candidate." Even soul-hunting Christian missionaries went from house to house, but they made very few converts.

In the evenings, people would walk over to their friends' homes or sit on their front porches conversing with their families and neighbors (they usually knew almost everyone on the block, as well as their neighbors' family histories and struggles) as a procession of ice cream, candy, and sometimes waffle vendors passed. Or they would sit on big wooden swings on their back porches. The elderly would sip hot tea from tall glasses, sucking the drinks through the sugar cubes held in their mouths. Before automobiles became so prevalent, many people would go to Garfield Park, or especially, to Douglas Park, where they would rent rowboats or listen to the free summer band concerts. Some would sleep in the park all night during the most stifling hot summer weather. There was plenty of company and little to fear in those days. Various groups belonging to Zionist, religious, social, and *landsmanshaften* organizations would meet in their "special" sections of the parks, where they often sang to mandolin music or danced into the late hours of the night.

Intellectuals congregated outside Silverstein's restaurant on Roosevelt Road and St. Louis Avenue to debate the issues of the day with the soapbox orators – communists, Trotskyites, socialists, anarchists, atheists, Zionists, and the like. The broad spectrum of opinions indicated the intellectual fervor in the area as well as the marked differences in religion, politics, culture, and economics that were heatedly discussed. Some ideological conflicts were carried over from the Old World. Rarely, however, were there overt acts such as the incident in 1929 when yeshivah boys burned the Yiddish communist newspaper, the *Freiheit,* in public on Roosevelt Road because it condoned the Arab massacre of Jews in Palestine.[13]

The youngsters of the area, as in most other Jewish communities in the city, when not in public or Hebrew school, would keep busy outdoors spinning tops, or playing marbles, kick-the-can, peg-and-stick, buck-buck how many fingers up, hide-and-seek, baseball, or football, or riding their homemade little orange-crate scooters. The girls would often also be seen jumping rope or playing jacks or hop-scotch. Older boys and young men would have their low-stake dice and card games hidden from the eyes of roving policemen. Baseball games in the schoolyards would often be interrupted until an intrepid youth would scale the building to retrieve the ball hit onto the roof. But most ball games were played on the streets where traffic was light, except when the Sears Roebuck complex workers started home. Renting bicycles was common as few owned their own.

Many of the boys of the area participated in the activities, mainly athletic, of the three youth centers in Lawndale: the ABC (American Boys' Commonwealth), the BBR (Boys' Brotherhood Republic), and the Marcy Center. All three were originally founded in the Maxwell Street area. While the ABC and BBR were Jewish-sponsored youth centers, Marcy Center was engaged in Christian missionary work and was not welcomed by the Jews it hoped to convert. However, some of the Jewish boys did use its athletic facilities, viewed movies there, and ate candy at its Christmas parties. Although Marcy Center had a well-equipped dispensary, Jewish people who were injured nearby usually refused to be taken to the center's clinic for treatment.

In addition to these centers, every few blocks there was a Social and Athletic Club (SAC), usually organized by young men. The youths would rent a small, cheap, sometimes run-down basement apartment for their clubhouse, clean it up, outfit it with old furniture, place their sign in the window and spend some

The BBR (Boys' Brotherhood Republic) on Hamlin Avenue near Sixteenth Street in Lawndale. The youth center had numerous athletic and craft programs and was noted for its policy of self-government by its members. (Photo by Irving Cutler.)

The intersection of Homan and Thirteenth Place in Lawndale. On the left is Lawson Elementary School, whose student body at one time was almost completely Jewish; on the right is the American Boys Commonwealth Building (the ABC), which was a boys' club featuring athletics and crafts; and in the background is the Douglas Library, which at one time had an outstanding Yiddish and Hebrew collection, and where for a short while in its earlier building there was a young librarian by the name of Golda Meir. (Photo by Irving Cutler.)

of their leisure time there. They often formed softball teams that played other SACs in the local parks and schoolyards. On weekend evenings they would invite girls into the clubhouse for dancing and a snack party. Like members of many other Jewish organizations, on summer Sundays they would sometimes pile into a fruit and vegetable truck outfitted with apple boxes for seats, which they would rent for five or ten dollars a day, and head for the forest preserves, the Fox River or Diamond Lake area, or the Indiana Dunes for a picnic, with the girls usually providing the sandwiches. They would sometimes sponsor dances to raise money to buy club jackets. Girls also often would have parties in their homes, and there would be dancing to radio or phonograph music.

Sunday morning, especially, was also the time of the impromptu neighborhood "pick-up" and "choose-em-up" softball games, played with a sixteen-inch ball. Players from sixteen to sixty years of age would choose sides and enjoy a spirited rivalry in the fresh air, while youngsters and oldsters watched and cheered from the sidelines. Because there were cash bets, the umpires would often be caught in the middle of heated arguments. There were also organized softball leagues that played in the school playgrounds, parks, and even stadiums of the various Jewish neighborhoods. Sunday was also often the day for family outings, such as going by street car to Navy Pier for carnival rides, boat rides, picnics, and musical entertainment and dancing. Riverview on Western Avenue was also a big attraction especially for the younger people, as were the city beaches.

Jews of all ages participated in the cultural, social, and recreational activities of the Jewish People's Institute (JPI) on Douglas Boulevard and St. Louis Avenue (declared a national historic place in 1979). The JPI exerted an enormous influence on the community. There, one could mingle with emerging fighters and writers, artists, politicians, and business leaders – Barney Ross, Nelson Algren, Stuart Brent, Leo Rosten, Todros Geller, Abraham Lincoln Marovitz, Maurice Goldblatt, and others. With its wide range of activities and facilities, and because the automobile had not yet expanded peoples' geographic range, the JPI was one of the busiest community centers the city ever had. One could attend a variety of lectures and classes, listen to the institute's own orchestra or to classical record concerts, visit Jewish museum exhibitions, see plays by Chekhov, Turgenev, and Hirschbein in English or Yiddish in the 792-seat auditorium performed by the excellent *Yiddishe Dramatishe Gezelshaft* (Jewish Drama Society of Chicago) or the Institute Players, attend Herziliah Hebrew School or Central Hebrew High School, or eat at the Blintzes Inn. One could also read in the library, swim in the large pool, exercise in the gym or health club, learn arts and crafts, enroll the children in the day or summer camp, vote for delegates to Jewish congresses, hold club meetings, or dance under the stars in summer on the roof garden on Sunday evenings (the dances rivaled the Old World matchmaker in successful pairings). In 1932, the JPI served as headquarters for some seventy clubs and organizations. On Sundays there would be three different public forums, many producing heated and impassioned audience participation.

Philip L. Seman, for decades the very capable general director of the Jewish People's Institute, gave this description of a typical day's use of the reference library in 1932:

> By two o'clock, thirty-two persons are studying; among them is a car conductor, who starting work at three, comes in daily for an hour and a half to be informed as to the work of Congress. Here are students from the Hebrew

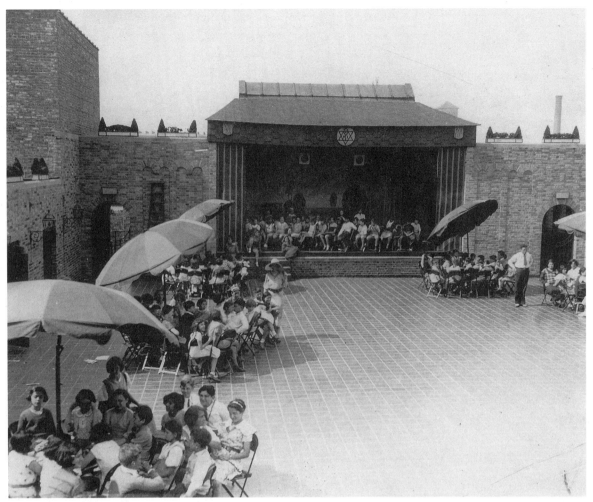

The roof garden of the Jewish People's Institute (JPI), located at Douglas Boulevard and St. Louis Avenue, was used during the warmer months by day camps, for popular Sunday evening dances, and for a variety of other events.

(Courtesy of the Chicago Historical Society.)

Theological College preparing their lessons for the next day from the volumes in the Judaica department, law students studying for the bar examination. . . .

By three o'clock the tables are fairly full of readers. . . . Some are reading a high type of literature, philosophy, art, biblical archaeology, etc. Into this group, too, fall the many ordinary enquirers, the person who wants to know whether a certain coin is worth anything, why Thanksgiving was celebrated, etc.

What is that man doing with the enormous dictionary which he has been using for almost two hours? He doesn't look as if he were exactly a philologist. He is a foreigner who is trying to get acquainted with the English language . . .

There is a second more important class made up of students and research workers . . . Here is a student of chemistry studying the composition of ether; here is a teacher reading up on literature of the early English period; there is a writer compiling data for his next work.

By nine o'clock in the evening the library is overcrowded. A student is asking for help with a certain Algebra problem; another wants to have a letter translated from French into English.

Thus the day wears on and when 10:30 P.M., closing time, approaches we can feel that nearly 400 persons know something that they did not know before. And such is a typical day's work.[14]

The lecture courses at the JPI, given by highly qualified instructors, were very well attended. The 1945–46 courses included these offerings: The Jewish World Yesterday and Today; New Trends in Medicine; Our Pan American Neighbors; Our Musical World; Which Way, Mr. & Mrs. Consumer; Post War Agriculture; From Cover to Cover (a literature course); and New World A-Coming (about the recent arrival of the atomic age).[15]

It was at the JPI that Leo Rosten taught English to adult Jewish immigrants, an experience that inspired his book *The Education of H*Y*M*A*N K*A*P*L*A*N*. Its hero was an indomitable Russian Jewish night-school student who insisted that Atlantic's opposite ocean was the "Specific," that the fourth president was Abram Lincohen, that "laktric" lights "short soicused," that the three pilgrims who followed the star to Bethlehem were the "Tree Vise Guys," and that the principal parts of the word "fail" were "fail, failed, bankrupt"; of "bad" were "bad, voise, rotten"; and of "good" were "good, better, and high class."

In the summer, those Jewish families who could afford it rented cottages in the Indiana Dunes or in the Union Pier and South Haven areas of Michigan, to which the husband of the family would usually commute on weekends, often loaded down with supplies for the vacationers. The largest Jewish resort area was South Haven, situated on the eastern shore of Lake Michigan and accessible by auto, boat, bus, and train. The German Jews during the same period often vacationed in nearby but separate areas such as Lakeside or Coloma, Michigan, where many owned their own, usually somewhat more elaborate, cottages.

South Haven developed as the major Jewish summer vacation center in the Midwest despite what many Jews perceived to be underlying anti-Semitism in the town. It contained summer camps, cottages, boardinghouses, and especially resort hotels, most of them kosher and some with big-name entertainment such as Martha Raye. The South Haven area was a miniature Catskills *borscht* belt – without the mountains. An estimated fifty-five resorts and boardinghouses were Jewish owned. Resorts such as Fidelman's and Mendelson's were like little villages. About seventy-five thousand people from all over the Midwest would jam into South Haven and its environs on a summer weekend; Jews especially frequented the North Shore section of South Haven. The community had two Jewish butchers, two Jewish grocers, a synagogue, a dance hall, and an illegal casino. There was daily boat service from Chicago in the summer.

South Haven declined as a Jewish resort area in the 1950s and 1960s, but Fidelman's, founded on an eighty-acre farm in 1911, lasted into the 1980s. Like the other resorts, it was the victim of the suburban movement, with people no longer living in sweltering apartments and also able to broaden their vacation horizons. Frequently, the resort-owners' children went into the professions rather than face the grueling pace of the summer resorts. It is said that one proprietor was so busy during the summer vacation season that when his own children would ask him a question he would answer, "Talk to me after Labor Day."

Through the years some Jews have continued to live in South Haven, which is currently experiencing something of a building resurgence. The synagogue

*An advertisement just after World War II for resorts and hotels of South Haven, Michigan — for almost half a century the most popular summer resort area for Chicago Jewry. In the summer there was daily steamship service from downtown Chicago across Lake Michigan to South Haven.* (Courtesy of the South Haven Chamber of Commerce.)

still functions and the Mount Pleasant subdivision, a summer cottage development built by Chicago members of the Workmen's Circle, mainly Yiddish-speaking tradesmen, is now used by the founders' doctor, lawyer, and scientist grandchildren.

While the Jews of Maxwell Street had been almost direct transplants from the poor, isolated European ghettos, the Jews of greater Lawndale were people who lived in pleasant physical surroundings and were working hard to achieve middle-class status. Despite the widespread severe hardships and setbacks of the Great Depression of the 1930s, upward mobility continued among the Jews, and their Old World cultural patterns and traditions were being steadily modified by "the American way." This acculturation happened among some of the more radical, irreligious immigrant Jews as well as among many younger Jews, usually American-born, who were sometimes ashamed of the Old World ways of their parents. Many preferred baseball to Hebrew school, basement social and athletic club "hangouts" to synagogues, and careers in the professions to careers in merchandising. Meyer Levin's novel *The Old Bunch* describes the strong secular forces that shaped the lives of the Lawndale Jewish youth, and even of the immigrants themselves, as they became increasingly associated with institutions outside of their neighborhood that helped to speed acculturation.[16] Despite the prejudice encountered in certain educational, job, and residential spheres, these changes took place because more openings existed for Jewish youth in Chicago than ever before.

Change was accelerating in Lawndale. As rapidly as Lawndale had been transformed from gentile to Jewish earlier in the century, so did it change from Jewish to black during the late 1940s and early 1950s, although some younger Jews had started leaving as early as the 1930s.[17] Other choice areas in Chicago and its suburbs began to open up for the Jews, and they leapfrogged over intervening sections to reach them. At this time, greater Lawndale had not physically deteriorated, even though its population was dense. But the Jews left the area because many of them had reached a point during the economic boom of the 1940s and 1950s where they could afford and wanted to own their own homes, and Lawndale had few single-family homes. They were interested in areas with more amenities, better schools, higher status, more space, and perhaps less concentrated ethnicity; and they were part of the general outward exodus that was facilitated by the improved mobility offered by the automobile and the government loans that were readily available, especially to veterans. Jews had been on the move for 2,500 years, although usually not voluntarily, and even in greater Lawndale they had frequently moved from one apartment to another to take advantage of better rent deals or better cleaning and painting incentives. The burgeoning black population coming from the area to the east, unlike in some other neighborhoods, met no resistance from the Jews. There was some prejudice but there was no name calling or brick throwing.

Relatively few members of the new generation of Jewish adults were interested in clinging to the great institutional structures that their parents and grandparents had labored so hard to build. Old World traditions, religious involvement, and the Yiddish language meant much less to those raised in the more secular environment of the New World. So they dispersed to areas with more amenities, mainly to the north – some to already Jewish neighborhoods in Albany Park and Rogers Park but more to West Rogers Park (West Ridge) and parts of the northern suburbs – new areas that were being built up after World War II. A much smaller number went to Austin, to the western suburbs, and to communities such as South Shore. By the late 1950s, what had been Chicago's largest and most institutionalized Jewish community was *Judenrein* (free of Jews), voluntarily, a situation never likely to be even remotely duplicated. The crowded Maxwell Street had been the place of first settlement for most of the immigrant Jews. Lawndale, with its two-family houses and middle-class apartments, was the place of second settlement, and the areas of third settlement consisted of finer apartments and single-family homes in the outer fringes of the city or in the suburbs, where the children of the immigrants were mainly settling.

Most of the Jewish institutions that once dotted the Lawndale area were transferred to other uses, though some were simply demolished and others abandoned. Mount Sinai Hospital and Schwab Rehabilitation Center (formerly Rest Haven) still serve the community. The ABC and BBR facilities were turned over to a community organization for use by the new youths of the area. Most of the former synagogues are now black churches, as is the Labor Lyceum. The Jewish People's Institute was sold for a nominal fee in 1955 to the Board of Education; it is now a public elementary school, as is the former Herzl Junior College. Most of the facilities occupied by Hebrew schools have been torn down, as have the buildings of the *Jewish Daily Forward,* the Douglas Park Day Nursery, the Jewish People's Convalescent Home, and the Orthodox Jewish Home for the Aged. These sites are now mainly littered empty lots. Much of the eastern part of the once busy Roosevelt Road commercial strip is now barren, its structures burned down in the 1968 riots following the assassination of Dr. Martin Luther King, Jr. The vacant expanse exposes to view the giant Sears Roebuck mail-order complex just to the north, which outlasted the numerous immigrant groups that have passed through the area and which itself has now been phased out. About half of the area's housing was lost between 1960 and 1990, although a few limited instances of redevelopment were visible by the mid-1990s.

A trip along Douglas and Independence boulevards today, about forty years after the neighborhood changed, reveals that most of the former synagogue buildings are still there, in generally good condition and still containing an occasional Star of David, faintly etched Hebrew letters, an identifying cornerstone, or the tablet of the Ten Commandments. But almost every block now has boarded-up buildings and vacant lots where once fine homes and three-story apartment buildings stood. Missing are the buildings of the Labor Zionists, the Religious Zionists, Beth Hamedresh Hagodol Synagogue, and the "mansion" of Jack Arvey. The Hebrew Theological College building, once a pride of the neighborhood, now stands boarded up.

Many of the Jewish institutions of greater Lawndale were reestablished on the North Side, especially on and around California Avenue in West Rogers Park, but usually not on the scale or with the grandeur found in Lawndale. Some synagogues of Lawndale were liquidated completely, one portion of their assets donated to a congregation in a new neighborhood that would preserve their name and their memorial plaques and another portion given to the Hebrew Theological College, which moved with the Jewish population from Douglas Boulevard to a bigger facility with an enlarged program in Skokie. Lawndale, like Maxwell Street before it, is part of the past of Jewish Chicago, etched not in the stone of its buildings but in the minds and hearts of the many thousands of immigrant Jews and their offspring who dwelt there when Lawndale was the great center of the Chicago Jewish community.

## THE WEST TOWN—HUMBOLDT PARK—LOGAN SQUARE AREA

The Jewish community on the Northwest Side of Chicago, in the vicinity of West Town, Humboldt Park, and Logan Square, reached a peak of almost thirty thousand people in the 1930s. Although small compared to Lawndale, the area preceded Lawndale chronologically by almost two decades and outlasted it by nearly the same amount of time. Unlike Lawndale, it was not a solidly Jewish neighborhood, as the Jews lived among sizable numbers of Poles, Germans, Italians, Ukrainians, Russians, and Scandinavians and never comprised more than perhaps one-quarter of the total population of the community. The construction of the Humboldt Park and the Logan Square branches of the elevated lines in the 1890s helped to speed the development of the area.

The nucleus of a Jewish community had been established in the late 1800s in the West Town area centering along Milwaukee Avenue and along Division Street, where many of the Jews had retail stores and where, as in the Old Coun-

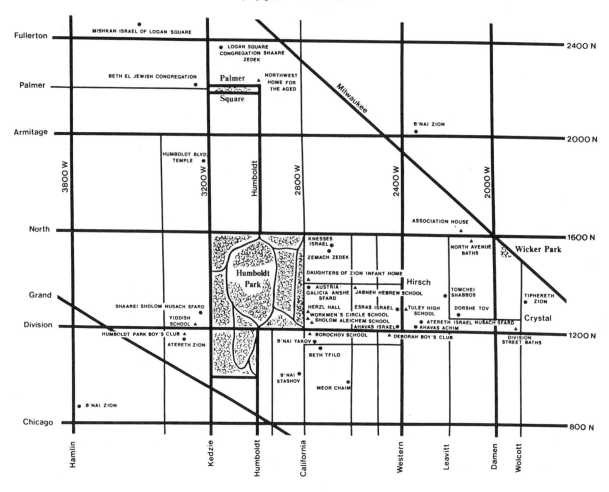

*Major Jewish and other institutions in the Humboldt Park–Logan Square area and adjacent West Town, 1948.*
(Map by Irving Cutler.)

try, they often dealt with Poles, Ukrainians, and Russians as well as with Jews. Some of the Old World tensions sometimes surfaced in skirmishes between Jewish and gentile youths. Many of the Jewish settlers were from Hungary, the Ukraine, and Galicia (mainly southeastern Poland). Originally concentrated in the part between Ashland and Western avenues, in the area known as Wicker Park, the Jews gradually moved westward until many lived on the blocks to the east and west of Humboldt Park.

The first synagogues in the West Town area were built in the 1890s. Eventually about twenty served a Jewish community that in time spread out not only to the more affluent neighborhood west of Humboldt Park but also into Logan Square. In addition to the synagogues there were a number of Hebrew schools, including the large Yavneh in the Humboldt Park area, sponsored originally by four Orthodox synagogues in the vicinity and serving Jews from many religious segments of the community. There were also Yiddish theaters, Yiddish bookstores, a day and night nursery, a home for the aged, an education center, a Deborah Boys' Club and a Humboldt Park Boys' Club, a community center, and a variety of *landsmanshaften,* clubs, and secular Jewish organizations. A large building at 1243 North Wood Street, in the early decades of the 1900s, housed at various times a Talmud Torah, the Marks Nathan Jewish Orphan

Humboldt Park, Chicago.

*Humboldt Park was a focal point for Jewish meetings, picnics, and a variety of social and athletic activities.* (Courtesy of the Chicago Public Library.)

Home, the Jewish Educational Alliance, a Poale Zion Yiddish school, and the Northwest Side branch of the Chicago Hebrew Institute. Nearby were the Marion Court Talmud Torah, the Boys Brotherhood Republic, the Daughters of Zion Jewish Day Nursery and Infant Home, and the Home for Jewish Friendless and Working Girls. There were a number of synagogues, including the large Tiffereth Zion on Lincoln Street (Wolcott), for many years led by Rabbi Yehudah Gordon, a noted Talmudic scholar; Beth El on Crystal Street; Moses Montefiore on Damen Avenue; and Ezras Israel on Artesian Avenue. Unlike Lawndale, which was largely Orthodox, this Northwest Side area also contained many Reform and Conservative Jews as well as members of Rabbi Yehoshua Heshel Eichenstein's Hasidic synagogue.

Many local Jews were inclined to emphasize Yiddish culture and somewhat radical philosophies. There were many intellectuals and activists espousing various causes and beliefs. Ideologically, the area contained many adherents of socialism, communism, secularism, and Zionism. It had a number of Yiddish schools for the young, including the Sholem Aleichem, Workmen's Circle, Zionist, and leftist-oriented schools. On Pierce Avenue there was the Northwest Fellowship Club.

Jewish radicals, fairly numerous in the area, frequently articulated their philosophies from soap boxes on the corners around Humboldt Park. Anarchists, socialists, communists, and "Wobblies" (Industrial Workers of the World), speaking either in Yiddish or English, would give their analysis of the news and idealistic solutions to world problems, while verbally sparring with questioners and occasional hecklers. At one such outdoor oration at North and Fairfield avenues the speaker for the IWW was Ralph Chapman, who had written the song "Solidarity Forever." Communists tried to break up the meeting by loudly singing that song, unaware that the speaker was also its composer.

Brown and Koppel Restaurant (right) at Division Street and Damen Avenue was a popular Jewish-style restaurant with a little discreet gambling on the side.
(Photo by Joseph G. Domin, courtesy of the Chicago Historical Society.)

The 207-acre beautifully landscaped Humboldt Park was itself a focal point of Jewish activity. Besides offering a spot for playing ball, boating, bicycling, swimming, skating, and romancing, the park was also the meeting ground for *landsmanshaften,* family clubs, and a variety of other Jewish organizations. The annual *Tashlich* was at the park's lagoon.

Fine residential areas were aligned along Sacramento, Humboldt, Logan, and Kedzie boulevards and in Wicker Park, but the area was generally middle class economically, with some families of lower income. There were a few sweatshops in homes, storefronts, and lofts interspersed in the West Town area. Many of the buildings were two-flats or larger apartment buildings.

For Jews, the area's principal commercial artery was Division Street, which had numerous Jewish stores to serve the community. Favorite gathering places were restaurants like those of Joe Pierce, Moishe Pippic, Brown and Koppel (also known for its gambling), and Itzkovitz; the Deborah Boys' Club; and Parklane (Humboldt Billiards). Another favorite meeting place, especially for writers and radicals, was Ceshinsky's Jewish bookstore.

Opposite Humboldt Park on California Avenue was the Herzl Hall (for meetings, classes, and dances); the large Austro-Galizien congregation led by Rabbi Moses Eichenstein and featuring such prominent cantors on the High Holy Days as Moishe Oysher, Yosele Rosenblatt, Richard Tucker, and Todros Greenberg; and the Parkview Home for the Aged (originally the Daughters of Zion Jewish Day Nursery building). Sabin, Von Humboldt, Schley, Columbus, Lowell, Bancroft, and Tuley high schools had large numbers of Jewish students.

The demise of the Jewish community in Logan Square is epitomized by the razing in 1977 of its last synagogue, Shaare Zedek, the Logan Square Conservative Congregation located on Fullerton Avenue near Kedzie Avenue. Erected in 1922, the synagogue had a seating capacity of 1,400, a large Hebrew and Sunday school, and a wide variety of educational and social programs. Toward the end it no longer had a rabbi or cantor and was being supported by rummage sales and by former members who returned for the High Holy Days.

(Photo by Irving Cutler.)

West of Humboldt Park on Spaulding Avenue was Atereth Zion Congregation, whose president for many years was Samuel Seligman, a Hebrew scholar and high school teacher who was instrumental in establishing Hebrew as a modern language course at Marshall High School.

In Logan Square the Jewish concentration was around Milwaukee and Kimball avenues, where at one time there were stores such as Goldblatts, Morris B. Sachs, and Kaufman's Fashion Forum, as well as the Lipsky Yiddish Theater. Nearby were Shulman's delicatessen and Kaufman's Bakery, which later moved into the Jewish areas of Albany Park and Skokie.

The Logan Square community, which included the Palmer, Kedzie, and Logan boulevard areas, was a step up economically from the adjacent West Town and Humboldt Park areas to the south. Eastern European Jews started moving into Logan Square before World War I, attracted by the spacious boulevards, good housing, and convenient transportation to the Loop. They lived mainly in well-kept two- or three-flats or apartment buildings on or near the boulevards. In 1930 an estimated seven thousand Jews lived in the area. Through the years, five synagogues were established in Logan Square, three of them Conservative, one Reform, and one Traditional.[18] The synagogues served as social centers for the community.

There were people in the West Town–Humboldt Park–Logan Square area who pursued the arts and literature, and there were a number of Jewish cultural groups. The area was once the home of many well-known celebrities, including movie impresario Michael Todd (Aaron Goldbogen), comedian Jackie Leonard (Fats Levitsky), and numerous writers, such as the noted columnist

Sydney J. Harris, National Book Award winner Nelson Algren, prolific song-writer Jule Styne, and the Nobel Prize-winning novelist Saul Bellow. Most of these men were alumni of the neighborhood Tuley High School. The Crowns and the Pritzkers, two families highly successful in business and very generous in philanthropy, had their American roots in this area. The former Wicker Park school is now named after its alumnus, A. N. Pritzker. Many of the early union leaders came from the area, including Sol Brandzel, who later became head of the Midwest region of the Amalgamated Clothing Workers of America. Another prominent resident was Dr. Max Dolnick, a dedicated family doctor, Yiddish scholar, and teacher who was an active Labor Zionist leader.

The Jewish population of the area, later concentrated largely in Humboldt Park and Logan Square, started to decline after World War II, although the decline was not as precipitous as in Lawndale. A few Jewish institutions and Jews remained into the 1970s. The last synagogues, B'nai Yakov on Haddon Avenue near Humboldt Park, and Logan Square Congregation Shaare Zedek (Shaare Zedek) on Kedzie and Fullerton avenues, closed in the mid-1970s as the neighborhoods became largely Hispanic. A few dozen Jewish families, often elderly people, continue to live in Logan Square along the boulevards. Additionally, some younger Jews (frequently in mixed marriages) have moved into the neighborhood as it has undergone rehabilitation.

### THE ALBANY PARK–NORTH PARK AREA

For decades there had been a slow, continuous movement of Jews out of the West Town–Humboldt Park–Logan Square area farther north into the region called Albany Park. Jews first began moving into Albany Park a few years after the completion of the Ravenswood Elevated in 1907 to its terminal at Lawrence (4800 North) and Kimball (3400 West) avenues. Later many also moved north into the adjacent North Park community, which, like Albany Park, had single-family houses and two-flats as well as many larger apartment buildings, especially to the east. The first Albany Park synagogue was the Reform Temple Beth Israel, founded in 1917 by German Jews. The congregation's first services were held above a store on Lawrence Avenue. Shimon Agranat, one of its members, later became one of the chief justices of Israel, and another member, Seymour Simon, became a justice of the Illinois Supreme Court. Its spiritual leaders for many years were Rabbis Felix Mendelsohn and Ernest M. Lorge. Founded in 1919 also above a store on Lawrence Avenue, by Orthodox Eastern European Jews, was Beth Itzchok (the "Drake Avenue Shul") whose rabbi for many years was Aaron Rine. By 1930, Albany Park contained about twenty-three thousand Jews, almost half of the total population of the community.

The Jews were concentrated largely in a 1¼-square-mile area bounded approximately by the North Branch of the Chicago River on the east, Pulaski Road on the west, Foster Avenue to the north, and Montrose Avenue to the south. Near the northern boundary of the community were large, open tracts of land that included the Bohemian National Cemetery, Eugene Field Park, and the Chicago Parental School. Just north of the North Branch of the river in North

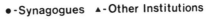

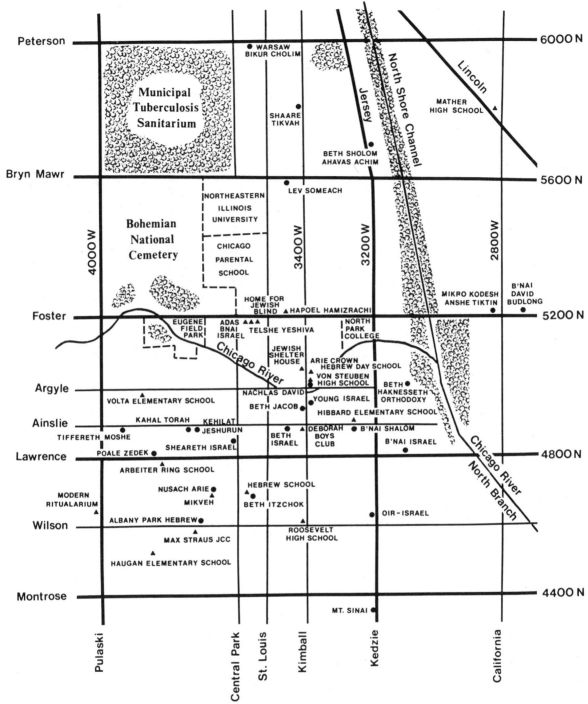

*Major Jewish and other institutions in the Albany Park–North Park area, 1965.*

*(Map by Irving Cutler.)*

Park, Swedes founded North Park College, whose bells – in a true ecumenical spirit – would chime the traditional Jewish melody "Sholem Aleichem," at the start of Sabbath at sunset each Friday.

For the Jews who moved into Albany Park from the northwest and west sides of Chicago, the community represented a movement upward into a more Americanized community as well as a transitional middle ground between the prevalent Orthodoxy of the West Side and the Reform Judaism of the South Side.

*Lawrence Avenue, the main commercial street of Albany Park, looking east from Kimball Avenue, 1929. At the right is the Ravenswood elevated terminal and the popular Purity Restaurant. (Courtesy of the Chicago Historical Society.)*

Albany Park was a diverse Jewish community somewhat like the Humboldt Park area. Along with adjacent North Park, it supported about fifteen Orthodox, Conservative, and Reform synagogues and had numerous other institutional facilities, including a Hebrew day school, a rabbinical college, a boys' club, a girls' club, a Yiddish school, and a home for the Jewish blind. The Max Straus Jewish Community Center on Wilson Avenue, established in 1941, was attended by all age groups until it closed in 1968. Its diversified program attracted more than 2,000 people a week for many years. It was located near one of the largest synagogues in the city, Albany Park Hebrew Congregation, which was established in 1923. By 1950, at the time the Jewish population of Albany Park reached its peak, that congregation had around 2,000 member, with 600 children in the Hebrew school. Rabbi Abraham E. Abramowitz was the spiritual leader there for about thirty years. Originally founded as an Orthodox synagogue, it joined the Conservative movement in 1939. Some 3,000 people would worship there during the High Holy Days, often listening to renowned cantors. Other fairly sizable synagogues in Albany Park included Beth Jacob, B'nai Sholom, Kehilath Jeshurun, and Nusach Ari.

(Top) The Max Straus Jewish Community Center on Wilson Avenue in Albany Park was established in 1941 and was attended by all age groups until it closed in 1968, after most of the Jewish population had moved out of the area.

(Courtesy of the Jewish Federation of Metropolitan Chicago.)

(Bottom) Beth Itzchok of Albany Park (the Drake Avenue Shul), 1990. It is one of the synagogues that barely survive in Albany Park. Its membership, once large, has been largely depleted and some former members have joined its offshoot, Congregation Beth Itzchok of West Rogers Park.

(Photo by Irving Cutler.)

A strong concentration of Jewish institutions clustered along Kimball Avenue, on which two major public high schools, Roosevelt and Von Steuben, were also situated. Both high schools had a predominantly Jewish student body and were virtually empty on major Jewish holidays. Lawrence Avenue, especially from Kedzie to Pulaski, was the main business street, and it was somewhat similar to Lawndale's Roosevelt Road in its concentration of Jewish stores. In fact, some of its stores – among them Rosenblum's Bookstore, St. Louis Fish Market, and B. Nathan Dress Shop – had been transplanted from Lawndale's major thoroughfare.

Each age group in Albany Park had its favorite places to gather. Many of the elderly would meet at the Workmen's Circle, attend occasional Yiddish movies at the Alba Theater on Kedzie Avenue, play pinochle at Eugene Field Park, or gamble at the Horseshoe Club on Kedzie Avenue. The younger people would go to dances at Eugene Field Park, attend the many functions at the Max Straus Center or Deborah Boys' Club, or roller skate at the Hollywood Roller Rink on Kedzie Avenue. Everyone would frequent the Purity Restaurant and Terminal or Metro theaters on Lawrence Avenue. At one time there were as many as twenty Kosher butcher shops and chicken stores and five Jewish bakeries in Albany Park. Newsstands selling Yiddish newspapers and journals were at many intersections, with a few serving also as "bookies," as did a few cigar stores.

The Jewish population of Albany Park was essentially middle class. Many people were upwardly mobile, but some were in the lower middle class and the laboring group. Although the area was hurt badly by the Depression of the 1930s, as was most of Chicago, a government relief agency reported that of the three thousand families on relief in Albany Park, only about one hundred were Jewish. Additionally, several dozen families received help from Jewish social service agencies.[19]

Albany Park was an active Jewish community with about fifty fraternal, social, communal, and political organizations in 1936, in addition to those associated with the synagogues. The groups ranged in scope from the American Jewish Congress to the IWO (International Workers Order). Many of them met in halls on Kedzie Avenue, on Lawrence Avenue, or at Jensen Park or Eugene Field Park.

During the post–World War II massive exodus from Lawndale, a large number of Jewish families, including many from among the Orthodox, settled in Albany Park and adjacent North Park. Albany Park was also the first place of residence for some young Israeli immigrants. However, by the 1950s over 70 percent of the Jews of Albany Park were native-born first-generation Americans.[20]

At the same time that Jews from declining Jewish neighborhoods were moving into Albany Park, some Jewish settlers of Albany Park were moving still further north. The Jewish move out of Albany Park accelerated during the 1960s until today a very small number of Jews remain, most of them elderly with limited financial means, who cannot or do not want to leave the area where they have deep roots. Their needs are met by several organizations, including the Ark, which was formerly in Albany Park but is now at 6450 North California Avenue, in a building funded by Seymour Persky, a real estate developer and

The changing proprietorship of the Congregation Beth Jacob synagogue, in the 4900 block of North Kimball Avenue, Albany Park, is reflected in the Korean script on the facade in this 1979 photograph.

(Photo by Irving Cutler.)

philanthropist. The Ark provides food supplies and hundreds of professional and lay volunteers, including doctors, lawyers, and social workers. A few small Orthodox synagogues still exist in Albany Park – mainly with a handful of aged members clinging to their traditions – but most of the large Jewish institutions have been closed or sold to other groups. The Deborah Boys' Club is now the Albany Park Community Center; many of the former synagogues are now Korean churches; and a number of the former Jewish businesses along Lawrence Avenue are now Korean owned. The Arie Crown Hebrew Day School moved to Skokie. Albany Park today is a place of great ethnic diversity with Koreans, Asian Indians, Filipinos, Hispanics, Yugoslavs, Arabs, Greeks, and Pakistani, but very few Jews.

Probably the largest concentration of remaining Jews in the area is the small Orthodox community in the few blocks around the Telshe Yeshiva, at Foster and Drake avenues. Jews also live in the neighborhoods just to the north, Peterson Park and Hollywood Park. The yeshivah's roots go back to the renowned Telshe Yeshiva in Telshe, Lithuania, which was wiped out by the invading Nazis. It was reestablished in Cleveland, Ohio, by personnel who escaped, and a branch was set up in Chicago in 1960. Today about 150 students from across the country diligently study in the ultra-Orthodox yeshivah's high school, college, or graduate-school levels. While some students go on to become practicing rabbis, most go into business, Jewish education, or the professions but maintain their love of Torah learning. The Telshe Yeshiva is one of the largest Jewish institutions remaining in the Albany Park–North Park section. Across the street is the Association of the Jewish Blind Home, which moved there from Lawndale's Douglas Boulevard in 1957. To the north on Peterson Avenue, until its recent move to Devon Avenue, was the newer Yeshivas Brisk, founded in Chicago in 1974 by Rabbi Aaron Soloveichik, who until then was Rosh Yeshiva and dean of the faculty of the Hebrew Theological College in Skokie. The yeshivah was named after the city of Brisk in Eastern Europe, where his ancestors had been heads of yeshivahs for generations. It has about fifty students.

Rogers Park, Chicago's most northeasterly community, owes its growth to the coming of the elevated line, which was extended to Howard Street in 1907. Before then it had been largely a farm area with some single-family frame houses. With the improvement in transportation, numerous large apartment buildings and apartment hotels were built, especially in the eastern portion adjacent to Sheridan Road and Lake Michigan. Jews – mainly those from Eastern Europe – started to move into the area after 1910. By 1920 two of Rogers Park's larger congregations, B'nai Zion and Temple Mizpah, had been established there, and within a decade about ten thousand Jews resided in the community. A somewhat larger number lived to the south in the communities of Uptown and Lakeview. Rogers Park was often the third site of settlement of many Jews who first settled in the Maxwell Street area and then lived either in Lawndale or on the Northwest Side.

From 1930 to 1960 the Jewish population in Rogers Park more than doubled to about twenty-two thousand and constituted the largest ethnic group in the area and over a third of the community's population.[21] There was an especially heavy Jewish concentration between Pratt Boulevard (6800 North) on the south and Touhy Avenue (7200 North) on the north and from Ashland Avenue (1600 West) eastward to the lake. About a dozen synagogues, including a number of large ones, served the area. Strip shopping areas used by the Jewish population were located along Sheridan Road, Glenwood Avenue, and Morse Avenue, where the popular Ashkenaz Restaurant once stood. The restaurant was at one time the largest Jewish delicatessen in Chicago, serving more than a half ton of corned beef monthly. The strip also was the site of a Jewish community center that opened in 1953. Good transportation, proximity to the lake, and a variety of housing units were among the neighborhood's attractive features.

In recent years, and despite an influx of thousands of newly arrived Russian Jewish immigrants in the 1970s and 1980s, the Jewish population of Rogers Park began to decline rapidly. By 1980 it was estimated at about thirteen thousand, or about 23 percent of the community's population.

Most of the Jews who now live in Rogers Park are elderly retirees, widows and widowers. Some reside in the numerous nursing homes along Sheridan Road. To the south on Argyle Avenue is the Self Help Home for the Aged, created to house German Jewish survivors of Nazi persecution. There are very few Jewish children in the area; the average age among the Jewish population of Rogers Park is about sixty. In 1965 an estimated 85 percent of the students at Sullivan High School in Rogers Park were Jewish, compared with fewer than 10 percent today. A 1946 study had shown that Sullivan had almost two thousand Jewish students and Senn High School had over one thousand. Elementary schools in Rogers Park such as Field, Gale, and Kilmer each then had over five hundred Jewish students. The decline of the Jewish population is due not only to the aging of the population and its westward and northward movement, but also to the loss of various "feeder" neighborhoods that had previously supplied Rogers Park with Jewish residents.[22] The appeal of the neighborhood also

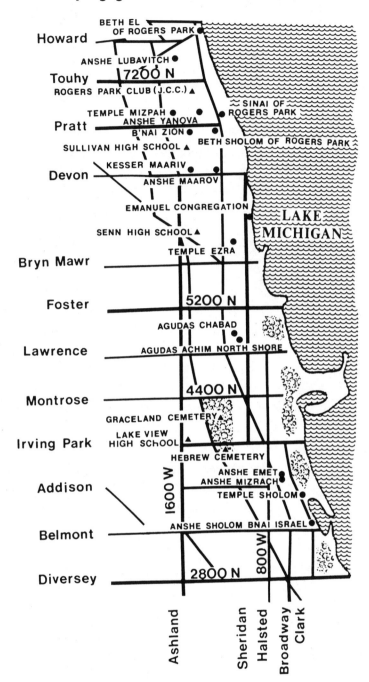

**•−Synagogues  ▲−Other Institutions**

Major Jewish and other
institutions in the Lakeview–
Uptown–Rogers Park area,
1960.
(Map by Irving Cutler.)

declined as the somewhat heterogeneous, transient character of parts of the area
increased and security problems arose. About half of the approximately dozen
synagogues that were in Rogers Park have closed and those remaining have
declining membership. Even formerly large synagogues such as Kesser Maariv
and Temple Mizpah have closed or moved, and B'nai Zion on Pratt Boulevard
has had its membership decline from over 1,000 to about 150. To the south of
Rogers Park at Clark Street and Irving Park Road there still remains the oldest
Jewish cemetery in the Chicago area, the Hebrew Benevolent Society Ceme-

One of the wheelchair-accessible minibuses of the Council for Jewish Elderly that bring people to doctors' offices, shopping, Jewish Community Centers, or other prearranged destinations. (Courtesy of the Jewish Federation of Metropolitan Chicago.)

tery (generally known as Jewish Graceland), which was established in the 1850s.

The Jewish community has responded to the characteristics of the changing Jewish population in Rogers Park through a number of new agencies. The citywide Council for Jewish Elderly, started in 1972, does much of its work in Rogers Park, where it assists the elderly with meals, housing, and transportation. Friends of Refugees of Eastern Europe (FREE) was organized in 1973 to help the Russian Jewish immigrants make the difficult adjustment to life in their new land and to act as contacts between the refugees and various governmental and community organizations. The Jewish Federation of Metropolitan Chicago set up a variety of programs to help the new immigrants.

Since the early 1970s over twenty thousand Soviet Jewish immigrants have settled in Chicago, most initially living in small apartments in the Rogers Park area, with increasing numbers in adjacent West Rogers Park. It is reported that Jews in Russia at holiday time would raise their glasses and toast to "next year in Rogers Park."[23] Chicago, with about 4 percent of the country's Jewish population, has taken in over 9 percent of the Soviet Jews settling in the United States. These recent immigrants already comprise about 5 percent of Chicago's Jewish population. They are mainly well-educated professional couples, typically with two children and often accompanied by an elderly parent or two. Many are doctors, scientists, lawyers, and engineers. They constitute one of the best-educated immigrant groups of recent years.

On arrival in Chicago they were welcomed by Jewish organizations, especially by agencies of the Jewish Federation of Metropolitan Chicago, who helped find them living quarters and jobs, and helped them financially and with language problems. Some twenty-one organizations participated in the resettlement program. In less than a year, 80 percent of the immigrants were considered self-sufficient and over 90 percent were working.[24] Only 25 percent had received any public assistance, most for less than three months.

*A protest against Soviet policy toward Jews in the 1970s in front of the Civic Opera House during a visit of the Bolshoi Ballet. A change in Soviet policy later allowed thousands of Russian Jews to come to Chicago.* (Courtesy of the Jewish Federation of Metropolitan Chicago.)

Adjustment to the American way of living was not easy for many of the Russian Jewish immigrants. They had come from a land of enormous bureaucracy where they were fearful of the government, which usually made the decisions regarding apartments, schooling, medical care, jobs, and vacations. The system they faced was one where petty bribery and aggressive behavior were necessary to obtain hard-to-get goods. In democratic America they had to fend for themselves. How they fared in America often depended on their age, profession, knowledge of English, and adaptability to a new system. Some in the more-needed professions became successful; others had to settle for jobs below their skill levels. Some experienced culture shock, and others complained of a vulgarity in American culture and the "pandering to common tastes which they found repulsive."[25] One irate mother even protested that her daughter in a nursery school was sleeping on a floormat "like a dog."

Many Jewish organizations, especially those with strong Orthodox ties, reached out to the immigrants to educate them about Judaism. Some of the immigrants were amenable to these efforts; others were indifferent. Many had come here mainly for the possibility of a better life and also for more opportunities for their children. Most of them had little religious background or knowledge of Jewish traditions. Their general lack of involvement in Jewish life in Chicago was a cause of concern for some in the Jewish community. It was felt by some that the Russian Jewish immigrants were not like the "teeming masses," Zionist zealots, or Torah scholars who had come from Russia almost a century earlier. Some of the new immigrants had never even heard of the Torah.

*Temple Sholom, the largest congregation in the Chicago area, with about 1,800 families, was founded in 1867 as North Chicago Hebrew Congregation. Located initially on Superior Avenue near Wells Street, it was the pioneer congregation on the North Side. In a series of moves northward through the years it moved into its present home at 3480 North Lake Shore Drive in 1930.*

*(Photo by Irving Cutler.)*

The hope was that the immigrants would not "go native" and forget their identity as Jews.[26]

In time, the efforts of the various Jewish organizations met with increasing success. Although the Russian Jewish immigrants still socialized mainly among themselves and had set up their own facilities, such as delis and restaurants, many were using the facilities of the Jewish Community Centers, sending their children to Jewish schools, undergoing circumcision, and, when they become financially successful, as many have, moving out of declining areas in Rogers Park and into predominantly Jewish areas of the northern suburbs such as Skokie or Buffalo Grove. Many have been energetic self-starters.

Thousands of Jews live in the vicinity of Lake Shore Drive southward from Rogers Park to near the downtown area, the southern stretch of which is referred to as the Gold Coast. They mainly occupy condominiums, cooperatives, and rental apartments in a nearly unbroken array of high rises that extends along Lake Shore Drive through the communities of Edgewater, Uptown, Lake View, Lincoln Park, and the Near North Side. They include many retirees as well as many young professionals. There are sizable numbers of singles, widows, and widowers but relatively few small children. In the late 1940s neighborhood elementary schools such as LeMoyne, Stewart, and Nettlehorst in Lake View and Uptown each had enrollments of more than five hundred Jewish students. The wealthier Jewish families generally lived east of Broadway. Now the Jewish students usually attend private schools or the Anshe Emet Day School.

As a whole, the lakeshore residents are comfortable economically; interest-

ed and involved in numerous Jewish organizations and causes; active politically, with a general socially liberal and independent stance; and supportive of some
of the largest congregations in Chicago, such as Temple Sholom, Anshe Emet,
and Emanuel congregations. They were led for long periods by Louis Binstock
(serving from 1937 to 1974), Solomon Goldman (serving from 1929 to 1953),
and Felix A. Levy (serving from 1908 to 1955), respectively, all well-known rabbis. Temple Sholom is the largest congregation in the Chicago area, with eighteen hundred families. There are also a number of smaller synagogues in the
area, such as the venerable Anshe Sholom B'nai Israel, whose roots go back to
the Maxwell Street area. In Lake View, Herman Davis was its rabbi from 1945
to 1978. Some members of the metropolitan area's wealthiest Jewish families –
now more likely to be of Eastern European descent than of German descent,
such as the Crowns, Pritzkers, and Klutznicks – live along the north lakefront.

### WEST ROGERS PARK

Since World War II, the largest intracity movement of Jews who have left
their former communities on the South, West, and Northwest sides has been
into the community of West Ridge, an area that in 1940 still contained considerable amounts of vacant land. Located just to the west of Rogers Park, the
area is popularly known as West Rogers Park. Its approximate boundaries are
Ridge Avenue to the east, Kedzie Avenue to the west, Peterson Avenue to the
south, and Howard Street and the Evanston border to the north. Today it contains the greatest concentration of Jews in the city and is the only Jewish community in Chicago with some characteristics of former major Jewish areas such
as Lawndale and Albany Park. In West Rogers Park almost half of the Jewish
households keep kosher and the majority are affiliated with a synagogue and
send their children to Jewish day schools.

There were fewer than 2,000 Jews in the area in 1930, out of a total population of about 40,000; by 1950 the number had reached about 11,000. In the
1950s, the Jewish population of West Rogers park quadrupled, and in 1963 it
reached an estimated 48,000, or about three-fourths of the total population.
Most Jews of West Rogers Park are of Russian-Polish descent but are mainly
second- and third-generation Americans. They came particularly from Lawndale and nearby Albany Park. Many purchased single-family homes in the
northern part of West Rogers Park, while others moved into the Winston Towers
condominium complex south of Touhy Avenue.

The Jewish presence in West Rogers Park has declined since the 1970s to an
estimated 33,000 Jewish residents, about half of the community's total population. But there is a determined effort to maintain a Jewish community there. The
neighborhood is physically attractive and has one of the higher median income
and educational levels in the city. Some recent immigrant Russian Jews, but mainly
religious Jews, many of them young families of ultra-Orthodox Jews, continue
to move into West Rogers Park, thereby maintaining the strength of institutions
and services they require, while secular Jews, Conservative and Reform Jews, and
some Orthodox Jews continue to move out. The Jewish Community Council of

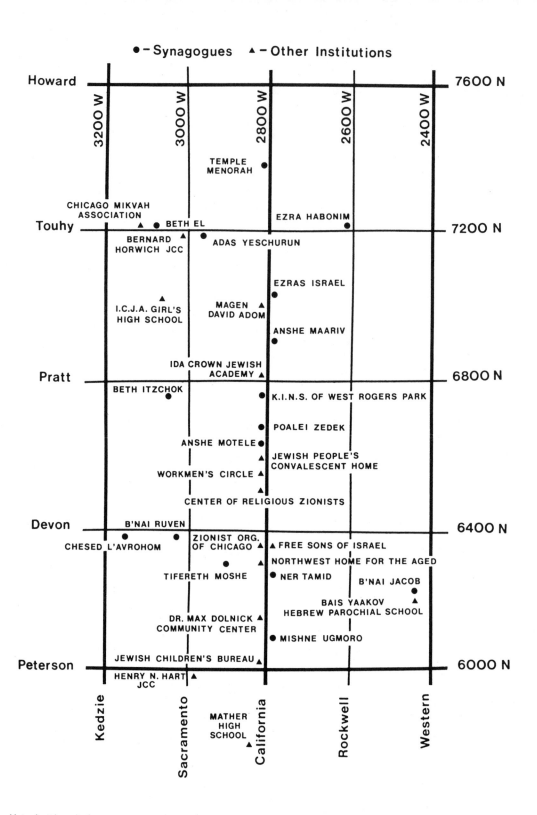

● – Synagogues   ▲ – Other Institutions

Howard ———————————————————————————— 7600 N

3200 W   3000 W   2800 W   2600 W   2400 W

TEMPLE
MENORAH ●

CHICAGO MIKVAH
ASSOCIATION ▲                    EZRA HABONIM
Touhy ——— ● BETH EL ———————————— ● ——— 7200 N
        BERNARD ▲
        HORWICH JCC    ● ADAS YESCHURUN

                            EZRAS ISRAEL
                            ●
I.C.J.A. GIRL'S ▲   MAGEN ▲
HIGH SCHOOL         DAVID ADOM   ANSHE MAARIV
                                 ●

        IDA CROWN JEWISH
        ACADEMY ▲
Pratt ——————————————————————————————— 6800 N
    BETH ITZCHOK ●    ● K.I.N.S. OF WEST ROGERS PARK

                     ● POALEI ZEDEK

         ANSHE MOTELE ●
                      ▲ JEWISH PEOPLE'S
                        CONVALESCENT HOME
    WORKMEN'S CIRCLE ▲
                     ▲
    CENTER OF RELIGIOUS ZIONISTS

        B'NAI RUVEN
Devon ——— ● —————— ● —————————————————— 6400 N
CHESED L'AVROHOM    ZIONIST ORG.
                   OF CHICAGO ▲ ▲ FREE SONS OF ISRAEL
                    ●          ▲ NORTHWEST HOME FOR THE AGED
    TIFERETH MOSHE    ● NER TAMID
                                  B'NAI JACOB
                          BAIS YAAKOV ▲
                          HEBREW PAROCHIAL SCHOOL
    DR. MAX DOLNICK ▲
    COMMUNITY CENTER   ● MISHNE UGMORO

    JEWISH CHILDREN'S BUREAU ▲
Peterson ——————————————————————————————— 6000 N
    HENRY N. HART ▲
         JCC

Kedzie   Sacramento   California   Rockwell   Western

        MATHER
        HIGH
        SCHOOL
         ▲

*Major Jewish and other institutions in West Rogers Park, 1979. Eighteen major Jewish facilities were aligned along a two-mile stretch of California from Peterson Avenue to Howard Street.* (Map by Irving Cutler.)

West Rogers Park, founded in 1974, is trying to preserve the Jewish character of the community by holding community forums, publishing a newsletter, having a welcome wagon (Sholom Wheels), and providing housing assistance to Jewish families who wish to settle in West Rogers Park.[27]

West Rogers Park today maintains more than fifty Jewish institutions and organizations, including twenty synagogues, most of which are Orthodox or Traditional. Despite the population decline, the number of Jewish institutions

*Some twenty-five Jewish organizations met in the Free Sons of Israel building on California Avenue in West Rogers Park, 1979.*
(Photo by Irving Cutler.)

has actually increased, with the new institutions mainly serving the growing number of ultra-Orthodox Jews, who generally have large families. A number of the congregations were founded in the Maxwell Street area about a century ago and reached West Rogers Park via Lawndale. Many of the institutions are aligned along California Avenue's "synagogue row," in the mile-and-a-half stretch between Peterson and Touhy avenues. In a small way, the distribution is reminiscent of that found along Douglas Boulevard in Lawndale. Rabbi Jerome Bass, a president of the Jewish Community Council of West Rogers Park, stated some time ago that West Rogers Park is "the last bastion of neighborhood Judaism in the city. . . . We love the Jewishness of the area. For a Jew, there is nothing better in Chicago. . . . A place where Jews can live and not be interfered with." It is the last Jewish area in Chicago where one can see numerous ultra-Orthodox, bearded Jews in their traditional dress of long black coats and black hats, youngsters with their long sidelocks and skullcaps, and women wearing *sheitels* (wigs) or having their hair covered. The area is the home of many of the city's Lubavitcher Hasidim, a movement that stresses strict religious observance, group cohesiveness, spiritual fervor, and less emphasis on the material world. This religious movement originated in Poland in the eighteenth century.

In West Rogers Park the rhythm of Orthodox life is still evident – ranging from the daily synagogue prayer services to the closing of stores for the Sabbath. On California Avenue are eight synagogues; two Hebrew elementary

parochial schools; a religiously oriented high school, the Ida Crown Jewish Academy, whose principal for thirty-five years was Rabbi Shlomo Rapoport; a home for the Jewish aged, whose driving force for decades was Judge Michael F. Zlatnick; the Ark; several children and family welfare centers; the Chicago Community Kollel (an adult religious study center); a number of Zionist groups; and the offices of various other Jewish organizations. A new *mikvah* (ritual bath) is nearby. The recently enlarged Bernard Horwich Community Center on Touhy Avenue is used intensively by a growing number of Soviet Jews, senior citizens, and Orthodox families. For the last few years the center has offered separate recreational classes for Orthodox Jewish boys and girls. Recently, with railroads, a canal, and strung wires used as boundaries, most of West Rogers Park has been established as an *eruv,* which allows observant Jews

*Devon Avenue, the main commercial street of West Rogers Park, showing Jewish stores, c. 1980. Once extensive, the Jewish commercial strip on Devon Avenue now is confined largely to sections between Kedzie and California avenues.*

(Photo by Irving Cutler.)

*Reflecting changes in West Rogers Park, the popular Jewish-style Bagel Restaurant closed its Devon Avenue facility in 1992, but it was replaced by the Orthodox Yeshivas Brisk.*

(Photo by Irving Cutler.)

to carry things on the Sabbath, something otherwise not allowed under Jewish law. The only other Chicago-area *eruv* is in Skokie.

The main commercial street in West Rogers Park is Devon Avenue, to which many of its Jewish merchants relocated from Roosevelt Road or Lawrence Avenue, major Jewish-oriented streets of the past. Until recently, Devon Avenue had resembled those old locations, but the street has become a thoroughfare of many other nations as increasing numbers of Asians (especially Indians and Pakistani), Greeks, Slavs, and others have moved into the community. Yet, on Thursdays and Fridays a few blocks of Devon Avenue still bustle with Jews doing their pre-Sabbath shopping in the Jewish butcher shops, bakeries, groceries, and bookstores. However, once-popular clothing stores such as Seymour Paisin, Young Debs, and Darzi; the Crawford Department Store; and the Bagel Restaurant are missing. On Saturdays and holidays the Jewish part of the street, now approximately from California Avenue west to Kedzie Avenue, a stretch given the honorary designation of Golda Meir Boulevard, becomes quiet as the activity switches to "synagogue row" along California Avenue and to a lesser extent along Touhy Avenue. But unlike along Roosevelt Road and Lawrence Avenue, the Yiddish language is heard less frequently and Hebrew and Russian are heard more often. The myriad of notices about Jewish activities and businesses posted in the stores are now mainly in English.

Even as other nationalities establish their own shopping sections on Devon Avenue, it is still the most Jewish street in Chicago's most Jewish neighborhood. In 1993 the street had five synagogues, three Jewish bakeries, three Jewish restaurants, four kosher food stores, two kosher fish stores, two Jewish bookstores, and a Russian bookstore, in addition to numerous other Jewish facilities, including a Jewish monument store, the Hannah Sacks High School for Orthodox Girls, and FREE (Friends of Refugees of Eastern Europe), which since 1973 has helped in the resettlement and religious training of Russian Jewish immigrants.

### THE EXODUS TO THE SUBURBS

By 1990, a survey by the Jewish Federation of Metropolitan Chicago showed that of the estimated 261,000 Jews in the Chicago Metropolitan area, only 87,600, or 33.5 percent, lived within the city of Chicago. Of these, about 77,700, or 89 percent, lived either in the north lakefront apartment communities (from the Loop to Rogers Park) or the contiguous communities inland, especially in West Rogers Park (West Ridge). A few thousand lived in the South Side communities of Hyde Park and Kenwood and the small remainder were thinly dispersed in other city communities.[28]

The majority of the Jews of the metropolitan area, about 67 percent, live in the suburbs – a remarkable change since 1950 when only about 4 percent of the Jews were suburban. A few thousand more Jews lived in more distant satellite cities such as Joliet, Aurora, Elgin, and Waukegan, each of which has a synagogue. It is estimated that over 80 percent of the entire Jewish population of metropolitan Chicago now lives north of Lawrence Avenue. The suburban Jewish population is dispersed over a wide area, in several dozen suburban communities, while the Jewish population in the city is still generally concentrated in a few communities, as in the past, though not as densely, and now mainly on the North Side.

The movement north, over time, was demonstrated in a 1989 reunion of graduates of the Lawndale-area Penn Elementary School from the classes of 1918 through 1957 (see table 5). The list of reunion attendees shows how these stu-

TABLE 5. *Current Residence of Penn Elementary School Graduates, 1918–57*[a]

| States | Number | Illinois Cities | Number |
|---|---|---|---|
| Illinois | 625 | Skokie | 143 |
| California | 42 | Chicago | 118 |
| Florida | 14 | Northbrook | 62 |
| Wisconsin | 4 | Highland Park | 40 |
| Arizona | 3 | Glenview | 33 |
| Nevada | 3 | Des Plaines | 25 |
| Texas | 3 | Lincolnwood | 24 |
| Iowa | 2 | Morton Grove | 24 |
| Minnesota | 2 | Buffalo Grove | 23 |
| Missouri | 2 | Wilmette | 23 |
| Other states | 9 | Niles | 16 |
|  | —— | Deerfield | 10 |
|  | 709 | Wheeling | 8 |
|  |  | Arlington Heights | 6 |
|  |  | Evanston | 5 |
|  |  | Prospect Heights | 4 |
|  |  | Glencoe | 3 |
|  |  | Glenwood | 3 |
|  |  | Schaumberg | 3 |
|  |  | Winnetka | 3 |
|  |  | Flossmoor | 2 |
|  |  | Naperville | 2 |
|  |  | Oak Park | 2 |
|  |  | Other cities | 43 |
|  |  |  | —— |
|  |  |  | 625 |

Source: From the *Penn-Y-Gram* issue of the Penn School Reunion, October 28, 1989, p. 15.

a. As tabulated of 1989 reunion attendees.

dents (virtually all of them Jewish) have dispersed through the years into other parts of the city, the suburbs, and other states. Of 625 living in the area, the northern and northwest suburbs of Chicago are, with 77 percent of the graduates, by far the dominant place of residence. Only about 4 percent live in the western and southern suburbs. About 19 percent live in Chicago. The out-of-state resident numbers are not definitive because many of the out-of-state graduates did not come to the reunion due to the distance involved, but the local numbers are revealing.

Since World War II the major Jewish population movement has been out of Chicago and into the suburbs – especially the northern and northwestern suburbs. Small numbers of Jews, mainly wealthy descendants of early German

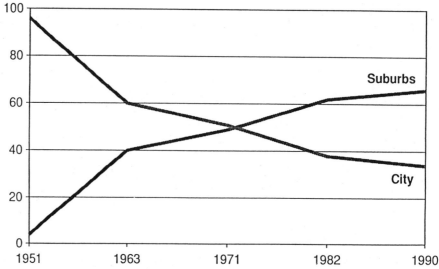

*Distribution of the Jewish population between city and suburbs, 1951–90. The post–World War II years witnessed a major shift of the Jewish population from the city to the suburbs, from 4 percent living in the suburbs in 1951 to about 67 percent living there in 1990.* (Courtesy of the Jewish Federation of Metropolitan Chicago.)

immigrants, had in the early decades of the twentieth century purchased homes in North Shore suburbs such as Glencoe and Highland Park. The first synagogue in the North Shore area was the "branch" of Chicago Sinai Congregation (Reform) of the south side of Chicago, established in Glencoe in 1920. It soon became the independent North Shore Congregation Israel. However, due to the Great Depression and the events of World War II, and because of restrictive residential covenants in many Chicago suburbs, few Jews were living in the suburbs before 1950.

The 1950s, however, saw a move to the suburbs by many groups of people for a variety of reasons: changes in city neighborhoods, invalidation of restrictive covenants, greater affluence, the desire for suburban amenities and status, better schools, improved transportation, the availability of government-backed mortgages, and an increase in the number and size of young families. During that decade, the Jewish population in the suburbs increased by almost 100,000. In the following quarter century the Jewish suburban population increased another 50,000, and currently there are approximately 174,000 Jews living in the suburbs.

In an era of general "white flight" from the city, the percentage of Jews living in the suburbs, according to the Jewish Federation of Metropolitan Chicago, rose dramatically from about 4 percent in 1950 to 39.5 percent in 1963, to 51.2 percent in 1973, and to an estimated 67 percent in the early 1990s. Some of the growth was because suburban Jewish families had more children than Jewish families in the city. Families with school-age children made up a large share of the Jewish families moving to the suburbs.[29]

## THE WESTERN AND SOUTHERN SUBURBS

Of the 174,000 Chicago Jewish suburbanites in 1990, only about 25,100, or 14.4 percent, lived in the western and southern suburbs.[30] A 1982 Federation of Metropolitan Chicago survey showed that compared to Jews in other suburban areas, the Jewish families in the western and southern suburbs have the

The Oak Park Temple is one of the oldest in the area, representing a merger of Zion Congregation (1864) and B'nai Abraham (1870), both originally located just west of downtown Chicago. When in Garfield Park, before it moved to Oak Park, it was known as the Washington Boulevard Temple.
(Photo by Irving Cutler.)

highest percentage of married adults (90 percent), the largest households (3.3 people), and the greatest percentage living in single-family households (81 percent). The western suburbs, despite the Jewish population's move west from Maxwell Street to Lawndale, Garfield Park, and Austin, never attained a large Jewish population. There were small, older Jewish communities in places such as Oak Park and Maywood, but the expected continued westward movement of Jews never developed. The western suburbs, being close to the core of the city, geographically, were generally densely populated before World War II. Furthermore, many of them, such as Cicero, Berwyn, and Melrose Park, were essentially blue-collar suburbs.

Today the small Jewish population of the western suburbs, estimated at 11,900 in 1990, is quite widely dispersed; its synagogues are located in Oak Park, River Forest, Westchester, Lombard, and Naperville – the latter two in DuPage County, which has a small but growing Jewish population estimated at about 4,000. Congregations assume special importance in the western suburbs because there are relatively few other significant Jewish institutions and organizations.

The Naperville congregation was organized in recent years as the region experienced an influx of young Jewish professionals who work in the rapidly growing high-tech research facilities of the area. Oak Park Temple (Reform), with Rabbi Samuel Schwartz as spiritual leader for many years, is one of the oldest in the Chicago area. It traces its origins to Zion Congregation, which was established on the western fringes of Chicago's downtown in 1864, and to B'nai Abraham, established in 1870 southwest of downtown. Until the congregation moved to Oak Park in the 1950s, it was, for a number of decades, known as the Washington Boulevard Temple and was located in West Garfield Park.

Located also in the western suburbs, in Forest Park, is the largest of the thirteen Jewish cemeteries in the Chicago area, Jewish Waldheim Cemetery. Over a century old, the cemetery is divided into nearly three hundred sections representing fraternal organizations, congregations, family circles, lodges, and *lands-*

*One of the numerous lands-manshaften sections of Jewish Waldheim Cemetery in Forest Park. This landsmanshaft represented two neighboring shtetlach in Ukraine.*

(Photo by Irving Cutler.)

*manshaften* ranging from Divinitzer to Ziditshover and from Woroshilevker to Warsaw. The thousands of monuments, bearing inscriptions in Yiddish, Hebrew, German, English, and even Portuguese and Ladino, reveal fragments of Chicago Jewish history and are testimony to the great diversity of Chicago's Jewish community through the years. With about 175,000 graves, the cemetery is one of the largest consecrated Jewish burial grounds in the world.

There were few Jews in the south suburbs until after World War II. Chicago Heights was the one community that had a small prewar concentration of Jews. It had the area's only synagogue, Beth Israel, founded about 1905, and also the first Jewish religious school, established in 1903. Geographically the most remote from the heart of Chicago, the southern suburbs were in a sector perceived as one that had somewhat lower income and a sizable minority populations. The area was heavily industrialized and lacked the lakefront, transportation, status, and other amenities of the North Shore suburbs.

Once substantial Jewish movement into the southern suburbs started after the war, it was accelerated by rapid movement out of such South Side communities as Hyde Park and South Shore and by the building of a number of expressways, which made the southern communities more accessible. Early rapid movement into the region took place especially in the newly planned community of Park Forest. Many young Jewish couples relocated there, among them war veterans who had completed their education under the GI Bill of Rights and who benefited from the veterans' housing program. The community's first congregation, Beth Sholom, was established there in 1952 and the religious

*Temple Anshe Sholom, a Reform congregation in Olympia Fields, established in 1952, is the largest Jewish congregation in the south suburbs, with a membership of over five hundred families.* (Photo by Irving Cutler.)

school in Park Forest at one time contained six hundred children. In 1958, it was estimated that of a total of four thousand Jews in the southern suburbs, three-quarters lived in Park Forest.[31] That suburb often served as the first home for families of professionals and young executives just starting out. The Jewish population in Park Forest declined in the 1970s and 1980s, a period that also witnessed an accelerated racial change.

Jews are now more concentrated in the contiguous strip of the south suburbs of Homewood, Flossmoor, Olympia Fields, and Park Forest, but only in Flossmoor do they comprise as much as perhaps 25 percent of the total population. Smaller numbers reside in such communities as Country Club Hills, Hazel Crest, and Glenwood. In 1990 there were an estimated 13,200 Jews living in the southern suburbs.[32]

The southern suburbs have developed a network of Jewish organizations, including ORT, B'nai B'rith, Hadassah, the National Council of Jewish Women, two country clubs, a number of religious schools, and five synagogues, two in Park Forest, two in Olympia Fields, and one in Homewood. Anshe Sholom, a Reform congregation in Olympia Fields, is the largest of the congregations and has a membership of over five hundred families. Some of the synagogues, especially through mergers, can trace at least part of their origins to Chicago. Temple B'nai Yehuda, for example, now in Homewood, was founded in Hyde Park in 1944 by German Jewish refugees from the Nazis. The congregation later moved to the South Shore area before reestablishing itself successfully in Homewood. Beth Torah of Beverly in Chicago merged into Anshe Sholom in 1974.

Small but often declining Jewish communities exist across the state line in the larger cities of northwest Indiana such as Hammond, East Chicago, Gary, and Michigan City. Many of the earlier Jews in these cities were merchants; more recently, the Jewish residents are members of the professions. There are synagogues in each of these four communities. However, in recent years there have been major racial changes in population, and some of the white population, including Jews, have moved into growing communities to the south, including Highland, Munster, and Merrillville, Indiana. Munster now has a Jewish day school and a chabad house of the Lubavitch movement.

The Jews of the southern Chicago suburbs, because of their small numbers and lack of services such as kosher butcher shops, bakeries, and other related facilities, often feel removed from the mainstream of the city's Jewry, which is concentrated over forty miles to the north. Efforts to overcome the sense of isolation and lack of a fair share of social services have resulted in a number of improvements, including the establishment of a south suburban Jewish community center, a branch of the Board of Jewish Education's high school, and extension courses of Spertus Institute of Jewish Studies.[33] Jewish Family and Community Services and the Jewish Children's Bureau, both sponsored by the Jewish Federation of Metropolitan Chicago, have been in the south suburbs since the 1970s. However, the Council for Jewish Elderly is not currently in the south suburbs, possibly due to the lack of a large population.

### THE NORTH AND NORTHWEST SUBURBS

At the very beginning of this century small numbers of wealthy German Jews, mainly from Chicago's South Side, had established homes near Lake Michigan in Highland Park. The residences were essentially summer homes used in addition to their city houses. In 1908, Jewish residents built the fashionable Lake Shore Country Club. It straddled the Highland Park–Glencoe border, exceeded three hundred acres in size, and was adjacent to the lake. Soon other Jews, including Julius Rosenwald, started moving into the area. (Rosenwald's estate was later donated to Highland Park and is now Rosewood Park.) By 1920 there were permanent German Jewish residents in the Highland Park–Glencoe area. When the North Shore branch of Chicago Sinai was established in Glencoe that year, it was the only synagogue between Chicago and Waukegan. Rabbi Edgar E. Siskin was its spiritual leader for many years. Highland Park, with its very diverse Christian denominations, and Glencoe, with its small black population, seemed more pluralistic, sensitive, and hospitable to Jews than did the other North Shore suburbs.

The first mass movement of Jews to the north suburbs was carried out mainly by those of Eastern European descent. Starting after World War II, they moved into Skokie and adjacent Lincolnwood. The first synagogue of these two suburbs, the Reconstructionist Niles Township Jewish Congregation, was founded in 1952. Skokie and Lincolnwood contained a large amount of vacant, relatively low-priced land, some of which had been prematurely subdivided during the 1920s, before the Great Depression and World War II halted construction. After building resumed, in the years between 1950 and 1960 the population of Skokie alone quadrupled to about sixty thousand people. The Edens Expressway facilitated the growth when it opened in 1951.

Thousands of chiefly single-family dwellings were built in Skokie and Lin-

colnwood, often by Jewish builders who advertised in Jewish neighborhoods. By the 1960s these suburbs were about half Jewish, and in 1975 the Jewish Federation of Metropolitan Chicago estimated that about forty thousand of Skokie's almost seventy thousand residents were Jewish. Since then, the community's Jewish population has declined an estimated 15 to 20 percent. Some of the decline came as people moved farther out, but much of it occurred as the pop-

More than four thousand gathered on Northwestern University's Deering Meadow in Evanston on October 19, 1980, to participate in a community-wide, interfaith, anti-Nazi demonstration.

(Photo by Irving Cutler.)

ulation aged, with the "empty nesters" remaining and many of the young leaving. Synagogues have adjusted to the situation by offering more education classes and programs aimed at adults and fewer children's Hebrew classes. In recent years some Orthodox Jews, mainly from West Rogers Park, have been moving into the area.

Skokie contains an estimated seven thousand survivors of the Holocaust and in 1978 was the target of a brazen attempt by a small band of American Nazis to march in the city's streets. After a series of conflicting court decisions, the Nazis, displaying swastikas, were allowed to make a quick entrance into and exit from Skokie under the protection of hundreds of police, while thousands of people of all faiths demonstrated against them. One day in 1987 a Holocaust memorial sculpture was dedicated in the village center. It was vandalized that same night.

At present, Skokie and Lincolnwood contain a dozen synagogues, most of which follow the Orthodox-Traditional or Conservative ritual. This contrasts with the greater concentration of Orthodox synagogues in West Rogers Park, which has much larger numbers of elderly and foreign-born, and with the preponderance of Reform congregations in the more distant North Shore suburbs. Skokie is also the site of the Lieberman Geriatric Health Centre, the large and very active Mayer Kaplan Jewish Community Center, the Skokie Soloman Schechter Day School (which, together with its Northbrook school, has about eight hundred students), the Hebrew Theological College, and the National Jewish Theater, located in the Mayer Kaplan Jewish Community Center.

The first major facility of the Hebrew Theological College was established in 1922 on Douglas Boulevard in Lawndale. Rabbi Saul Silber was its president from its early days until his death in 1946. The nucleus of the college had been started in 1902 in the Maxwell Street area with the chartering of Yeshivath Etz Chaim, which later merged through the efforts of Ben Zion Lazar and others

The Holocaust memorial sculpture was dedicated in 1987 in the village center in Skokie. It was desecrated that same night with Nazi swastikas.

(Photo by Irving Cutler.)

with Beth Hamedrash La Rabonim, founded in 1916, to form the Hebrew Theological College. It moved to its present sixteen-acre Skokie campus in 1958 during the presidency of Rabbi Oscar Z. Fasman. Through the years, over 500 Orthodox rabbis have been ordained by the college, and thousands of others have attended classes at its ancillary institutions, such as the Ann Blitstein Teachers Institute for Women, Fasman Yeshiva High School, the Max Bressler College of Advanced Hebrew Studies, the Jewish University of America, and various postgraduate and outreach programs. The school is authorized to confer master's degrees and doctorates in Hebrew letters and attracts students from across the country and around the world. Its Yeshivah program has about 200 students and the high school about 130 students. Nearby is the Hillel Torah North Suburban Day School founded in 1962, which has an enrollment of about 550 students in its modern Orthodox elementary and middle school.

*(Top) The Hebrew Theological College at 7135 North Carpenter Road in Skokie, 1993. The institution moved to this sixteen-acre site in 1958 after being in Lawndale for about thirty-five years.*
(Photo by Irving Cutler.)

*(Bottom) Skokie's Lieberman Geriatric Health Centre of the Council for Jewish Elderly offers social, recreational, and rehabilitation programs to 240 residents. The facility features private rooms and community services such as a health center, synagogue, beauty shop, craft center, and a library.*
(Courtesy of the Jewish Federation of Metropolitan Chicago.)

Dempster Street in Skokie has a number of stores that cater to the Jewish populace. But the presence of Jewish facilities on the street is minor compared to the concentration of Jewish merchants on the main shopping streets of older Jewish areas of the past, such as Maxwell Street, Division Street, Roosevelt Road, Lawrence Avenue, and the present Devon Avenue.

In the early 1980s the near north inland suburbs – home to many Jewish "empty nesters" (20 percent of the households) – had the highest median age (40.6 years) of any of the Chicago metropolitan suburban areas and had the smallest size of Jewish household (2.6 persons). Jews have also lived for a longer period of time in their present near north suburban residences than Jewish suburbanites have resided in other areas. While Skokie, Lincolnwood, Niles, Morton Grove, and Des Plaines contained an estimated 53,700 Jews in 1990,

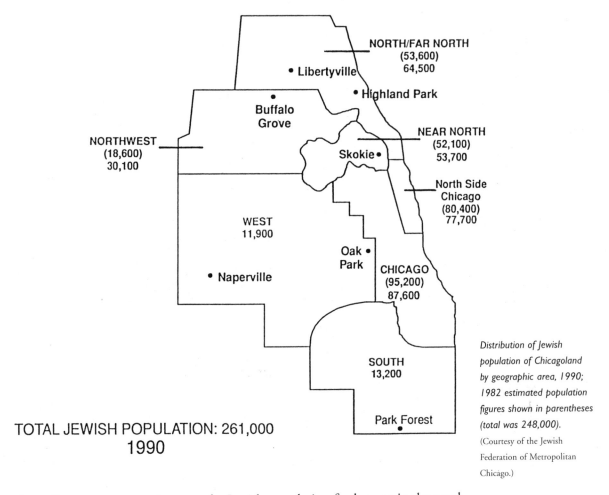

NORTH/FAR NORTH
(53,600)
64,500

• Libertyville

• Highland Park

Buffalo
Grove

NORTHWEST
(18,600)
30,100

Skokie •

NEAR NORTH
(52,100)
53,700

North Side
Chicago
(80,400)
77,700

WEST
11,900

Oak •
Park

CHICAGO
(95,200)
87,600

• Naperville

SOUTH
13,200

Park Forest
•

TOTAL JEWISH POPULATION: 261,000
1990

*Distribution of Jewish
population of Chicagoland
by geographic area, 1990;
1982 estimated population
figures shown in parentheses
(total was 248,000).*
(Courtesy of the Jewish
Federation of Metropolitan
Chicago.)

down from some 57,000 in 1970, the Jewish population farther out in the north
and far north suburbs continued to grow, reaching an estimated population of
64,500 in 1990, up from about 53,000 a decade earlier.[34] These suburbs stretched
north along the lake from Evanston and inland to Libertyville. In 1950, Rabbi
David Polish had established in Evanston the Reform Congregation Beth Emet
The Free Synagogue. The Jewish population in these communities started growing rapidly, especially in the more southerly suburbs, after World War II, although growth was initially slow in Lake Forest and Kenilworth, areas that had
been essentially closed to Jews. As late as 1963 an Anti-Defamation League
survey showed that about 20 percent of the North Shore suburban real-estate
listings were still closed to Jews, although the discrimination was often disguised
in coded or seemingly innocuous phrasing.[35] Many Jews moved into the newer western part of the lakeshore suburbs such as Wilmette, Glencoe, and Highland Park and into the inland tier of suburbs such as Glenview, Northbrook,
and Deerfield, where vacant land was available and land values were lower than
near the lake. The Jewish areas of the north suburbs show relative residential
stability, high income, a high percentage of home ownership, and significant
Jewish affiliation. Stable Jewish residential areas generally correlate with higher Jewish communal activity and number of institutions.

The frontier of Jewish suburban settlement now seems to be to the northwest in such suburbs as Hanover Park, Schaumburg, Hoffman Estates, Wheel-

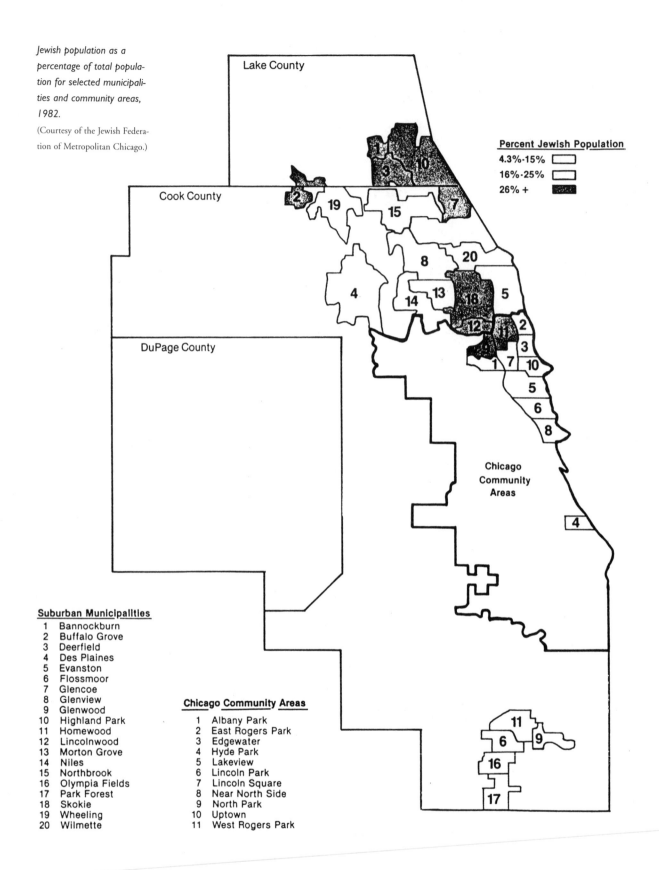

*Jewish population as a percentage of total population for selected municipalities and community areas, 1982.*

(Courtesy of the Jewish Federation of Metropolitan Chicago.)

Lake County

Cook County

DuPage County

**Percent Jewish Population**

4.3%-15%
16%-25%
26% +

Chicago Community Areas

**Suburban Municipalities**
1  Bannockburn
2  Buffalo Grove
3  Deerfield
4  Des Plaines
5  Evanston
6  Flossmoor
7  Glencoe
8  Glenview
9  Glenwood
10  Highland Park
11  Homewood
12  Lincolnwood
13  Morton Grove
14  Niles
15  Northbrook
16  Olympia Fields
17  Park Forest
18  Skokie
19  Wheeling
20  Wilmette

**Chicago Community Areas**
1  Albany Park
2  East Rogers Park
3  Edgewater
4  Hyde Park
5  Lakeview
6  Lincoln Park
7  Lincoln Square
8  Near North Side
9  North Park
10  Uptown
11  West Rogers Park

ing, Vernon Hills, and Buffalo Grove. Affordable housing was a more important factor in the movement than Jewish identity, although virtually all of these communities now contain synagogues. The fastest growing of them all, the Buffalo Grove area, has a half dozen. The estimate of more than 30,000 Jews

in 1990 in the northwest area also includes some older parents who moved there to be closer to their grown children, as has happened in some of the other suburbs. The Jewish population of the area more than tripled since 1970.

The movement of Jews into newly developing areas such as the northwest suburbs has created some unique situations for the Jews who first settled there. While the earlier arrivals were somewhat isolated in an all-gentile area, they had many things in common and tried to find each other. They were young, usually around thirty, and had small children, relatively little money, and a Jewish neighborhood upbringing that they initially missed. Many of the husbands commuted by train to Chicago so that the wives could have the car. One settler said, "I used to go to delicatessens in Skokie just to smell the atmosphere."[36] Their isolation precipitated the formation of chapters of ORT, Hadassah, B'nai B'rith, and other Jewish organizations. To obtain members for newly forming synagogues, some people would drive through all the new subdivisions looking for Jewish names on mailboxes. One former South Sider reminisced about her first Passover in the northwest suburbs: "When I selected a check-out line at the supermarket I went to one where the people in front of me also had boxes of matzos in their shopping carts."[37] But to get the matzos into the store, the Jewish women first had to educate the supermarket manager and help him make up his Passover order. In recent years an annual Synagogue Affiliation Fair has been held at the Jewish Community Center in Buffalo Grove, where representatives from all of the synagogues in the area are available so that unaffiliated Jewish families can compare and select a synagogue to join. In some of the outlying suburbs the only indications of a Jewish presence are the synagogues, which become especially important as a cohesive force for the Jews living there and may lead to contact with fellow Jews.

In time, the northwest suburbs have developed a large, growing, and viable Jewish community. They have had the help of various Jewish institutions such as the Jewish Federation of Metropolitan Chicago, which established a Jewish Community Center in Buffalo Grove; the Board of Jewish Education and the Associated Talmud Torahs, which assisted in establishing religious schools; the Spertus Institute of Jewish Studies, which provided extension courses; and es-

The extreme frontier of Jewish settlement, the McHenry County Jewish Congregation. The Conservative congregation was founded in 1979 and is located in a former township public school in Ridgefield, Illinois, just north of Crystal Lake. It serves a small but growing Jewish population in the county.

(Photo by Irving Cutler.)

tablished congregations that helped new congregations with guidance, prayer books, and even Torahs. The region has the lowest median age, 29.8 years, of any of the suburban areas. Generally, the further-removed suburban Jewish families are larger than those in the close-in suburbs and even more so than those in the city.

With the recent growth in the northwest suburbs, the Jewish population to the northwest and north of Chicago now numbers about 150,000, compared with just a few thousand who lived in the area immediately after World War II. Scattered throughout the area are numerous Jewish institutions that serve the population. A number of the suburbs have high concentrations of Jewish people. The population of such suburbs as Niles, Evanston, Morton Grove, Glenview, Northbrook, Wilmette, and Winnetka is now estimated at 10 to 25 percent Jewish, and Glencoe, Highland Park, Skokie, and Lincolnwood are close to 50 percent Jewish.[38] As the Jewish population continues to move north and northwest, there is even a synagogue now in the once-rural McHenry County. Unlike in Chicago, where the Jewish population has become largely concentrated in fewer neighborhoods such as West Rogers Park, the Lake Shore Drive vicinity, and Hyde Park, the suburban population continues to disperse over a widening geographic area. Despite the suburban dispersal, the majority of Jews in the suburbs are clustered on blocks whose population is more than half Jewish. Orthodox and Conservative Jews are more likely to live on blocks with more Jews than are Reform or the unaffiliated. However, the dispersal of much of the Jewish population to the suburbs at a lower population density has made it more difficult to supply certain services desired by Jews.

The movement of Jews such as "empty nesters" from the suburbs to the city, while increasing, is still relatively small. Conversely, a small but growing number of "empty nesters" are selling their homes in Chicago or the Near North suburbs and moving into condominium or apartment complexes in some of the more distant outlying suburbs such as Northbrook, Deerfield, Des Plaines, Glenview, or Buffalo Grove, where they can be relieved of the requirements of house ownership and possibly be closer to their children. It is estimated that in recent years about four times as many Jews have moved from the city to the suburbs as have moved in the opposite direction.

### CHICAGO-AREA JEWRY TODAY: PROBLEMS AND PROGRESS

In addition to major geographic changes, recent decades have witnessed substantial changes in the characteristics and demographics of the Chicago Jewish community. The Jewish Federation study of 1990 showed that despite a low birth rate, movement to the Sun Belt, intermarriage, and relatively small Jewish immigration compared to the past, the Chicago-area Jewish population has hardly declined in recent decades. In 1990 it was estimated at 261,000, up from 248,000 in 1982 but down from 269,000 in 1960. (See table 6.) The Jews comprise almost 4 percent of the total area population, but that percentage is down from almost 7 percent in 1930. About 3 percent of Chicago's population is Jewish, as is about 4 percent of the suburban population. The Jewish population has aged and there are fewer children and more small households, reflecting the fact that there are more singles, elderly people, and childless couples.

Jews have made advances both educationally and professionally, and they can now enter into most fields of endeavor. The number of Jewish women in the workforce has increased rapidly. The average Chicago Jewish family median income in 1980 was 40 percent higher than that of the general population, although there were still some 20,000 Jews with incomes below the poverty lev-

TABLE 6. *Estimated Jewish Population in Chicago Area*[a]

| Year | Jewish Population |
|------|-------------------|
| 1850 | 200 |
| 1860 | 1,500 |
| 1870 | 4,000 |
| 1880 | 10,000 |
| 1900 | 75,000 |
| 1920 | 230,000 |
| 1940 | 290,000 |
| 1960 | 269,000 |
| 1970 | 253,000 |
| 1980 | 248,000 |
| 1990 | 261,000 |

a. Based on numerous surveys and estimates through the years by a variety of Jewish organizations.

el and another 18,000 who were considered economically vulnerable.[39] These categories include many elderly people, some recent immigrants, the handicapped, and some large ultra-observant families who have special education and food expenses.

The high median income reflects the fact that about twice as many Jews attend college as do members of the general urban population.[40] About 90 percent of young Jews now attend college and 62 percent of Jewish men and women are now college graduates. A Jewish Federation of Metropolitan Chicago survey in 1990 found that vocationally, 31 percent of the area's Jews were in the professions and related fields, 18 percent were in management, 18 percent in sales, 18 percent in clerical/support, and 11 percent in service/blue-collar fields.

There are some major demographic differences between the Jews of Chicago and those of the suburbs. Of the 38,000 Jews who had incomes near or below the poverty level, over 80 percent lived in Chicago. While the estimated median Jewish household income in the near north, northwest, south, and west suburbs was around $30,000 in a 1982 survey, and $45,760 in the north and far north suburbs, in Chicago itself the median income was $21,594.[41] Despite Chicago's having only 38 percent of the total Jewish population of the area in 1982, it had 49 percent of the households, reflecting the city's large population of single Jewish people. In 1982 the city contained about 70 percent of those over sixty-five years of age (26 percent of the city's Jewish population) and 60 percent of the singles (unmarried). Conversely, the suburbs contained about 75 percent of the Jewish youths under eighteen. The city also contained a much higher proportion of Jewish renters (more than half of them rent) than do the suburbs, where the single-family home is the prevailing place of residence. However, the city, probably reflecting the concentration and growing number of Jewish singles in their twenties and thirties, ranks as high as or even higher than most suburban areas in the number of professionals (36 percent) and those having higher degrees (27 percent). An important and rapid demographic change revealed in the 1990 survey was that slightly over half of the Jewish elderly now live in the suburbs.

Statistics show many positive changes in recent decades for the Jewish population in the Chicago area and in the United States in general, which have somewhat transformed life patterns. For example, Jews have achieved a position of relative influence and prosperity never before realized in the Diaspora. Yet, many of the old festering problems, such as sporadic evidence and acts of anti-Semitism, job discrimination, and concern for Israel's safety and survival, still remain along with some new problems. The concern for Israel is manifested in many ways, including at the ballot box, as evidenced by the many Jews who voted against Senator Adlai Stevenson II and Senator Charles Percy probably because of their questionable stance on Israel.

Some people fear that the open society that replaced the European ghetto is creating a dangerous challenge to their continuity and survival as Jews. The earliest immigrants are usually the most assimilated. Rising levels of education, occupation, and income and general Jewish acceptance seem to increase assim-

The annual walk by thousands, mainly youths, to show support and raise money for Israel.
(Courtesy of the Jewish Federation of Metropolitan Chicago.)

ilation levels.[42] Of major concern is the uncertain direction American Jewry will take. Threats to its future lie in the lessening of the synagogue as a religious force, changing family values, limited education in Judaism, uncaring attitudes of some Jewish youth toward Jewish institutions and communal life, the attraction of cults for a considerable number of Jewish youths, the fragmentation caused by suburbanization, and the alarming rate of intermarriage. At one time the mark of an intermarriage was when an Eastern European Jew married a German Jew. Today the apprehension and distress is over the rapidly increasing interfaith marriages. Some studies attribute the increase of such marriages to a number of factors, including the lack of intensive Jewish education for many of the Jewish youth, the greater contact between Jews and non-Jews in a free society, and diminishing cultural differences between Jew and gentile. Although for all Jewish age groups in the Chicago area, 83 percent of all marriages involve couples in which both partners are Jewish, over one-third of marriages between people under forty years of age involve non-Jewish spouses, with the percentage being even higher for more recent marriages. A national Jewish population survey has shown that since 1985 only 48 percent of Jewish marriages involve partners who were born Jewish, down from 91 percent of those who married before 1965. Conversion to Judaism takes place in fewer than 20 percent of these marriages, and more than half of these eventually end in divorce. Additionally, 90 percent of the children of mixed marriages marry outside the Jewish faith.

Maladies of society such as alcoholism, drugs, spousal abuse, and divorce, all of which had been rare in the Jewish community in the past, are now also increasing, although they are still well below national levels. One of the many explanations for this is that Jewish couples have "a highly developed art of quarreling which resolved disputes. . . . A Jewish husband and wife will spend hour after hour stormily ventilating differences of opinion while other couples stew quietly all the way to the divorce court."[43] Nevertheless, about one-third of Jewish marriages do end in divorce, possibly due to the changing attitude toward the sanctity of marriage and the changing position of women, which has opened many jobs to them and made them more independent. Family stress also often results from the fact that about two-thirds of Jewish families with young children have both parents working, thereby restricting the time available for many essential family needs.

There is a constant debate about the need for more Jewish education for Jewish youth. Statistics by age categories show that about 60 percent of children six to thirteen years of age are receiving some formal Jewish education, even if it is only one day a week. But only 20 percent of Jewish teenagers are still attending Jewish education classes after Bar or Bat Mitzvah. Nonetheless, there is still good attendance at Jewish day schools; Jewish-oriented camps run by religious, Zionist, and other Jewish organizations; Hebrew classes in high school; and Jewish studies courses in college. In addition, young people still travel and work in Israel. By contrast, the secular Yiddish schools of Chicago fostered by such groups as the Arbeiter Ring, Poalei Zion, International Workers Order, the Borochov School, the procommunist Non-Partisan Labor Children's Schools, and the politically neutral Sholem Aleichem schools that flourished during the immigrant period in the first part of this century disappeared in the period after World War II. They had originally been developed to serve as a bond for the Jewish people by perpetuating Yiddish language, Jewish literature, history, and folklore. They closed because of financial stress, frequent political bickering among radical groups, the decline of Yiddish speech, and, particularly, the rapid Americanization of the Jewish population.[44]

The long-established afternoon and Sunday Jewish schools, most of which are synagogue sponsored, had until the last few years experienced enrollment losses due to the decline of the Jewish school-age population. Of the 18,300 enrolled in 1991 in formal Jewish education classes, about 80 percent were in these afternoon or Sunday programs. However, there has been rapid growth of all-day Jewish elementary schools and high schools, both Orthodox and non-Orthodox, many of them recently organized, such as the first Reform Jewish day school in 1987, as some parents try to upgrade their children's secular education as well as teach them about their cultural heritage. While many Jewish families are strong supporters of public school education, a number are discontent with the quality of education now received in public schools. The total local day school enrollment in 1991 was 3,900 students, with 68 percent of the children attending Orthodox schools.[45] After many proposals for mergers, the schools are still run by two separate boards, the Associated Talmud Torahs, which primarily serves the Orthodox and Traditional groups, and the Board of Jewish Education, which primarily is associated with the Reform, Conservative, and Reconstructionist movements. The boards now supervise about

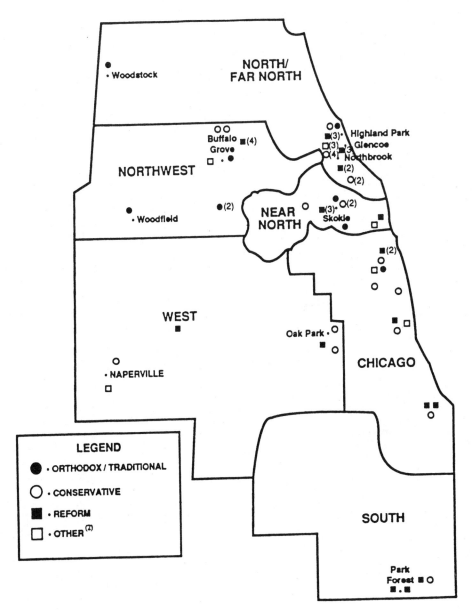

NORTH/
FAR NORTH

• Woodstock

NORTHWEST

Buffalo
Grove ■(4)

Highland Park
■(3)•
□(3)• Glencoe
○(4) Northbrook
■(2)
○(2)

• Woodfield
●(2)

NEAR
NORTH
Skokie
■(3)• ○(2)

WEST
■

Oak Park •○

CHICAGO

○ • NAPERVILLE
□

LEGEND
● • ORTHODOX / TRADITIONAL
○ • CONSERVATIVE
■ • REFORM
□ • OTHER (2)

SOUTH

Park
Forest ■ ○
■ • ■

*Distribution of Associated Talmud Torahs (ATT) and Board of Jewish Education (BJE) supplementary schools (part-time schools usually offering Judaic studies in the late afternoon and/or on weekends) located within the Chicago Metropolitan area. Multiple sites in the same community are shown by numbers within parentheses. "Other" includes two Recon-structionist supplementary schools and six Early Child-hood Programs. In 1991 there were 14,400 students enrolled in these schools compared to 3,900 in day schools.*

(From the Commission on Jewish Education of the Jewish Federation of Metropolitan Chicago, *Insuring Our Future: A Report on Jewish Education in Chicago,* 1991.)

ninety schools throughout the metropolitan area, including about twenty all-day schools. In 1993 a partnership of the Conservative, Reform, and Reconstructionist synagogue movements, the Board of Jewish Education, and the Jewish Federation of Metropolitan Chicago was organized. Its purpose was to enhance the quality of Jewish life and to ensure the continuity of the Chicago Jewish community by supporting in various ways the strengthening of formal and informal Jewish education programs for children and adults. The Community Foundation for Jewish Education was thus established.

Jewish study courses for adults have also been benefitting from a renaissance of interest among many Jews in their heritage and from their concern about Israel's future and survival. These courses, often part of a family education program, are offered by many religious institutions and Jewish organizations, local colleges, and universities, as well as at the fully accredited Spertus Institute of Jewish Studies. The institute was established in 1924 as the College of Jew-

The Ida Crown Jewish
Academy, an all-day high
school for Orthodox boys
and girls at 2828 West Pratt
Avenue in the West Rogers
Park area.

(Photo by Irving Cutler.)

ish Studies, mainly to train teachers for the Jewish schools. Despite periods of
financial stress and some community indifference, since 1974 it has been cen-
trally located in good quarters at 618 South Michigan Avenue; in the late 1980s
it had an enrollment of around six hundred students and a faculty of twenty-
three.[46] It awards bachelor's and graduate degrees in several aspects of Jewish
studies and has a reciprocal course credit agreement with most major universities in the area. Its 73,000-volume Asher Library is recognized as one of the best
of its kind in the country. The same building contains the Chicago Jewish
Archives and the Spertus Museum of Judaica, founded in 1967, which contains
more than three thousand Jewish artifacts.

Some members of the older generations occasionally exhibit antagonism to
reminders of their Jewish heritage. In a letter to the editor of the *Sentinel,* a
Jewish weekly, a Jewish orchestra leader complained that about eight or ten
times a year at a Jewish wedding or Bar Mitzvah he would receive orders from
"mine host" right at the outset: "Do not play any Jewish music." He wrote that
he plays for many different ethnic groups and has never been told not to play
their folk music. "Is it that they are afraid they will offend the gentiles present
or that they no longer wish to be reminded of their humble beginnings when
the parties were always held in a broken down hall with three *klezmorim* playing folk music? What is with our people? Where will it end?"[47]

American Jews are often torn between differing American societal values and

The Spertus Institute of Jewish Studies, 618 South Michigan Avenue, was founded in 1924 as the College of Jewish Studies. The building also houses the Chicago Jewish Archives, the Asher Library, the Chicago Jewish Historical Society, and the Spertus Museum of Judaica.

(Photo by Irving Cutler.)

their Jewishness. But, in general, when faced with problems dealing with their youth, family relationships, and changing values, the offspring (now often fourth generation) of Chicago's earlier Jewish settlers, most now living in the suburbs, are still usually buoyed up by the residual effects of their culture and Jewish self-consciousness, the immigrant experience, and the transmitted values of their parents and grandparents, which help to soften the effects of their problems. And although the *Yiddishkeit* diminishes and the identity problems increase with each generation and with movement upward economically and outward geographically, many cherished fundamental values remain. Emphasis on education, peaceful conduct, respectability, liberality, culture, and a sense of charity generally continues unabated, as does achievement. The once-prevalent Jewish ethnic antagonisms and divisions about Zionism and religion have given way to a Jewish community that is united on most issues, although differences still remain in regard to Israeli policies and to religion, especially between the Orthodox and the non-Orthodox. However, the influence of religion seems not as important to some Jews as in the past, but divisiveness on these issues still remains an important challenge. There is also some indication that as Jews become more comfortable economically and socially, their commitment to liberal causes may not be as great as in the past. Still, in the mayoral elections of the 1980s the Jews seemed to give the strongest support to Harold Washington of any of the white groups.

The Jews remain important book buyers and supporters of the universities, the Chicago Symphony, Ravinia, the Art Institute, and the Lyric Opera. The tradition of *tzedaka* and helping in the area of community responsibility continues to be strong both in the city and in the suburbs. Jewish efforts at self-taxation for charity are rarely equalled by any other group.

The Jewish Federation of Metropolitan Chicago is the main Jewish agency providing needed services today for the Jewish community. This model community umbrella organization was founded in 1900 as the successor to somewhat similar but smaller agencies. Since its founding, its professional executive leadership has included Louis M. Cahn, Samuel A. Goldsmith, James P. Rice, and, since 1980, Dr. Steven B. Nasatir, assisted by staff colleagues, lay leaders, and board members. Many of the area's most esteemed and dedicated Jews have served it in leadership roles. The Jewish Federation of Metropolitan Chicago maintains or helps support numerous community, social welfare, health care, cultural, religious, and educational services and organizations that encompass many facets of Jewish life, including aid to refugees, orphans, students, the elderly, the unemployed, the sick, and the poor. Through the years it has replaced many abandoned communal institutions of the city with new ones erected in areas into which the Jews have moved. About a dozen city and suburban Jewish community centers and senior adult centers operate under the aegis of the Jewish Federation of Metropolitan Chicago. One of its agencies, the Jewish Family and Community Service (or its predecessors), had its beginnings as far back as 1859.

The increased dispersal of a more eclectic Jewish population makes such services much more difficult to provide and more costly. Money for the support of the numerous local services and for Israel is raised through the efficient appeals campaign of the Jewish United Fund–Israel Emergency Fund, working largely through some four thousand dedicated campaign volunteers. In 1994 about forty-five thousand families gave over $54,000,000 for the fund; additionally, in the last five years nearly $50,000,000 was contributed for Operation Exodus to help resettle Russian and other Jews.[48]

The numerous *landsmanshaften,* the Workmen's Circle, the Farband, and other groups that were once an integral part of the immigrant's life have declined sharply as most of the Jewish immigrants have passed from the scene. Gone also is the benevolence and intimacy of the shtetl-like communities where

The Jewish Federation of Metropolitan Chicago has been headquartered since 1958 at 1 South Franklin Street (Ben Gurion Way). (Photo by Irving Cutler.)

*Yiddishkeit* came naturally and stores and organizations were all within walking distance. In their places are a broad range of local, regional, and national organizations that have been formed for fraternal, charitable, religious, or educational purposes, as well as groups that have been formed to aid various institutions in Israel. For some, support of Israel is a major focal point of their Jewish identity, and they wonder what will happen if Israel becomes a secure land. However, only 40 percent of the Jewish households now have membership in nonreligious Jewish organizations, compared to about 50 percent in 1971. Membership does not always mean active participation, and as more and more women work, they have less time for organizations.

Today there is a great diversity in types of religious Judaism among Jews, ranging from the religious fervor of the Lubavitch Hasidim to the humanistic Reform congregations. There are also specialized synagogues for the deaf, the blind, homosexuals, and the alienated. Yet, according to a 1990 Jewish Federation of Metropolitan Chicago survey, an estimated 56 percent of the area's Jewish households are not affiliated with a synagogue. Religious convictions may no longer always be the chief motivation for joining a particular congregation; the social, cultural, and local attractions are often just as, if not more, important. The change in religious affiliation that has coincided with the rapid decline of earlier Jewish immigrant groups and the movement of Jews to the suburbs is shown by the increase in the percentage of Conservative and Reform Jews. The mass movement out of Lawndale and the Northwest Side probably

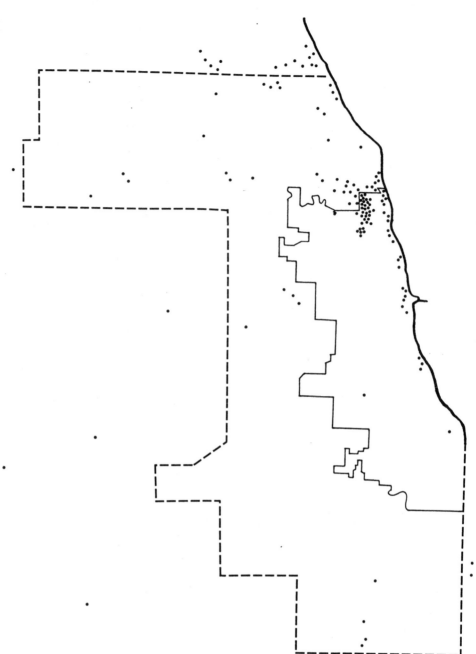

*Synagogue distribution in Chicagoland, 1990. One dot equals one synagogue location. The number of synagogues in 1990, about 120, has been about the same during the last few decades, but the size, religious affiliation, and location of the synagogues have changed. For example, the number of synagogues in southern Lake County, Illinois, has increased to seventeen, more than double the number there a dozen years ago.*

(Map by Irving Cutler.)

had the greatest disruptive effect on the Orthodox institutions, as did some internal fragmentation and the generally elderly membership. More than in other groups, many of the Orthodox, including some leaders, have moved to Israel.

A survey by the Jewish Federation shows that of those households affiliated with Jewish congregations, 44 percent belong to Conservative congregations, 37 percent to Reform, 17 percent to Orthodox-Traditional, and 2 percent to Reconstructionist congregations.[49] The number of synagogues in the Chicago area today – about 120 – remains about the same as it was a quarter of a century ago, but the location and size of these synagogues and their division among religious denominations have changed markedly, as has, in all probability, the intensity of religious dedication of their members. While many Jews, through

TABLE 7. *Indicators of Trends in Jewish Identity and Involvement Comparing Chicago Jews and the National Jewish Populace*[a]

| | Chicago 1982 | Chicago 1990 | National 1990 |
|---|---|---|---|
| Celebrate Passover | 84.6% | 93.0% | 78.2% |
| Celebrate Hannukah | 75.0 | 84.1 | 71.2 |
| Identify with denomination | 86.0 | 86.0 | 74.0 |
| Contribute to Jewish philanthropy | 68.0 | 75.0 | 56.0 |
| Close friends Jewish (most–nearly all) | 61.5 | 58.2 | 38.0 |
| Synagogue affiliated | 44.0 | 43.5 | 37.0 |
| Jewish organizational member | 37.0 | 40.3 | 28.0 |
| Visited Israel | 30.0 | 39.6 | 27.0 |
| Close friends/relatives in Israel | — | 36.7 | 32.0 |
| Read/subscribe to Jewish periodicals | 33.0 | 35.0 | 23.4 |
| Volunteer work for Jewish organizations | — | 30.3 | 18.0 |
| Participated in adult Jewish education | 24.7 | 29.0 | 14.0 |

a. Results are based on a scientific sample of 1,247 completed interviews in 1982 and 2,248 such interviews in 1990 in the Chicago area by the Jewish Federation of Metropolitan Chicago. The 1990 results show a slight trend of increasing Jewish involvement and also a substantially higher involvement than that of the national Jewish populace.

the years, have moved further away from the heart of Jewish life, there is a smaller group, often young people, who have fervently embraced their Jewish heritage, traditions, and obligations into their daily living, often more so than their parents (see table 7).

While strong differences occasionally exist concerning some issues among the various denominations, and most have their own auxiliary arms such as rabbinical organizations, publications, camps, and programs, the factions generally unite on many of the issues affecting the Jewish community. The Chicago Board of Rabbis, headed for many years by Rabbi Mordecai Simon, serves as an umbrella association that is open to all of the religious groups. It carries on extensive education, broadcasting, and chaplaincy programs as well as playing an important role in many communal activities.

The once tripartite division of virtually the entire Jewish community into North, South, and West Side neighborhoods in Chicago, with certain social, economic, ethnic, and religious implications, has long been erased as the Jews have dispersed into many communities over a wide geographical area, especially into the north and northwest suburbs. The literally extended family may now have the grandparents living in West Rogers Park, their children in Wilmette, and their grandchildren in Buffalo Grove.

The sharp dichotomy that once existed between German and Eastern European Jews has essentially disappeared, as the process of acculturation has progressed rapidly. The transition from European shtetlach and cities to Chicago suburbs is but a fleeting moment in the long history of the Jews. It is a noteworthy American – and Jewish – success story, and one of many contributions to the city and nation, though it was not written without hardship, toil, and perseverance.

# Glossary

*aliyah* : being called to the Torah reading in the synagogue; migration to Israel

*balebatim* : men of substance and high standing; the burghers

*bet din* : Jewish court employing religious and Talmudic law and principles

*bimah* : reader's stand in synagogue; pulpit

*Bundist* : member of the Jewish workers socialist movement, mainly in Eastern Europe, strongly in favor of Yiddish language and culture but opposed to Zionism

*challah* : a white bread, often braided, usually served on the Sabbath and for holidays and special occasions

*chazan* : the cantor who sings the liturgy in a Jewish religious service

*cheder* : elementary Hebrew school

*chutzpah* : nerve, excess of gall, outrageous gutsy behavior

*di alte haim* : the Old Country home

*dorf (*pl., *derfer)* : a small village

*eruv* : a boundaried area within which observant Jews are allowed to carry things on the Sabbath, something otherwise not allowed under Jewish law

*etrog* : citrus fruit used to celebrate Sukkot

*farfel* : noodle flakes

*Gabbai* : once a collector of synagogue funds and charitable contributions; now an honorary synagogue official with certain ritual functions

*Galitzianer* : persons from Galicia, an area in southeastern Poland and northwestern Ukraine

*hamentash* : a small triangular cake baked especially for the Purim holiday, which celebrates the foiling of the plot of Hamen

*Hasidism* : a religious, mystical revival movement in Judaism which evolved in Eastern Europe in the eighteenth century and which was in opposition to many of the prevailing religious concepts of the time

*Haskalah* : the movement for enlightenment, intellectual emancipation, and secular education that arose among Jews in Germany and Eastern Europe during the eighteenth and nineteenth centuries

*Judengasse* : Jewish street; Jewish area

*Judenrein* : free of Jews – as in Germany after the Nazis

*kaddish* : mourner's prayer

*kapote* : traditional long coat that originated in Eastern Europe, usually black, worn especially by very observant Jews

*kashrut* : kosher practices in regard to the Jewish dietary code

*kehillah* : an organized Jewish communal self-government

*klezmorim* : Eastern European Jewish musicians who played traditional folk songs and dances at weddings and other celebrations

*landsman* : someone who comes from one's hometown in the Old Country

*landsmanshaften* : an organization of immigrants from the same town in the Old Country

*latke* : a potato pancake served especially on Chanukah

*Litvak* : a Jew from Lithuania or adjacent regions

*lulav* : a palm branch used during the Sukkot services

*mama loshen* : mother tongue, especially Yiddish

*mazel tov* : good luck, congratulations

*melamed* : teacher, especially of young children

*menshlikhkeit* : humaness

*meshumed* : apostate; religious renegade

*minche* : daily afternoon prayer service

*mikvah* : ritual bath used mainly by married women after menstruation

*minyan* : the minimum of ten Hebrew males over thirteen years of age required for communal services; many non-Orthodox congregations include women in a minyan

*mitzvah (*pl., *mitzvot)* : a good deed; commandment

*mohel* : a person trained and authorized to perform a circumcision

*naches* : joy or pride usually derived from one's offspring

*pecklach* : bundles, packages

*pogroms* : organized massacres of Jews

*proste Yidn* : the unlettered common Jew, the humble folk

*pushkas* : small metal boxes used for donations to Jewish causes

*rosh Yeshivah* : head of a Talmudic institution

*schnapps* : whiskey, brandy

*schnorrer* : a beggar, a moocher, an impudent indigent

*shadchans* : marriage arrangers, matchmakers

*sheitel* : a wig worn by very Orthodox married women to cover the head for reasons of modesty

*shep* : derive, garner

*shmatte* : rag; cheap or old clothes

*shochet* : a person authorized to kill fowl, cattle, or lamb according to Jewish ritual

*shomer shabbas* : one who observes the Sabbath to the letter of the law; an observant Jew

*shtetl (pl., shtetlach)* : small rural village or town in Eastern Europe inhabited primarily by Jews

*shtiebl* : a house used at least partially as a synagogue; often a room in a rabbi's house for praying and learning

*shuckling* : to shake or sway in fervent prayer

*shul* : a synagogue

*Shulchan Aruch* : authoritative code of Jewish law and practice

*shulen* : Jewish secular schools

*siddur* : daily prayer book

*Talmud Torah* : Hebrew religious school

*Tashlich* : symbolically casting off one's sins in a nearby body of water on the first day of Rosh Hashonah

*tzedakah* : charity; righteousness

*unsere leite* : our people; one of us

*verein* : an organization or society, usually of people from the same community in the Old Country

*yarmulke* : a skullcap worn by observant Jewish males

*yeshivah* : a school of higher and intensive Jewish study where Talmud, law, and ritual are generally the major subjects; an Orthodox seminary

*yichus* : distinguished ancestral background; status by virtue of family station, learning, or wealth

*Yiddishkeit* : Jewishness; the practices and customs of traditional Judaism and Jewish folkways and mores

*yizkor bikher* : a memorial book commemorating those slaughtered in a given community during the Holocaust

*zemirot* : songs, hymns, and melodies usually sung at the Sabbath table

# Chronology of Chicago Jewish History

1833    Chicago, with 350 inhabitants, incorporated as a town.

1841    First permanent Jewish settlers arrive in Chicago.

1845    First Jewish High Holy Day services held above store on Lake and Wells streets.

        Jewish Burial Ground Society founded – first Jewish organization in Chicago.

1846    Jewish cemetery established near Lake Michigan just north of North Avenue, now Lincoln Park.

1847    Kehilath Anshe Maariv (KAM), first Jewish congregation in Chicago, established with Rev. Ignatz Kunreuther as religious leader.

        Henry Meyer, first Jewish farmer in Cook County, settles in the Schaumburg area.

1849    First Jewish wedding in Chicago, between Jacob Rosenberg and Hannah Reese (of the Michael Reese family).

1850    Jewish population in Chicago estimated at 200 out of total population of about 30,000.

1851    Hebrew Benevolent Society of Chicago organized; establishes a second Jewish cemetery at Clark and Grace streets.

        KAM constructs first synagogue building in Illinois at Clark and Quincy streets.

1852    Kehilath B'nai Sholom is organized as the second Jewish congregation in Chicago, now part of KAM–Isaiah Israel.

1857    First B'nai B'rith Lodge established – Ramah Lodge No. 33.

1859    United Hebrew Relief Association established.

        KAM establishes an all-day school and also a Sunday school.

1860    An estimated 1,500 Jews live in Chicago; total city population is 112,000.

1861    Chicago Sinai Congregation organized on Monroe Street near La Salle Street as Chicago's first Reform temple, with Dr. Bernard Felsenthal as its first spiritual leader.

        Abraham Kohn, city clerk of Chicago, presents president-elect Abraham Lincoln with an American flag inscribed with a biblical quotation in Hebrew.

1862    A volunteer company of Jewish soldiers, the Concordia Guards, is organized to fight for the Union in the Civil War.

        City directory lists eleven Jewish organizations.

1864    Zion Congregation organized as a Reform temple and first Jewish house of worship on the West Side, now part of Oak Park Temple.

1865    The first Orthodox Congregation of Eastern European Jews, B'nai Jacob, is organized.

1866    Congregation Beth Hamedrash Hagodol established.

1867    North Chicago Hebrew Congregation founded as first congregation on the North Side, now Temple Sholom.

1868    First Jewish hospital opened on La Salle Street between Schiller and Goethe streets.

1869    The Standard Club founded.

        First Jewish periodical in Chicago, *Zeichen der Zeit* (Signs of the Times), a monthly in German, is started and published by Dr. Isaac Chronic, rabbi of Chicago Sinai Congregation.

1870    B'nai Abraham Congregation founded, the first in Maxwell Street area, now part of Oak Park Temple.

        Congregation Ohave Sholom Mariampoler founded, now part of Anshe Sholom B'nai Israel, the city's oldest existing Orthodox congregation.

        An estimated 4,000 Jews live in Chicago; total city population is 299,000.

1871    The Great Chicago Fire leaves 500 Jewish families homeless, destroying the Jewish hospital, four of the B'nai B'rith lodges, and consuming or badly damaging most of the city's synagogues.

        Beth El Congregation, founded as Rodef Sholom, the first Jewish congregation on the Northwest Side.

        Dr. Liebman Adler is appointed rabbi of KAM.

1873    The first Jewish periodical in English, the *Occident,* is started.

Congregation Anshe Emet founded.

1874    Congregation Rodfei Zedek established in stockyards area.

1875    Congregation Anshe Kneseth Israel, the "Russishe Shul," founded.

1876    Jewish Educational Society founded.

1877    *Israelitische Press,* the city's first Yiddish newspaper, is published.

Zion Literary Society founded.

1878    Hebrew Free School started; later became Moses Montefiore Hebrew Free School.

1880    Dr. Emil G. Hirsch becomes rabbi at Chicago Sinai Congregation.

Congregation Emanuel founded as a German-speaking Orthodox congregation, now Reform.

An estimated 10,000 Jews live in Chicago; total city population is 503,000.

1881    Michael Reese Hospital opened.

1882    Chicago Women's Aid founded.

1886    First Jewish labor groups formed.

First Zionist group organized in Chicago, Hovevi Zion (Lovers of Zion).

Protesting Jewish workers beaten by police on the day after the Haymarket Riot.

1887    *Daily Jewish Courier,* Yiddish newspaper, founded.

1889    United Hebrew Charities chartered.

1890    Jewish Training School, a forerunner of manual training classes in public school systems, is organized.

Chicago Cloak Makers Union chartered city's first formal Jewish trade union.

Jewish leaders raise money to assure the founding of the University of Chicago.

1891    *Reform Advocate* founded and edited by Dr. Emil G. Hirsch.

Hebrew Literary Society founded.

1893    World's Columbian Exposition featured the World's Parliament of Religion, which included the Jewish
            Denominational Congress and the Jewish Women's Congress.

National Council of Jewish Women organized, with Hannah G. Solomon as president and Sadie
            American as secretary.

Maxwell Street Settlement founded at 185 Maxwell Street, modeled after Hull-House.

Chicago Home for Jewish Aged opened at Sixty-second Street and Drexel Avenue.

Eastern European intellectuals organize the Self-Educational Club.

Chicago Rabbinical Association is organized (now Chicago Board of Rabbis).

1894    Independent Western Star Order formed.

1896    Chicago Zionist Organization, No. 1, the first Herzilian Zionist group in the country, is organized, with
            Bernard Horwich as president; name later changed to Knights of Zion.

1899    Chicago Home for Jewish Orphans established at 3601 Vernon Avenue.

1900    Associated Jewish Charities formed to coordinate charitable activities.

Samuel Alschuler nominated for governor of Illinois.

An estimated 75,000 Jews live in Chicago; total city population is 1,698,000.

1901    Home for Jewish Friendless and Working Girls organized.

1902    Yeshivat Etz Chaim incorporated, first Orthodox Talmudic school.

1903    Chicago Hebrew Institute founded at 224 Blue Island Avenue; forerunner of present Jewish Community
            Centers.

Orthodox Jewish Home for the Aged at Ogden and Albany avenues established.

First branch of Arbeiter Ring established.

1905    Poale Zion group established.

Upheavals in Russia increase Jewish immigration to Chicago.

1906    Marks Nathan Jewish Orphan Home founded.

1907    Deborah Boys' Club founded.

Jewish Home Finding Society organized.

Kishinev Massacre in Russia provokes anxiety in Chicago Jewish community.

Albert Abraham Michelson received Nobel Prize for physics.

1908    Harry Auerbuch, a Russian Jewish immigrant, killed by Chicago police chief in mysterious circumstances.

Chicago Hebrew Institute relocated to much larger facility at Taylor and Lytle streets.

1910    Strike of 40,000 garment workers, mainly Jewish, led by Sidney Hillman and Bessie Abramovitz.

Conference of Jewish Women's Organizations organized under leadership of Hannah G. Solomon.

1911    The *Sentinel*, weekly journal, starts publication.

1912    Federated Orthodox Jewish Charities formed.

Hebrew Immigrant Aid Society (HIAS) established in Chicago.

Arbeiter Verband (Jewish National Workers Alliance) fraternal order established.

Maimonides Hospital (now Mount Sinai) opened.

1913    Hadassah established in Chicago.

Rest Haven (now Schwab Rehabilitation Center) established for the care of convalescing women and girls.

Mizrachi Zionist group established in Chicago.

Chicagoans founded the B'nai B'rith Anti-Defamation League.

Daughters of Zion Infant Home and Day Nursery established on Northwest Side.

1914    Sam Meisenberg, first American to die in Mexican incursion, honored with official city parade.

1915    Major campaign by Orthodox Jews to raise funds to aid Jews in war-torn Eastern Europe.

Increased movement of Eastern European Jews out of Maxwell Street area to Lawndale.

1917    The Covenant Club established.

Yavneh Hebrew School established on the Northwest Side and Grenshaw Street Talmud Torah established in Lawndale.

The Balfour Declaration by England strengthens the Zionist movement.

1919    Glickman's Palace Theatre (Yiddish) opened on Roosevelt Road and Blue Island Avenue.

1920    The *Forward* begins publication of a Chicago edition.

An estimated 230,000 Jews live in Chicago; total city population is 2,702,000.

1921    Jewish artists group, Around the Palette, organized.

Camp CHI for girls established at Loon Lake, Illinois.

Jewish Training School closed.

1922    Hebrew Theological College opened at Douglas Boulevard and St. Louis Avenue.

1923    Associated Jewish Charities and Federated Orthodox Jewish Charities of Chicago merge and become Jewish Charities of Chicago; Julius Rosenwald is first president.

First Hillel organization in the nation established at the University of Illinois at Urbana, Illinois, with backing of Chicago Jewish leaders.

Jewish Education Committee formed, predecessor to the Board of Jewish Education.

1924    The murder of Bobby Franks by Nathan Leopold and Richard Loeb, all three from wealthy South Side German Jewish families, shocks and troubles the Jewish community.

1925    Board of Jewish Education formed.

College of Jewish Studies started.

1926    Jewish People's Institute (JPI), formerly the Chicago Hebrew Institute, relocated from Taylor and Lytle streets to 3500 West Douglas Boulevard.

Queen Marie of Romania attends services at the Romanian synagogue on Douglas Boulevard.

1927    Four Yiddish theaters operating in Chicago.

1928    Pioneer Women branch established.

1929    An Orthodox *kehillah* is established to control kosher practices and tend to other Orthodox needs.

1930    An estimated 280,000 Jews live in Chicago; total city population is 3,376,000.

1932    Judge Henry Horner elected first Jewish governor of Illinois, reelected in 1936.

1933 • Hitler assumes power in Germany; Chicago Jewish community begins to take steps to help beleaguered German Jews.

First Women's American ORT group established in Chicago.

1934 • American Jewish Congress chapter established.

1936 Associated Talmud Torahs established to direct Orthodox education.

Chicago elects delegates to first World Jewish Congress.

Jewish Welfare Fund formed to raise funds for the needs of overseas Jews.

1937 • Chicago Rabbinical Council (CRC), comprised of Orthodox rabbis, is founded. It oversees the laws of *kashrut* and guides and assists the Orthodox community in other ways.

1938 Douglas Park Theatre (Yiddish) opened in Workmen's Circle building at Ogden and Kedzie avenues.

1940 An estimated 290,000 Jews live in Chicago; total city population is 3,397,000.

1941 United States enters World War II; over 45,000 Chicago Jews served in the armed forces, with almost 1,000 killed and 1,400 wounded.

Max Straus Center established in Albany Park.

1942 • Chicago Home for Jewish Orphans (Woodlawn Hall) closed.

1944 *Daily Jewish Courier* ceases publication after fifty-seven years.

1948 Chicago celebrated the rebirth of Israel; volunteers, money, and arms funneled into Israel.

Marks Nathan Jewish Orphan Home (Marks Nathan Hall) closed.

1950 Reflecting its broadening activities, the Jewish Charities becomes the Jewish Federation of Metropolitan Chicago.

1956 Jewish agencies assist in the settlement of Hungarian Jewish refugees.

1960 Bernard Horwich Jewish Community Center built in West Rogers Park.

An estimated 269,000 Jews live in Chicago metropolitan area; total city population is 3,550,000.

1961 • Spertus Museum started at 72 East Eleventh Street.

1964 Jewish Council on Urban Affairs established to have a voice in addressing Chicago's urban problems.

1968 Jewish United Fund replaces Combined Jewish Appeal, with Philip M. Klutznick as first general chairman.

1970 • College of Jewish Studies becomes Spertus College of Judaica; now Spertus Institute of Jewish Studies.

An estimated 253,000 Jews live in Chicago metropolitan area; total city population is 3,369,000.

1971 Council for Jewish Elderly established.

Mayer Kaplan Jewish Community Center opens in Skokie.

Jewish Community Centers opens Hyde Park JCC, initiates program in south suburbs.

1974 Jewish Federation and Jewish Welfare Fund merge.

1976 Milton Friedman received Nobel Prize for economics and Saul Bellow awarded Nobel Prize for literature.

1978 Small band of American Nazis enters and exits Skokie quickly as thousands demonstrate against them.

Lincoln Park/Lakeview Jewish Community Center opens.

1979 Herbert C. Brown receives Nobel Prize for chemistry.

1980 An estimated 248,000 Jews live in the Chicago Metropolitan area; 38 percent live in the city and 62 percent in the suburbs.

Anita M. Stone Jewish Community Center dedicated in Flossmoor.

1981 • Drexel Home for the Aged closed after ninety years of service; most residents moved to the new Lieberman Centre in Skokie.

1983 First Chicago Jewish Film Festival.

Jewish Federation study showed that there are 37,000 poor and economically vulnerable Jews in the Chicago area.

1985 Jacob Duman Jewish Community Center opened in Buffalo Grove.

1986 National Jewish Theater established in Skokie.

1987 On the anniversary of the Kristallnacht devastation in Germany, vandals deface and damage three synagogues and a number of Jewish-owned shops in West Rogers Park and Albany Park.

In a close race, Bernard Epton loses mayoral race to Harold Washington.

1988     Leon M. Lederman receives the Nobel Prize for physics.

Fiftieth anniversary of Kristallnacht commemorated by numerous community events.

1990     An estimated 261,000 Jews live in Chicago metropolitan area; total city population is 2,784,000.

1991     Jewish community distressed as Scud missiles strike Israel during the Gulf War.

1992     Gary S. Becker receives the Nobel Prize for economics.

Anita M. Stone Jewish Community Center moves into large facility in Flossmoor.

1993     Robert W. Fogel receives the Nobel Prize for economics.

Jews have conflicting opinions over Israel-PLO peace negotiations.

1995     Over 22,000 Soviet Jewish immigrants have now been resettled in Chicago since the 1970s.

# Notes

**Chapter 1** The First Wave

1 Patrick Shirreff, *A Tour through North America: together with a Comprehensive View of Canada and the United States* (Edinburgh: Oliver and Boyd, 1835), p. 226.

2 John Lewis Peyton, *Over the Alleghenies and Across the Prairies, Personal Recollection of the Far West One and Twenty Years Ago (1848)* (London: Simpkin, Marshall and Co., 1869), pp. 325–29.

3 Marvin Lowenthal, *The Jews of Germany* (Philadelphia: Jewish Publication Society of America, 1939), pp. 211–12.

4 Ibid., p. 210.

5 Bildarchiv Preussischer Kultubestz, *Jews in Germany under Prussian Rule* (Berlin: 1984), p. 33.

6 *Allgemeine Zeitung des Judentums,* Apr. 2, 1899, quoted in Abrhaham J. Karp, *Golden Door to America* (New York: Penguin Books, 1977), pp. 37–38.

7 Lowenthal, *Jews of Germany,* pp. 249–50.

8 Hyman L. Meites, ed., *History of the Jews of Chicago* (Chicago: Jewish Historical Society of Illinois, 1924), pp. 35–36. This classic book is a voluminous, comprehensive history of Chicago Jewry with special emphasis on important individuals, organizations, and institutions. It was an indispensable source of early Chicago Jewish history in the writing of this volume. The book was republished in 1990 by the Chicago Jewish Historical Society and Wellington Publishing, Inc.

9 Meites, *History of the Jews of Chicago,* p. 38.

10 Bernhard Felsenthal and Herman Eliassof, *The History of Kehillath Anshe Maarabh* (Chicago: Privately published, 1897), pp. 12–13. Also Mark Mandle, *Society News of the Chicago Jewish Historical Society* (Chicago, June 1986), p. 7.

11 Meites, *History of the Jews of Chicago,* p. 44.

12 Louis Wirth, *The Ghetto* (Chicago: University of Chicago Press, 1928), p. 158. This book, by a distinguished sociologist, is an account of the historical development of the "ghetto," with the last half of the book devoted largely to Chicago. Has good understanding of the Jewish immigrant.

13 Irving Cutler, *Chicago: Metropolis of the Mid-Continent,* 3d ed. (Dubuque: Geographic Society of Chicago and Kendall/Hunt Publishing Co., 1982), p. 282.

14 *Chicago Journal,* Nov. 14, 1899.

15 *The Asmonean,* vol. 2 (1850), pp. 126, 132, as quoted in Morris A. Gutstein, *A Priceless Heritage* (New York: Bloch Publishing Co., 1953), p. 60. Rabbi Gutstein's book is a well-documented, detailed study of Chicago Jewry in the nineteenth century, with especial emphasis on the community's religious and educational structure.

16 *Chicago Daily Democrat,* June 14, 1851.

17 *The Israelite,* May 4, 1857.

18 Meites, *History of the Jews of Chicago,* p. 58.

19 Ibid., p. 106.

20 *Chicago Tribune,* Aug. 16, 1862.

21 Meites, *History of the Jews of Chicago,* p. 97.

22 Ibid., p. 110.

23 Standard Club of Chicago, *The Standard Club's First Hundred Years* (Chicago: Standard Club of Chicago, 1969), p. 7.

24 Herman Kogan and Robert Cromie, *The Great Fire: Chicago 1871* (New York: G. P. Putnam's Sons, 1971), p. 9.

25 Gutstein, *Priceless Heritage,* p. 37.

26 Cutler, *Chicago: Metropolis of the Mid-Continent,* p. 30.

27 *The Israelite,* Oct. 20, 1871.

28 Ron Grossman, "Touring Chicago's Older Jewish Neighborhoods," *Jewish Chicago* (Sept. 1982): 45.

29 Cutler, *Chicago: Metropolis of the Mid-Continent,* p. 31.

30 Meites, *History of the Jews of Chicago,* p. 133.

31 Wirth, *The Ghetto,* p. 174.

32 Meites, *History of the Jews of Chicago,* p. 141.

33 Walter Roth, "Who Was Lazarus Silverman," *Chicago Jewish History* (Fall 1994): 1, 4–5.

34 M. R. Werner, *Julius Rosenwald: The Life of a Practical Humanitarian* (New York: Harper, 1939), p. 86.

35 Sarah Gordon, ed., *All Our Lives: A Centennial History of Michael Reese Hospital and Medical Center* (Chicago: Michael Reese Hospital and Medical Center, 1981), pp. 1–7.

36 Standard Club of Chicago, *First Hundred Years,* p. 31.

37 Grossman, "Touring Chicago's Older Jewish Neighborhood," p. 45.

38 Pamphlet, Jewish Educational Society of Chicago, Sept. 15, 1876, as quoted in Wirth, *The Ghetto,* pp. 176–77.

## **Chapter 2** The Second Wave

1 Jacob Frumkin, Gregor Aronson, and Alexis Goldenweiser, eds., *Russian Jewry (1860–1917)* (New York: Thomas Yoseloff, 1966), p. 17.

2 S. M. Dubnow, *History of the Jews in Russia and Poland,* 3 vols. (Philadelphia: Jewish Publication Society of America, 1916), 1:255. Simon Dubnow, a Russian Jew, was an eminent historian whose lifework was concentrated on Jewish history. This three-volume edition is a definitive history of Russian and Polish Jewry and was translated into several languages. Dubnow was murdered by the Nazis in 1941 at the age of eighty-one.

3 Chaim Potok, *Wanderings: Chaim Potok's History of the Jews* (New York: Knopf, 1978), p. 338.

4 Irving Howe, *World of Our Fathers* (New York: Harcourt Brace Jovanovich, 1976), pp. 7–8.

5 Diane K. Roskies and David G. Roskies, *The Shtetl Book* (New York: Ktav Publishing House, 1975), pp. 36–37.

6 Mark Zborowski and Elizabeth Herzog, *Life Is with People* (New York: Schocken Books, 1952), p. 71.

7 Eliezer L. Ehrmann, *Readings in Modern Jewish History* (New York: Ktav Publishing House, 1977), pp. 73–75.

8 Zborowski and Herzog, *Life Is with People,* pp. 233–34.

9 Maurice Samuel, *The World of Sholem Aleichem* (New York: Knopf, 1943), pp. 26–27, as quoted in Howe, *World of Our Fathers,* p. 10.

10 Abba Eben, *My People: The Story of the Jews* (New York: Random House, 1968), pp. 238–43.

11 Simon Rawidowicz, ed., *The Chicago Pinkas* (Chicago: College of Jewish Studies, 1952), p. 115.

12 Abram Leon Sachar, *A History of the Jews* (New York: Knopf, 1940), p. 322.

13 Salo W. Baron, *The Russian Jew under Tsars and Soviets,* 2d ed. (New York: Macmillan, 1976), p. 50.

14 Ibid., p. 29.

15 Milton Meltzer, *World of Our Fathers: The Jews of Eastern Europe* (New York: Farrar, Straus and Giroux, 1974), pp. 45–46.

16 Howe, *World of Our Fathers,* pp. 6–7.

17 Dubnow, *History of the Jews in Russia and Poland,* 3:33.

18 Ibid., p. 76.

19 Howard Morley Sachar, *The Course of Modern Jewish History* (New York: Delta, 1958), pp. 245–46.

20 Baron, *The Russian Jew under Tsars and Soviets,* p. 71.

21 Howe, *World of Our Fathers,* p. 27.

22 George W. Stevens, *The Land of the Dollar* (New York: Dodd, Mead, 1897), p. 144.

23 Wirth, *The Ghetto,* p. 205.

24 Seymour Jacob Pomrenze, "Aspects of Chicago Russian-Jewish Life, 1893–1915," in *The Chicago Pinkas,* ed. Rawidowicz, pp. 130–31.

25 Meites, *History of the Jews of Chicago,* pp. 150–51.

26 *Reform Advocate* (Chicago), July 22, 1899.

27 *Chicago Record Herald,* Apr. 2, 1905.

28 *Chicago Tribune,* July 19, 1891.

29 Residents of Hull-House, *Hull-House Maps and Papers* (New York: Thomas Y. Crowell, 1895), pp. 94–95.

30 Charles Bernheimer, *The Russian Jew in the United States: Studies of Social Conditions in New York, Philadelphia, and Chicago, with a Description of Rural Settlements* (Philadelphia: John C. Winston, 1905), p. 328.

31 Ibid., p. 320.

32 Harry Golden, *Travels through Jewish America* (Garden City, N.Y.: Doubleday, 1973), p. 206.

33 Bernheimer, *The Russian Jew in the United States,* p. 135.

34 Wirth, *The Ghetto,* pp. 232–33.

35 Ibid., p. 235.

36 Bernheimer, *The Russian Jew in the United States,* pp. 94–95.

37 Ibid., pp. 173–74.

38 *Report of the Religious School Work Committee of the Council of Jewish Women,* 1902.

39 Lottie Lavin, "The Jewish Educational System in Chicago" (Master's thesis, University of Chicago, 1938), pp. 21–22.

40 Philip P. Bregstone, *Chicago and Its Jews: A Cultural History* (Chicago, 1933), p. 69. This valuable, privately published book deals in a nonchronological manner with Chicago Jewish history from approximately the late 1880s to the early 1930s. The author, an attorney, public official, and reporter, reminisces and frequently offers opinions about numerous events and individuals, many personally familiar to him.

41 *Jewish Advance,* Aug. 12, 1884.

42 "The Jewish Manual Training School," *Occident,* June 22, 1888.

43 Harold Korey, "The History of Jewish Education in Chicago" (Ph.D. diss., University of Chicago, 1942), p. 73.

44 Reported in *Illinois Staatszeitung,* June 27, 1891.

45 Meites, *History of the Jews of Chicago,* p. 187.

46 Irving Cutler, "The Jews of Chicago: From Shtetl to Suburb," in *Ethnic Chicago,* ed. Melvin G. Holli and Peter d'A. Jones (Grand Rapids: Eerdmans, 1984), p. 85.

47 Howe, *World of Our Fathers,* p. 187.

48 Ibid., p. 186.

49 Sidney Sorkin, "Landsmanschaften," in *The Sentinel's History of Chicago Jewry, 1911–1986* (Chicago: Sentinel Publishing Co., 1986), p. 241. Sorkin in his extensive research on Landsmanshaften has found that the organizations have 160 numbered and named gates at Waldheim Cemetery.

50 Walter P. Zenner, "Chicago's Unknown Jews: Story of Local Sephardim," *Chicago Jewish History* 12, no. 3 (Mar. 1989): 1, 8–9.

51 Nathan Glazer, *American Judaism* (Chicago: University of Chicago Press, 1957), p. 66.

52 Bernard Horwich, *My First Eighty Years* (Chicago: Argus Books, 1939), pp. 131–32.

53 Bregstone, *Chicago and Its Jews,* p. 48.

54 *The Occident,* Dec. 31, 1886.

55 Wirth, *The Ghetto,* pp. 183–84.

56 Quoted in Bregstone, *Chicago and Its Jews,* p. 26.

57 Bregstone, *Chicago and Its Jews,* p. 67.

58 Joe Kraus, "Manny Abrahams Led Checkered Career as 'Boss of the Ghetto,'" *Chicago Jewish History* 16, no. 2 (Spring 1993): 1, 4–7.

59 Wirth, *The Ghetto,* p. 245.

60 Cutler, "The Jews of Chicago," p. 89.

61 Ira Berkow, *Maxwell Street* (Garden City, N.Y.: Doubleday, 1977), pp. 10–11.

62 *Chicago Chronicle,* Jan. 16, 1925.

## Chapter 3 Through the World Wars

1 Meites, *History of the Jews of Chicago,* p. 180.

2 Ibid., p. 177.

3 Ibid., p. 178.

4 Ibid., p. 201.

5 Jane Addams, *Twenty Years at Hull-House* (New York: Macmillan, 1910), pp. 285–87.

6 Walter Roth, "The Story of Samuel 'Nails' Morton: A 20th Century Chicago Golem?" *Chicago Jewish History* (Oct. 1989): 1, 6–9.

7 Bregstone, *Chicago and Its Jews,* p. 173.

8 Meites, *History of the Jews of Chicago,* p. 301.

9 Horwich, *My First Eighty Years,* p. 349.

10 Meites, *History of the Jews of Chicago,* pp. 290–91.

11 Walter Roth, "Chicago Minister Sought Palestine for Jews," *Chicago Jewish Historical Society News* (Sept. 1987): 3–6.

12 Milton J. Silberman, "Zionism – The Chicago Movement 1910–1960," in *The Sentinel's History of Chicago Jewry, 1911–1961* (Chicago: Sentinel Publishing Co., 1961), p. 169.

13 Ibid., pp. 169–70.

14 Louis L. Mann and Gerson B. Levi, *Glimpses of the Jewish Exhibit* (Chicago, 1934), pp. 5–6.

15 Letter, collection of Chicago Jewish Archives.

16 Meites, *History of the Jews of Chicago,* p. 319.

17 Ibid., p. 323.

18 Anita Libman Lebeson, "Recall to Life," in *The Sentinel's History of Chicago Jewry, 1911–1961,* pp. 30–31.

19 Thirty-fourth Annual statement of the Jewish Charities of Chicago, condition as of January 2, 1934, Jewish Federation of Metropolitan Chicago.

20 Lebeson, "Recall to Life," p. 27.

21 Alexander Dushkin, "Six Years of Jewish Education," *Jewish Education Magazine* (Jan. 1930): 45.

22 Meites, *History of the Jews of Chicago,* p. 332.

23 Lebeson, "Recall to Life," p. 25.

24 Ibid., p. 23.

25 Ibid., p. 37.

26 Tom Littlewood, *Horner of Illinois* (Evanston: Northwestern University Press, 1969), p. 182.

27 Morris J. Nathanson, "In Defense of Country," in *The Sentinel's History of Chicago Jewry, 1911–1961,* pp. 85–86.

28 Bureau of Jewish Employment Problems, *Fair Employment News Report* 2, no. 1 (May 25, 1953): 1–3.

29 Nathanson, "In Defense of Country," p. 86.

30 Lebeson, "Recall to Life," p. 46.

31 Ibid., p. 49.

## Chapter 4 Moving Upward

1 Gutstein, *Priceless Heritage,* p. 380.

2 Edward Herbert Mazur, "Minyans for a Prairie City: The Politics of Chicago Jewry, 1850–1940" (Ph.D. diss., University of Chicago, 1974), p. 63.

3 Isaac Metzker, ed., *A Bintel Brief* (Garden City: Doubleday, 1971), pp. 12–17.

4 Benjamin Weintraub, "People of the Book," in *The Sentinel's History of Chicago Jewry, 1911–1961,* pp. 115–18.

5 Irwin J. Suloway, "People of the Book: The Contribution of Chicago's Jewish Authors," in *The Sentinel's History of Chicago Jewry, 1911–1986,* pp. 151–56.

6 Ibid, p. 155.

7 Louise Dunn Yochim, "Artists," *The Sentinel Presents 100 Years of Jewish History* (Chicago, 1948), p. 29.

8 Louise Dunn Yochim, "Art that Endures," in *The Sentinel's History of Chicago Jewry, 1911–1986*, pp. 137–40.

9 Meites, *History of the Jews of Chicago*, p. 371.

10 Ibid., p. 367.

11 George Perlman, "And there was music," in *The Sentinel's History of Chicago Jewry, 1911–1986*, pp. 145–50.

12 Ibid., p. 150.

13 George Perlman, "Let There Be Music," in *The Sentinel's History of Chicago Jewry, 1911–1961*, pp. 99–104.

14 Harry Heller, "The World of Chicago Jewish Sports," in *The Sentinel's History of Chicago Jewry, 1911–1986*, pp. 129–35.

15 Gordon, ed., *All Our Lives*, pp. 23–24.

16 Ibid., p. 50.

17 Ibid., p. 86.

18 Ibid., p. 193.

19 Sidney J. Kaplan, ". . . the art of healing is so vast," in *The Sentinel's History of Chicago Jewry, 1911–1986*, pp. 125–28.

20 Ibid., pp. 125–26.

21 *Reform Advocate* (Chicago), Apr. 8, 1916.

22 Kaplan, ". . . the art of healing," p. 126.

23 Walter Roth, "New Book Explores Life of Colorful Local Character," *Chicago Jewish History* (Mar. 1987): 4–7.

24 Samuel H. Zakon, "They Heal the Sick," in *The Sentinel's History of Chicago Jewry, 1911–1961*, p. 92.

25 Harry Barnard and Samuel H. Baskin, "Oh, How Love I Thy Law, It Is My Meditation of All the Day," in *The Sentinel's History of Chicago Jewry, 1911–1986*, pp. 93–97.

26 Ibid., p. 96.

27 Bregstone, *Chicago and Its Jews*, p. 77.

28 Ibid., p. 301.

29 George L. Siegel, "Contribution of Chicago Jewry to Law," in *The Sentinel's History of Chicago Jewry, 1961–1986*, pp. 98–100.

30 Ibid., p. 98.

31 Nathan E. Jacobs, "Building a Greater Chicago," in *The Sentinel's History of Chicago Jewry, 1961–1986*, pp. 101–13.

32 Ibid., p. 111.

33 Ibid., p. 102.

34 Ibid.

35 Lawrence A. Mesirow, "The Contribution of Chicago Jews to Commerce and Industry," in *The Sentinel's History of Chicago Jewry, 1961–1986*, pp. 114–18.

36 Ibid., p. 117.

37 Berkow, *Maxwell Street*, p. 165.

38 Ibid., pp. 358–71.

39 Mesirow, "Contribution of Chicago Jews," pp. 115–16.

40 Howe, *World of Our Fathers*, p. 306.

41 Meites, *History of the Jews of Chicago*, p. 454.

42 Joseph M. Jacobs, "From Gompers to Goldberg," in *The Sentinel's History of Chicago Jewry, 1911–1961*, pp. 79–84.

43 Amalgamated Clothing Workers of America, *The Golden Anniversary of the Great 1910 Strike* (Chicago: Amalgamated Clothing Workers of America, 1960), pp. 3–5.

44 Meites, *History of the Jews of Chicago*, p. 460.

45 Bregstone, *Chicago and Its Jews*, 210.

46 Jacobs, "From Gompers to Goldberg," pp. 83–84.

47 Meites, *History of the Jews of Chicago,* p. 465.

48 Ibid., p. 468.

49 Jacobs, "From Gompers to Goldberg," p. 81.

50 Ibid., p. 122.

51 Jerome R. Reich, "How Radical Were Chicago's Russian Jewish Immigrants?" *Chicago Jewish Historical Society News* (Dec. 1987), p. 8.

52 Jacobs, "From Gompers to Goldberg," p. 81.

## **Chapter 5** The Last Half-Century

1 Data compiled from W. A. Goldberg, "Jewish Population of Chicago, 1931, by Community Areas and Census Tracts," Jewish Charities of Chicago, 1934, mimeographed.

2 Erich Rosenthal, "Acculturation with Assimilation? The Jewish Community of Chicago, Illinois," *American Journal of Sociology* 66, no. 3 (1960): 276.

3 Irving Cutler, "The Story Continues," in *The Sentinel's History of Chicago Jewry, 1961–1986,* pp. 74–75.

4 Daniel I. Leifer, "The Great Debate: The Latke vs. the Hamentash," *Chicago Jewish Historical Society News* (Dec. 1980) pp. 8–12.

5 Cutler, "The Jews of Chicago," p. 90.

6 Anne Friedman, "Life among the Poles in Old South Chicago," *Chicago Jewish History* (June 1989): 1, 4–5.

7 Wirth, *The Ghetto,* p. 191.

8 Leonard C. Mishkin, "Orthodoxy: Saga of Chicago's Great West Side," in *The Sentinel's History of Chicago Jewry, 1911–1961,* p. 127.

9 Irving Cutler, "The West Side Story," *JUF News* (May 1988): 15.

10 From report given by Charles I. Herron at the annual meeting of the Marks Nathan Orphan Home, January 18, 1920.

11 *Chicago Sun-Times,* Aug. 19, 1968.

12 Mazur, "Minyans for a Prairie City," p. 345.

13 Leonard C. Mishkin, "Jerusalem in Chicago," *Sentinel,* Feb. 12, 1981, p. 38.

14 Philip L. Semen, "Community Culture in an Era of Depression," *Chicago Hebrew Institute Reports* (1932): 82–84.

15 "A Training Ground for Life in a Democratic World," *Jewish People's Institute* (1945), pp. 10–16.

16 Rosenthal, "Acculturation with Assimilation?" p. 287.

17 Erich Rosenthal, "This Was North Lawndale: The Transplantation of a Jewish Community," *Jewish Social Studies* 22 (Apr. 1960): 74.

18 Beatrice Michael Shapiro, "Logan Square: Memories of the Jewish Neighborhood that Was," *JUF News* (Dec. 1989), p. 20.

19 Jewish Welfare Board, *The Jewish Community of Albany Park* (New York; Jewish Welfare Board, 1937), pp. 5–6.

20 The Chicago Fact Book Consortium, *Local Community Fact Book, Chicago Metropolitan Area* (Chicago: Chicago Review Press, 1984), p. 37.

21 Ibid., p. 3.

22 Gail Parks Welter, *The Rogers Park Community* (Chicago: Center for Urban Policy, Loyola University of Chicago, 1982), p. 12.

23 Ron Grossman, "Visiting Jewish Chicago," *Present Tense* (Winter 1982): 10.

24 Donald J. McKay. "Soviet Jewish Emigration to Chicago, 1970–1980," (Ph.D. diss., University of Illinois at Chicago, 1986), p. 140.

25 Ibid., p. 155.

26 Ibid., p. 146.

27 Irwin H. Berent and Joy Liljegeren, *Guide to the Records of Jewish Community Institutions of West Rogers Park* (Chicago: Chicago Jewish Archives of Spertus College of Judaica, 1984), p. 62.

28 Jewish Federation of Metropolitan Chicago, *Metropolitan Chicago Jewish Population Study: 1990* (prepublication report, Chicago, 1992), table 9.

29 Charles Jaret, "Recent Patterns of Chicago Jewish Residential Mobility," *Ethnicity* 6 (1979): 237.

30 Jewish Federation of Metropolitan Chicago, *Metropolitan Chicago Jewish Population Study: 1990*, table 9.

31 Rachel Heimovics, "Chicago's South Side Jewish Community Update, Part II," *Jewish Chicago* (June 1983): 44.

32 Jewish Federation of Metropolitan Chicago, *Metropolitan Chicago Jewish Population Study: 1990*, table 9.

33 Heimovics, "Chicago's South Side Jewish Community Update, Part II," p. 45.

34 Jewish Federation of Metropolitan Chicago, *Metropolitan Chicago Jewish Population Study: 1990*, table 9.

35 Cutler, "The Story Continues," p. 63.

36 Ruth G. Silverman, "The Great Northwest: Jewish Territories Beyond Chicago," *Jewish Chicago* (Jan. 1983): 12.

37 Ibid.

38 Jewish Federation of Metropolitan Chicago, *A Population Study of the Jewish Community of Metropolitan Chicago* (Chicago, 1985), p. 21.

39 Ibid., pp. 14–18.

40 Cutler, "The Story Continues," p. 63.

41 Jewish Federation of Metropolitan Chicago, *A Population Study of the Jewish Community of Metropolitan Chicago* (Chicago, 1985), pp. 21–24.

42 Nathan Glazer, "New Perspectives in American Jewish Sociology," *American Jewish Yearbook 1987* (New York: American Jewish Committee and the Jewish Publication Society, 1987), pp. 3–4.

43 Cutler, "The Story Continues," p. 67.

44 Leonard C. Mishkin. "Out of the Past: Secular Yiddish Schools," in *The Sentinel's History of Chicago Jewry 1961–1986*, pp. 258–61.

45 Commission on Jewish Education of the Jewish Federation of Metropolitan Chicago, *Insuring Our Future: A Report on Jewish Education in Chicago* (Chicago: Commission on Jewish Education of the Jewish Federation of Metorpolitan Chicago, 1991), p. 18.

46 Howard A. Sulkin, "Spertus College of Judaica," in *The Sentinel's History of Chicago Jewry 1961–1986*, p. 201.

47 Cutler, "The Story Continues," p. 67.

48 Information provided by the Jewish Federation of Metropolitan Chicago.

49 Jewish Federation of Metropolitan Chicago, *A Population Study of the Jewish Community of Metropolitan Chicago* (Chicago, 1985), pp. 42–43.

# Selected Bibliography

## Books

### EUROPEAN JEWISH BACKGROUND

Association of Latvian and Estonian Jews in Israel. *The Jews in Latvia.* Tel Aviv, 1971.

Baron, Salo W. *The Russian Jew under Tsars and Soviets.* 2d ed. New York: Macmillan, 1976.

Bildarchiv Preussischer Kulturbestz. *Jews in Germany under Prussian Rule.* Berlin, 1984.

Chesler, Evan R. *The Russian Jewry Reader.* New York: Behrman House, 1974.

Cohen, Naomi W. *Encounter with Emancipation: The German Jews in the United States, 1830–1914.* Philadelphia: Jewish Publication Society of America, 1984.

Dawidowicz, Lucy S., ed. *The Golden Tradition: Jewish Life and Thought in Eastern Europe.* New York: Schocken, 1984.

Dubnow, S. M. *History of the Jews in Russia and Poland.* 3 vols. Philadelphia: Jewish Publication Society of America, 1916–1920.

Ehrmann, Eliezer L. *Readings in Modern Jewish History.* New York: Ktav Publishing House, 1977.

Frumkin, Jacob, Gregor Aronson, and Alexis Goldenweiser, eds. *Russian Jewry (1860–1917).* New York: Thomas Yoseloff, 1966.

Greenberg, Louis. *The Jews in Russia: The Struggle for Emancipation.* Edited by Mark Wischnitzer. New York: Schocken, 1976.

Israel, Gerard. *The Jews in Russia.* New York: St. Martin's, 1975.

Jewish Publication Society of America and the Society for the History of Czechoslovak Jews. *The Jews of Czechoslovakia.* Philadelphia, 1968.

Lowenthal, Marvin. *The Jews of Germany.* Philadelphia: Jewish Publication Society of America, 1939.

Meltzer, Milton. *World of Our Fathers: The Jews of Eastern Europe.* New York: Farrar, Straus and Giroux, 1974.

Porath, Jonathan D. *Jews in Russia – The Last Four Centuries.* New York: Ktav Publishing House, 1973.

Roskies, Diane K., and David G. Roskies. *The Shtetl Book.* New York: Ktav Publishing House, 1975.

Shulman, Abraham. *The Old Country: The Lost World of East European Jews.* New York: Charles Scribner's Sons, 1974.

Weinryb, Bernard D. *The Jews of Poland: A Social and Economic History of the Jewish Community in Poland from 1100–1800.* Philadelphia: Jewish Publication Society of America, 1972.

Zborowski, Mark, and Elizabeth Herzog. *Life Is with People.* New York: Schocken Books, 1952.

### CHICAGO: GENERAL

Abbott, Edith. *The Tenements of Chicago, 1908–1935.* Chicago: University of Chicago Press, 1936.

Addams, Jane. *Twenty Years at Hull-House.* New York: Macmillan, 1910.

Allswang, John Meyers. *A House for All Peoples: Ethnic Politics in Chicago, 1890–1936.* Lexington: University of Kentucky Press, 1971.

Amalgamated Clothing Workers of America. *The Golden Anniversary of the Great 1910 Strike.* Chicago, 1960.

Andreas, Alfred T. *History of Chicago.* 3 vols. Chicago: A. T. Andreas and Co., 1884–86.

Carsel, Wilfred. *A History of the Chicago Ladies Garment Workers Union.* Chicago: Normandie House, 1940.

Chicago Fact Book Consortium. *Local Community Fact Book, Chicago Metropolitan Area.* Chicago: Chicago Review Press, 1984.

Chicago Joint Board of Amalgamated Clothing Workers of America. *The Clothing Workers of Chicago, 1910–1922.* Chicago: Privately printed, 1922.

Cutler, Irving. *Chicago: Metropolis of the Mid-Continent.* 3d ed. Dubuque: Geographic Society of Chicago and Kendall/Hunt Publishing Co., 1982.

*Edwards 13th Annual Directory of the Inhabitants, Incorporated Companies, and Manufacturing Establishments of the City of Chicago Embracing a Complete Business Directory for 1870.* Chicago, 1870.

Grossman, Ron. *Guide to Chicago Neighborhoods.* Piscataway, N.J.: New Century Publishers, 1981.

Halper, Albert. *This Is Chicago: An Anthology.* New York: Henry Holt, 1952.

Holli, Melvin, and Peter d'A. Jones, eds. *Ethnic Chicago.* 4th ed. Grand Rapids: Eerdmans, 1995.

Kogan, Herman, and Robert Cromie. *The Great Fire: Chicago 1871.* New York: G. P. Putnam's Sons, 1971.

Lane, George A. *Chicago Churches and Synagogues.* Chicago: Loyola University Press, 1981.

Mayer, Harold M., and Richard C. Wade. *Chicago: Growth of a Metropolis.* Chicago: University of Chicago Press, 1969.

Pierce, Bessie Louise. *A History of Chicago.* 3 vols. New York: Knopf, 1937, 1940, 1957.

Residents of Hull-House. *Hull-House Maps and Papers.* New York: Thomas Y. Crowell, 1895.

Welter, Gail Parks. *The Rogers Park Community.* Chicago: Center for Urban Policy, Loyola University of Chicago, 1982.

CHICAGO: JEWISH

*American Jewish Art Club Golden Anniversary Exhibition, 1928–78.* Chicago, 1978.

*Anshe Emet Synagogue.* Chicago: Anshe Emet Synagogue, 1973.

*Anshe Sholom Congregation.* Chicago: Anshe Sholom Congregation, 1937.

Barnard, Harry. *The Forging of an American Jew: The Life and Times of Judge Julian W. Mack.* New York: Herzl Press, 1974.

———. *This Great Triumvirate of Patriots.* Chicago: Follett Publishing Co., 1971.

Berent, Irwin H., and Joy Liljegeren. *Guide to the Records of Jewish Community Institutions of West Rogers Park.* Mimeographed. Chicago: Chicago Jewish Archives of Spertus College of Judaica, 1984.

Berkow, Ira. *Maxwell Street.* Garden City, N.Y.: Doubleday, 1977.

Berman, Morton M. *Our First Century: A History of Temple B'nai Sholom – Isaiah Israel.* Chicago: Privately printed, 1952.

Bernheimer, Charles. *The Russian Jew in the United States: Studies of Social Conditions in New York, Philadelphia, and Chicago with a description of Rural Settlements.* Philadelphia: John C. Winston, 1905.

Bregstone, Philip P. *Chicago and Its Jews: A Cultural History.* Chicago: Privately published, 1933.

Byrne, Frank L., and Jean Powers Soman. *Your True Marcus: The Civil War Letters of a Jewish Colonel.* Kent, Ohio: Kent State University Press, 1985.

Chicago Board of Rabbis. *Jews and the World's Parliament of Religions.* Chicago, 1976.

Chicago Bureau of War Records, National Jewish Welfare Board. *War Record of the Jewish Population of Chicago, Illinois, in World War II.* Chicago, 1947.

*Chicago Hebrew Institute – Prospectus, 1907–1908.* Chicago, 1907–8.

*Chicago Jewish Community Blue Book.* Chicago: Sentinel Publishing Co., 1918.

Chicago Jewish Historical Society. Doris Minsky Memorial Fund Publication No. 1. *Chicago's Jewish Street Peddlers,* by Carolyn Eastwood; *Memories of Lawndale,* by Beatrice Michaels Shapiro. Chicago: Chicago Jewish Historical Society, 1991.

———. Doris Minsky Memorial Fund Publication No. 2. *The Chayder, the Yeshiva and I,* by Morris Springer; *Memories of the Manor,* by Eva Gross. Chicago: Chicago Jewish Historical Society, 1993.

Commission on Jewish Education of the Jewish Federation of Metropolitan Chicago. *Insuring Our Future: A Report on Jewish Education in Chicago, 1991.* Chicago, 1991.

Conference of Jewish Women's Organizations of Metropolitan Chicago. *Annual Directory.* Chicago, 1990–91.

Cutler, Irving. "The Jews of Chicago: From Shtetl to Suburb." In *Ethnic Chicago,* ed. Melvin G. Holli and Peter d'A. Jones. Grand Rapids: Eerdmans, 1995.

Cutler, Irving, Norman D. Schwartz, and Sidney Sorkin, eds. *Synagogues of Chicago.* 2 vols. Chicago: Chicago Jewish Historical Society, 1991.

Felsenthal, Bernhard, and Herman Eliassof. *The History of Kehillath Anshe Maarabh.* Chicago: Privately published, 1897.

Felsenthal, Emma. *Bernhard Felsenthal: Teacher in Israel.* New York: Oxford University Press, 1924.

Finfer, June Kraus, ed. *Generations of Young Men: Young Men's Jewish Council, 1907–1982.* Chicago, 1982.

Fishbein, Morris, with Sol Theron De Lee. *Joseph Bolivar De Lee, Crusading Obstetrician.* New York: E. P. Dutton, 1949.

*German-Jewish Emigration of the 1930s and Its Impact on Chicago.* Symposium report. Chicago: Chicago Jewish Historical Society, 1979.

Gertz, Elmer. *A Handful of Clients.* Chicago: Follett Publishing Co., 1965.

Gordon, Sarah, ed. *All Our Lives: A Centennial History of Michael Reese Hospital and Medical Center.* Chicago: Michael Reese Hospital and Medical Center, 1981.

Gutstein, Morris A. *A Priceless Heritage.* New York: Bloch Publishing Co., 1953.

Gutstein, Morris A., and Lauren Weingarden Rader. *Faith and Form: Synagogue Architecture in Illinois; an*

*Exhibition Organized by the Maurice Spertus Museum of Judaica.* Chicago: Spertus College Press, 1976.

*Hebrew Theological College Twentieth Anniversary Publication.* Chicago: Hebrew Theological College, 1942.

Heimovics, Rachel Baron. *The Chicago Jewish Source Book.* Chicago: Follett Publishing Co., 1981.

Hirsch, David Einhorn. *Rabbi Emil G. Hirsch.* Chicago: Whitehall, 1968.

Hirsch, Emil G. *My Religion.* N.Y.: Bloch Publishing Co., 1925.

Horwich, Bernard. *My First Eighty Years.* Chicago: Argus Books, 1939.

Jewish Federation of Metropolitan Chicago. *Metropolitan Chicago Jewish Population Study: 1990.* Report. Chicago: Jewish Federation of Metropolitan Chicago, 1992.

———. *A Population Study of the Jewish Community of Metropolitan Chicago.* Chicago, 1985.

Jewish National Fund. *Guide to Jewish Chicago.* Chicago: Jewish National Fund of America – Illinois Region, 1989.

Jewish Welfare Board. *The Jewish Community of Albany Park.* New York, 1937.

Kern, Janet. *Yesterday's Child.* Philadelphia: J. B. Lippincott Co., 1962.

Kramer, Sydelle, and Jenny Masur. *Jewish Grandmothers.* Boston: Beacon, 1976.

Kraus, Adolf. *Reminiscences and Comments.* Chicago: Toby Rubovits, 1925.

Krucoff, Carole. *Rodfei Zedek: The First Hundred Years.* Chicago: Congregation Rodfei Zedek, 1976.

Littlewood, Tom. *Horner of Illinois.* Evanston: Northwestern University Press, 1969.

Mann, Louis L., and Gerson B. Levi. *Glimpses of the Jewish Exhibit.* Chicago, 1934.

Mazur, Edward Herbert. "Minyans for a Prairie City: The Politics of Chicago Jewry, 1850–1940." Ph.D. diss., University of Chicago, 1974. Garland, 1990.

Meites, Hyman L., ed. *History of the Jews of Chicago.* Chicago: Jewish Historical Society of Illinois, 1924; Chicago Jewish Historical Society/Wellington Press, 1990.

Rawidowicz, Simon, ed. *The Chicago Pinkas.* Chicago: College of Jewish Studies, 1952.

Reform Advocate. *The Jews of Illinois.* Chicago: Bloch and Newman, 1909.

*Report of the Religious School Work Committee of the Council of Jewish Women, 1902.*

Seman, Philip L. *A Jewish Community Center in Action: The Immigrants' Adjustment to a New Environment.* Chicago: Chicago Hebrew Institute, 1921.

*The Sentinel Presents 100 Years of Chicago Jewish Life.* Chicago: Sentinel Publishing Co., 1948.

*The Sentinel's History of Chicago Jewry, 1911–1961.* Chicago: Sentinel Publishing Co., 1961.

*The Sentinel's History of Chicago Jewry, 1911–1986.* Chicago: Sentinel Publishing Co., 1986.

Silber, Rabbi Saul. *Selected Essays of Rabbi Saul Silber.* Chicago: International Printing Co., 1950.

Sklare, Marshall, and Benjamin Ringer. *Jewish Identity on the Suburban Frontier.* New York: American Jewish Committee, 1967.

Solomon, Hannah C. *Fabric of My Life: The Autobiography of Hannah G. Solomon.* New York: Bloch Publishing Co., 1946.

Sorkin, Sidney. *Bridges to an American City: A Guide to Chicago's Landsmanshaften, 1870–1990.* New York: Peter Lang Publishing, 1993.

Spray, John C. *Chicago's Great South Shore.* Chicago: Southshore Publishing Co., 1930.

Standard Club of Chicago. *The Standard Club's First Hundred Years.* Chicago: Standard Club of Chicago, 1969.

Union of American Hebrew Congregations. *Judaism at the World's Parliament of Religions.* Cincinnati, 1894.

Weinstein, Jacob J. *History of the Kehilath Anshe Maariv: Congregation of the Men of the West.* Chicago: Privately published, 1951.

———. *Solomon Goldman – A Rabbi's Rabbi.* New York: Ktav Publishing House, 1973.

Werner, M. R. *Julius Rosenwald: The Life of a Practical Humanitarian.* New York: Harper, 1939.

Westerman, Maxwell P., and Stan Tymorek. *Mount Sinai Hospital Medical Center. Sixty-five Years of Research* Chicago: Mount Sinai Hospital Medical Center, 1971.

Wirth, Louis. *The Ghetto.* Chicago: University of Chicago Press, 1928.

JEWS AND JUDAISM: GENERAL

Eben, Abba. *My People: The Story of the Jews.* New York: Random House, 1968.

Elbogen, Ismar. *A Century of Jewish Life.* Philadelphia: Jewish Publication Society of America, 1944.

Faber, Eli, Hasia Diner, Gerald Sorin, Henry Feingold, and Edward Shapiro. *The Jewish People in America.* Baltimore: Johns Hopkins University Press, 1992.

Feldstein, Stanley. *The Land That I Show You: Three Centuries of Jewish Life in America.* Garden City, N.Y.: Anchor Press/Doubleday, 1978.

Glazer, Nathan. *American Judaism.* Chicago: University of Chicago Press, 1957.

Golden, Harry. *Travels through Jewish America.* Garden City, N.Y.: Doubleday, 1973.

Grayzel, Solomon. *A History of the Jews.* Philadelphia: Jewish Publication Society of America, 1952.

Handlin, Oscar. *The Uprooted.* New York: Little, Brown, 1951.

Hirshler, Eric E., ed. *Jews from Germany in the United States.* N.Y.: Farrar, Straus, 1955.

Howe, Irving. *The World of Our Fathers.* New York: Harcourt Brace Jovanovich, 1976.

Karp, Abraham J. *Golden Door to America: The Jewish Immigrant Experience.* New York: Penguin, 1977.

Korn, Bertram Wallace. *American Jewry and the Civil War.* Philadelphia: Jewish Publication Society of America, 1951.

Metzker, Isaac, ed. *A Bintel Brief.* Garden City, N.Y.: Doubleday, 1971.

Potok, Chaim. *Wanderings: Chaim Potok's History of the Jews.* New York: Knopf, 1978.

Sachar, Abram Leon. *A History of the Jews.* New York: Knopf, 1964.

Sachar, Howard Morley. *The Course of Modern Jewish History.* New York: Delta, 1958.

Sklare, Marshall, ed. *The Jewish Community in America.* New York: Behrman House, 1974.

———. *The Jews: Social Patterns of an American Group.* New York: Free Press, 1958.

Yaffe, James. *The American Jews.* New York: Paperback Library, 1969.

FICTION: CHICAGO JEWISH SETTING

Bellow, Saul. *The Adventures of Augie March.* New York: Viking, 1961.

———. *Herzog.* New York: Fawcett, 1965.

Caspary, Vera. *Thicker than Water.* New York: Grosset and Dunlap, 1932.

Ferber, Edna. *Fanny Herself.* New York: F. A. Stokes, 1917.

Halper, Albert. *The Chute.* New York: Viking Press, 1937.

———. *The Foundry.* New York: Viking, 1934.

———. *The Golden Watch.* New York: Henry Holt, 1936.

———. *On the Shore.* New York: Viking, 1934.

Hecht, Ben. *Erik Dorn.* Chicago: University of Chicago Press, 1963.

Howland, Bette. *Blue in Chicago.* New York: Harper and Row, 1978.

Levin, Meyer. *Compulsion.* New York: Simon and Schuster, 1956.

———. *The Old Bunch.* New York: Citadel, 1937.

Rosenfeld, Isaac. *Passage from Home.* New York: World Publishing Co., 1946.

Ross, Sam. *Sidewalks Are Free.* New York: Farrar, Straus, 1950.

———. *Windy City.* New York: G. P. Putnam's Sons, 1979.

Rosten, Leo Calvin (Leonard Q. Ross). *The Education of H*Y*M*A*N K*A*P*L*A*N.* New York: Harcourt Brace Jovanovich, 1937.

Sigal, Clancy. *Going Home.* Boston: Houghton Mifflin, 1962.

Zara, Louis. *Blessed Is the Man.* New York: Bobbs-Merrill, 1935.

## Periodicals

Berrol, Selma. "Germans versus Russians: An Update." *American Jewish History* (Dec. 1983): 142–56.

Bureau of Jewish Employment Problems. *Fair Employment News Report, Vol. 2, No. 1.* Chicago, May 25, 1953.

Eliassof, Herman. "The Jews of Chicago." *Publications of the American Jewish Historical Society* 11 (1903): 117–30.

Felsenthal, Bernhard. "On the History of the Jews in Chicago." *Publications of the American Jewish Historical Society* 2 (1894): 21–27.

Gans, Herbert J. "Park Forest: Birth of a Jewish Community." *Commentary,* Apr. 1951, pp. 330–39.

Grossman, Ron. "Touring Chicago's Older Jewish Neighborhoods." *Jewish Chicago* (Sept. 1982): 43–49.

Handlin, Oscar, and Mary Handlin. "A Century of Jewish Immigration in the United States." In *American Jewish Year Book,* pp. 1–84. New York: American Jewish Committee and Jewish Publication society of America, 1949.

Heimovics, Rachel. "Chicago's South Side Jewish Community Update, Part 2." *Jewish Chicago* (June 1993): 44–47.

Jaret, Charles. "Recent Patterns of Chicago Jewish Residential Mobility." *Ethnicity* 6 (1979): 235–48.

Krug, Mark. "The Yiddish Schools in Chicago." *YIVO Annual of Jewish Social Science* 9 (1954): 276–307.

Mishkin, Leonard C. "Jerusalem in Chicago," *Sentinel,* Feb. 12, 1981, pp. 32, 34, 36, 38, 40, 42–45.

Paradise, Viola. "The Jewish Immigrant Girl in Chicago." *Survey* 30 (Sept. 6, 1913): 694–704.

Rosenthal, Erich. "Acculturation with Assimilation? The Jewish Community of Chicago, Illinois." *American Journal of Sociology* 66, no. 3 (1960): 275–88.

———. "This Was North Lawndale: The Transplantation of a Jewish Community." *Jewish Social Studies* 22, no. 2 (Apr. 1960): 67–80.

Seman, Philip L. "Community Culture in an Era of Depression." *Chicago Hebrew Institute Reports* (1932): 82–84.

Szajkowki, Zosa. "The Attitude of American Jews to East European Jewish Immigration, 1881–1893." *Publications of the American Jewish Historical Society* 40 (1951): 221–80.

## Unpublished Material

Ament, Jonathon I. "Being Jewish and Political in West Rogers Park and the Lakefront: A Comparison of Two Chicago Political Cultures." Master's thesis, University of Chicago, 1990.

Charney, Michael. "An Analytical Study of the Economic Life of the Jews in Chicago, 1870–1872." Seminar paper, Hebrew Union College, 1974.

Cressey, Paul F. "The Succession of Cultural Groups in the City of Chicago." Ph.D. diss., University of Chicago, 1930.

Frazin, Robert P. "The Public Life of Julius Rosenwald." Master's thesis, Hebrew Union College, 1964.

Goldberg, W. A. "A Jewish Population of Chicago, 1931, by Community Areas and Census Tracts." Mimeographed. Chicago: Jewish Charities of Chicago, 1934.

Guysenir, Maurice Glenn. "Jewish Voting Behavior in Chicago's Fiftieth Ward." Ph.D. diss., Northwestern University, 1957.

Jaret, Charles L. "Residential Mobility and Local Jewish Community Organization in Chicago." Ph.D. diss., University of Chicago, 1977.

Korey, Harold. "The History of Jewish Education in Chicago." Ph.D. diss., University of Chicago, 1942.

Lavin, Lottie. "The Jewish Educational System in Chicago." Master's thesis, University of Chicago, 1938.

Lewis, Sarah Florence. "Social Aspects of the Post-War Immigrant Jew." Master's thesis, University of Chicago, 1922.

McKay, Donald J. "Soviet Jewish Emigration to Chicago, 1970–1980." Ph.D. diss., University of Illinois at Chicago, 1986.

Oppenheimer, Michael A. "Jewish Life in Chicago as Reflected in the Reform Advocate." Seminar paper, Hebrew Union College, 1965.

Rosenthal, Erich. "The Jewish Population of Chicago, Illinois: Its Size and Distribution as Derived from Voters' Lists." Ph.D. diss., University of Chicago, 1949.

Weinberg, Leonard. "Aspects of Jewish Political Behavior." Master's thesis, University of Chicago, 1962.

# Index

After serving as a naval officer in World War II, IRVING CUTLER went on to receive a master's degree in social science at the University of Chicago and a Ph.D. in geography at Northwestern University. For twenty-four years he was on the faculty of Chicago State University, ten years as chairman of the geography department. He has been a consultant to a number of government agencies and educational publishers. Cutler is the author of several books and numerous articles, including many on the Jews of Chicago, and gives tours and talks on various aspects of Chicago. He is on the board of directors of a number of historical and geographic societies, including the Chicago Jewish Historical Society, of which he was a founding member, and the Geographic Society of Chicago, which he served as president.